University of Michigan Publications

LANGUAGE AND LITERATURE

VOLUME I

STUDIES IN SHAKESPEARE, MILTON AND DONNE

STUDIES IN SHAKESPEARE, MILTON AND DONNE

CONTRIBUTIONS BY . . .

Oscar J. Campbell
Charles C. Fries
James H. Hanford
Louis I. Bredvold

EDITED BY
Eugene S. McCartney

PHAETON PRESS
NEW YORK
1970

ORIGINALLY PUBLISHED 1925
REPRINTED 1970

LIBRARY OF CONGRESS CATALOG CARD NUMBER 78-93244

PUBLISHED BY PHAETON PRESS, INC.
SBN #87753-020-3

CONTENTS

PAGE

Love's Labour's Lost Re-studied. O. J. Campbell . . . 1

The Two Gentlemen of Verona and Italian Comedy. O. J. Campbell 47

Shakespearian Punctuation. Charles C. Fries 65

The Youth of Milton: An Interpretation of His Early Literary Development. James Holly Hanford 87

Samson Agonistes and Milton in Old Age. James Holly Hanford 165

The Religious Thought of Donne in Relation to Medieval and Later Traditions. Louis I. Bredvold 191

LOVE'S LABOUR'S LOST RE-STUDIED

LOVE'S LABOUR'S LOST RE-STUDIED

O. J. CAMPBELL

UNTIL very recently, *Love's Labour's Lost* has not received the critical attention to which its position in Shakespeare's dramatic work entitles it. It is probably his first comedy and often thought to be the first play that he wrote without collaboration. A thorough study of this drama might, therefore, be expected to reveal what Croce would call Shakespeare's "comic presuppositions." It might have discovered the bases of his entire comic technique. Such a genetic study might have simplified the history of Shakespeare's development as a writer of comedy and given it a coherence now lacking. It might even have thrown light upon his puzzling beginnings as a playwright.

No study of *Love's Labour's Lost* has cast such illumination upon Shakespeare's career. The comedy, rather, has been considered as a little apart from the straight course of his development, as a kind of experiment which yielded its author few permanent results either intellectual or technical. Moreover, a sort of unrecognized mystery has hung over this drama. No source for the plot has been discovered. To be sure, the scene is laid at the court of Henry of Navarre and the action is supposed to have been suggested by historical and social events in the life of that monarch, vaguely like those presented in the play. The style or dramatic manner of the play has been almost universally recognized as very like that of John Lyly. The dialogue has been thought to be in every way an approximation to that developed by Lyly, and the spirit and tone of the social life of the courtly ladies and gentlemen as depicted by both writers to be identical. One play of the earlier dramatist, in particular, *Endimion,* is believed to have furnished in Sir Tophas and his page, Epiton, models for Armado and Moth. One other derived character appears, Holofernes, the Latinizing pedagogue, who is a stock character in the sixteenth century comedy of France and Italy.

Except for these slight echoes of earlier comic practice, this drama, according to orthodox critical opinion, is Shakespeare's own invention, — his sustained travesty of contemporary court life, and of the fashions in speech and behavior that prevailed there. In this satire he adverts to incidents of current social and political life, and in it he directly satirizes figures well known in that world. In brief, *Love's Labour's Lost* has been regarded as Shakespeare's *Precieuses Ridicules*.[1]

Some of the elements of this rounded theory have been called into question. The sceptics, for example, have pointed out that it was extraordinary that a young man who had come, but meagrely educated, from the provinces a few years before, should show, at the outset of his career, enough familiarity with the uses and temper of a court to satirize them before an audience composed largely of courtiers. This was pointed, but negative criticism. Recently, newly discovered facts about this play have yielded positive results and have made a partial revision of the traditional estimate necessary. Indeed, they have rendered a complete reëxamination of the comedy highly desirable.

The most important of these new truths is the discovery that the central fable of the play reflects faithfully some definite historical events which took place at the court of Henry of Navarre, at Nérac in 1578. This important discovery is due to the researches of M. Abel Lefranc, published in *Sous le Masque de William Shakespeare*.[2] Inasmuch as the thesis of this book has prevented most American scholars from acquainting themselves with the sound historical investigations which it contains and which in no way depend upon the author's contention that the plays of Shakespeare were written by the sixth Earl of Derby, I shall review briefly his evidence on this question of historical fact.

[1] The facts are thus presented in Sir Sidney Lee's *William Shakespeare* (third revised edition, London, 1922), pp. 103 ff.

[2] *Sous le Masque de William Shakespeare* (Paris, 1919), II. 17 ff.

Vague correspondences between the play and events at the contemporary court of Navarre had been recognized since 1880. In that year Sir Sidney Lee suggested[3] that the plot of *Love's Labour's Lost* reflected events occurring at the court of Henri Quatre in the year 1586. At that time Catherine de Medici, the dowager queen of France, journeyed to Saint Bris, with the ladies of her court, in an attempt to settle the perennial disputes between Henry of Navarre and the King of France. General similarities between the meeting of Navarre and the princess in the play and the historical interview at Saint Bris undoubtedly exist. The social atmosphere of the two is identical, but the political objects are utterly different.

Queen Catherine's expedition was concerned principally with an attempt to persuade Navarre to divorce his dissolute wife, Marguerite of Valois, who had left her husband for fear of his resentment at her moral vagaries.[4] This accomplished, the dowager queen was to persuade Henry to marry Christine, a daughter of the Duke of Lorraine.[5] The expedition in Shakespeare's comedy is not concerned in the remotest degree with this project. Furthermore, the historical embassage was led by Catherine, then old and grievously afflicted with gout.[6] She is not a likely prototype of the lovely princess in *Love's Labour's Lost,* nor is her expedition a seed from which would grow naturally a comedy of amorous persiflage.

Now M. Lefranc shows that an expedition made to the court of Navarre in 1578 by Catherine and her daughter, Marguerite, is much more nearly like the fictitious one. The political object of this mission is identical with that in the play. It sought the settlement of the question of sovereignty in Aquitaine, which in the drama is accurately called "the dowry of a queen,"[7] and of a dispute over the payment of a hundred thousand

[3] *The Gentleman's Magazine,* October, 1880.

[4] There was also a declared intention to convert Henry from Protestantism, but that event can hardly have been expected.

[5] Davila, *Memoirs of Civil Wars in France* (trans. London, 1758), I. 505 ff.

[6] *Ibid.*

[7] *Love's Labour's Lost,* II. i. 8.

crowns to Navarre by the King of France.[8] Furthermore, contemporary accounts of this diplomatic mission show that its social atmosphere was very like that presented in the play. Marguerite of Valois in her *Mémoires* herself describes the occasion as follows: " faisant la pluspart de ce temps-là (quatre ou cinque ans que je fus en Gascogne) nostre séjour a Nérac, où nostre cour estoit si belle et si plaisante, que nous n'envions point celle de France, y ayant Madame la Princesse de Navarre sa soeur, qui depuis esté mariée à Monsieur le Duc de Bar mon nepveu, et moy avec bon nombre de dames et filles; et le Roy mon Mary estant suivy d'une belle trouppe de seigneurs et gentils-hommes, aussi honnestes gens que les plus galants que j'aye veu à la cour; et n'y avoit rien a regretter en eux, sinon qu'ils estoient huguenots." [9]

As one of the historians of the period remarks, the presence of the two queens transformed the town into a capital of the rank which it held in the reign of Henri d'Albert.[10] It is not strange, then, for Marguerite to confess that the court was so brilliant that she and her ladies did not envy the life at the greater court in Paris.[11] These descriptions invoke the essence of the social atmosphere of the diplomatic mission in *Love's Labour's Lost*. In the play, as doubtless at Nérac, the diplomatic questions are early referred to the experts and the social gaiety is all that meets the eye. The diplomats become courtiers and the political aims of the ladies are completely hidden by the social brilliance which attends them.

The dramatic figures, too, have some curious personal traits in common with the historical personages whom they represent. Ferdinand of *Love's Labour's Lost*, as he now appears in the comedy, is obviously not Henry of Navarre, yet he inherits one of the monarch's foibles as a courtly lover. The princess describes a *billet doux* which she receives from Ferdinand as follows:

[8] Cf. *Sous le Masque,* II. 67 ff.; also Batz-Trenquelleon, *Henri IV en Gascogne, 1553–1589* (Paris, 1885), pp. 75 and 122.

[9] *Mémoires et Lettres de Marguerite de Valois* (ed. par M. F. Guessard, Paris, 1842), p. 163. (Société de l'Histoire de France.)

[10] Batz-Trenquelleon, p. 129. [11] *Mémoires,* p. 163.

As much love in Rime
As would be cram'd up in a sheet of paper,
Writ on both sides the leafe, Margent and all
That he was fain to seale on Cupid's name.[12]

M. Lefranc reports[13] that an authentic original of one of Navarre's poems, *Charmante Gabrielle,* which was sent in the form of a letter to Gabrille d'Estreés, presents these same characteristics. Strophes are written in the margin and the letter is sealed with the seal of which the word *Amor* forms the center.

Similarities of a like sort exist between the princess of the play and Marguerite of Valois. It is significant for this identification that the princess was obviously called "queen" in the early editions of the play. In the first quarto she is called "queen" a number of times;[14] and many of these designations are retained in the Folio edition. Moreover, there are clear references in the comedy to journeys that Marguerite had made with her ladies in the years just previous to this historical visit to Nérac.[15] They have no dramatic point in their context and can be regarded as introduced only for the sake of "local color." M. Lefranc finds other rather cryptic references in the plays made clear by regarding them as adversions to events in the history of the entourage of Marguerite which are narrated in her *Mémoires,* or to actual conditions of life in the little court at Nérac.[16]

[12] *Love's Labour's Lost,* V. ii. 6–9.

[13] *Sous le Masque,* II. 64.

[14] II. iv, once; IV. i, eighteen times; V. iii, once. All of the eighteen of IV. i are retained in the Folio.

[15] II. i. 60–65. There is a reference to a visit made upon her brother, the Duke of Alençon in 1578: cf. *Mémoires,* pp. 156–57. Berowne's "Did I not dance with you in Brabant once?" is a reference to a trip to Flanders made by Marguerite and her train in 1577: cf. *Mémoires,* pp. 88 ff., particularly the ball referred to on page 97.

[16] V. ii. 13 ff. contains a reference to the death of Katherine's sister from unrequited love which may be a recollection of the sad fate of Helène de Tournon referred to in the *Mémoires,* pp. 110–114. The taunt (V. ii. 574) hurled at the actor playing Alexander: "You will be scraped out of the painted cloth," may refer to certain tapestries decorated with images of *The Nine Worthies* which we know hung in the royal apartments, sometimes at Pau and sometimes at Nérac.

Taken in their entirety, these similarities between Shakespeare's comedy and historical conditions at the court of Nérac in 1578 during an embassy of Catherine, Queen Marguerite of Valois and their ladies-in-waiting are completely convincing. The author of the fable of *Love's Labour's Lost* was evidently well acquainted not only with the spirit, but with the details of the life there.

One aspect of the picture, however, seems inharmonious with the facts of history. How could an author familiar with this gay life and undoubtedly also with the notorious love intrigues of the youthful Henry of Navarre, present him and his court as tinged with asceticism and determined intellectuality? The device of the oath, as I shall show later, may have been an invention necessary to solve a distinctly theatrical problem of the dramatist. However, in the solution of a technical problem an author must not destroy more important sorts of verisimilitude. As a matter of fact, the court at Navarre had the reputation among Englishmen of the time of being an exceedingly decorous place, — a safe spot for the completion of the continental education of Protestant Englishmen. M. Lefranc calls attention to a letter written June 9, 1583, by Cobham, the English ambassador to the Court of France to Walsingham.[17] In this report he remarks that Navarre has furnished his court with distinguished gentlemen of his religion and reformed his house. He ends with this significant phrase: "There are divers special persons of quality of intention to resort to that Court, and others send their children, understanding the honorable order that is there observed."

To Cobham, at least, it would have seemed not improper to speak of Navarre's court as a "little achademe." To the gay and licentious Marguerite of Valois this atmosphere of study seemed less admirable. She writes contemptuously to her husband, "Si j'osais dire, si vous etiez honete homme vouz quitteriez l'agriculture et l'humeur de Timon pour venir vivre parmi les

[17] *Calendar of State Papers. Foreign Series of the Reign of Elizabeth, June–January 1583* (London, 1913), P. 394.

hommes."[18] Such a woman would obviously enjoy thrusting herself and her flying squadron into such a world, with the deliberate purpose of enticing the students from their sobrieties into a society devoted to courtly love with all its artificial gallantries and barren felicities. At every point the knowledge of the court of Navarre during this expedition of 1578 reflected in *Love's Labour's Lost* proves to be, in the highest degree, intimate and accurate.

This hitherto unsuspected fact can be made to throw light upon the youthful Shakespeare's methods of composition from two angles. In the first place, we are able to say now what was, in effect, the source of this play and so we are able to determine by familiar methods of genetic cricitism what parts of this comedy are the product of Shakespeare's dramatic invention. In the second place, M. Lefranc's discovery may aid in the solution of some of the ever puzzling questions of Shakespeare's early relations to persons of the very highest social station and of the part that they played in stimulating and directing his early literary activity. The second of these problems I shall discuss first, because it will be seen to have a bearing on determining what material the dramatist found ready to his hand when he began to write.

The first question that comes to mind is how could Shakespeare have possessed this accurate and detailed knowledge of life at Navarre's court.[19] We must dismiss at once the possibility of Shakespeare's having himself been at the court at Nérac. In none of the wide journeys from Elsinore to Venice, postulated

[18] It is interesting to remark that Berowne seems to refer to the King as Timon (IV. iii. 170 ff.):

> "O me, with what strict patience have I sat
> To see a king transformed to a Gnat,
> And Critticke Tymon laugh at idle toyes."

[19] Marlowe's knowledge of French history shown in *The Massacre at Paris;* Chapman's, shown in his five plays dealing with the same subject; or Dekker's and Drayton's, undoubtedly exhibited in their plays on *The Civil Wars in France,* recorded by Henslowe, is not analogous to that of Shakespeare shown in *Love's Labour's Lost.* Their knowledge is of public political fact; Shakespeare's is of intimate personal incident.

to explain fancied local color detected in his plays, has he been made to visit this little Protestant court. The chance of the poet's having had access to any printed account of such intimate details of social life at this court of Henry IV as *Love's Labour's Lost* reflects, seems equally remote. The remaining possibility [20] is that the information was given to him in some form by one of the many English gentlemen who in the age of Elizabeth made this court one of the principal places of sojourn on their *grands tours*.[21]

The peculiar nature of *Love's Labour's Lost* lends this theory plausibility. It was clearly not written for a popular audience. The form in which we now possess the drama is that which had been newly corrected for a court performance in the Christmas season of 1597–1598, but its original version was undoubtedly intended for a similar occasion. Professor Baker has presented effectively the reasons for believing that the essential character of the entire comedy was determined by a prospective courtly, — nay royal — audience. He says, "The general attitude toward women, the sonneteering, and, above all, the eulogy of women which Biron utters near the end of Act IV, suggests strongly that originally, as in 1598, it may have been performed before the queen and her court, or that, as first written, it was given before an audience mainly composed of women. Throughout, the characters so much play with love rather than become its subjects, that one wonders whether it was not composed as a whole with a definite view of pleasing the Virgin Queen, who was such an adept in coquetry and was so fond of putting off her admirers just as they seemed nearest to the attainment of their wishes." [22]

Furthermore there is reason to suppose that the comedy was originally composed not for one of the professional companies, but for the children. An unusually large number of parts has been provided for boy actors. Moth, the Princess, her three ladies in waiting, Jaquenetta, and possibly Don Adriana de

[20] Except, of course, the one sponsored by M. Lefranc that Shakespeare did not write the comedy. [21] *Vid. sup.* 5.

[22] Baker, G. P., *The Development of Shakespeare as a Dramatist* (N. Y., 1907), pp. 107–108.

Armado, were rôles to be played by boys.[23] Surely six, and possibly seven, parts were written for child-actors. This number is nearly twice as large as that usually provided for boys in Shakespeare's comedies. None of these figures, furthermore, has been excluded by any critics who have sought to reconstruct the hypothetical original version. Their presence, therefore, suggests that the play, as originally conceived, was written for the children, and so not for Shakespeare's company and its London stage, but for a special occasion.

In such a fête as the one conjectured above a gentleman of the court would have a special interest. He might be concerned as the host to the Queen on the occasion for which the play was planned, or he might wish the drama to advert allegorically to facts or projects in which he had a personal interest. Guesses as to the identity of such a person have been made. Professor Austin K. Gray[24] seeks to prove that the drama was devised at the instigation of Southampton as part of his entertainment for the Queen when he received her at Tichfield Park in 1591. He furthermore attempts to show that part of it is the young Earl's plea under the guise of an allegory to have his proposed marriage with Lady Elizabeth de Vere, Burleigh's granddaughter, postponed for at least a year. Southampton later obtained release from this undesired engagement through the payment of a round sum. The correspondences between the dramatic situation and this real one are close and entertaining; but however ingenious this sort of study, such facts as it seeks to establish, are, I believe, now quite beyond proof. Such conjecture, however, serves to strengthen the plausibility of the view that the drama was composed under the eye of some gentleman of the court.

There is nothing intrinsically improbable in such a dramatic collaboration or coöperation between an actor-playwright and an Elizabethan gentleman, particularly in the construction of an occasional play. Hamlet's reception of the travelling players

[23] This fact is mentioned by Austin K. Gray in *The Secret of Love's Labour's Lost and the Earl of Southampton. Publ. of the Modern Language Association,* vol. XXXIX (Sept., 1924), No. 3, p. 602.

[24] *Op. cit.*

and, in particular, his discussion of dramatic composition with the first actor may be regarded as a realistic picture of an interesting phase of Elizabethan life.[25] Hamlet greets this player affectionately with " O my old friend " and discusses with him the play that was "caviare to the general " in such a way as to suggest that the actor was himself the author. Then he asks him to " study a speech of some dozen or sixteen lines " which he " could set down and insert " in one of their plays.[26]

In the frequent sojourns of travelling companies at the castles of nobility in Elizabethan times lay natural opportunities for the establishment of acquaintance and friendship between young literary nobles and talented actor-playwrights. At no time since have such occasions existed. The great concern of the Derby family for the drama, and particularly of the sixth Earl, whose interest as dramatist and patron M. Lefranc has abundantly established, is an example of an interest of which the scene in Hamlet is a dramatic picture. Shakespeare's later close friendship with Southampton is proof that he became the object of such an interest to one of the greatest nobles of his time. Such facts give us ample warrant for supposing that some travelled gentleman had established close enough relations with Shakespeare to induce the dramatist to use his personal reminiscences of the court of Navarre as a nucleus for his play.

From whatever source derived, this material would surely contain a description of the diplomatic mission, of its object, its methods, and its results. The Queen and her ladies would appear in the account with their atmosphere of graceful, half-sportive love-making and with their courtly badinage. The narrative, if true to history, would close not with marriages, nor with promised consummation of the half-playful wooing, but with the indicated success of the ladies' diplomatic mission and their regretful departure. The desire of the directing genius for an allegorical suggestion of some contemporary social situation may have determined other features of the play, such as the

25 *Hamlet,* II. ii. 446 ff.

26 In the play *Sir Thomas More,* Sir Thomas himself steps in and improvises a part for " Good Councell " until the fellow Luggins comes in to take the rôle.

grouping of the lovers and the abrupt termination of the projects of the lovers by the surprising death of the father of the visiting princess.

Let us suppose, then, that Shakespeare received such a story from a source which must remain unknown. Upon this he was to build a comedy. To what events within the range of his experience would he most naturally turn, in order to find details which could give his play verisimilitude to an Elizabethan audience? The one obvious source for this sort of dramatic material was the entertainment given to Queen Elizabeth when she visited the country houses of the great lords of her kingdom. Shakespeare and his audiences would agree that in these elaborate and diversified Progresses were to be discovered the approved methods of honoring and amusing a sovereign. Catherine de Medici or Margaret of Valois on the English stage would be expected to receive a similar form of entertainment from Henry of Navarre when they visited him at Nérac.[27]

The influence of these Progresses upon *Love's Labour's Lost* has been suggested before, but in an unfortunate manner. Efforts have been made to discover in the play reflections of one particular Progress. For example, Arthur Acheson in his recently published *Shakespeare's Lost Years in London*,[28] believes that *Love's Labour's Lost* reflects the events which took place at Cowdray House in August 1591[29] at the Honorable Entertainment given by Lord Montecuto (*sic*). The evidence which he presents in support of this theory is not convincing. His thesis proves to be mere interesting conjecture. Indeed attempts to discover reflections of any one particular Progress in *Love's Labour's Lost* seem doomed to failure. However, the constructive dramatic principle of this comedy proves to bear close resemblance to that of a Progress, regarded as a dramatic type.

[27] Shakespeare could readily have obtained knowledge of the nature of these Progresses either through personal experience or through a perusal of the accounts of these fêtes, which were often printed within a year of their occurrence. For a comparison of the dates of the Progresses with those of the printed accounts, see Nichols' *Progresses, passim*.

[28] *Shakespeare's Lost Years in London* (London, 1920), p. 186.

[29] Nichols, Vol. II.

The Progresses of the Queen comprised a series of highly diversified sorts of out-of-door amusement, lasting from four to ten days. Modern students think of these shows as consisting mainly of spectacular classical and allegorical pageants, like the sumptuous water-fête at the Earl of Hertford's entertainment in 1591. They may also remember that there were masque-like shows in which Daphne, or Pan appeared, or in which there was graceful dancing by Ceres and her nymphs before her Majesty. But in truth these features formed but a small part of the entire entertainment. Upon her arrival at the castle of her host the Queen is invariably greeted with some sort of oration; and verbal devices in prose and poetry pursue her wherever she walks. She hunts, in her youth riding to the hounds, in her more mature age shooting at the game from a covert. She is encountered by wild men.[30] She dines often in the walks of the garden, at tables sometimes as long as forty-eight yards. She is honored by the folk of the country-side, who present various forms of rustic and popular dramatic sport. She attends plays given by professional actors. All these forms of entertainment are presented out of doors, so that the Queen is constantly in some part of the park surrounding the castle of her host. When she is kept within doors by inclement weather, no pastime worth chronicling is offered to her. Just such a situation is presented in *Love's Labour's Lost.*

The first striking similarity of the play to the Progress lies in its setting. The scene of the entire play is the park of the King of Navarre. This, it will be noted, is not at all the pastoral wood which serves as the scene of *As You Like It;* nor is it the enchanted Arcadia of *The Tempest.* Furthermore the audience is constantly reminded by place notes[31] that the action is

[30] For the meaning and tradition of this "wild man," cf. Chambers, *Mediaeval Stage* I. 182; also note 2.

[31] Cf. Boyet's explanation of the King's reception of the ladies, II. i. 91–94:

> "He rather means to lodge you in the field,
> Like one that comes here to besiege his court
> Than seek a dispensation for his oath:
> To let you enter his unpeopled house."

continuously laid in the park. The critic is indeed almost justified in conjecturing that the ascetic vows of the gentlemen were introduced to enable the poet to use the story of the visit to the court of Navarre and yet to keep all the action out in the purlieus of the castle. In this way he could give the comedy the first essential of a Progress,—the setting and the atmosphere of an English park.

Another peculiarity of this comedy may be attributed to its Progress-like nature. Critics have often noted the disproportionate length of the last two acts. Henry David Gray speaks of it as "A disproportion as amazing as it is unique in Elizabethan drama."[32] Various explanations of this fact have been given. Sir Sidney Lee thinks it a fault of the original writing,—a youthful blemish. Professor Gray, on the other hand, believes that it is due to additions made to the play when Shakespeare revised it for presentation at court. These were largely made for the purpose of introducing the *Pageant of the Nine Worthies.*

A more satisfactory explanation for this apparent lack of proportion may be found in regarding the play as a drama intended to represent the events and the atmosphere of a royal Progress. Such dramatic disproportion as the critics have lamented would not have been noticed in this sort of comedy. It professed to be only a counterfeit presentment of a mere series of diverse entertainments. A division of such a sequence of scenes into acts was extrinsic to the nature of the play and clearly forced upon it when it was prepared for publication.

Furthermore, such a performance as that presented by the clownish figures was a conventional part of a prolonged Progress. I do not refer to the appearance of the people of the countryside in native costume in folk-dance and folk-song. Such

---

Also II. i. 181–183:

"You may not come, fair Princess, in my gates,
But here without you shall be so received,
As you shall deem yourself lodged in my heart."

[32] Gray, Henry David, *The Original Version of "Love's Labour's Lost" with a conjecture as to "Love's Labour's Won," Leland Stanford Junior Publications,* 1918, p. 19.

picturesque entertainment was common.[33] But "countrie shows," either intentionally or inadvertently burlesques, were often presented. These inventions the courtly audience was supposed to receive, not with respect, but with raillery, like that rained upon Holofernes and his fellows. At least two shows of this sort are described by Laneham in his famous epistolary report of the Progress at Kenilworth. One was a mock nuptial celebration made a burlesque by the actors, who were louts or pretended to be. They presented their show with a portentous seriousness that aroused a gay spirit of ridicule in the audience, as the following extract from Laneham will show:

"Then followed the worshippful bride, led (after the countrie maner) between two auncient parishioners, honest toownsmen. But . . . ill-smelling was she: a thirtie-five yeer old, of colour broun-bay, not very beautiful indeed, but ugly, fooul, ill-favor'd: yet marveyloous faine of the offis, because shee hard say she woould dauns before the Queen, in which feat shee thought shee woold foot it az finely az the best."

It is exactly this combination of eagerness and ineptitude that makes Holofernes and his actors so amusing to the courtly audience in *Love's Labour's Lost.* Laneham's delight at this rustic fooling was fully as hearty as that of the ladies and gentlemen at the bombast of the *Nine Worthies.*

"By my Trooth," he exclaims, "twaz a lively pastime, I believe it would have moved sum man to a right merry mood, though had it be toold him hiz wife lay a dying."

The hock-tide play presented on the same occasion by the men of Coventry led by one Captain Cox was received by the Queen in the same spirit of ridicule.[34] The first time that the

[33] Cf. The Earl of Hertford's Entertainment, Nichols, Vol. II: "Three musicians under the window disguised in ancient country attire did greet her with a pleasant song of Coridon and Phyllida." In the Cowdray Entertainment (*ibid.*), we read the following: "On Thursday — in the evening the Countrie people presented themselves to her Majestie in a pleasant dance with taber and pipe."

[34] Chambers (*The Mediaeval Stage,* I. 155) points out the fact that the germ of this play is clearly a very old festival celebration, and, like Hock-tide customs, found in many places throughout England. Its folk significance, however, had been entirely lost at this time and it was merely sport for the people and humor for the gentry.

folk played this pageant she was able to see but little of it. She therefore commanded that it be repeated on the following Tuesday "to have it full oout. Accordingly it waz prezented; whereat her Majestie laught well."[35] *The Pageant of the Nine Worthies* has been related to dramatic forms slightly different from these. It is well known that on the Progresses of the Queen the village schoolmaster, or some equally self-important local functionary often prepared a show. Some of the crude plays of this origin have been thought to have suggested Shakespeare's burlesque in the pageants of Holofernes and Bottom.[36] But it is more probable that such burlesques as those presented at Kenilworth suggested to the playwright the dramatic propriety of making a similar form of comic entertainment an integral part of his stage version of a royal Progress.

The curious detachment from the rest of the play of the *Pageant of the Nine Worthies* and the men who enact it has been often unfavorably commented upon. Professor Baker remarks that an audience must take an entirely fresh start with the announcement of the play that Holofernes and his fellows are to present. He says, "The interests in the final act have been, so to speak, thrust in from the outside, rather than developed from elements of story started in earlier acts."[37] Henry David Gray cannot accept this patchwork construction as evidence of Shakespeare's limitations, even at the outset of his career. He believes that the first edition of the play was shorter than that represented by the quarto of 1598, and that the *Nine Worthies* and the men who presented it were not a part of the original version. Holofernes and Nathaniel are abruptly introduced in the fourth act, because they are needed for the play, which has been rather loosely appended to the original comedy. Professor Gray asserts that "they have not the faintest excuse for being in the play, except to take part in the 1597 version of the masque."[38] But if the dramatic mould of *Love's Labour's Lost*

[35] Laneham, p. 25, in Nichols, Vol. II.

[36] Thorndyke, Ashley, *The Pastoral Element in the English Drama before 1605. Modern Language Notes,* 1889, p. 230.

[37] *Op. cit.*, p. 112.

[38] *Op. cit.*, p. 15.

be the essentially loose and episodic Progress, the late introduction of Holofernes and Nathaniel is natural and proper. Like the country folk in the burlesques presented at Kenilworth, their presence would not have been expected or tolerated until the time for their performance approached. Obviously the fortunes of the visiting Queen could not be involved in any plot-like fashion with these clowns. They were actors expected to appear only to furnish certain moments of amusement for their sovereign and then to vanish.

Light may be cast upon still another original and puzzling aspect of the comedy by considering it a dramatic initiation of a Progress. No satisfactory reason has been given for the unique and indeterminate ending of the drama.[39] When the ladies, at the moment of their departure, are sought in marriage by their lovers, they put them off for an entire year. This is an heretical ending for a romantic comedy, which never before had deliberately postponed love's felicity. Biron remarks the unconventionality of this close:

> Our wooing doth not end like an old play
> Jack hath not Gill: these ladies courtesy
> Might well have made our sport a Comedy.[40]

But this ending is harmonious with the origin of the drama as here presented and to the type as here conceived. In the first place, the story of the visit of the two queens at Nérac offered just this sort of indeterminate ending. No marriages were arranged. Marguerite of Valois was already the King's wife. The expedition resulted in a treaty between Navarre and France; and the flying squadron of ladies, its diplomatic service rendered, departed. In *Love's Labour's Lost,* too, the Princess seems to have succeeded in her diplomatic mission. In her farewell to the King she says:

> Excuse me so comming so short of thankes
> For my great suite, so easily obtained.[41]

[39] The only explanations are (1) that Shakespeare at this time, like all youthful genius, aimed at novelty of form (cf. H. D. Gray, *op. cit.,* p. 14; also Grant White, quoted *ibid.*), or (2) that the play was written as a plea of Southampton to have his projected marriage postponed.

[40] V. ii. 950 ff.

[41] V. ii. 811–812.

In the second place the Progresses of the Queen ended in the same way. However alluring the coquetry of Elizabeth and her ladies, however ardent the gallantry of the gentlemen, the imperial vot'ress passed on in maiden meditation fancy free. Therefore if *Love's Labour's Lost* had closed with the marriages of a typical romantic comedy, it would have departed in an important feature from the dramatic form which Shakespeare had chosen for it.

What hypothesis of the genesis and growth of *Love's Labour's Lost* have our studies up to this point enabled us to form? It occurred, we may suppose, to some Elizabethan gentleman that life at the court of Navarre, reflected at a moment when it was stirred into brilliant and picturesque movement by a famous visit of Marguerite of Valois and Catherine de Medici, would form an admirable foundation for an English court play. Whether his attraction was purely aesthetic or whether he saw in the possibilities of the situation an opportunity to make some personal plea in his own private interest, cannot now be determined. This idea became the property of Shakespeare. He believed that this situation would find its most suitable dramatic investiture in a play modelled on the royal Progresses of Elizabeth. It would be a new and piquant experience for the Queen to behold, as a spectator, the drama of a typical Progress, in which so many times she had been the central figure. Consequently as many as possible of the characteristics of these royal entertainments were preserved in the play. The scene of all the action was set in such a spacious park as surrounded many of the castles at which the Queen had been received. The play itself was not given any closely knit structure, but was deliberately planned as a chronicle of entertainments such as were provided for Elizabeth on successive days. The royal guest was given her inevitable opportunity to shoot deer from a covert. The gentlemen presented a merry anti-mask; the clowns, a burlesque show intended to provoke raillery. Finally there was a lyrical debate between the owl and the cuckoo and innumerable social conflicts of wit and dainty devices of speech and repartee. No one of these bits of entertainment in the Progress bore any intrinsic relationship to any other. Consequently Shakespeare felt no obligation to bind his dramatic pictures of such episodes any more closely together. They remain, as it were, a number of acts of the highest sort of Elizabethan vaudeville. Finally the Progress, as a dramatic form, would impose upon the playwright a kind of obligation to give his comedy an indefinite ending. The revels are over and the guests depart: "You that way; we this way."

In the Progress, therefore, we seem to have discovered the structural principle of *Love's Labour's Lost*. Other features of the play remain to be explained. They come from various sources. After the Progresses Shakespeare's most natural source for suggestions for the dramatization of his French story would be the plays of John Lyly, particularly the following comedies of court life: *Sapho and Phao, Endimion, and Midas*. Shakespeare's debt to these dramas in *Love's Labour's Lost* has often been assumed to be all-embracing. Bond expresses this opinion in the enthusiastic form of a special pleader. "In comedy," he says, "Lyly is Shakespeare's only model — and Lyly's influence is of a far more permanent nature than any exercised on the great poet by other writers. It extends beyond the boundaries of mechanical style to the more important matters of structure and spirit." [42] Professor Baker regards *Love's Labour's Lost* as a play constructed on the model of Lyly's work. He believes that it follows the earlier dramatist's method as it appears in his court comedies.[43]

In the latter statement there is much justice, if the critic be referring primarily to Shakespeare's style in this early play. The younger playwright may be said to have learned from Lyly the following important lessons, all of which he incorporated into *Love's Labour's Lost:*

1. How to present the intercourse of refined people conducted with the ease and grace of people to whom verbal ingenuity in conversation has become the supreme form of social delight.

[42] Bond's *Lyly,* II. 243.

[43] Baker, *op. cit.,* p. 114.

2. How to write dialogue, most of it in prose, which is the proper conversation for such a group. It is always witty, brisk, and adorned with fancy and learning; it sometimes degenerates into a somewhat artificial wit combat.
3. How to make love the principal subject of this conversation, which is guided largely by the women who treat their lovers in a tantalizing, flippant manner.
4. How to lay so much emphasis upon dialogue that both plot and characterization become unimportant by comparison.
5. How to introduce many songs.

The influence of Lyly upon *Love's Labour's Lost* in all these respects is indisputable. The conversation of the ladies and gentlemen deals almost exclusively with love. Biron and Rosaline occasionally peer over their flying words to behold each other as man and woman. The others, however, are too completely engrossed in their verbal encounters for such human entanglements; they are blind mouths skilled only in the play of amorous words. This atmosphere of gay badinage is that of Lyly and the witty dialogue a mere echo of his.

The characters in this game of words are grouped somewhat as Lyly's are. The Princess is balanced by the King, and the three ladies, Rosaline, Maria and Catherine are wooed by the three gentlemen, Biron, Longaville and Dumain. In Lyly's plays the same sort of formalism often exists. In *Midas*, for example, there are three councillors, three pages, a group of ladies and a group of shepherds; in *Endimion* there are three pages, two councillors and two philosophers.

All of these elements appear in *Love's Labour's Lost* in greatly altered form. There they have been deepened until they form a somewhat definite comic view of life. Bond says, with warrant, that "there is however, a humanity behind the trifling, the jokes and the affectations to which Lyly in his ripest work never attains." [44] In *Love's Labour's Lost* true love stories emerge, fitfully at least, from what would have remained in Lyly mere verbal trifling. Some critics, as has been noted, have seen in

[44] Bond, II. 262.

Shakespeare's comedy an "obvious satire on the notion that polite society, its sayings, and its doings was life in any real sense at all." All these differences serve to emphasize the fact that none of the structural elements of *Love's Labour's Lost* were derived from Lyly. His comedies were little more than manuals to which the younger dramatist referred for authentic details of proper courtly behavior.

Certain writers have believed Lyly's influence much more extensive. They maintain that most of the comic characters in Shakespeare's drama are copies of similar figures in Lyly. "The comic figures," says Baker, "except Costard and Jaquenetta, owe much both in the content and the phrasing of their speech to John Lyly.[45] Elsewhere Baker says that Shakespeare "presents somewhat caricatured figures of the day, in place of Lyly's exaggerated classic comic figures."[46] Bond says, a little more specifically: "The pretentious Sir Tophas, the ridicule of him by the pages and his pairing with Bagoa, are the originals of the magnificent Armado, of his relation in the Moth and his declension upon the country wench Jaquenetta."[47]

Shakespeare's imitation of Lyly in these respects seems very much more doubtful. Indeed upon examination these comic characters in *Love's Labour's Lost* prove to resemble the corresponding ones in Lyly only in the most general features.

The generally noted resemblances between Sir Tophas in Lyly's *Endimion* and Don Armado are the following:

1. They are both braggarts.
2. They are both in love with ill-favored rustic wenches.
3. The adventures of both reflect in humorous fashion the action of the main plot.
4. Each has, as an attendant, a derisive page or boy.

These similarities exist, but they are characteristics held in common by all the descendants of the Plautine and Terentian braggart soldier. Within the limits of that wide-spread tradition the two figures will be seen to differ so strikingly that it can be clearly shown that one is in no sense a model for the other, but

[45] Baker, p. 113. [46] *Ibid.*, p. 114. [47] I. 297.

that they attach themselves to the hoary tradition at quite different points. Sir Tophas is a farced *miles gloriosus*, a descendant of such exaggerated figures as Thersites in the English interlude of that name, sometimes attributed to John Heywood. His boasts are extravagant to the point of folly. He threatens to do bloody execution upon the mildest of God's creatures. He will slay the monster *Ovis*. "I will draw their guts out of their bellies," he shouts, "and tear the flesh with my teeth, so mortal is my hate." [48] He beholds two pages who he insists are wrens. Epiton, his boy, tells him that the objects are two lads. But Tophas replies, "Byrdes or boyes, they are both but a pittance for my breakfast." [49]

Now in the drawing of Armado no stress whatever is placed upon his grandiose boasting or such display of his military process. In fact, if he were not called "braggart" throughout the play, we should hardly recognize him as belonging to the *miles gloriosus* type. He is introduced rather as a voluble traveller, nice in his speech to the point of affectation. He speaks of himself as "Armado, a soldier, a man of travel, that hath seen the world." [50] Biron says:

> Armado is a most illustrious wight
> A man of fire, new words, fashions owne Knight.[51]

Ferdinand just a moment before has referred to him as

> A refined traveler of Spain
> A man in all the world's new fashion planted
> That hath a mint of phrases in his brain

This figure is no swashbuckler and windy braggart, but a fop in manners and a virtuoso in speech.

This Armado in many of these important respects in which he differs from Sir Tophas and the *miles gloriosus* resembles the

[48] *Endimion,* I. 11.

[49] Thersites, when he catches sight of a snail, makes a similarly absurd remark:

> "But what a monster do I see now
> Come hitherward with an armed bow?
> What is it? Ah it is a sow."

[50] V. i. 103.

[51] I. i. 189–190.

braggart as he had become conventionalized in the Italian popular comedy or the *Commedia dell' Arte.*[52] There, too, he was usually a Spaniard.[53] This transformation of the Latin braggart into a Spanish swashbuckler was a natural result of political conditions in Italy during the sixteenth century, when the Spaniards held much of the country as conquered territory. Their rule in many places, in Naples, for example, was cruel and repressive and provoked many uprisings and revolutions. The unpopular Spanish soldier quartered upon the unwilling Italian inhabitants was satirized by means of the age-old stage figure. Hence the *miles gloriosus* became the *Matamoras.* He was made to affect Spanish stateliness, to talk Castilian, and to adopt a vocabulary of magnificent high-sounding phrases.[54]

In this process of change most of the roughness and noisy extravagance of the rôle disappeared to be replaced by the polished elegance of a gloved gentleman, who carries on his warfare with the utmost dignity and seriousness.[55] A contemporary pen-sketch of the character, reproduced by Rasi,[56] shows the figure to be in no sense grotesque in form or in his

[52] Winifred Smith has noticed this general resemblance. She says (*Italian and Elizabethan Comedy, Modern Philology,* V. 561), " Not less important is Shakespeare's Holofernes, whose name, manner of speech, and general imbecility place him far nearer to the Italian stage-type than to a possible village personage of Shakespeare's acquaintance."

[53] Luigi Riccoboni says that the character was introduced into Italian drama comedy from Spanish drama. — *Histoire du Théâtre Italien depuis la Décadence de la Comédie Latine* (Paris, 1730), I. 56. This statement, of course, ignores the obvious relation of this figure with its Latin prototype. Cf. also Scherillo, Michele, *La Commedia dell' Arte in Italia* (1884), p. 96, and Lee, Vernon, *Studies of the Eighteenth Century in Italy* (1880), p. 235.

[54] Contemporary Italian critics declared that the Spanish tongue was admirably suited to this verbal extravagance. Cecchini (*Frutti delle Moderne Commedie,* 1628) says, " Questa iperbolica parte par che suoni meglio nella spagnuola che nella Italiana lingua, come quella a cui vediamo esser più proprii a più domestici gl'impossibili."

[55] Rasi, L., *I Comici Italiani; biografia, bibliografia, iconografia* (Firenze, 1897), I. 63: " La maschera chiassona, urlona che atterrà un reggimento di soldati con un semplice Guarda voi, ha ceduto il campo al gentiluomo, inguantato, levigato, compassato, che offre a tutti e non da al alcuno, che spara bombe colassali colla maggior calma e serietà del mondo."

[56] Rasi, I. 513.

costume. His sword does not protrude behind at an absurd angle. His hat is embellished with two huge feathers, but he has no trace of the long pointed nose. On the whole he is a graceful gentleman overnicely clad.

Francesco Andreini, the most important impersonator of the *capitano* in the sixteenth century, was a captain of this sort, and became famous for the verbal virtuosity that he exhibited in his reading of the part. This Andreini was a contemporary of Shakespeare; he acted in the company of the Gelosi in 1571, 1574, 1576, 1599 and 1603–4 before the French court and in Paris at the Hotel de Bourgogne.[57] He was so famous as an actor and a writer that an English actor and playwright of any intellectual curiosity could hardly have failed to hear of him and his work.

This actor-dramatist was a highly intelligent man, a member of a Florentine academy, and interested primarily in the entertainment he could afford by twisting *concetti* and every sort of literary allusion into the speech of his captain,[58] whom he called Capitano Spavento of Hell-Valley. These speeches were so much admired that he collected and published them in two different collections.[59] Of this braggart, as of Armado, it could be truthfully said that he had " a mint of phrases in his brain." At least it need surprise no one that the influence of a *Commedia dell' Arte* figure upon a farcical character like the *miles gloriosus* has been to refine it in much the same fashion in which Armado has been refined.

Shakespeare's figure certainly shows more points of relationship with this Italian re-creation than with Sir Tophas. It is, of course, probable that Shakespeare, like all literary artists, drew upon his personal experience when fashioning a character. He may have had his eye on the fantastical *monarcho,* a Span-

[57] Baschet, A., *Les Comédiens italiens à la cour de France sous Charles IX, Henri III, Henri IV, et Louis XIII* (1882), pp. 67 ff.

[58] Rasi, II. 513.

[59] Belwacqua, Enrico, in *Giornale Storico,* XXIII. 87: " Egli cita spesso il Petrarca, l'Ariosto e il Tasso, cita il Marino, il Chiabrera, il Caporali, reporta in verso di Dante, sebbene per isbaglio dica che e del Petrarca, recorda molti scrittori greci e latini."

iard who for years hung about the court of Elizabeth, when drawing Armado. However, the more we know of Shakespeare's sources, the more we realize that he usually had dramatic warrant for his so-called innovations, — that his original conceptions were poured into dramatic moulds already cast. Such a rude mould existed in the Spanish braggart of the *Commedia dell' Arte.*[60]

Strong corroborative evidence of this origin can be found in the fact that each one of Don Armado's clownish associates in *Love's Labour's Lost* bears a close resemblance to a corresponding type-figure in the picturesque clown-group of Italian comedy. Such likenesses between characters as individuals, and as members of a conventionalized group, can hardly be fortuitous.

Before these points of similarity are indicated, a word should be said about the term "Italian comedy." This term is commonly applied to two types of drama: the *Commedia Erudita*, or "learned" comedy, of which Gascogne's *Supposes*[61] is the best known English example; and the *Commedia dell' Arte*, the professional or improvised comedy. The differences between the two in the essential qualities of plot and character were never very great. The same authors often wrote both sorts of comedy and brought the same literary conventions, the same notions of construction, and the same comic devices to both sorts of work.

The extent of the knowledge of *Commedia Erudita* in Elizabethan England can be fairly easily determined. That of the *Commedia dell' Arte* is obviously more difficult to fix. Yet the probabilities that this more popular form exercised an influence

[60] Indeed in Elizabethan drama the term "braggart" came to be applied to this Armado type rather than to the traditional "Miles." Braggardino in Chapman's *The Blind Beggar of Alexandria* is such a creature; and Osric in *Hamlet* once in the first quarto (V. ii) in a stage direction is called a "braggart gentleman." Shakespeare was probably not the first English dramatist to introduce this Spanish braggart to the Elizabethan stage. Basilisco in Kyd's *Soliman and Perseda* is a mixture of braggart and virtuoso in the use of inflated verbiage, as Bond has noted in his introduction to this play. Miss Smith (*Italian and Elizabethan Comedy*, *Modern Philology,* V. 562) calls this Basilisco "the forerunner of Shakespeare's Armado and Parolles."

[61] A free translation of Ariosto's *Gli Suppositi,* appearing in 1575.

upon Elizabethan dramatists in general, and upon Shakespeare in particular, are strong.

The evidence in the records, of various sorts, of the presence of Italian actors and Italian companies in England during the later half of the sixteenth century has been often presented.[62] Payments were made by the Privy Council to Italians both singers and actors from 1550 on,[63] and there are occasional references in the Revels Accounts to representations by the Italian Players.[64]

The first notice of the appearance of an Italian company in England concerns a reward "gevin to the Italyans for serteyne pastymes that they showed before Maister Mear and his brethen"[65] in September, 1573. This company apparently stayed on into the next year, because we find in the Revels Accounts various payments and furnishings and properties of some Italian actors who "followed the progresse and made pastyme first at Wynsor and afterwards at Reading."[66] The next Italian company apparently visited England early in the year 1578; at any rate the Treasurer of the Chamber paid "Alfroso Ferrabolle and the rest of the Italian Players"[67] for an entertainment presented at court on February 27, 1576. Finally, on January 13, 1578, The Privy Council ordered "The Lord Mayor of London to give orders that one Drousiano, the Italian, a commediante, and

[62] (a) Schücking, L. L., *Studien über die Stöfflichen Beziehungen der englischen Komödie zur italienischen bis Lilly,* Halle, 1901.
(b) Wolf, Max, *op. cit.*, pp. 1–20.
(c) Smith, Winifred, *The Commedia dell' Arte* (1912), pp. 172 ff.
(d) The latest and most complete account of Italian companies in England is to be found in E. K. Chambers, *The Elizabethan Stage* (1923), II. 261–265. This I follow rather closely.

[63] *Acts of the Privy Council,* II. 88.

[64] Edited by Feuillerat, A., *Documents relating to the Office of Revels in the Time of Queen Elizabeth . . . (London,* 1903), pp. 225 ff.

[65] Murray, J. T., *English Dramatic Companies 1558–1642,* II. 374.

[66] Chambers (*op. cit.*, p. 262) points out that "Queen Elizabeth was at Windsor on 11 and 12 July; on 15 July she removed to Reading and remained there to July 22."

[67] Chambers suggests that this is probably a clerical error for Alfonso Ferrabosco, the first of three generations of that name attached to the English Court. Cf. G. E. P. Arkwright, *Notes on the Ferrabosco Family* (*The Musical Antiquary*), III. 221; IV. 42.

his companye may play within the Cittie and the liberties of the same between this and the first weeks of Lent." [68] This Drousiano was first identified by Collier as Drusiano Martinelli; [69] and this identification has been accepted by practically all subsequent historians of Italian comedy. He was the brother of Tristano Martinelli,[70] the Arlecchino of the Gelosi. He was probably associated with this famous troupe himself, although there is no direct proof to establish this as a fact. However, this was the only company known to have been in France during the summer of 1577 and Italian players universally left some trace of their presence in France on their way to England. We can, therefore, say with assurance that Drusiano took certain members of this troupe across the Channel to perform before popular London audiences.[71] Later he took the leading rôles in the Duke of Mantua's company of comedians.[72] The nature of the repertory of this company can be inferred from the plays acted by the Gelosi in Paris and by Drusiano's company while it was in Mantua. Besides the *Commedie dell' Arte,* he almost surely presented some of the *Commedie Erudite* written by members of the bourgeois academies to which many of the actors belonged.[73]

This company and others of a similar nature which probably followed it [74] evidently made a profound impression upon Eng-

[68] *Acts etc.,* X. 144. Quoted by Smith, 175.

[69] *History of English Dramatic Poetry* (1826), III. 398, note.

[70] Cf. Rasi, *op. cit.,* under " Martinelli."

[71] Dr. Furness, referring to the visit of this company, remarks (*Much Ado About Nothing,* Variorum ed., Intro., p. xxvii) that it is evidence of " an intimate relationship at that early date between the English and the Italian stage, of which too little account is made by those who wish to explain Shakespeare's knowledge of Italian manners and names."

[72] D'Ancona, Alessandro, *Teatro Montovano nel Secolo XVI, Giornale Storico,* VI. 37.

[73] Winifred Smith, in *Italian and Elizabethan Comedy*, *Modern Philology,* V. 557, says that there is no particular reason why the Inganni of Alessandro Piccolomini, which many have compared to *Twelfth Night,* may not have been given in London by the Italian actors.

[74] Miss Smith (*ibid.*) says that Coryat in his *Crudities* (London, 1776, from ed. of 1611), II. 16, 17, must be alluding to such a company in his comment on a play he attended in Venice. " I saw women acte, a thing I never saw before, though I have heard it hath been sometimes used in

lish authors and audiences. Nash's famous attack upon "the players beyond the sea" as "a sort of squirting baudie comedians that have whores to play women's parts — forbeare no immodest speech or unchast action that may procure laughter"[75] is but one of a score of references,[76] complementary and, like this, condemnatory, made during the final quarter of the sixteenth century.

Indeed there is evidence to suggest that the comic dramaturgy of these years in England was permeated with the ideals of Italian comedy. Stephen Gosson in his *School of Abuse,*[77] and his *Plays Confuted in Five Actions,*[78] uses the terms "comedies" and "Italian devices," or variations of this latter phrase, practically synonymously. His own comedy, an indiscretion of his youth, of which he heartily repents in his obscurantist maturity, he calls "a cast of Italian devices" with the title *The Comedie of Capitaine Mario.*

Plays, he is certain, came from the Devil, who first corrupted Englishmen by giving them wanton Italian books to read,[79] but "not contented with the number he hath corrupted with reading Italian bawdry, because all cannot read, presented us comedies cut by the same pattern." This trash is called "new-learning" by those which "bear a sharper smack of Italian devices in their heads, than of English religion in their hearts." "Compare London to Rome," he cries in *The School of Abuse,* "and England to Italy. You shall find the theatres of one, the abuses of the other to be rife among us." Repetition of more of these familiar passages should be unnecessary. Gosson's description of the constituent elements of comedy as he understands it fits Italian comedy best. "The Grounde Work of

London." Visiting Italians were the only ones who in those days could have had women actors in their troupes.

[75] Nash, *Pierce Penilesse* (1592, ed. Grosart), p. 92.

[76] Cf. Smith, *Commedia dell' Arte,* p. 177; also Schucking, pp. 58 ff.

[77] For the text, see *The Shakespeare Society Publications,* No. 2, 1841.

[78] For the text, see Hazlitt, *The English Drama and Stage under the Tudor and Stuart Princes: 1543–1664* (Roxburgh Library, 1859), pp. 157 ff.

[79] It is well known that the age of Shakespeare's youth was, as Schelling says (*Foreign Influences in Elizabethan Plays,* p. 49), "literally soaked in Italian literature and fiction."

Comedies," he says, " is love cosenedge, flatterie, bawderie, slye conveyhance of whoredom; the persons cookes, queans, knaves, baudes, parasites, courtezannes, lecherous olde men, amorous young men." Allowing for the zealot's exaggeration, this passage might refer to either sort of Italian comedy, or even to that of Plautus or Terence; but taken in connection with the passage to be cited, it seems clearly intended as a description of the popular comedy.

The Devil, continues the implacable Gosson, seduces man by way of comedies, particularly through the eye, because he sendeth in " gearish apparell, maskes, vauting, tumbling, dancing of gigges, galiandes, morisces, hobbi-horses, showing of iudgeling castes."

The properties and devices here mentioned are of the very essence of the *Commedia dell' Arte.* The passage is primarily a description of the *lazzi* of the clowns with which the improvised comedy was replete. Moreover, it is highly probable that the word " maskes " in this context refers to the actual masks that the typical figures in this comedy wore. It obviously does not refer to the highly refined court show of the same name.[80] " Gearish apparell " obviously refers to costume and describes nothing so accurately as the fantastic parti-coloured garments of the popular Italian comedy. " Maskes," Gosson opines, are equally designed to seduce the eyes of the vulgar. They must be, therefore, something related to " gearish apparell " and so probably the word refers to the grotesque half-faces which the clowns like Harlequin and Pulchinella habitually wore.

These passages tend to confirm our *a priori* judgment in this matter. Of the two sorts of Italian comedy one would expect the *Commedia dell' Arte* to have the more definite influence upon English drama.[81] Only those few literary comedies which were translated into English could have exerted any pervasive influ-

[80] The word was frequently used to mean a disguise or mumming. In the *Documents relating to the Office of Revels 1559–60* one may read such entries as " A Maske of Patriarkes " and " A Maske of Italyen Women."

[81] The almost universal knowledge of Italian among Elizabethan courtiers and gentlemen of distinction (cf. Schelling, *Foreign Influences in Elizabethan Plays,* p. 41) did not extend to the popular playwrights.

ence. The appeal of the *Commedia dell' Arte,* on the other hand, was largely independent of language. It flourished in nearly every capital and important city of the continent during the latter half of the sixteenth century. English travelling comedians are known to have played at the same places with Italian companies for prolonged periods. Before 1580, London had at least once submitted itself to the charm of the *Commedia dell' Arte.* Its appeal was striking, picturesque, unique. Such plays, once seen, would be held securely in memory and all their comic devices cherished.

The historical facts adduced and such utterances as these of Gosson show that English dramatic life during the seventies and eighties of the sixteenth century was permeated by the form and spirit of Italian comedy,— largely of the popular sort. What reason is there to suppose that Shakespeare during the latter part of this period fell under the wide-spread influence of this striking comedy?

At the end of his career, Shakespeare knew well a certain type of Italian comic scenario. It has recently been shown that the story of *The Tempest* and many of its distinctive theatrical features are undoubtedly derived from a romantic type of *Commedia dell' Arte.*[82] A group of five scenarios, written down first in 1622, but representing much older traditions of the masked players, contains practically all of the constructive and distinctive histrionic features of *The Tempest,* in a combination which makes the evidence for their influence upon Shakespeare absolutely convincing. These newly discovered facts justify our assuming that by 1610 he had direct and specific knowledge of the *Commedia dell' Arte.* His general or traditional knowledge seems to have been much older. Specific allusions to the various Italian "masks" can be found throughout his work.[83] Even in

[82] See Neri, Ferdinando, *Scenari delle Maschere in Arcadia* (Città di Castello, 1913). Number I of *Documenti di Storia Letteraria Italiana,* edited by Pietro Mattiacci, for the text. Cf. also Gray, Henry David, *The Sources of The Tempest, Modern Language Notes,* XXXV (1920), 321.

[83] He refers to Pantalone as "the old Pantaloon" in *The Taming of the Shrew,* III. i. 37; as "the lean and slippered Pantaloon" in *As You Like It,* II. vii. 158; as "the old Magnifico" in *Othello,* I. ii. 12. Cf.

the comedy under discussion Biron speaks of "some carry-tale, some pleseman, some slight zany." [84] These facts simply confirm what is an almost inevitable inference, — that a young writer like Shakespeare, who throughout his career showed himself to be closely in touch with all the dramatic tendencies of his time, could hardly have failed, especially in the opening years of his career, to be aware of the spectacular action and striking stage-figures of the *Commedia dell' Arte.* Its influence, perhaps next to that of Lyly, would be the most natural one to draw Shakespeare within its sphere. His clowns, indeed, would almost inevitably be related to that comedy of clowns. That the character of Armado should resemble the Spanish braggart of Italian comedy, then, and not the Latinate Sir Tophas of Lyly, need astonish no critic familiar with the European dramatic situation in the years when Shakespeare began to write for the stage.

All the points of likeness usually asserted as existing between Sir Tophas and Armado can now be recognized as traditions of the *capitano.* For example, Sir Tophas is said to be the prototype of Armado because he is forced to marry an ugly wench Bagoa, just as Armado pairs with the country lout Jaquenetta. But this is one of the conventional ways of disposing of the *capitano.* Thus are his amorous conceit and amorous ambition broadly satirized. He is regularly either utterly humiliated and driven off in disgrace at the end of the play or he is married to some clownish and ill-favored female. Francisco Andreini, for example, in one of the discourses which he composed for this part of the *capitano* [85] presents the plight of the *capitano* who is married to the terrible fury Megara.[86] A less extravagant situation of this sort is that of Captain Crackstone in *The Two*

Smith, *op. cit.,* pp. 178 ff., where references of a similar sort by other Elizabethan dramatists are also collected.

[84] *Love's Labour's Lost,* V. ii. 463.

[85] *Le Bravure del Capitano Spavento . . . di Francesco Andreini da Pistoria Comico Geloso* (*Venetia,* 1607), Ragiomento ventesimo, 134–141.

[86] Cf. 138: "Quella notte tremo più volte l'Inferno, mentre ch'io rompeva lancie con la mia bella sposa, e per quando io mi sapessi fare non hebbi gratia di renderla gravida di me, peresser ella troppo furiosa negli amorosi conflitte et per haver la matrice arsa, e bruciata."

Italian Gentlemen, an English adaptation of an Italian comedy.[87] This braggart woos the vulgar maid Attilia and apparently wins her. "How saist those Alice tittle tattle," he cries in the last lines of the play "art thou content by love to be bound?" Sir Tophas and Armado decline upon sorry wenches, then, because that amorous disaster is in the typical *capitano's* part.

A relationship between Lyly's and Shakespeare's figure has been assumed because each is accompanied by a page, who ridicules the self-importance and the extravagant assumptions of his braggart master, particularly his rôle of lover. But here again Sir Tophas and Armado have merely both inherited a common appendage of the *capitano.* He was invariably accompanied by such a servant. In the *Commedia dell' Arte* this fellow was one of the clowns, often Arlecchino, and his relation to his master was that of the page to Sir Tophas or to Armado. This figure, the zany, was originally the clown or mountebank, whose first requisite was the physical agility demanded for the performance of his *lazzi* or bits of horse-play. His brains in time came to be as swift as his muscles, because his function in the plot became more and more that of managing events in the interest of the *amorosa.* His quick wit was also shown more and more in puns, in word-play of all sorts, and in satiric repartee. He assumed so many forms and inherited so many characteristics of the "servus" of Latin comedy and resembled so closely the clown in native English drama that it is impossible to prove that a figure like Moth is a direct descendant of the zany attached to the *capitano.* However, the two belong to the same family, and it is reasonable to suppose that the servant would come from the same source as the master. If Armado came into English comedy as an Italian type, Moth probably had a similar origin.

A strong confirmation of this theory may be found in the fact that all the members of the subsidiary comic group have prototypes in the figures of the *Commedia dell' Arte:* Costard, the slow-witted rustic, in Pagliaccio, a similar heavy lout; Holofernes, in a figure with various names, charlatan, pedagogue, and pedant, with his speech habitually crammed with macaronic

87 *Il Fedele,* written by Luigi Pasqualigo.

Latin and Bolognese riddles; Nathaniel, in the Parasite or *affamato,* who only in the *Commedia dell' Arte* is attached to the Pedant. Even Dull, English to the core in his particular form of conscientious stupidity, has a prototype in Italian comedy.

Costard's ancestor, a stupid rustic, appears in the earliest scenario that we possess.[88] There he evokes laughter only by his ridiculous clothing and rustic behavior,[89] and bears no relation whatever to the plot. The proper " business " for an actor presenting this character is explained in a dialogue about scenic performances composed between 1567 and 1590 by an actor-manager, Leone di Sommi.[90] His advice to the âctor on this point is " If he plays a fool, besides answering off the point (which the poet will teach him by his words) he must be able to act the imbecile, catch flies, kill fleas, and do like foolish actions."

This rustic or fool first became an integral part of the bourgeois group who form the vehicle of the love plot, in the company of the Gelosi. He there usually bears the name of Pedrolino,[91] and is the servant of Pantalone. He is generally outwitted by the other servants, stupidly falls asleep at his post, or gets drunk with the *capitano* and his servant. In particular, he made himself ridiculous when encountering the principal zany and becoming involved in the toils of his wit. By the time of Barbieri's *Il Supplica,* written in 1634, the dramatic contrast between the two servants had become a thoroughly established dramatic convention and treated as such in this book of dramaturgy. Barbieri says, " The first servant provokes laughter by most subtle tricks and ready replies, the second by foolishness."

[88] In a description, written by Massuno Trojano, of an improvised comedy which he, as court choir-master, wrote for presentation at the Duke of Bavaria's wedding in 1568. Cf. Smith, *op. cit.,* p. 70.

[89] He is introduced " alla Cavajola." That is, he impersonated the peasant as he appeared in the " farse caviole," which represented the life of the folk in the southern Italian town of Cava. Cf. Torraca, F., *Il teatro italiano nei secoli XIII, XIV, XV* (Firenze, 1885), pp. 431 ff.

[90] Cf. Smith, *op. cit.,* p. 70.

[91] He inherits certain traits of a Pagliaccio of an earlier company and of a character called Bertoldino. Cf. the present author's *The Comedies of Holberg,* pp. 175 and 350.

The dramatic contrast between these two servants Shakespeare did not develop strongly until he wrote *The Two Gentlemen of Verona.* However, the possibilities of humor in such a contrast are suggested in *Love's Labour's Lost.* Costard, at any rate, is a very close equivalent of this Italian fool. Like his prototype described by Leone di Sommi, his humor is rustic behavior and the vice of mistaking the word or of answering off the point. Every time that he appears, he contributes bits of verbal misunderstanding like the following:

Armado. Sirra, Costard. I will infranchise thee.
Clown. O, marrie me to one Francis, I smell some Lenvoy, some goose in this.[92]

The following dialogue illustrates the same point:

Ber. O my good Knave Costard, exceedingly well met.
Clown. Pray you sir, How much Carnation Ribbon may a man buy for a remuneration?
Ber. What is a remuneration?
Cost. Marrie, sir, halfe pennie farthing.[93]

Shakespeare naturally gave this Costard traits of English rustics, but the character is very clearly cast in the dramatic mould of the Italian figure.

Holofernes, another permanent member of the group of clowns, is also modelled on the very popular Italian figure of the pedant. Many critics, following the lead of Warburton, have attempted to see in this character Shakespeare's satire of some individual whom he knew and scorned. Warburton asserted without any apparent warrant that Holofernes was intended to represent John Florio.[94] Karl Elze makes the unsupported assertion that Shakespeare's pedant is a satirical picture of Thomas Hunt, the poet's teacher from 1572 to 1577.[95] Abel Lefranc, finding a manuscript play on the *Nine Worthies* by Richard Lloyd, the

[92] Act III, Scene ii.
[93] *Ibid.*
[94] Variorum of 1821, p. 479: "By Holofernes is designed a particular character, a pedant and schoolmaster of our author's time, one John Florio . . ."
[95] *William Shakespeare* (translated by L. Dora Schmitz, 1888), p. 37: "There is, probably, little doubt that the poet has immortalized Thos. Hunt as Holofernes.

tutor of the Sixth Earl of Derby, concludes that Holofernes is comic portrait of this schoolmaster. Arthur Acheson believes that Holofernes represents Chapman and that "In the pedantry and verbosity of Holofernes he (Shakespeare) caricatures Chapman's style, and in the person of Holofernes excoriates Chapman himself."[96]

These theories, by no means all of the sort that have been advanced, besides being impossible of proof, ignore the existence of one of the most wide-spread and popular of the Italian stage conventions of the time, — that of the pedant. The model from which this character was drawn was an international figure, the product of Renaissance culture. With the coming of the new learning the intellectual methods of the scholastics or medieval school-philosophers naturally became the objects of ridicule. This sort of scholar came to appear as an absurd combination of the rigid logician and formal rhetorician. In drama he was made to argue according to all forms of the syllogism, — to concede the major and deny the minor. He fatuously came forward on all occasions with some general rule which he considered applicable to the particular case in hand.

Later the exaggerations of the humanist himself were made the object of satire, — his confident and superior wisdom, which yet rendered him helpless in any difficult situation, and his motley tongue, half Italian and half Latin. He is particularly prone to use his learning in colloquies with people of the lower class, among whom he produces misunderstandings which fill him with rage. He usually falls in love, in which state his insatiable quotation of Latin maxims and classical precedents render him particularly ridiculous. He is always cozened and misled, but he seeks to make his learning yield him comfort. He thinks of the great men of the past who have been pursued by misfortune and hopes that thought will bring him equanimity. Occasionally he is made a philosopher in words and a licentious hyprocrite in fact. As such he is exposed and driven off the stage with scorn.

In Italian comedy, also, the pedant is usually the school

[96] Acheson, *Shakespeare and the Rival Poet* (1903), p. 83.

teacher or tutor. In *Gl'Ingannati*[97] (1526), for example, one of the principal characters is Piero, the tutor of Fabrizio. In *The Two Italian Gentlemen,* Pedante, the tutor of Fidele, enters "attired in a gown and cap like a schoolmaster." Both of these teachers fill their discourse with Latin and are particularly eloquent in that tongue before dolts who cannot understand them.

In *The Two Italian Gentlemen*[98] Attilia, the loutish maid, is the object of the pedant's attentions and is forced to listen to much incomprehensible Latin.

Attilia:
I pray Sir, what was it you sayde of love?
Pedante:
Est Deus in nobis agitante calescimus illo.

I dare not tell you the meaning, lest I make your cheeks glow. This pedant, too, inserts Italian into his discourse with a freedom only once or twice attempted by Holofernes:

Andante allegramente, you are right under her window now

or

Oche cricca di vacche? What cattell have we heare?

To be sure these Italian schoolmasters are in love and show their Latinate folly most completely in this situation.

Holofernes clearly belongs to this type.[99] He is a schoolmaster who "teaches boys the Horne-book." He apostrophizes good old Mantuan, whose Eclogues were a favorite text for study in the schools. Nathaniel, his parasite, praises his work as follows: "Sir, I praise God for you, and so may my parish-

[97] This play has been considered to be a possible source of *Twelfth Night.* Dr. Furness goes so far as to suggest that this might be one of the dramas brought to England by Drousiano in 1577–78 (*New Variorum Twelfth Night,* p. xxi). This play was also translated into Latin under the title of *Laelia* and presented at Queens College, Cambridge, in 1590 and again in 1598. Cf. Churchill and Keller, *Shakespeare Jahrbuch,* XXIV (1898), 286, 291.

[98] The characteristics of this pedant are important for our purpose, because he is one of a very few representatives of the Italian type who appeared in extant plays written before Shakespeare began to compose.

[99] See note 52.

ioners, for their Sonnes are well tutor'd by you, and their Daughters profit very greatly under you; you are a good member of the Common-wealth." [100] Later in this same scene Holofernes says, " I do dine today at the fathers of a certaine Pupill of mine."

He crams his discourse with Latin and is outraged at the ignorance of the clowns who cannot understand him.

> *Nath.* . . . but sir, I assure ye, it was a Bucke of the first head.
> *Hol.* Sir Nathaniel, haud credo.
> *Dul.* 'Twas not a haud credo, 'twas a Pricket.
> *Hol.* Most barbarous intimation: yet a kind of insinuation, as it were in via, in way of explication *facere,* as it were replication, or rather *ostentare,* to show as it were his inclination after his undressed, unpolished, uneducated, unpruned, untrained, or rather unlettered, or ratherest unconfirmed fashion, to insert againe my haud *credo* for a dear.[101]

Holofernes is also keenly on the lookout for false Latin.

> *Clowns:* Goe to, thou hast it ad dungil, at the finger ends, as they say.
> *Peda:* Oh, I smell false Latin, dunghel for unguam.[102]

Furthermore he now and then falls into Italian as in his apostrophe to Mantuan, " Ah good old Mantuan, I may speake of thee as the traveller doth of Venice, 'Venetia, Venetia, chi non te vede, non te pregia.' " [103]

The verbal affectations and flourishes of Holofernes in the use of his mother-tongue are of definite sorts. In the first place he shows his mastery of a vocabulary by uttering on every possible occasion a mass of synonyms. He says that the braggart is " too picked, too spruce, too affected, too odde, as it were, too peregrinat." He comments as follows on Don Armado's use of the term " posteriors of this day " for afternoon as follows: " The posterior of the day, most generous sir, is liable, congruent, and measurable for the afternoone: the word is well culd, chose,

[100] Act IV, Sc. ii.
[101] Act IV, Sc. ii, ll. 10 ff.
[102] Act V, Sc. i, ll. 75–77.
[103] In the Folio text this is written as gibberish: " Venice, venchie, que non te unde, que non te perreche." Theobald was the first to discern the Italian proverb in this hash. Scherillo (*La Via italiana nel seicento,* p. 336) finds this like similar speeches of the Dottore Gratiano, the pedant in the Gelosi company.

sweet and apt. I doe assure you."[104] He speaks of his own talent in making rhymes in the following way: "This is a gift that I have simple: simple, a foolish extravagant spirit, full of forms, figures, objects, ideas, apprehensions, motions, revolutions."[105]

In the second place, Holofernes indulges a passion for over-ingenious etymologies. He exclaims pompously, "But for elegancy, facility and golden cadence of poesie, caret. Ovidius Naso was the man. And why indeed Naso, but for smelling out the odoriferous flowers of fancy, the jerks of invention."[106] He answers Jaquenetta's "God give you good morrow, Master Parson," in the following jocose fashion: "Master Parson, quasi pers-on. An if one should be pierced, which is the one?"[107]

In the third place, he is sometimes given to false pronunciations. For example, he says to Nathaniel, after he has read the love letter, "You find not the apostrophas and so miss the accent. Let me supervise the cangenet (canzonet)."[108]

The following somewhat puzzling passage, in which Holofernes comments on Don Armado's pronunciation, is also an indication of bookish ignorance of the spoken idiom: "He clepeth a Calf; Caufe halfe, haufe; Neighbour vocabitur nebour: neigh abbreviated ne: this is abhominable, which he would call abbominable."[109] To assume that the pedant here is talking merely as a purist is to attribute to him a subtlety of humor not in harmony with his character as drawn elsewhere in the play. He is rather presented in this speech as a man essentially

[104] Act V, Sc. i, ll. 14–15.

[105] Act V, Sc. i, ll. 87–90.

[106] Act IV, Sc. ii, ll. 80–83.

[107] Act V, Sc. i, l. 25. This speech is given to Nathaniel in the Folio, but obviously belongs to Holofernes, as Theobald was the first to see. After the first eighty lines of this scene there is much confusion in the attribution of speeches to Holofernes and Nathaniel. Fleay first (*Life*, p. 203) finds the origin of the confusion in the hurried retouching of the scene for a court performance. Later (*Anglia*, VII. p. 229) he says that in the first draft of the play Holofernes was curate and Nathaniel the pedant. Dr. Furness (Variorum, p. 136) prefers the traditional scapegoats, — the compositors or compositors' reader. I follow the attribution of the Cambridge editors.

[108] Act IV, Sc. ii, l. 135.

[109] Act V, Sc. i, ll. 24–26.

bookish, who has learned his words from a printed page, and is oblivious and contemptuous of their career in the living speech. His own mispronunciation of "abominable," based upon a false etymology, gives satiric emphasis to his ponderous ignorance of idiomatic pronunciation.

Now every one of these verbal affectations of Holofernes, with the necessary exception of his use of Italian, is a recognized convention of the pedantic doctor in the *Commedia dell' Arte*, and particularly of the rôle as played by Ludovico Bianchi of the Gelosi troupe. This *dottore*, generally called Graziano, is usually from Bologna, and his humors are exactly the same as those just catalogued. Rasi thus enumerates his foibles: "The doctor is always the invariable ignoramus and pedant, who utters wise saws in the inevitable mixture of macaronic Latin, of foolish quotations and absurd etymologies . . . clear proof that the true type of Graziano had, in the eyes of the public, as distinctive and fundamental characteristics, ignorant pretension to learning, stupid etymologizing, grotesque mispronunciation of words and the buffoonery of Latin quotation." [110] Later Rasi mentions the doctor's penchant for synonyms and gives as an example the following: Pero essend' tra un allegad et culigad la grazia, l'affabilita, la benignita, l'allegrezza, and so on for forty-eight synonyms.[111]

In this record of the practice of an actor in the Gelosi troupe are to be found all of the verbal extravagances of Holofernes: the inevitable medley of macaronic Latin, the whimsical etymologies, the mispronunciations, and the interminable lists of synonyms.

This doctor is a pedant, though not expressly so called. In Scala's Collection at least once the pedant is introduced by that knew. But the solidity of framework which this group gave

[110] Rasi, I. 407: Il Dottore è sempre il solito ignorantone, saccentone, che sputa sentenze, con mescolanza inevitabile di latino maccheronico, di citazioni spropositate, di etimologie bislacche. . . . Segno evidente che il tipo vero del Graziano ebbe al cospetto del pubblico per base unica la saccenteria ignorante, la etimologia insula, la storpiatura grottesca di vocaboli, la buffoneria delle citazioni latine.

[111] *Ibid.*, p. 412.

name.[112] This Cataldo is also a tiresome Latinate pedant, but is primarily a hypocrite. Under cover of giving Isabella, the beautiful young wife of Pantalone, the counsel that she needs to keep her from betraying her husband with the captain, he attempts to seduce her himself. Isabella traps, and exposes him, and so holds him up to ignominy and ridicule. Cataldo is thus a sort of skeleton for Tartuffe. This aspect of the pedant was not uncommonly treated in Italian comedy. Indeed several passages in *Love's Labour's Lost* show that Holofernes was sometimes under the sway of similar wanton desires.[113] This Shakespearian pedant thus seems to exhibit most of the absurdities conventionally the humorous property of the *Commedia dell' Arte* pedant.

The attempt to find any specific dramatic figure who served as a definite literary prototype for Holofernes is probably futile. These characteristics of the *dottore* did not join in any figure before Holofernes in a combination enough like his own to furnish Shakespeare a serviceable model. In English literature before *Love's Labour's Lost,* the pedant played a comparatively insignificant rôle. Rombus in Sidney's *Lady of May* is one of the few. He exhibits many of the characteristics of the Italian type in his predilection for Latin quotation and his grandiloquence in his native idiom. However he is ridiculous principally because he is excessively prone to formal rhetoric and the forms of the syllogism. He is a belated scholastic. Churchill and Keller, in the article already cited,[114] suggest that Shakespeare might naturally have known the Cambridge University play *Paedantius*[115] and have used the comic protagonist there, as a

[112] *Il Pedante, Giorno XXXI.*

[113] Compare the following speech of Holofernes: "Me hercule, if their Sonnes be ingennuous, they shall want no instruction. If their daughters be capable, I will put it to them. But *vir sapis qui pauca loquitur.*" Numerous editors, beginning with Steevens and Malone, have caught a *double entendre* in these lines. In spite of good Dr. Furness's irritation at the ignoble minds of the critics, the double meaning seems to be in the text.

[114] *Shakespeare Jahrbuch,* XXXIV (1898), 256 ff.

[115] Sir John Harington in his *Apology for Poetry,* written in 1591, speaks of the play, so that it was performed before this date.

model for Holofernes. However none of the similarities between the two lie in common deviations from the type figure, so that this assumption is hardly warranted. The pedant in *The Two Italian Gentlemen* is much more like Holofernes than either of these figures; doubtless because he bears a closer relationship to the Italian figure.

These facts pretty clearly establish the truth that Holofernes left a home in popular Italian comedy to travel with his clownish associates into Shakespeare's workshop. Naturally the English dramatist has transformed the figure in many ways. Some of his new traits may well have been derived from country schoolmasters whom he had known, but they never obscure Holofernes' relationship to the Italian type figure.

Nathaniel is a parasite who, like hundreds of his prototypes from classical comedy down, flatters and toadies to the person to whom he attaches himself, so that he may satisfy his insatiable appetite for food.[116] It is only in Italian comedy, however, that the parasite attaches himself to the pedant. Moland [117] says that it is only in the *Commedia dell' Arte* that he is thus placed, but in *The Supposes* Pasiphilo divides his allegiance between Erostrato and the pedant Cleander.[118] Nathaniel is, of course, a character of very minor importance. Yet the slight indications that the author has given us prove that he is a representative of the parasite in the form that he came to assume in Italian comedy.

Even Dull has a prototype in the Italian comedy. A stupid

[116] Churchill and Keller (*op. cit.*) think that the presence of a second pedant Dromodotus in the school-comedy *Paedantius* proves that Shakespeare had this situation in this Latin play in mind when he introduced both Holofernes and Nathaniel into *Love's Labour's Lost*. Dromodotus is called Philosophus and is a scholastic ridiculously wedded to his medieval jargon. Nathaniel is not a second pedant; he is a lightly-sketched parasite or "affamato," as he was called in Italian Comedy. Only in the confused attribution of speeches in Act IV, Sc. ii, of the Folio text does he seem to be a second pedant.

[117] *Molière et la Comedie Italienne,* 2d ed., Paris, 1867.

[118] *Supposes,* I. 3: "I am of the householde with this scholer Erostrato (his rival) as well as with Domine Cleander; now with the one, and then with the other, according as I see their caters provide good cheere at the market."

magistrate was one of Francesco Andreini's most successful rôles. In one of Bartoli's scenari, *La Regina d'Inghilterra,* Trappola plays an officer with the same portentous stupidity as does Dull. In *The Two Italian Gentlemen,* described above, there is a representative of the same type-character in Sberri, captain of the watch. Examples could be multiplied. Even the presence of the multiform love story may be due to *Commedia dell' Arte* influence. There were nearly always, in these plays, a *prima donna* and a *secunda donna.* Each of these ladies had to be provided with a lover. Occasionally there was even a third lady who made a like demand of the author. This was in addition to the inevitable love-making among the servants and clowns. Shakespeare's multiform love stories in this comedy and elsewhere may be regarded as a natural expansion and complication of this structural feature of Italian comedy.

The *capitano,* upon examination, seems to have brought all of his Italian familiars with him into *Love's Labour's Lost.*[119] Certain members of this famous group had appeared in plays in English before this one, but this is the first English comedy in which the entire group appears as a veritable *société joyeuse.*

The young dramatist evidently felt that the clever courtly badinage of Lyly-like ladies and gentlemen, even when associated with a more natural and sincere love story than any that Lyly had ever presented, did not give enough comic substance to his play, which we have agreed to regard as a sort of dramatic Progress. Accordingly, turning for material to the enormously popular characters of contemporary Italian Comedy, he imported thence not isolated figures, but the entire group of clownish masks. Their mere presence gave his comedy a firm foundation for laughter. He forced them moreover to meet some of the structural needs of his drama, as when he assigned to them the presentation of the burlesque pageant of *The Nine Worthies.* Each one of them was also modified as a result of Shakespeare's observation of contemporary life, and perhaps occasionally by his impulse to satirize certain ridiculous individuals whom he

[119] Birowne enumerates them all except the constable (V. ii. 545), "The Pedant, the Braggart, the Hedge-Priest, the Foole, and the Boy."

knew. But the solidity of framework which this group gave his tenuously connected episodes and the perennial mirth which it aroused must have been their main recommendation to the young dramatist.

Love's Labour's Lost, therefore, proves to have had a somewhat complicated history of construction. The nature of the play shows clearly enough that even in its earliest form, it was connected in some way with the English court. Indeed its central plot reveals such an intimate familiarity with nearly contemporary events and social conditions at the court of Navarre as the author could scarcely have gained from his own personal experience. This fact points to Shakespeare's association with some gentleman of the court in the composition of this *Love's Labour's Lost.* Who he was or what his purposes were in this collaboration will probably never be known. To a student of Shakespeare's early methods of composition, these interesting personal questions are of only minor importance. Once given his central idea, the playwright invested it with vitality and diversity by bringing to it constructive principles and comic motifs from three sources clearly within the range of his knowledge, — the progresses of Queen Elizabeth, the court comedies of John Lyly, and Italian comedy, particularly the *Commedia dell' Arte.*

We find Shakespeare then, at the outset of his career as a writer of comedy, not, as Bond asserts, having one master and one only, — John Lyly. Nor do we find him working carefully in imitation of this one author in an effort to discover what qualities of his own would emerge during this process. Such a method is scarcely calculated to develop the great versatility in comic composition which Shakespeare shows early in his career. What he seems actually to have done is to have found dramatic suggestions for his own practice in many places. Fortunately his imagination kindled at many smouldering fires.

Moreover each one of his borrowed ideas he developed with a joyous creative exuberance. He was not to be satisfied with one love story in this play or even with two. He arranged four or five. He developed, intensified, and diversified Lyly's courtly conversation until it became a veritable dramatic symphony on the theme of Euphuistic speech. He introduced into it not single figures from Italian comedy, but all of the comic masks at once and made each one of them contribute his traditional humor, in a sublimated form, to the gorgeous Progress given by the King of Navarre to his royal guests.

This imaginative abundance appears in all of Shakespeare's early plays,—tragedies and historical. It is the temper of *The Comedy of Errors*, of *Titus Andonicus*, and of *Richard III*. May we not say it is the universally approved and natural method of all youthful genius?

THE TWO GENTLEMEN OF VERONA AND ITALIAN COMEDY

THE TWO GENTLEMEN OF VERONA AND ITALIAN COMEDY

O. J. CAMPBELL

SHAKESPEARE'S *The Two Gentlemen of Verona* occupies an important position in the history of English drama. It is usually regarded as "the earliest surviving romantic comedy of England and almost of Europe."[1] At all events in this play, so the approved criticism runs, the distinctive qualities of Shakespeare's romantic comedy appear for the first time. "In this play," writes Mr. Warwick Bond, "he opens the vein he worked so richly afterwards—the vein of crossed love, of flight and exile under the escort of generous sentiments; of disguised heroines, of sufferings endured and virtues exhibited under their disguise; and of Providence kinder than life, that annuls the errors and forgives the sin; and here first he lays the scene in Italy."[2]

The sources and provenience of a play of so great importance in the history of English drama are of more than ordinary interest. Yet the relations of this comedy to the continental drama contemporary with it and immediately anterior to it have, I believe, never been properly understood.

The commonly accepted notion is that the story of Julia and Proteus was derived, in all of its characteristic features, from the tale of Felix and Felismena in the romance *Diana Enamorada*, written in Spanish by the Portuguese poet Jorge de Montemayor, and first printed at Valentia in 1542. That story runs as follows. Felismena is wooed by the gentleman Don Felix, whose advances she at first repulses but later receives with pleasure. His father disapproves their love and sends his son away to court.

[1] This phrase comes from the work of R. Warwick Bond, the Arden edition of *The Two Gentlemen of Verona* (London, 1906), p. xxxii.

[2] *Ibid.*

Felismena, disguised as a page, follows him thither. The first night that she spends in the city, the host of her inn takes her to a place where she may hear music. He conducts her to a spot not far from the inn where she listens to a passionate serenade addressed by the false Felix to the lady Celia. Felismena next day sees him at court gorgeously arrayed in the colors of this new mistress. The deserted maiden enters his service as a page and bears his messages and gifts to Celia. This lady falls in love with Felismena, and realizing that it is impossible to win her love, she dies of a broken heart. Felix then mysteriously disappears and is thought to have died also of grief. Felismena becomes a shepherdess. One day long after she beholds an unknown knight pursued and hard pressed by three foemen. Through almost miraculous skill in archery she slays the pursuers and rescues the knight, and then discovers that he is her lost Felix. His love for her immediately revives and they are united.

The general similarities between this romantic tale and the story of Julia and Proteus are evident. At two points the likenesses extend to comparatively unimportant details. These are the effort of the lady's maid to deliver the lover's first letter to her mistress and the circumstances under which the girl-page overhears the serenade given by her faithless lover to his new flame. In Montemayor's romance Rosina's first attempt to deliver Felix's declaration of love is met by an angry rebuke by Felismena. The next morning, however, the maid allows the letter to fall, as if by accident, in the lady's chamber. Felismena, by this time eager to see the missive, pretends not to know what the dropped article is, and insists upon seeing it. Lucetta, in *The Two Gentlemen of Verona,* also lets the love letter fall where it will be certain to attract the attention of her mistress. Julia affects to believe it a missive from one of the maid's lovers, and insists upon seeing it. After she has it in her possession, she tears it into pieces. Then dismissing Lucetta, she eagerly gathers the fragments from the floor and pieces them together in an effort to recover some of its precious love-phrases.

The second point of similarity in detail between the two plays is to be found in the page's overhearing of the serenade. Felismena, at the suggestion of the host of the inn at which she is staying, goes to a spot where she hears Felix serenade Celia. Similarly it is the host in *The Two Gentlemen of Verona* who takes Julia to hear the serenade arranged by Thurio and incidentally to learn of her lover's infidelity.

The consensus of critical opinion seems to be that such points of similarity in unessential details make Shakespeare's knowledge of Montemayor's tale practically certain. Shakespeare, however, probably did not know Spanish. Scholarly ingenuity has therefore been severely taxed to discover a form of tale which he might have read. The facts are these. *The Two Gentlemen of Verona* was written certainly no later than 1592, while the first English translation of *Diana Enamorada,* that made by Bartholomew Yonge, was not printed until 1598.[3] To be sure, the translator says in his preface that the work had existed in manuscript for more than sixteen years, that is since 1582. There is no reason to suppose, however, that Shakespeare saw this document. Another translation was dedicated by Thomas Wilson to the Earl of Southampton in 1596. There was a French translation of the work made in 1578, which was reprinted with additions in 1587 and re-issued in 1592.[4] This French translation Shakespeare might conceivably have seen, although he was apparently not an habitual reader of French. The English version most apt to come within the range of Shakespeare's notice was that probably contained in the lost play *Felix and Philiomena,* which we know was acted before the queen on January 3, 1584–85.[5]

The assumption that the tale of Felix and Felismena, in the form which it assumes in Montemayor's romance, is the

[3] *Diana* (with a second part by A. Perez and also a continuation entitled *Enamoured Diana* by G. Gil Polo), translated out of Spanish by B. Yong. E. Bollifant: Imprensis G. B., London, 1598.

[4] *Le Diane* de G. de Montemayor. Divisée en trois parties . . . e traduites d'Espagnol en François (Pt. I by N. Colon, Pts. II and III by G. Chapuis.

[5] Feuillerat, Albert, *Documents relating to the office of the Revels in the Time of Queen Elizabeth,* p. 365. Bangs, *Materialien,* Vol. XXI.

sole source for the central story in *The Two Gentlemen of Verona* has led to two sorts of rather extreme views about this comedy. The first is that of Bond, part of which I have quoted above. He believes that Shakespeare is practically the inventor of most of the distinctive comic traits of this play and therefore of Elizabethan romantic comedy. It is undoubtedly true that the part played by Shakespeare in giving to this type of play its poetry and imaginative reach cannot be overestimated; yet the essential nature of this aspect of his genius and the interesting course of its development have been partially obscured by the belief that romantic comedy as a type sprang full-grown from his brain.

Professor George P. Baker's critical opinion of this play, which is based on the same notion of its inception and growth, is quite different from that of Bond. He assumes that the entire comedy, with the exception of the Proteus-Julia story, is Shakespeare's invention and so to be studied as evidence of his power to construct a complicated plot. Thus regarded *The Two Gentlemen of Verona* proves to be a weak and tentative effort. Shakespeare now recognizes the value of a complicated plot, Professor Baker believes, but he cannot develop with any firmness, the story that he has so constructed. He also realizes the need of creating suspense in his audience, but he does not know how to satisfy the suspense when once he has aroused it. Consequently the critic believes that the dénouement of the play is a "complete confession of dramatic ineptitude." [6]

These two somewhat contradictory views of the work, each one rather extreme, are at least partly the result of a narrow view of the origin of *The Two Gentlemen of Verona,* and of its relation to similar drama on the Continent,—particularly to that of Italy. There are, to be sure, other critics of the comedy who have recognized that parts of it other than the Proteus-Julia story smack of Italian ingenuity. Some scholars have pointed out certain definite Italian plays which Shakespeare may have had in mind when he composed this comedy. Sir

[6] Baker, George P., *The Development of Shakespeare as a Dramatist* (1907), p. 120.

Sidney Lee believes that the dramatist "had clearly studied *the pleasant and conceited comedy of Two Italian Gentlemen,* issued anonymously in London in 1584." [7] Klein asserts that Shakespeare took the elopement and double wooing from Parabosco's *Il Viluppo,* 1547,[8] a knowledge of which on Shakespeare's part would have been a kind of miracle. In 1817 Treck pointed out [9] a resemblance between *The Two Gentlemen of Verona* and a German drama called *Tragoedia von Julio,* published first in 1620 as one of the collection entitled *Englishe Comoedien und Tragoedien.*[10] Finally Max Koch has suggested [11] that the source of Shakespeare's play is a popular Italian comedy, *Flavio Tradito.* A scenario of this play is number five in Flaminio Scala's collection of scenarios of the *Commedia dell' Arte* published in 1611.

Resemblances certainly do exist between all of the Italianate comedies suggested by these learned critics and *The Two Gentlemen of Verona.* However, they occur, without exception, in situations which are commonplaces of Italian comedy as a type, both of the literary and popular sort. This form of drama, it will be remembered, possesses rigid conventionality of both plot and incidental device. Characters and situations recur indefinitely. This fact suggests the difficulty of finding the one Italianate play among those still extant which was the source of *The Two Gentlemen of Verona.* A search for time-worn commonplaces of Italian comedy in this drama, however, has convinced me that practically all its important structural elements are patterned after recurrent features of "Italian comedy." [12]

If this be true, certain general truths in regard to the inception of *The Two Gentlemen of Verona* become evident. If, for

[7] *A Life of William Shakespeare* (1922 edition), p. 107. This play is commonly assigned to Anthony Munday.

[8] *Geschichte des Dramas* (1866), IV. 785–791. Some of the similarities in detail are rather close.

[9] *Deutsches Theatre* (Berlin, 1817), I, xxiii–xxvii.

[10] It is possible that this drama may represent Henslowe's lost play, *Phillipo and Hewpolyta,* marked as old under date of July 9, 1594.

[11] *Shakespeare Jahrbuch* (1910), p. 10.

[12] For meaning of this term, see "*Love's Labour's Lost*" *Re-studied,* p. 26.

example, Shakespeare possessed a definite dramatic source for this comedy, such as the lost *Felix and Philiomena,* that must have been a thoroughly Italianate play. If, on the other hand, he had only a slender thread of story, such as that in Montemayor's *Diana,* upon which to build, he must have made all his additions to it from devices chosen from the wide-spread traditions of Italian comedy. In either case we shall have to recognize Shakespeare's contributions to the growth of romantic comedy, not in new forms of dramatic ingenuity, but in the emotional deepening of elements taken bodily from a drama which was at once comedy of intrigue and high complicated farce.

The plot structure of *The Two Gentlemen of Verona* is modelled on that of a typical Italian comedy. Ideally the play is a conflict between love and friendship illustrated by the love of two friends, Proteus and Valentine, for the same girl, Silvia. In the story Proteus, faithless to his friend, supersedes him in the favored position of suitor. Silvia's father prefers a third wooer, the foolish Thurio, a sort of braggart captain.[13] Eventually Proteus finds himself in danger of death, whence he is rescued by Valentine. Whereupon he repents, surrenders his claim to Silvia, and takes for his wife his first love Julia, who has followed him from Verona and served him in the disguise of a page. The various scenes in this double story are interrupted by intermezzi of verbal wit and horseplay carried on by two clowns, one intensely keen-witted and verbally adroit,—Speed; the other loutish and stupid,—Launce.

All of these elements are commonplaces of Italian comedy. Many of them appear in the play of Scala's collection mentioned above, *Flavio Tradito.* In this scenario Flavio, a Florentine gentleman, is in love with Isabella, the daughter of Dr. Gratiano. Oratio, his sworn friend, falls in love with the same girl. Thus is precipitated in the latter's mind a struggle like that of Proteus. The intellectual strife between love and friendship was a favorite

[13] *The Two Gentlemen of Verona,* V. iii. 15 ff.
Thurio: "How likes she my discourse?"
Proteus: "Ill when you talk of war. . . ."

theme of debate in all the bourgeois academies of Renaissance Italy; and this subject naturally became the intellectual substance of comedies composed by the cultivated members of the Gelosi troupe.[14] Isabella, like Silvia, has a third lover, the Capitano Spavento, who, like Thurio, is favored by her father, the Duke of Milan. This contest of the three rivals, two young men and one clown, invariably the father's favorite, for the hand of the *prima donna*, is a time-worn convention of Italian comedy. It is one of the commonest variations of the multiform love story which is a constant feature of both sorts of Italian comedy and particularly of the *Commedia dell' Arte*.[15]

Oratio in *Flavio Tradito*, renouncing the obligations of friendship, contrives to make Flavio believe that Silvia has been false to him, with the result that he abandons her.[16] Flavio learns of his friend's falseness through the craftiness of a servant, but bides his time for unmasking Oratio and exposing his treachery. His opportunity comes one day when the false friend is defeated in a duel and about to be slain. Flavio exhibits his unswerving friendship by rescuing him from this pressing danger. This generous act fills Oratio with so great remorse that he forthwith gives up Isabella to Oratio and consoles himself immediately with the ever willing Flaminia. Friendship thus triumphs, as it should in the soul of a Renaissance gentleman. However, Oratio, by quick thinking and equally quick acting, enables the comedy to close with the rigorously prescribed double marriage.

This dénouement is like that in *The Two Gentleman of Verona*. Valentine arrives in the nick of time to rescue Silvia from the unwelcome embraces of an outlaw, who proves to be the false Proteus. As soon as the mutual recognition takes place, Proteus immediately asks, and as immediately receives, forgiveness. Then follows a generous passing back and forth of the

[14] See *"Love's Labour's Lost" Re-studied*, p. 25.

[15] Two extant Italianate plays evidently known in some form to Shakespeare contain this feature. In *The Two Italian Gentlemen* there is presented the rivalry of Fortunio, Fedele and Captain Crackstone; in *Gl'Ingannati* that of Fabrizio, Flaminio and Gherardo. This is also an aspect of some of the comedies in Scala's Collection. In *Il Ritratto*, two old men and the Capitano seek the favor of the *Comédienne*.

[16] Exactly the same situation appears in *The Two Italian Gentlemen*.

ladies without any regard for their wishes. This naturally seems to a modern critic like Professor Baker "complete dramatic ineptitude." To the author of this sort of Italianate comedy, it was the expected indisputable proof of the complete victory of friendship in its mortal struggle with love. Moreover it precipitated neatly the situation demanded for the proper ending of a *Commedia dell' Arte*. The *prima donna* and the *secunda donna* had each to be provided with a husband before the final curtain. Consequently when the author's attention had been largely devoted to his intrigue, the husbands were thrust upon the ladies almost *all' improviso,* utterly without psychological preparation for the author's beneficence.[17]

The larger features even of the Julia-Proteus plot are also conventions of the Italian drama. The male disguise of the girl was the authorized solution of a universal problem of stage realism. The scene of all the action in Italian comedy, both learned and professional, was a public place. But Italian customs of the cinquecento forbade the appearance of a respectable citizen's daughter on the street with the men.[18] If the girl, therefore, was to have any sort of extended speech with the men in these comedies, she had either to talk to them from a window or a balcony, or to assume some sort of male disguise. Consequently, all Renaissance comedy is filled with these two situations.

As the writers of the comedies became more skillful in giving their plots unity, they naturally wished the disguised girl to bear some intimate relation to the love intrigue. The disguise of page was hit upon as solving most successfully this problem of unity. A girl could most realistically impersonate a page and in this character she could naturally attach herself to one of the *amorosi*.

In at least three of Scala's collection of scenarios, the heroine

[17] Cf. also *The Two Italian Gentlemen.*

[18] R. Warwick Bond in his *Early Plays from the Italian* (Oxford: The Clarenden Press, 1911) quotes on page xxxix the following passage from Geraldi Cinthio's *Sulle Comedie* (p. 103): "Serva, messer Giulio, la comedia una certa religione che mai giovane vergine, o polzella, non viene a ragionare in iscena."

is disguised as a page. In two of these, *Il Ritratto* and *La Fortunata Isabella,* she follows her errant lover to a distant city where he has fallen in love with another girl. In *Il Ritratto,* written before 1578, Silvia follows her former lover, in this case the *capitano,* from Milan to Parma. There she assumes the name and guise of a page Lesbino and becomes the captain's servant. Act II, Scene XV, is a discussion, carried on by these former lovers, of the man's recent infatuation for *la Comédienne.* A significant sentence in the *scenario* reads, "She asks him if he has never loved before. The captain replies that he has loved at Milan a very beautiful young girl named Silvia."[19] A situation in *The Two Gentlemen of Verona* (Act IV, Scene V, ll. 75 ff.) between Julia and Proteus exactly similar to this one displays Julia in one of her most charming and wistful moments.

The girl who disguises as a page and takes service in that capacity with the lover is an equally common figure in the *commedia crudita.* Parabosco's *Il Viluppo,* 1547, Ceechi's *I Rivali,*[20] the same author's *Le Pellegrine,* 1567, and *Gl'Ingannati,*[21] written by the Intronate of Siena, are some of the best known of a large number of plays in which the heroine assumes some form of masculine disguise. In the two last mentioned she serves as the page of her lover. In *Gl'Ingannati,*[22] some version of which is now commonly supposed to be the source of the serious part of *Twelfth Night,*[23] Lelia disguises herself

[19] It is perhaps significant that one *amorosa* in each of these plays is called Silvia.

[20] Winnifred Smith in *The Commedia dell' Arte,* p. 98, note 56, says that this play and *Gl'Ingannati* are the best known of "innumerable written plays in which the heroine resorts to masculine disguise."

[21] Furness in the Variorum edition of *Twelfth Night* suggests that the Italian company led by Drusiano which played in London in 1577–78 (cf. "*Love's Labour's Lost*" Re-studied, p. 28) may have brought this popular play to England. This seems hardly probable.

[22] *Commedia dell' Arte* companies did sometimes play *Commedie erudite* in Italy, but practically never when touring abroad. The play was first performed in Siena in Carnival week of 1531 and printed first in 1537. The drama is undoubtedly the source for Bandello's novella of Nicuola and Lattanzio, which is Number XXXVI of *Le Novelle* in *Scrittori d'Italia,* Bari, 1911, Vol. I, Part. II, pp. 252 ff.

[23] A Latin version of the play called *Laelia* has sometimes been re-

as the page and takes service with her faithless lover Flaminio. In this disguise she carries on a conversation with Flaminio about his first love[24] even more like the scene in which Julia reproaches Proteus than the one from *Il Ritratto* mentioned above. Julia's grief-evoked "alas" and her subsequent swoon are paralleled in Lelia's actions when Flaminio urges her to press his suit upon Isabella.

> *Flam:* I will give Isabella to understand that I love Lelia no longer, rather that I hate her, and cannot bear to hear her named, and will pledge my faith never to go where she may be. Tell Isabella this as strongly as you can.
>
> *Lelia:* Oh, me.
> *Flam:* What has come over you? What do you feel?
> *Lelia:* Oh, Me.
> *Flam:* Lean on me. Have you any pain?
> *Lelia:* Suddenly. In the heart.[25]

These examples should be sufficient to show that all the structural points of similarity between the Proteus-Julia story and that of Felix and Felismena are commonplaces of Italian comedy. Indeed, one might pronounce them the most frequently recurrent features of that drama. Only the circumstances attendant upon the dropping of the love-letter and the conditions under which the disguised page overhears the serenade remain as evidence of a direct relationship between the plot of *The Two Gentlemen of Verona* and the story from the *Diana Enamorada*. To these details I shall recur later.

Still other conventions of Italian comedy appear in the play. Critics have remarked the large number of Petrarchan conceits and of the half-lyrical *tirades* on love and on the conflict between

---

garded as the direct source of Churchill, Geo. B., *Die lateinischen Universitäts-Dramen Englands in der Zeit Königen Elisabeth, Shakespeare Jahrbuch,* XXXIV (1898), 286.

24 Act II, Scene i.

25 Quoted from the translation of T. L. Peacock called *The Deceived* (*The Works* [London, 1875], III. 284). This situation between the *amorosa* and his abandoned and disguised mistress is indicated as a recurrent one by its appearance in collections of conceits written in dialogue form. There is one in the collection of Domenico Bruni, in which the man agrees with his former love, who is now disguised as his page, that his present lady is fairer and worthier than his first one. (Cf. Rasi, I. 521 ff.; also Smith, *The Commedia dell' Arte*, p. 90.)

love and friendship in which this drama abounds.[26] This curious mixture of sincere emotional exaltation and mere imaginative ingenuity, sometimes called Petrarchism, permeated the lyrical poetry of nearly every nation of Europe during the years of the sonneteering vogue. Shakespeare's non-dramatic works written about the same time as *The Two Gentlemen of Verona,* — *Venus and Adonis, The Rape of Lucrece* and *The Sonnets* are filled with this sort of lyrical decoration. Though widely diffused, in no drama of the time did it assume a form so close to that employed in *The Two Gentlemen of Verona* as in the love tirades contributed by Isabella Andreini to the *Commedia dell' Arte* as played by the Gelosi troupe.[27] Her letters,[28] a series of carefully wrought literary exercises, preserve these tirades in a form very like that which they must have assumed in the plays.[29] Here appear the subtle sentimentalities of the sonneteers expressed in a slightly inflated style. Here are the elaborate puns, the conventional love-laments and the fine-spun debates on the nature of love and on its distracting conflicts with friendship.

The vogue of this intellectual exercise was so wide-spread that verbal parallels between the *tirades* of Isabella, the *amorosa,* and the speeches of characters in *The Two Gentlemen of Verona* would not prove a direct relationship between the two. The significant fact is that the nature of the dramatic conversations about love in this play of Shakespeare's — the very essence of romantic comedy — is of exactly the same sort as the similar dialogue of the most highly developed form of *Commedia dell' Arte* that was composed in Shakespeare's time. The romantic story of *The Two Gentlemen of Verona,* then, and the dramatic form which it assumes are close reflections of the narratives of Italian comedy.

[26] For a list of such conceits cf. Bond, *op. cit.,* p. xxxi.

[27] Cf. "*Love's Labour's Lost*" *Re-studied,* p. 25.

[28] Andreini Isabella: *Lettere d'Isabella Andreini. Comicà Gelosa, et academica intenta, nominata l'Accesa, Venetia,* 1607.

[29] As I have explained in my study of *Love's Labour's Lost,* certain fixed and typical speeches made by the characters were not left to the invention of the moment, but were carefully composed and committed to memory. The *tirades* of Francesco Andreini spoken in his rôle of Capitano Spavento (cf. "*Love's Labour's Lost*" *Re-studied,* p. 25) were also of this sort.

The fun provided by Speed and Launce in their *intermezzi* is of the essence of this comedy, particularly of the *Commedia dell' Arte.* The traditional view is that these clowns bear at least a general likeness to Lyly's pages. Courthope states definitely that they are modelled on the characters of Licio and Petulus in *Mydas.*[30] He also asserts that the dialogue between Launce and Speed, in which the latter gives a catalogue of his mistress's qualities and Launce makes a feebly witty comment upon each item,[31] is founded on a similar conversation between Licio and Petulus.[32] This latter fact seems highly probable, inasmuch as it is certain that Shakespeare when writing these early comedies imitated the dramatic style of Lyly.[33] In these encounters between Launce and Speed, however, Shakespeare develops and emphasizes the amusing contrast between the quick-witted rogue and the slow-minded rustic which he presented only tentatively in *Love's Labour's Lost,*[34] but which Lyly does not suggest. Even in the scene under discussion in which the conventional form of the dialogue obscures a little the firm outlines of Launce's character as established elsewhere in the play, his replies do not ever display the ingenuity of those habitual to Petulus. On the contrary, they are pretty consistently heavy-footed and stupid.

In the *Commedia dell' Arte,* however, by the end of the sixteenth century, this relationship had become one of its firmest traditions.[35] The books of dramaturgy laid down the conventions which had to be observed in conceiving and presenting these characters. Both Moth and Costard, and Speed and

30 *A History of English Poetry* (London, 1903), IV. 89.

31 *The Two Gentlemen of Verona,* Act III, Scene ii. 281 ff.

Speed: Item, She can wash and scour."

Launce: "A special virtue: for then she need not be washed and scoured."

32 *Mydas,* Act II, Scene i.

Licio: "Well, she hath the tongue of a parrot."

Pet: "That's a leaden dagger in a velvet sheath, to have a blacke tongue in a fair mouth."

33 *"Love's Labour's Lost" Re-studied,* p. 21.

34 *Ibid.,* p. 35.

35 *Ibid.,* pp. 34 ff., for the development of these two figures in the *Commedia dell' Arte.*

Launce conform closely to the types. The dramatic possibilities of the two contrasted clowns are naturally more thoroughly realized in the later play. There, also, the nationalization of the booby's stupidity has proceeded further, so that Launce seems a typical English country lout whose Italian origin is never obvious.

Launce's immortal dog, who gives occasion to much "unforced unageing humor" seems to be English to the core. Yet even he may have escaped from some Italian scenario. At least live animals of all sorts, particularly dogs, were often introduced upon the stage of the *Commedia dell' Arte* and very seldom elsewhere. I have not forgotten Balaam's ass and the boisterous comedy that he provoked in both French and English Miracle plays.[36] However, other live animals seem not to have found their way upon the English stage in his company; but the farcical atmosphere of the *Commedia dell' Arte* was very congenial to the incalculable improvisation in which animals might indulge. In Scala's collection they appeared frequently. In *La Caccia* we have the following extraordinary directions: "Enter Graziano with a live cock on his wrist for a sparrowhawk. Claudione with a cat on a leash. Burattino with an ape on a leash."[37] Among the properties required for another one of Scala's scenarios were "a live cat, a live cock and four hunting dogs." Occasionally live animals are introduced into a *Commedia erudita,* where they obviously harmonize less naturally with the comic temper of the play. In Luigi Grotto's *Il Tesoro* (1590), for example, when the old woman Donnola goes to consult a lawyer, she is informed that he is conferring with the gentlemen. Upon being admitted she finds him playing with two kittens which are on his lap.

In the dialogue on scenic performances composed by Leone de Sommi, and referred to above,[38] one of the directions given

[36] Prof. Gayley remarks that "Once the donkey thrust his head within the church door, liturgy and drama were lost in the stupor of his ears or the bathos of his braying." — *Plays of Our Forefathers* (N. Y., 1901), p. 33.

[37] Giorn., 36: "Graziano che viene con un gallo vivo in pugno per sparviere, Claudione con una gatta alla lassa, Burattino con una scimmia alla lassa."

[38] P. 34.

to actors is the following: "If the poet brings in a cowherd, let him wear rustic clothes that he may appear peasantlike — and it adds much pleasure if the shepherd have with him at times one or more dogs, so also would it please me if the nymphs, too, had some, but gentler with pretty collars and delicate little coats."

The rustic or stupid clown in Italian comedy, if he follows the authoritative directions of Leone di Sommi, would as often as possible bring his live dog with him. Launce, inheriting the rôle of this Italian figure, inherited his cur also and brought the beast with him into *The Two Gentlemen of Verona,* to the delight of every reader of Shakespeare's comedy.

These parallels between essential situations and mere incidental comic devices of *The Two Gentlemen of Verona* and Italian comedy show with reasonable certainty that Shakespeare's source was some thoroughly Italianate play. If that was by chance the lost *Felix and Philiomena,* we may assume that this drama was a conventional Italian comedy into which some of the details of the Spanish story had been inserted to give the play its distinctive features.[39] In these Italian plays, particularly in the *Commedia dell' Arte,* it was the new or unusual element in its which determined its title. That was obviously the thing to advertise. This method of naming comedies was that employed by Menander [40] and by authors of every sort of so-called "new comedy." Indeed, this is the inevitable method of choosing titles for plays in any sort of drama in which the stable, unchanging element was as large as it was in most forms of Italian comedy.

By being thus able to assume that this *Felix and Philiomena,* or whatever the play that served as the source of *The Two Gentlemen of Verona,* supplied Shakespeare with many more

[39] The writers of scenarios took plot material avidly from every sort of available source and naturally often from novella and romance. Sometimes, to be sure, the borrowing was in the opposite direction, from the play to the novella. For the purpose of this argument the exact history of this relationship does not need to be determined.

[40] Cf. Post, C. R., *The Dramatic Art of Menander, Harvard Studies in Classical Philology,* XXIV. 116.

elements of his comedy than has hitherto been suspected, we are able to revise the traditional opinion in regard to Shakespeare's contribution to the development of Elizabethan romantic comedy. He can no longer be regarded as having invented the type in all of its distinctive features. Nor can he be regarded as an experimenter attempting to graft foreign material upon a slender romantic story and producing an ill-constructed play.

His method must be conceived, rather, as much more nearly analogous to that which he applied to the development of other types, such as Senecan tragedy and Chronicle history. He found in his source his plot in all its constructive elements, and he found there many of the type-figures needed to animate it ready to his hand. This perfectly conventional material occasionally appears in *The Two Gentlemen of Verona* in its original stiff caricature of reality, as in the hurried dénouement. Usually it is made to assume new forms of authentic life through Shakespeare's creative sympathy with youthful emotion, particularly in the soul of the woman. This interest expressing itself in dramatic form completely changed the spirit of Italian comedy. It released the love story from its bondage to the intrigue and gave it the central point of interest through its revelation of the beauty and the poetry of youthful love. The result was a comedy, new in kind, which was to develop into one of the most characteristic manifestations of Elizabethan art.

The formative influence of Italian comedy upon *Love's Labour's Lost* and *The Two Gentlemen of Verona*, which these two essays have tried to reveal, is but an example of its effect upon much of Shakespeare's early work in comedy. To a study of its influence upon *The Taming of the Shrew*, *The Comedy of Errors* and *The Merry Wives of Windsor*, I shall turn in the near future.

SHAKESPEARIAN PUNCTUATION

SHAKESPEARIAN PUNCTUATION

CHARLES C. FRIES

EDITORS of the text of Shakespeare have hitherto cast aside as utterly worthless the punctuation of the early Quartos and of the 1623 Folio. The usual attitude has been that expressed by the editors of the Cambridge edition of 1894–1895,

> . . . in many places, we may almost say that a complete want of points would mislead us less than the punctuation of the Folios. The consequence is that our punctuation is very little dependent upon the Folios and Quartos, but generally follows the practice which has taken possession of the text of Shakespeare, under the arrangement of the best editors, from Pope to Dyce and Staunton.[1]

And the principle underlying this practice could almost be summed up in the words of Dr. Samuel Johnson,

> In restoring the author's (Shakespeare's) works to their integrity, I have considered the punctuation as wholly in my power. . . .[2]

On the other hand, the editors of the new *Cambridge Shakespeare* (1921–), Sir Arthur Quiller-Couch and Mr. John Dover Wilson, in their "attempt . . . at a complete recension of Shakespeare's text"[3] have daringly adopted a punctuation of their own which aims "to translate into symbols convenient to the modern eye"[4] the pointing of the 1623 Folio. This revolutionary point of view cannot help arousing discussion with the appearance of each volume of the new edition,[5] and a question-

[1] Preface, p. xxi.

[2] *Preface to Shakespeare, The Works of Samuel Johnson* (Oxford, 1825), 5. 148.

[3] *The Tempest, General Introduction,* p. vii.

[4] *Ibid., A Note on Punctuation,* p. lvii.

[5] *The Tempest* and *The Two Gentlemen of Verona* appeared in 1921; *Merry Wives of Windsor,* in 1922; *Much Ado About Nothing,* in 1923.

ing of the grounds upon which the practice of two centuries has been repudiated.

The statements of the new theory of the reliability of the punctuation of the Folio and the early Quartos and the evidence upon which it rests are contained in a number of articles published during the last twenty-five years.[6] In the views of those who have argued for the new theory there seems to be considerable diversity.

The suggestions of the first two, Mr. Wyndham and Mr. Thistelton, substantially agree. The substance of their view is as follows:

(*a*) There is an order and system, not chaos, in the punctuation of the early Quartos and the 1623 Folio;

(*b*) There are two possible principles of punctuation: one based upon elocution, indicating pauses for delivery; the other

[6] The most important contributions to the discussion of Shakespearian punctuation are the following:

George Wyndham, *The Poems of Shakespeare* (1898), Notes on the Sonnets, pp. 265–268.

A. E. Thistelton, *Textual Notes on Measure for Measure* (1901), pp. 43–46.

———, *Textual Notes on Cymbeline* (1902), pp. 52–56.

———, *Textual Notes on A Midsummer Night's Dream* (1903), pp. 80–87.

Percy Simpson, *Shakespearian Punctuation* (1911).

A. W. Pollard, *Shakespeare's Fight with the Pirates, . . .* (1917), pp. 91–97.

———, 2d edition (1920), *Introduction,* pp. xv–xxi.

———, Introduction to *A New Shakespeare Quarto, the Tragedy of King Richard II, printed for the third time by Valentine Simmes in 1598,* edited by William A. White (1916).

Sir Edward Sullivan, *Punctuation in Shakespeare* (1921), *The Nineteenth Century,* 90. pp. 995–1006.

John Dover Wilson, *The Tempest* (1921), Textual Introduction, and a Note on Punctuation, pp. xxxvii, lvii.

William Poel, *Shakespeare's Prompt Copies* (1921), *London Times Literary Supplement,* Feb. 3, 1921, pp. 75, 76.

Sir Sidney Lee, *A Life of Shakespeare* (1922), Preface, pp. xiii–xvi.

Percy Simpson (A letter replying to the objections offered by Sir Sidney Lee), *London Times Literary Supplement,* July 13, 1922, p. 476.

As this paper was going through the press there appeared in the *Publications of the Modern Language Association* (XXXIX. 555–580) an article by the late Professor Raymond M. Alden, entitled *The Punctuation of Shakespeare's Printers.* Professor Alden examines with care the claims of the "elocutionary theory" in the light of the actual practice of the Folio and the early Quartos and concludes that the case for the new theory, so far as the evidence goes, has not as yet been proved.

based upon construction to distinguish structural additions to the sentence;

(*c*) In Shakespeare's work *both* principles are employed. The stops mark the syntax but they also frequently indicate elocutionary pauses unrelated to syntax. In the somewhat unsettled punctuation of the times the two principles seem to be striving for mastery.

The next four, Mr. Percy Simpson, Mr. A. W. Pollard, Sir Edward Sullivan, and Mr. John Dover Wilson, accord with the view just given in respect to denying the chaos and affirming the soundness and reasonableness of the punctuation of the Folio and the early Quartos. They differ, however, in objecting to the essential relation of the grammar and the syntax to the punctuation and insist upon the rhythmical or elocutionary principle as *the* guide to its interpretation. Even with these men there is considerable diversity between the cautious statement of Mr. Pollard,

> In Shakespeare's day . . . all the four stops, comma, semicolon, colon, and full stop, could be, and (on occasion) were, used simply and solely to denote pauses of different length irrespective of grammar and syntax. . . .[7]

and the unconditional assertion of Mr. John Dover Wilson, that

> . . . this punctuation is dramatic . . . a question of pause, emphasis and intonation; and is quite independent of syntax. . . . The stops, brackets, capital letters in the Folio and the Quartos are in fact stage directions, in shorthand. They tell the actor when to pause and for how long, they guide his intonation, they indicate the emphatic word, often enough they denote stage business.[8]

Among those who have supported this view of dramatic punctuation there seems to be fairly general agreement that the punctuation of the Folio and the early Quartos reproduces with substantial fidelity the pointing of Shakespeare's manuscript. In this respect even Mr. Pollard becomes so enthusiastic for the rhythmic effect of certain marks of punctuation that he feels that the " colons and commas [of one set speech of Richard

[7] A. W. Pollard, *Shakespeare's Fight with the Pirates* (1917), p. 92.
[8] John Dover Wilson, *The Tempest*, pp. lvii, xxxvii.

II] take us straight into the room in which *Richard II* was written and we look over Shakespeare's shoulder as he penned it."[9] A more cautious statement of the significance attached to the new theory comes from Sir Edward Sullivan,

> . . . there is thus a high probability that the long derided punctuation of the First Folio gives us a very fair idea of how Shakespeare's lines were being spoken within a few years of his death by actors who had been, directly or indirectly, in close touch with him.[10]

In support of this very interesting theory that Shakespeare by means of punctuation in his manuscript endeavored to instruct actors in the elocutionary or dramatic delivery of his lines there is offered very little tangible evidence; nothing, indeed, except a rather large number of instances given by Mr. Thistelton to fit his "rules," and by Mr. Simpson in forty-two roughly classified groups. Of the other men, Sir Edward Sullivan and Mr. Pollard also set forth and analyze a few additional instances of noteworthy "elocutionary" pointing. No attention is paid to instances which do not fit the classifications or the theory proposed.[11] One ought also to remark in passing that, although Mr. Simpson is attempting to prove by his accumulation of instances that the Shakespearian punctuation was based upon rhythmical rather than grammatical or logical considerations, of the forty-two classes in which these instances are grouped, at least eighteen are formed on the basis of the grammar of the sentence and seven others have a logical basis. No more than twelve of the classes given seem to rest on rhythmical or logical considerations.[12] So far as I am aware, such instances

[9] A. W. Pollard, *Shakespeare's Fight, etc.* (2d edition, 1920), p. xxi.

[10] Sir Edward Sullivan, *Punctuation in Shakespeare, Nineteenth Century,* 1921, p. 998.

[11] Mr. Simpson seems to consider this system of punctuation so flexible that no *negative* instances are possible. See his reply to Sir Sidney Lee, *London Times Lit. Suppl.,* July 13, 1922, p. 476.

[12] The following classes seem to rest on grammatical considerations. I give the numbers and titles as they appear in Mr. Simpson's book:

2. Vocative followed, but not preceded by a comma.
10. Comma marking logical subject.
11. Comma marking off adverbial phrase and clause.
14. Comma before a noun clause.

constitute the whole of the evidence upon which the case for the theory of elocutionary and dramatic punctuation rests.

On the other hand, both Mr. William Poel and Sir Sidney Lee present a negative argument of three objections:

---

15. Comma before the defining relative.
22. Comma with inversion.
23. Relative followed by a comma.
24. Comma marking ellipse of copula.
25. Comma marking the omission of the relative.
27. Semicolon with preliminary clauses.
34. Colon introducing reported speech, etc.
12. Comma between accusative and dative.
13. Comma between object and complement.
39. Brackets " mark off words, phrases, or clauses which interrupt the direct grammatical construction."

The following classes rest on grammatical considerations, but differ from those above in having no marks of punctuation:

3. Vocative without comma.
4. Imperative without comma.
5. Appositional phrase without comma.
41. Absence of punctuation to mark an interruption.

The following are the classes referred to above as having a logical basis for the grouping:

8. Comma equivalent to a dash.
16. Comma before " as."
17. Comma before " but " (= " except ").
18. Comma before " than."
19. Comma before " and," with no comma after.
20. Comma before " or " and " nor," with no comma afte.
21. Comma before " not," with no comma after.

The following classes accord more or less with a rhythmical basis for the grouping:

1. Light stopping.
6. Comma marking a metrical pause.
7. The emphasizing comma.
9. Comma marking interrupted speech.
28. Semicolon marking interrupted speech.
29. The emphasizing semicolon.
31. Colon marking an emphatic pause.
32. Colon marking an interrupted speech.
33. Antithetic colon.
35. The full stop in an incomplete sentence.
36. Full stop ending an interrupted speech.
38. The metrical hyphen.

(*a*) The avowed practice of actors is and has been against the usefulness of such punctuation in the manuscript of an author.[13]

(*b*) The punctuation of the Folio and the Quartos when followed in accord with this elocutionary theory often indicates a word as the key-word of a passage which is impossible in the light of the whole context.[14]

(*c*) It is unlikely that such a system of punctuation could have been employed by Shakespeare with no knowledge or mention of it among contemporaries.[15]

In support of these negative contentions the evidence offered is also exceedingly meager.

From this discussion of Shakespeare's punctuation three questions arise upon which it seems possible to offer some definitely objective evidence:

[13] William Poel, *Shakespeare's "Prompt Copies," London Times, Literary Suppl.*, Feb. 3, 1921, pp. 75, 76.

Mr. Poel quotes two actors' opinions:

Coquelin: "When I have to create a part, I begin reading the play with the greatest attention five or six times."

———: "I pay no attention to punctuation, because this would impede the natural movement of the voice from expressing the various shades of thought and feeling which are indicated by the sliding of the voice up and down."

———: "Before a passage can be tuned, the key-word to its meaning must be found. Find that and bring it out forcibly, and the other words will take care of themselves."

Talma: "The hunting for the key-word gives you the eyes of a lynx in searching all the corners of the sentence, and compels you to study closely the thought of the author and to weigh all his words."

[14] Mr. Poel objects to the illustration Mr. Pollard offers as an excellent example of rhythmical pointing in these words: "If, like Coquelin, Mr. Pollard had read the scene over, in which the quotation appears, five or six times, he might then, perhaps, have discovered a more suitable key-word than the one he thinks Shakespeare has indicated. . . . The scene does not deal with the question of Mowbray's treasons, but with that of who is the traitor, Bolingbroke or Mowbray. If so, the colon after the word 'treasons' has no elocutionary value."

[15] Sir Sidney Lee rests this contention on the ground that "Jonson, who was as well acquainted with the technique of the drama and the customs of the stage as any contemporary, knew nothing of any 'rhetorical' or 'elocutionary' mode of Elizabethan or Jacobean punctuation, which should convey to actors the dramatist's conception of emphasis." And he refers to the treatment of punctuation in Jonson's *Grammar* as evidence.

(1) Was there an *accepted system* of punctuation at the end of the sixteenth and the beginning of the seventeenth century?

(2) What connection existed between the marks of punctuation used and the structure and syntax of the sentence, and between the punctuation and oral reading?

(3) In what respects does the use of punctuation in the sixteenth and seventeenth centuries differ from the modern theory of punctuation?

Upon these questions a search of the grammars, rhetorics, and books to teach reading and speaking, published during the late sixteenth and early seventeenth centuries, yields some facts worthy of consideration.

On mere a priori grounds it would seem necessary that whenever or wherever punctuation is generally used in printed texts there must exist something of an accepted or general interpretation of its use. A peculiarly individual system of pointing without a key could have no meaning for others than the author. It seems very difficult indeed, therefore, to accept Mr. John Dover Wilson's assertion, " Punctuation, spelling, and the use of capitals were, in Shakespeare's day, personal matters, subject solely to the individual practice of a particular author,"[16] or to reconcile such a view with either of the two theories of punctuation, even that which insists that Shakespeare used his punctuation to convey stage directions or delivery hints to readers of his lines.

Against the idea of a generally *accepted system* of Elizabethan punctuation, however, and in harmony with Mr. Wilson's assertion, might be urged (1) the silence of a number of the books of grammar, rhetoric, and the art of reading, in which we should expect to find the subject of punctuation treated,[17] and (2) the

[16] John Dover Wilson and A. W. Pollard, *The " Stolne and Surreptitious " Shakespearian Texts, London Times Literary Suppl.*, Jan. 16, 1919, p. 30.

[17] The following books contain no statement of the use of punctuation:
Thomas Smith, *De recta & emendata Linguae Anglicae Scriptione,* 1568.
J. B. Gen. Ca., *Le Maistre d'Escole Anglois,* 1580.
W. Bullokar, *Bullokars Booke at large, for the Amendment of Orthographie for English speech,* 1580.
——, *Bref Grammar,* 1586.

fact that printers even as late as the eighteenth century regarded punctuation as a matter of so little consequence that neither the " Corrector " nor the " Compositor " was expected to refrain from " changing and thrusting in Points, capitals, or anything else that has nothing but fancy and humour for its authority and foundation."[18]

On the other hand not only does Shakespeare himself mention

P. Gr., *Grammatica Anglicana,* 1594.
George Mason, *Grammaire Angloise,* 1622.
John Wallis, *Grammatica Linguae Anglicanae,* 1653.

Nor does any mention of punctuation appear in
Thomas Wilson, *The Arte of Rhetoryke,* 1553.
Leonard Cox, *The Arte or Crafte of Rhethoryke,* 1532.

[18] P. Luckombe, *The History and Art of Printing,* 1771, p. 441:

" But where a Corrector understands the language and characters of a work, he often finds occasion to alter and to mend things that he can maintain to be either wrong or else ill digested. If therefore a Corrector suspects Copy to want revising, he is not to postpone it, but to make his emendations in the Manuscript before it is wanted by the Compositor, that he may not be hindered in the pursuit of his business; or prejudiced by alterations in the proof, especially if they are of no real signification; such as far-fetched spelling of Words, changing and thrusting in Points, Capitals, or any thing else that has nothing but fancy and humour for its authority and foundation."

Ibid., p. 263: " 'Tis true, that the expectation of a settled Punctuation is in vain, since no rules of prevailing authority have yet been established for that purpose; which is the reason that so many take the liberty of criticizing upon that head; yet when we compare the rules which very able Grammarians have laid down about Pointing, the difference is not very material; and it appears, that it is only a maxim with humourous Pedants, to make a clamour about the quality of a Point; who would even make an Erratum of a Comma which they fancy to bear the pause of a Semicolon, were the Printer to give way to such pretended accuracies. . . . It must be allowed, that all Matter is not pointed alike; for some require more stops than others. Thus, Historical and Narrative subjects do not take up so many points as Explanatory Matter; and that, again, not so many as English Statute Law —— But, happy! that Mispointing is not of the same consequence with Misnomer; otherwise, Where would be the end of Law-quibbles!

" It must likewise be owned, that every Compositor is not alike versed in pointing; and therefore such as are dubious whether they can maintain their notion of Pointing, ought to submit to the method, or even humour, of Authors, and authorized Correctors, rather than give them room to exclaim about spoiling the sense of the subject, because the Points are not put their right way. . . ."

punctuation and use pointing as a source of humor,[19] but a definite treatment of the uses of punctuation does appear in each of the following:

George Puttenham, *The Arte of English Poesie,* 1589.
Alexander Gil, *Logonomia Anglica,* 1619, 1621.
Charls Butler, *The English Grammar,* 1633.
Ben Jonson, *The English Grammar* (written before 1637).
Simon Daines, *Orthoepia Anglicana,* 1640.

The character of the discussions in these five books (set forth below, pages 76–79) with their points of similarity provides fairly safe ground for the conclusion that there was in the late sixteenth and early seventeenth centuries something of a *generally accepted system* of punctuation. The attitude of the printers, however, and the silence of some grammarians, or rather the few statements of the uses of punctuation which appear, point to two equally important provisions: that this system must have been loosely and somewhat variously applied and considered of rather small importance; and that the pointing of any printed book of this period cannot be assumed to be the author's without definite and unmistakable evidence.

II

That punctuation should serve as a guide to oral reading and indicate to the eye places of pause has been true throughout its history. Books and teachers of reading have all emphasized and still do insist that a reader should observe the pauses indicated by the commas and periods; that he should sustain the tone of his voice at the former but drop it at the latter. Many have objected to the system of punctuation as an inadequate guide to the pauses of oral reading, but throughout the last three centuries practically all agree that the two are essentially related.[20]

[19] See examples given below, pages 81–82.

[20] J. F. Genung, *The Working Principles of Rhetoric* (1900), p. 333: " By way of premise it should be borne in mind that, well furnished as it is, the existing scale of punctuation is by no means a complete represen-

The question at issue in this discussion of punctuation is whether the pauses indicated by the punctuation have been placed as dictated by the syntax and structure of the sentences or whether they are dramatic pauses indicating elocutionary emphasis and placed with no relation to structural divisions. On this question we have as evidence, first of all, the five summaries of the practice of the times listed above (page 75) — all by contemporaries of Shakespeare. The most important parts of these summaries of the uses of the four marks indicating pause are the following.

George Puttenham, *The Arte of English Poesie,* 1589:

" it is therefore requisit that leasure be taken in pronuntiation, such as may make our wordes plaine & most audible and agreable to the eare; also the breath asketh to be now and then releeued with some pause or stay more or lesse; besides that the very nature of speach (because it goeth by clauses of seuerall construction & sence) requireth some space betwixt them with intermission of sound, to th'end they may not huddle one vpon another so rudly & so fast that th'eare may not perceiue their difference. For these respectes the auncient reformers of language inuented three maner of pauses, one of the lesse leasure then another, and such seuerall intermissions of sound to serue (besides easment to the breath) for a treble distinction of sentences or parts of speach, as they happened to be more or lesse perfect in sence. The shortest pause or intermission they called *comma,* as who would say a peece of a speach cut out of. The second they called *colon,* not a peece, but as it were a member for his larger length, because it occupied twise as much time as the *comma.* The third they called *periodus,* for a complement or full pause, and as a resting place and perfection of so much former speach as had bene vterred, and from whence they needed not to passe any further, vnless it were to renew more matter to enlarge the tale. . . . I will say no more in it then thus, that they be vsed for a commodious and sensible distinction of clauses in prose, since euery verse is as it were a clause of it selfe, and limited with a *Cesure* howsoeuer the sence beare, perfect or imperfect, which difference is obseruable betwixt the prose and the meeter." [21]

---

tation of the pauses actually made in speaking or reading aloud. In every sentence there are rhetorical pauses that go unmarked and need no marking; they make themselves. And the more lucid and well organized the sentence, the more safely these pauses may be left to the reader. In a well-written passage the syntax dictates the place of the stops, and is not dependent on them. When a pause has to be lugged in to bolster up the construction, and above all when without the pause it would be left ambiguous or uncertain, the sentence itself is wrong, — it needs amendment."

[21] Book II. iv (v), pp. 77–80.

Alexander Gil, *Logonomia Anglica*, 1619, 1621:

" Accentui inseruiunt interpunctiones: quia illae ut sensū aperiunt, ita quantū possunt accentui viam sternunt. Eaedē sunt nobis quae Latinis, & usus idem: sunt autem κόμμα siue incisum (,), ποδιαστολή aut subdistinctio (;), κῶλον siue membrum (:) περίοδος siue sententiae & sensus. integra complexio (.) " [22]

Charls Butler, *The English Grammar*, 1634:

(The *special* symbols of Butler's phonetic spelling are here changed to the usual letters of normal spelling.)

" Points serving for the better understanding of Woords ar either Primari, or Secondari.

" Primari Points, which shew their Ton', Sound, and Pauses, ar eight: 4 simple and mor' common; Period, (.) Colon, (:) Semicolon, (;) Comma; (,) and 4 mixt and les freqent.

" Period is a point of perfect sens, and perfect sentenc': which, in the last woord, falleth the Ton' of the voic' below its ordinari tenour, with a long paus.

" Colon is a point of perfect sens, but not of perfect sentenc': which falleth the Ton' of the voic', with a shorter paus.

" Colon beeing a point of imperfect sentenc', the part following soomtim' dooth perfect the sam' . . . soomtim' it on'ly maketh perfect sens; (as the former part) but dooth not perfect the sentenc': so that ther' may bee many Colons in on' Period: . . . But wher' such perfect members ar both many and short; Semicolon dooth wel suppli' the Colons room': . . . And wher' they go' by par's, answering on' an other; . . . every second member is noted with a Semicolon, and every first with a Comma; . . .

" Semicolon is a point of imperfect sens, in the midle of a Colon, or Period: commonly, when it is a compound axiom; whos' parts ar joyned together, by a dubble, and soomtim' by a single, conjunction: . . . and it continueth the tenour or ton' of the voic' to the last woord, with a Colon-paus: . . .

" Comma is a point of mor' imperfect sens, in a simple axiom, or in either part of a compound: which continueth the tenour of the voic' to the last, with the shortest paus.

" Many single woords, of the sam' sort, cooming together, ar distinguished by Commas: . . . But if they bee *antitheta* answering on' another; every second, for distinction of the par's, is fitly pointed with Semicolon." [23]

Ben Jonson, *The English Grammar* (written before 1637):

" For, whereas our breath is by nature so short, that we cannot continue without a stay to speak long together; it was thought necessary as well for the speaker's ease, as for the plainer deliverance of the things spoken,

[22] P. 135.
[23] Pp. 58, 59.

to invent this means, whereby men pausing a pretty while, the whole speech might never the worse be understood.

" These distinctions are either of a *perfect* or *imperfect sentence.* The distinctions of an imperfect sentence are two, a *subdistinction* and a *comma.* A *subdistinction* is a mean breathing, when the word serveth indifferently, both to the parts of the sentence going before and following after, and is marked thus (;).

" A *comma* is a distinction of an *imperfect* sentence, wherein with somewhat a longer breath, the sentence following is included; and is noted with this shorter semicircle (,). . . . The distinction of a *perfect* sentence hath a more full stay, and doth rest the spirit, which is a *pause* or a *period.*

" A *pause* is a distinction of a sentence, though perfect in itself, yet joined to another, being marked with two pricks (:).

" A *period* is the distinction of a sentence, in all respects *perfect,* and is marked with one full prick over against the lower part of the last letter, thus (.). . . . These distinctions (whereof the first is commonly neglected,) as they best agree with nature, so come they nearest to the ancient stays of sentences among the Romans and the Grecians." [24]

All four thus far quoted show remarkable agreement concerning the point at issue. One cannot mistake the basis of their theory of punctuation. The pauses, comma, semicolon, colon, and period, with their graded values are to be placed according to the " sense " or structure of the sentence, with a discrimination of a more or less " imperfect sense " or a " perfect sense." In the views expressed in these summaries, the placing of the marks of punctuation which indicate pause is to be determined upon a structural basis, with no hint of an elocutionary system.

The basis of the directions given by the fifth author, Simon Daines, seems at first somewhat less certain.[25] One cannot at

[24] Pp. 144–147.

[25] Simon Daines, *Orthoepia Anglicana,* 1640, pp. 69–74.

The full statement of the uses of these marks of punctuation as given by Daines follows:

" . . . it onely remaines, that we say somewhat of the stops, or pauses, between sentence and sentence, for the more renable (as we call it) and distinct reading . . . the knowledge of these stops or points is no lesse conducible and hypothetically necessary to distinct and ready reading (the perfection of Orthoepie) than to Orthographie, or right writing: though I will not further inferre, knowing it so requisite to both.

" These stops therefore are by the Latines termed *Comma; Commacolon; colon; periodus; Interrogatio; Parenthesis; Exclamatio; Apostrophe, sive contractionis nota, vel signum.*

" Their number (you see eight) their figure and use ensues.

" The *Comma* hath its place at the foot of the line, . . . The use onely once definitely conclude that he agrees with the others in making structure determine the stops, although the following statements do look in that direction:

> This [the period] is altogether used at the end of every speech or sentence, as the name it selfe implies . . . and signifies *conclusion.*
>
> It [the colon] is chiefly used in the division of sentences, and exacts halfe the pause of a Period.
>
> The *Comma-colon* . . . to make some short deliberation as it were of little sentences, as the *Comma* doth of words.

Even the following remark concerning the comma,

---

in long sentences, in the most convenient places to make a small pause for the necessity of breathing; or in Rhetoricall speeches (where many other words are used to one effect) to make a kind of Emphasis and deliberation for the greater majesty or state of Elocution.

" The *Comma-colon,* as you see by the name, participates of both the *Comma* and the *Colon;* . . . This to the Ancients was not knowne; but now in no lesse use than estimation, especially among Rhetoricians. Who in their long winded sentences, and reduplications, have it as a constant pack-horse, to make some short deliberation as it were of little sentences, as the *Comma* doth of words; the time of pause about double that of the *Comma* generally, which yet is very small.

" The *Colon.* . . . It is chiefly used in the division of sentences and exacts halfe the pause of a *Period;* and halfe as much againe as a *Comma Colon.*

" The *Period.* . . . This is altogether used at the end of every speech or sentence, as the name itselfe implies (being derived from the Greek) and signifies *conclusion.* The pause or distance of speaking hereto appropriate is sometime more, sometime lesse: for . . . when in the middle of a line it cuts off any integrall part of a complete Tractate, which goes not on with the same, but begins a new line, it requireth double the time of pause, that it doth when the Treatise persists in the same line: being then foure times as long as a *Colon,* which in the same line is but twice.

" I remember my singing-Master taught me to keep time, by telling from 1, to 4, according to the nature of the time I was to keep, and I found the practice thereof much ease and certainty to me, till I was perfect in it. The same course I have used to my pupils in their reading, to inure them to the distinction of their pauses, and found it no lesse successefull."

One sentence from the example given to illustrate the use of the points follows. This sentence is the shortest one that contains all four points.

" Travellers, Merchants, Historiographers, report, assure, relate, partly what themselves have seen; partly what approved in their wofull companions, left to be entombed in the bellies of those monsters: while they themselves with much adoe escaped, onely to be the dolefull narratours of so sad a story."

> The use onely in long sentences, in the most convenient places to make a small pause for the necessity of breathing; or in Rhetoricall speeches (where many other words are used to one effect) to make a kinde of Emphasis and deliberation for the greater majesty or state of Elocution,

which, indeed, comes nearest to the elocutionary-emphasis theory of punctuation, indicates the separation of words in a series "where many other words are used to one effect," a structural relation, as the peculiar function of this point. But when these statements of the uses of the points are completely analyzed and viewed in connection with the example "annexed [by Daines] to exemplifie further the use of the precedent Points in their severall kinds" there seems to be little doubt that this grammarian also would place the pauses on the basis of structural considerations.

Some significance attaches to the fact that all five grammarians refer to the use of these terms, *comma, colon,* and *period* in classical rhetorical theory. Indeed, Alexander Gil (1619) definitely insists, "Eaedē sunt nobis quae Latinis, & usus idem." In Aristotle, in Cicero, in Quintilian, these names refer not to punctuation but to parts of the sentence.[26] The *period* is a

[26] Aristotle, *Rhetoric,* III. 9. 4, 5, 6: δεῖ δὲ τὴν περίοδον καὶ τῇ διανοίᾳ τετελειῶσθαι, καὶ μὴ διακόπτεσθαι . . . . . περίοδος δὲ ἡ μὲν ἐν κώλοις ἡ δ' ἀφελής. ἔστι δ' ἐν κώλοις μὲν λέξις ἡ τετελειωμένη τε καὶ διῃρημένη καὶ εὐανάπνευστος, μὴ ἐν τῇ διαιρέσει ὥσπερ ἡ εἰρημένη περίοδος, ἀλλ' ὅλη. κῶλον δ' ἐστὶ τὸ ἕτερον μόριον ταύτης. ἀφελῆ δὲ λέγω τὴν μονόκωλον. δεῖ δὲ καὶ τὰ κῶλα καὶ τὰς περιόδους μήτε μυούρους εἶναι μήτε μακράς.

Cicero, *Orator,* 66. 222, 223 (referring to sentences just quoted): "Prima sunt illa duo, quae κόμματα Graeci vocant, nos *incisa* dicimus; deinde tertium κῶλον illi, nos *membrum;* sequitur non longa — ex duobus enim versibus, id est membris, perfecta comprehensio est et in spondios cadit."

Quintilian, *Institutionis Oratoriae,* IX. 4. 22. 122, 123: "At illa connexa series tres habet formas: incisa quae κόμματα dicuntur, membra quae κῶλα, περίοδον, quae est vel ambitus vel circumductum vel continuatio vel conclusio.

"Dicimus igitur esse incisa, membra, circuitus. Incisum (quantum mea fert opinio) erit sensus non expleto numero conclusus, plerisque pars membri. . . . Fiunt autem etiam singulis verbis incisa; *Diximus, testes dare volumus;* incisum est diximus. Membrum autem est sensus numeris conclusus, sed a toto corpore abruptus et per se nihil efficiens. . . . Quando ergo incipit corpus esse? cum venit extrema conclusio. . . . Itaque, fere incisa et membra mutila sunt et conclusionem utique desiderant. Periodo plurima nomina dat Cicero, *ambitum, circuitum, comprehensionem, continuationem, circumscriptionem.* Genera eius duo sunt, alterum simplex, cum sensus unus longiore ambitu circumducitur, alterum, quod constat membris et incisis, quae plures sensus habent."

complete sentence; the *colon* a member; the *comma*, a small part or phrase. Starting from this use in classical rhetoric these names for the parts of the sentence attached themselves to the particular points used to set them off. The word *period* thus not only means a sentence, but also the point (.) indicating its end; *colon* becomes the name of the " two pricks " (:) commonly used to separate the *cola* of a sentence; and *comma*, the name for the point (,) separating the *commata* or smaller parts of a sentence member. These names for the points thus indicate their earliest use, the separation of the structural parts of the sentence. That a structural basis should underlie the explanations of the uses of the marks of punctuation as set forth in the early grammars is thus to be expected, for these books depend upon classical grammar and rhetoric for their ideas and apparatus.

Although the practice of the times might easily not strictly conform to the theory of the grammarians (and very probably in any case only loosely conformed) it seems unlikely that that practice could have been consciously based upon another principle differing so fundamentally from that expressed in contemporary grammars and opposed to the early structural connection of the names employed.

If that were the case with Shakespeare we should at least expect his comments upon punctuation to accord with the principle of his practice. In the footnotes are given five instances from Shakespeare's plays and poems.[27] Of these, in *a* the word

27

a Timon of Athens, I. i. 39–50.

Poet: . . . My free drift
Halts not particularly, but moves itself
In a wide sea of wax. No levell'd malice
Infect one comma in the course I hold;
But flies an eagle flight, bold and forth on,
Leaving no tract behind.

b Hamlet, V. ii 36–47.

Hamlet: . . . Wilt thou know
The effect of what I wrote?
Horatio: Ay, good my lord.
Hamlet: An earnest conjuration from the King,
As England was his faithful tributary,
As love between them as the palm should flourish,

comma is used in its original structural meaning of a short member of a sentence or period, a group of words less than a colon.

As Peace should still her wheaten garland wear
And stand a comma 'tween their amities,
And many such-like *as*-es of great charge,
That, on the view and know of these contents,
Without debatement further, more or less,
He should the bearers put to sudden death,
Not shriving time allow'd.

c Midsummer Night's Dream, V. i. 89–105.

Theseus: Where I have come, great clerks have purposed
To greet me with premeditated welcomes;
Where I have seen them shiver and look pale,
Make periods in the midst of sentences,
Throttle their practis'd accent in their fears,
And in conclusion dumbly have broke off,
Not paying me a welcome.

d Lucrece, 561–567.

Her pity-pleading eyes are sadly fixed
In the remorseless wrinkles of his face;
Her modest eloquence with sighs is mixed,
Which to her oratory adds more grace.
She puts the period often from his place;
And midst the sentence so her accent breaks,
That twice she doth begin ere once she speaks.

e Midsummer Night's Dream, V. i. 108–126.

Enter (Quince for) the Prologue.

Pro. If we offend, it is with our good will.
That you should think, we come not to offend,
But with good will. To show our simple skill,
That is the true beginning of our end.
Consider then we come but in despite.
We do not come as minding to content you,
Our true intent is. All for your delight
We are not here. That you should here repent you,
The actors are at hand, and by their show
You shall know all that you are like to know.

The. This fellow doth not stand upon points.

Lys. He hath rid his prologue like a rough colt; he knows not the stop. A good moral, my lord: it is not enough to speak, but to speak true.

Hip. Indeed he hath play'd on this prologue like a child on a recorder; a sound, but not in government.

The. His speech was like a tangled chain; nothing impaired, but all disordered.

The figurative use of a word *comma* in *b* seems to have no meaning in harmony with an elocutionary or stress principle of punctuation. In *c* and *d* the end of the sentence is recognized as the proper place for the period but under embarrassment or great emotional stress one may *break off* before the meaning is complete or make several false starts. Such " making a period in the midst of the sentence " seems to me to have structural significance rather than to be, as the elocutionary theory implies, the indication of a long pause of emphasis upon the word preceding the period. In *e* the humor of the mispointing and wrong pausing arises out of the changed meaning conveyed by the joining of wrong structural elements or the separation of essential parts of the sentences. If the punctuation here has significance only for stress and no relation to syntax and structure, the humor loses much of its point.

III

Those who support the elocutionary theory of Elizabethan punctuation insist that punctuation " has radically changed in the last three hundred years," in that (1) " modern punctuation is, or at any rate attempts to be, logical; the earlier system was mainly rhythmical," and (2) " modern punctuation is uniform; the old punctuation was quite the reverse . . . a flexible system . . . to express subtle differences of tone." [28] One who attempts to trace the development of our system of punctuation as that system is expressed in the grammars of the last three hundred years [29] receives an impression quite different from that

[28] Percy Simpson, *Shakespearian Punctuation* pp. 8, 10.

[29] In addition to the books referred to above, pages 73–75, the following texts were examined with considerable care:

C. Cooper, *Grammatica Linguae,* 1685, pp. 154–160.

J. Jones, *Practical Phonography,* 1701, pp. 141–144.

Anon. (Brightland) *English Grammar,* 1710, pp. 127 ff.

I. Watts, *The Art of Reading and Writing English* (6th ed., 1740), pp. 35 ff.

Robert Lowth, *A Short Introduction,* etc., 1762, pp. 177–193.

Thomas Sheridan, A *Prosodial Grammar* (prefixed to dictionary), 1780, pp. li–lv.

of these assertions. In all the grammars examined, dated from 1589 to 1900, the structural basis of placing the points of punctuation appears without exception. Changes during the last three hundred years have not shown themselves in the underlying general principles of the uses of the stops. Lindley Murray's general statement of the use of the comma,

> The Comma usually separates those parts of a sentence, which, though very closely connected in sense and construction, require a pause between them [30]

closely parallels that of Charls Butler (of 1634),

> Comma is a point of mor' imperfect sens, in a simple axiom, or in either part of a compound: which continueth the tenour of the voic' to the last, with the shortest paus

and that of J. F. Genung in 1900,

> *The Comma.* Just as the semicolon is the mark of the added clause, with its clear though appreciably remote logical relation, the comma is the mark of the closer dependent clause . . . and of the phrase or the word that does duty *as* a phrase. It is still a mark of separation, but not enough, ordinarily to break into the grammatical continuity of the passage.[31]

The difference in treatment from that of the early seventeenth century, however, shows itself in Lindley Murray's twenty specific rules for the comma in which he attempts to indicate very definitely all the applications of the general statement he first gives. If the grammars can be trusted as evidence, the development of our punctuation has not resulted in a changed

---

Anon. (Thomas Dodson), *Comprehensive Grammar,* 1780, pp. 155–173.
Ralph Harrison, *Rudiments of English Grammar,* 1783, pp. 67–78.
Charles Coote, *Elements of the Grammar of the English Language,* 1788, pp. 260–267.
Noah Webster, *An American Selection of Lessons in Reading and Speaking* (9th ed., 1794), pp. 3 ff.
———, *A Philosophical and Practical Grammar,* pp. 214–220.
William Hazlitt, *A New and Improved Grammar* 1810, pp. 145–148.
John Walker, *Rhetorical Grammar,* 1814, pp. 50–77.
Lindley Murray, *English Grammar* (1795, 5th ed., 1824), pp. 392–415.
A number of later 19th century texts were also examined, but with much less care.

[30] Lindley Murray, *English Grammar,* p. 392.

[31] J. F. Genung, *The Working Principles of Rhetoric,* 1900, p. 328.

basis or *theory* of its use, but rather in this attempt to make more definite and regular the application of the points in matters of detail. This particular tendency appears to have reached its highest point at the end of the eighteenth century and during the first half of the nineteenth. The best modern practice, according to Professor Genung,[32] probably tends to a much more flexible, artistic use of punctuation, more open to the individualities of style.

These facts in the history of punctuation have some significance for our immediate problem. If Elizabethan punctuation is based on the structure of the sentence, then it is directly in line both with the meanings of the names, comma, colon, and period, as these were used in classical rhetoric and with the theory of punctuation expressed in the grammars from 1589 to 1900. If, on the other hand, Elizabethan punctuation is based on elocutionary emphasis unrelated to syntax and structure, then there must be found some means to account for the development of that elocutionary principle out of the earlier structural applications of the names, comma, colon, and period, in classical rhetoric, and for the later progress from that elocutionary principle back to structural considerations after the Elizabethan era.

From the materials here presented one cannot by any means insist that an elocutionary system of Shakespearian punctuation is impossible. But when they are all gathered in a single view it seems much more reasonable to conclude that we have in Elizabethan books a structural punctuation, in line both with the modern principle of punctuation and with the earlier history

[32] *Op. cit.*, pp. 333, 334: "The modern tendency is to reduce punctuation: cutting down semicoloned relations, where possible, to the comma, and leaving many of the comma pauses to the unmarked rhetorical pause. . . . With this general reduction of punctuation the field is left clearer for special effects. Accordingly we find that in modern writing punctuation is a much more flexible thing, and more open to individualities of style, than was formerly the case. It may for greater stress be augmented,—that is, pushed up from comma to semicolon; it may also be attenuated for greater rapidity. It is this skilful employment of punctuation as a flexible, living, artistic thing which makes it so truly a cardinal factor in the organism of the sentence."

of the names for the points used.[33] One must add, however, that this early structural punctuation, especially that in the Quartos and the Folio, was much more loosely and variously applied than modern punctuation and represents so much possibility of printers' interference that it can have very slight value for our interpretation of Shakespeare.

[33] Not only is the elocution-emphasis theory of punctuation applied to the use of the stops but frequently also to the use of capital letters. Mr. Simpson's statement (*Shakespearian Punctuation,* p. 103) is typical: "Capitals emphasize: hence the implied courtesy in their use with proper names. When a word derived special significance from its context, it was the rule to use a capital."

Although the use of capital letters is treated even more frequently in Elizabethan grammars than is the use of the stops, there is no hint of such an emphasis use of capitals in any of these books. The statements, despite considerable variation, do not essentially differ from that contained in *Bullokar's Booke at large, for the Amendment of Orthographie for English speech,* 1580 (Section XXXV):

"Note farder, that capitall or great letters, are to be placed onely at the beginning of words, that begin a full, perfect, and seuerall sentence: or in the beginning of words, that signify great countries, nations, sects, & proper names of men, Cities, Castles, Sheres, Villages, Hils, Riuers, and other proper names which be specially notorious."

THE YOUTH OF MILTON

AN INTERPRETATION OF HIS EARLY LITERARY DEVELOPMENT

THE YOUTH OF MILTON

AN INTERPRETATION OF HIS EARLY LITERARY DEVELOPMENT

JAMES HOLLY HANFORD

THE part of Milton's life which falls between his eighteenth and his thirty-second years has never, I think, been made the subject of a special and independent critical study. Its various outward episodes — the residence at Cambridge, the retreat at Horton, the continental journey, the return to England — are presented in full detail by Masson and more interpretatively by Mark Pattison and other writers. Critical comment on the early poems, often of the most brilliant sort, of course abounds. What one misses in the discussions is a recognition of the fact that these years, comprising as they do the epoch of Milton's transition from boyhood to maturity and the first full cycle of his poetry, constitute, both from the psychological and from the literary standpoint, a unit.

Even the recent admirable study of the Latin poems by Professor E. K. Rand,[1] which greatly enriches our understanding of these remarkable compositions and is so full of suggestion to the Milton student, makes no systematic attempt to integrate them with other phases of the poet's early work or to set forth in detail their significance in relation to his personality. Outwardly the Latin verse is sharply distinguished from the contemporary English poetry as belonging to a different literary tradition, and, indeed, the whole product of Milton's youthful imagination has the appearance of being highly miscellaneous. More carefully considered, it is seen to be marked, not alone by the normal growth of his powers, but by a singularly coherent progression of experience.

[1] *Milton in Rustication, Studies in Philology,* April, 1922.

The failure of Milton students generally to interpret his development in what seem to me its most essential aspects results, I believe, from an overvaluation of known outward incident and historical circumstance as determining factors in the constitution of the poetic mind. The mass of biographical detail and the still larger mass of information regarding the setting of Milton's career presented by Masson is, after all, of little avail toward an understanding of the actual unfolding of his genius. These things are, of course, not to be neglected, but they can be used only tentatively and in subordination to the all-important evidence of the poet's self-expression. Such evidence, modestly interpreted, may yield us less, but what it yields will be definite and assured, whereas conclusions based on assumptions regarding the relation between biographical incident and the subjective consciousness of the artist remain at the mercy of conjecture. A recent important work, M. Denis Saurat's *La Pensée de Milton,* which aims to give a comprehensive map of the poet's mind, is frequently liable to objection on these grounds. A weight of inference is attached, for example, to Milton's first marriage, which, even if we possessed complete understanding of the facts, the episode will by no means bear. Another contemporary student, Heinreich Mutschmann (*Milton und das Licht*), who approaches his subject equipped with all the paraphernalia of psychoanalysis, is shipwrecked by a wild thesis concerning Milton's supposed physical degeneracy. Finally the able and industrious Liljegren in his *Studies in Milton* stakes everything on the demonstration of two facts, that Milton did not, as he claims, meet Galileo in Italy, and that he did, as his enemies affirmed, craftily insert the Pamela prayer into the *Eikon Basilike* for the purpose of finding it there, facts sensational enough, certainly, but of purely speculative relevance even if true. The present writer, while confessing himself, in his attempt to envisage Milton's personality more clearly, indebted to these works, even to that of Mutschmann, professes to avoid their waywardness by virtue of a stricter dependence on the poet's written words.

The proper use of these materials involves, first of all, a careful attention to their chronology. There have been errors here which it is now possible to correct. It involves also a due proportioning of emphasis. Milton critics have in the past inclined to center attention too much on the Horton period, to the comparative neglect of that which immediately preceded it. From the standpoint of literary values such an emphasis is natural enough; but for the comprehension of the mental processes and habits which underlie his creative activity and of the moulding effects of the intellectual and imaginative forces with which he was in contact, the significance of his less mature work, of his failures, even, and of documents not literary at all may be greater than that of the Horton masterpieces.

But the Horton period itself has not, I think, been altogether rightly understood. Romantic critics like Raleigh and Moody go to great lengths in idealizing Milton's " long vacation," painting it as a moment of sweet serenity in which the poet reflects without emotional disturbance the joyous spirit of the English Renaissance. Such a view is based too exclusively on the evidence of four poems, and, with regard to these poems, it fails to take account of the effects of a studied decorum, the result of a strong personal reserve and of the strict tradition in which Milton had so carefully schooled himself, which compelled him to conceal his more instinctive emotions under a mask of formal beauty. This is generally true of the poet's early work in verse; it is particularly so of that done between 1632 and 1637. The aesthetic objectivity of the Horton poems was in considerable degree an artificial thing.

Beneath it, and in the entire body of Milton's youthful writing, we may read the evidence of disturbing experiences and intimate reactions which belong characteristically to the period of adolescence. We may read also a part, at least, of the record of Milton's awakening to the potential influences of his intellectual and artistic environment. To indicate as definitely as possible the stages in this awakening and to trace the effects of the emotional and imaginative forces thus released in him upon the developing processes of his art, is the object chiefly aimed at in the present discussion.

The record of Milton's more individual experience does not begin significantly before the period of the Latin elegies. Of his really distinctive boyhood traits we know nothing directly. Even the untimely seriousness and ambition, the deliberate purpose to fulfill expectation by becoming something good and great, are, as regards his childhood, matters of inference. We may assume him to have taken his bent thus early, but it is only later that we can study his temperament at first hand. We have Milton's own later statement to the effect that his literary talents early attracted the attention of his elders. It would be interesting to know under precisely what conditions and stimuli his first compositions were written. Given the cultural tradition of the Renaissance, it was entirely natural that he should write verses before any powerful original impulses asserted themselves in him. Latin composition was an important feature of the curriculum in all the public schools of Milton's time, a "preposterous exaction," the poet describes it in the *Tractate of Education,* "forcing the empty wits of children to compose themes, verses, and orations which are the acts of ripest judgment, and the final work of a head filled by long reading and observing, with elegant maxims and copious invention." The writing of English verse was required at Westminster and may have been at St. Paul's.

Beside this we have the special influences of Milton's home environment. It should not be forgotten that to cultivate music meant, throughout the English Renaissance, to cultivate song, and that the known compositions of Milton's father are all settings of English words. This fact presumably determines the character of Milton's first approach to poetry, and it is of far-reaching importance in its effect upon his art. Particularly suggestive, in view of the fact that the father had contributed tunes to five of the Psalms in Ravenscroft's psalter of 1621, is the preservation of two metrical Psalm paraphrases written by Milton in his sixteenth year. One surmises collaboration between the musician father and the poet son. In any case some of the sweetest of his later verses — the *Song on a May Morning* and the lyrics in *Arcades* and *Comus* were composed for music.

Milton's own musical training and his sense of the analogy between the sister arts of music and poetry clearly underlie the conception of *L'Allegro* and *Il Penseroso*.

A less obvious result of this early influence is to be found in the aesthetic character of his enthusiasm for language. The terms in which he expresses in the poem *Ad Patrem* his gratitude to his father for his linguistic education suggest the meeting point in him of humanistic learning and the sense of beauty:

Tuo, pater optime, sumptu
Cum mihi Romuleae patuit facundia linguae,
Et Latii veneres, et quae Iovis ora decebant
Grandia magniloquis elata vocabula Graiis,
Addere suasisti quos iactat Gallia flores,
Et quam degeneri novus Italus ore loquelam
Fundit, barbaricos testatus voce tumultus,
Quaeque Palaestinus loquitur mysteria vates.[2]

His feeling for English is a home-felt delight, implying a still closer discrimination of the harmonies and ornaments of speech:

Hail, Native Language, that by sinews weak
Didst move my first endeavouring tongue to speak,
And madest imperfect words with childish trips,
Half unpronounced, slide through my infant lips,
Driving dumb Silence from the portal door,
Where he had mutely sat two years before. . . .
But haste thee straight to do me once a pleasure,
And from thy wardrobe bring thy chiefest treasure,
Not those new-fangled toys, and trimming slight
Which takes our late fantastics with delight;
But cull those richest robes and gay'st attire,
Which deepest spirits and choicest wits desire.[3]

There is no reason to suppose that these enthusiasms do not go back to the early years of Milton's schooling. They are, like

[2] "When, at your cost, dear father, I had mastered the tongue of Romulus and seen all the graces of it, and had learned the noble idiom of the magniloquent Greeks, fit for the great mouth of Jove himself, you persuaded me to add to these the flowers which France boasts; and the speech which the modern Italian pours from his degenerate lips, bearing witness in every accent of the barbarian tumults; and the language in which the singers of Palestine speak their mysteries." — W. V. Moody's translation, revised by E. K. Rand, Moody, *Milton's Complete Poems*, revised edition, 1924.

[3] *At a Vacation Exercise*, vv. 1 ff. The text employed for the quotations from the English and Latin poems is W. A. Wright's, *The Poetical Works of Milton*, Cambridge, 1903.

the born artist's love of color, his initial gift as a poet, and they antedate the need which he later felt to find an expressive medium for those

> naked thoughts that rove about
> And loudly knock to have their passage out.[4]

According to a statement made by Aubrey on the authority of Milton's brother Christopher he was already a poet at the age of ten and " composed many copies of verses which might well become a riper age." [5] The anonymous biographer, who is well informed regarding Milton's early life, says that in his school days he "wrote several grave and religious poems, and paraphrased some of David's Psalms." [6] The first of these experiments and exercises, of whatever sort they may have been, are lost, but the two Psalm paraphrases, the only pieces which survive from his school period, will serve as slightly more mature examples. They were preserved and printed in the 1645 edition of the *Poems,* not, presumably, for their own sakes but as evidences of the poet's early devotion to the Muse of his native land, and they bear accordingly the careful superscription " This and the following Psalm were done by the Author at fifteen years old." This would be in 1624, the year preceding his matriculation at the University. The choice of subject was dictated by a time when Psalm paraphrase was not merely a habit but an obsession. An illustrious line of poets had swollen the records of failure in this attempt. A pious and learned sovereign, who was not a poet, had magnanimously lent his hand. More directly responsible for Milton's endeavor in this common task were the elegant Latin versions of Buchanan, which he had doubtless studied at St. Paul's.[7]

[4] *Ibid.*, vv. 23–24.

[5] *Collections for the Life of Milton* reprinted in L. E. Lockwood's *Of Education,* etc., Riverside Edition, 1911, p. xl.

[6] *Op. cit.,* p. xxiv.

[7] There are perhaps eight or ten instances in which Milton clearly owes his turn of phrase to Buchanan's rendering. Thus in v. 3 of Psalm cxxxvi, where Scripture has simply " Lord of Lords " Buchanan paraphrases " Cui domini rerum submittunt sceptra tyranni," and Milton, with a similar republican touch, " That doth the wrathful tyrants quell." Buchanan's " auricomum solem " becomes " the golden-tressed sun; " his unscriptural

Milton was to return on two later occasions to Psalm paraphrases. In 1648 he undertook to supply the need of an accurate and doctrinally sound Puritan version to supplant the Sternhold and Hopkins Psalter for congregational singing. In 1653, when he had become blind, he did the first eight Psalms (on successive days) as a combined spiritual discipline and metrical exercise, probably in anticipation of a renewal of work on the composition of *Paradise Lost.* The two early pieces differ strikingly in character from these uninspired works of his maturity. The latter are severely plain in language, and the first set, at least, as nearly literal as Milton could make them. The early versions, on the other hand, are independent poems. They are characterized by a freedom of rhythm which marks them as the products of a genuine though immature poetical enthusiasm, and their original Hebrew substance is all but lost in the ornamental phraseology which Milton adopts from the religious verse of seventeenth century England. More specifically their stylistic inspiration is Sylvester, whose rich and elaborate though somewhat undignified language apparently satisfied Milton's youthful sense of verbal beauty.[8] The choice of the 114th and 136th Psalms and the manifest enthusiasm which Milton puts into the compositions is evidence also of a deeper sympathy with the poetic substance of Sylvester, whose broad and pious sense of the greatness and goodness of God as witnessed by the excellence of created nature Milton reproduces not ineffectively. We have here the beginning of a strain in Milton's poetry the importance of which, far more than any mere consideration of style, justifies the claim of Sylvester's *DuBartas* to be counted among the permanent

---

epithet for Og, " confisum viribus Ogum," is repeated in Milton's " large-limbed Og." In Psalm cxiv, " Pharian fields " goes back to Buchanan's " arva Phari " and the phrase " among their ewes," which is added to the literal rendering of v. 4, has its original in Buchanan's " ut dux gregis inter oves."

For the prevalent use of Buchanan's Latin Psalms as school texts see P. Hume Brown, *Buchanan as Humanist and Reformer,* 1890, p. 146; Foster Watson, *English Grammar Schools to 1660,* 1908, p. 472. I have no evidence that Buchanan was used at St. Paul's.

[8] See C. Dunster, *Considerations on Milton's Early Reading and the prima stamina of " Paradise Lost,"* 1800.

sources of his inspiration, a strain which reaches its culmination and full Miltonic glory in the morning hymn of Adam and Eve in the fifth book of *Paradise Lost.*[9]

In such a passage as this Milton has, of course, far transcended Sylvester's humbler muse. In it, too, more than in any attempt to reduce the Psalms to meter, does he approach their spirit, as he elaborates with his own imagery and in his own majestic idiom the great theme " The Heavens declare the glory of God." Yet the animating motive of the hymn and the quality of religious feeling manifested in it are essentially the same as in the work of his Puritan predecessor. It is an elevated and impersonal enthusiasm, having as its appropriate expression precisely the ornate magniloquence of which Sylvester is a humble and Milton the consummate master. Essentially literary in origin and developing naturally from boyhood tastes and influences this emotion and the style which attended it became characteristic of one whole phase of Milton's poetry, and of this phase the early Psalms are clear though faint precursors. With the more individual aspects of his genius, on the other hand— with such subjective experience as is embodied, for example, in the invocations in *Paradise Lost* and in the lyric parts of *Samson Agonistes,* the two paraphases have not the slightest discernible relation.

Of analogous significance in Milton's literary biography, is the poem *On the Death of a Fair Infant Dying of a Cough,* published along with other material which he apparently had not at first considered worth printing, in the edition of 1673, and dated " Anno aetatis 17." Allowing for Milton's peculiar usage in the Latin designation of his age and assuming that the poem was composed immediately after the event which it commemorates, the death, namely, of the infant daughter of his sister Anne Philips, its date would be between December 8, 1626, and the following spring, when Milton was in his second year of residence at the University. The piece was conceived in a mood of tender grief and sympathy, not untouched with a larger sense of the mystery of death and immortality, motives

[9] Lines 153–208.

toward which his mind had naturally been drawn by the ravages of the plague in London, even before they were brought home to him in a domestic sorrow. The literary influence under which his emotion characteristically shapes itself is the seventeenth century poetry of death. In style it belongs, as is evident both from its meter and its language, to the Spenserian tradition as represented particularly by Giles and Phineas Fletcher. The verbal conceits which chill the feeling in all but a few stanzas show Milton in the toils of a fashion which he was later to repudiate. There are, however, beyond this, some definitely marked Miltonic traits which suggest the beginnings of a more individual style. Such expressions as "the ruined roof of shaked Olympus," the "golden-winged host," "the middle empire of the freezing air," "thy heaven-loved innocence" surely enough reveal his touch. The lovely opening anticipates the delicate perfection of the Horton poetry:

> O fairest flower, no sooner blown but blasted,
> Soft silken primrose fading timelessly,
> Summer's chief honour, if thou had'st outlasted
> Bleak Winter's force that made thy blossom dry.

We have, too, the introduction of favorite motives which he was later to employ more happily. Thus lines 38–40,

> Tell me, bright Spirit, where'er thou hoverest,
> Whether above that high first-moving sphere,
> Or in the Elysian fields (if such there were),

establish the verbal form for *Lycidas*, 155 ff.,

> where'er thy bones are hurled,
> Whether beyond the stormy Hebrides, . . .

and the parenthesis, "if such there were," is the first of those conscientious reservations with which Milton checks himself in his instinctive use of classical mythology. Again, the allusion to Astraea in the eighth stanza, and the mask-like imaging of Mercy and "that crowned Matron, sage white-robed truth . . . let down in cloudy throne to do the world some good," while suggesting the Fletcherian personifications, anticipate familiar passages in the poem *On the Morning of Christ's Nativity*, and the references to the guardian spirit introduce a motive to which Milton returns again and again.

These things are specifically and characteristically Miltonic. Where, however, in Stanza V, he reaches for a moment the heights of poetic utterance it is on the wings of the great tradition of Elizabethan and Jacobean song:

> Yet can I not persuade me thou art dead,
> Or that thy corse corrupts in earth's dark womb,
> Or that thy beauties lie in wormy bed,
> Hid from the world in a low-delved tomb.

A striking parallel to these lines is to be found in the words of Christ in Book III of *Paradise Lost*:[10]

> Though now to Death I yield, and am his due
> All that of me can die, yet, that debt paid,
> Thou wilt not leave me in the loathsome grave,
> His prey, nor suffer my unspotted soul
> Forever with corruption there to dwell;
> But I shall rise victorious, and subdue
> My vanquisher, spoil'd of his vaunted spoil.
> Death his death's wound shall then receive, and stoop
> Inglorious, of his mortal sting disarm'd;
> I through the ample air in triumph high
> Shall lead Hell captive maugre Hell, and shew
> The powers of Darkness bound.

The poetic essence of this passage, apart from its theological implications, is something, one feels, which Milton has carried over from his youth. It shows that he could still respond with the full energy of maturity to the Christian sentiment of Donne's "Death, be not proud" or of Giles Fletcher's *Christ's Victory and Triumph.* But such moments in Milton's later work are rare. His mature spiritual life is normally ministered to by other emotions than those which associate themselves with the Resurrection, and it is only by reviving an old emotion and by falling back on his unfailing stylistic resources that he avoids the danger of mediocrity in dealing with this theme. The more striking, therefore, is its pervasiveness in the work of the Cambridge and Horton periods, where the idea of future bliss held,

[10] Lines 245–256.

as we shall see, an increasingly strong and glowing appeal to his imagination.

It is, I think, significant that the poems just described stand alone among Milton's works at this period of his career. There is nothing further in English before the *Vacation Exercise* of 1628 and the *Nativity* of 1629. On the other hand, we have no less than six Latin poems dated, like the English elegy, "Anno aetatis 17," a larger number than belongs to any other single year in his life. We may, perhaps, infer a deliberate postponement of further English composition in favor of an assault on the citadels of poetry in a medium dictated by the humanistic ideals of his day and rendered attractive by a growing sense of the rich beauties of Latin style.

Four of the poems, all written in the autumn of 1626, are laments occasioned by the deaths of dignitaries associated in one way or another with the University, namely, the Bishops of Winchester and Ely, alumni and former masters of Pembroke Hall, John Gostlin, the vice-chancellor, and Richard Riddle, the University beadle. The poem on the vice-chancellor is simply a meditation on the inevitableness of death, with praise of Gostlin's skill in medicine and the usual conceits regarding the failure of his art to procure him release from the common doom.

The elegies for the bishops are more elaborate and are constructed on an identical plan, having evidently been written within a short time of each other. The poet represents himself as in the act of exclaiming against Death when he is vouchsafed a vision of the abode of the blessed. In the earlier piece, *In Obitum Praesulis Wintoniensis,* Milton describes this vision in detail, painting in colorful imagery the landscape of Heaven, with its flowers, its silver streams playing over golden sands, its bejewelled angelic presences, its fanfare of celestial music. The passage anticipates both *Lycidas* and the *Epitaphium Damonis* and is the first of a series of Paradisiac pictures elaborated from antique models and enriched by the more luxuriant poetic tradition of the Renaissance, a series which culminates in the account of Eden in *Paradise Lost.* In the second piece he forbears to repeat the description of the Heaven of Heavens, but elaborates instead the journey on which he is borne by the Muse into the broad spaces of the sky, past Boötes and Orion, above the moon and the starry sphere, to the threshold of Olympus. The theme is an equally congenial one and foreshadows some of the best known and most characteristic passages in his mature poetry. The remaining elegy, *In Obitum Praeconis Academici Cantabrigiensis,* is a mere trifle, exhibiting the same conceitful humor, not untempered by kindliness, which marks the later English poems on the death of the old carrier Hobson. The attitude is oddly but appropriately expressive of the sentiments of young academic gentlemen toward those minor functionaries who are ridiculed during their lives and offices only to have it faintly remembered at their passing that they were human. In style it is, like the others, laden with verbal ornament. Milton is making himself free of the realm of classic vocabulary and allusion as, in the Psalms and the English elegy, he was free of seventeenth century poetic phrase. All three pieces are largely devoid of the personal note which characterizes Milton's expression of sorrow for the loss of his sister's child. Yet one feels that he has been sincerely moved by realization of the fact of death and that it costs him no effort to accept the obligation of celebrating these successive occasions of academic mourning. Witness the sober and beautiful opening of the elegy on the Bishop of Winchester:

> Moestus eram, et tacitus, nullo comitante, sedebam,
>   Haerebantque animo tristia plura meo:
> Protinus en subiit funestae cladis imago
>   Fecit in Angliaco quam Libitina solo;
> Dum procerum ingressa est splendentes marmore turres
>   Dira sepulchrali Mors metuenda face,
> Pulsavitque auro gravidos et iaspide muros,
>   Nec metuit satrapum sternere falce greges.
> Tunc memini clarique ducis, fratrisque verendi,
>   Intempestivis ossa cremata rogis;
> Et memini Heroum quos vidit ad aethera raptos,
>   Flevit et amissos Belgia tota duces.
> At te praecipue luxi, dignissime Praesul,
>   Wintoniaeque olim gloria magna tuae.[11]

[11] Sad and silent I sat, comradeless; and many griefs clung about my soul. Then suddenly, behold, there arose before me an image of the

Also the tenderly melancholy lines with which he brings to a close the lament for the vice-chancellor, dismissing his body to the grave and his spirit to the Elysian Fields:

> Colende Praeses, membra precor tua
> Molli quiescant cespite, et ex tuo
> Crescant rosae calthaeque busto,
> Purpureoque hyacinthus ore.
> Sit mite de te iudicium Aeaci,
> Subrideatque Aetnaea Proserpina,
> Interque felices perennis
> Elysio spatiere campo! [12]

These Latin poems, then, as clearly as the English elegy, are something more than mere poetic exercises or prescriptive tasks. They spring spontaneously enough from a mood of reflective melancholy forced upon the youthful poet by the ravages of the plague, and they definitely suggest the birth in him of a more inward poetic impulse than would have been natural in his earlier boyhood. Of rather less interest is the long hexameter poem, *In Quintum Novembris,* a miniature epic, written just after the Latin elegies and describing the origin and progress of the gunpowder plot. There is perhaps a relation between this piece and the equally elaborate *Locustae* of Phineas Fletcher, but the idea of a demoniac origin of the plot was a commonplace and the anti-catholic bitterness of Milton's poem represents the prevailing and appropriate sentiment for the occasion. Thus early does the gentle and humane spirit of the youthful artist

---

deadly plague which Libitina spread on English soil, when dire Death, fearful with his sepulchral torch, entered the glorious marble towers of the great, shook the walls heavy with jasper and gold, and feared not to lay low with his scythe the host of princes. Then I thought on that illustrious duke [Duke Christian of Brunswick, a victim of the War of the Palatinate] and his worshipped brother-in-arms, whose bones were consumed on untimely pyres; and I thought on those heroes whom all Belgia saw snatched away to the skies, — saw, and wept her lost leaders. But for you chiefly I grieved, good Bishop, once the great glory of your Winchester.

[12] Loved master, I pray that your limbs may rest quiet beneath the gentle sod, and that from your grave roses may spring, and marigold, and the purple-mouthed hyacinth. May Aeacus pronounce judgment mildly on you, and Proserpina, maid of Aetna, give you a smile, and may you walk forever in the Elysian fields among the blessed.

who could already invest the pain of death with beauty and send his Muse beyond the " flaming walls of space and time " receive his schooling in the harsh animosities which were for his day a necessary ingredient of patriotism and Protestant zeal. The remarkable thing is that he can throw himself so fully into the spirit of his alien theme. It is another evidence of the protean responsiveness of his genius to the divers and even contradictory influences of the various literary traditions in which he happens from time to time to be writing. The range and character of these influences I have barely indicated. To trace them in detail would be beyond my purpose. The point to observe is that Milton's poetry, as we have thus far surveyed it, is essentially imitation, though imitation of a peculiarly generous and dynamic kind. The process of literary composition is with him in each case the result of a cultural enthusiasm which enables the poet to identify himself so completely with a literary mode that he can express himself in it freely and spontaneously without having to resort to a particular model. In the act of reproducing such a tradition Milton makes it permanently his own. The successive contacts open to him new ranges of poetic thought and expression and their influence is, as we have seen, definitely traceable in his maturest work.

It remains to consider a set of reactions of a more positive nature, reactions which belong peculiarly to the period of Milton's adolescence and which have a very different bearing on the problem of the development of his poetic personality. The first evidence of the dawn in him of an emotional experience more inwardly disturbing than the artistic melancholy which he has elaborated out of the incidents of the plague is to be found in the poem which he afterwards printed as the first of his Latin elegies. This poem, written presumably in the same spring which saw the composition of the lament for the Fair Infant, is significantly addressed to Charles Diodati, the friend who for many years served Milton as the confidant of his deepest experiences and most cherished dreams. The occasion is the incident of the poet's rustication in consequence of a quarrel with his University tutor, and *Elegy I* teaches us to look to that event as marking an important moment in the breaking down of the carefully schooled docility of Milton's boyhood. The fact of a real and fundamental change in the poet's experience is confirmed by all that we know of his relations to the University. Our fullest information comes from Christopher Milton through the biographer Aubrey, as follows: " He was a very hard student in the University and performed all his exercises there with very good applause. His first tutor there was Mr. Chapell, from whom receiving some unkindness (whipped him), he was afterwards (though it seemed opposite to the rules of the college), transferred to the tuition of one Mr. Tovell, who died parson of Lutterworth." [13] The other early biographers say nothing of any trouble, though Wood, after repeating from his authorities the statement that Milton won the admiration of all by his exercises and was esteemed to be a virtuous and sober person, adds the qualification "yet not to be ignorant of his own parts." [14] The fact and date of the rustication are established by the elegy and Aubrey's parenthetical explanation of its cause apparently confirmed by the poet's mention of a " harsh master's threats " and "other things not to be endured by my nature." The circumstances are not difficult to reconstruct if we bear in mind the liberal environment from which Milton had just come and the atmosphere of intelligent appreciation which so evidently surrounded him at home and at school. The letters written from the University to Young and Gill [15] are evidence of the friendly relations in which he stood to these admired mentors of his boyhood. In Chapell he doubtless encountered an individual of smaller mould whose methods and attitude he resented.

Much light is thrown on Milton's situation at the University by later utterances in which he expresses a hostile point of view toward the discipline and ideals in vogue there in his time. There is contemporary evidence of still greater value. It is quite clear that he allied himself almost from the first with the group of intellectual liberals who carried on into the seventeenth

[13] Lockwood, p. xl.

[14] Lockwood, p. xlv.

[15] *The Works of John Milton in Prose and Verse,* ed. John Mitford, VII. 368–371.

century the old battle of humanistic culture against the narrow and jejune scholasticism which had taken its last refuge in the universities and which still dominated the thought and practice of the academic body as a whole. This is the basis of Milton's disparaging remarks about the students themselves in the letter already referred to. (*Alexander Gillio,* Cantabrigia, Julii 2, 1628): "Sane apud nos, quod sciam, vix unus atque alter est, qui non Philologiae, pariter et Philosophiae, prope rudis et profanus, ad Theologiam devolet implumis." [16] In the same letter he refers to certain Latin verses which he had just been writing for a friend who was Respondent in the philosophical disputation at the commencement of that year. These verses have been very plausibly identified with the poem "*Naturam non pati senium,*" which Milton included in the edition of 1645, and Masson assumes that the general subject of the disputation must have been suggested by the publication in the preceding year of George Hakewill's *Apologie or Declaration of the Power of God in the Government of the World, Consisting in an examination and Censure of the Common Errour Touching Nature's Perpetual and Universal Decay.*

The importance of Hakewill's point of view in the campaign against the vestiges of medievalism in the philosophy of the time is well recognized by the historians of thought. In championing the idea of progress against the fatalistic conception of a decline of human achievement Hakewill joins forces, as Mr. Richard Jones has recently pointed out,[17] with Francis Bacon and with the whole intellectual movement of which he was the prophet. Particularly important is his exaltation of the attainments of the moderns in such fields as mathematics, geography, and astronomy. The opposite theory of a necessary decay of nature Hakewill recognizes to be fundamentally disheartening to human endeavor: "For being once thoroughly persuaded in

[16] "Among us, as far as I know, there are only two or three, who without any acquaintance with criticism or philosophy, do not instantly engage with raw and untutored judgments in the study of theology.—*Milton's Prose Works,* Bohn Library edition. So throughout for the translations from the *Familiar Letters.*

[17] *The Background of the "Battle of the Books," Washington University Studies, Humanistic Series,* vol. VII (1920), No. 2, pp. 107 ff.

themselves," he writes of the maintainers of the more orthodox point of view, "that by a fatall kinde of necessitie and course of times, they are cast into those straights that notwithstanding all their striving and industrie, it is impossible they should rise to the pitch of their noble and renowned Predecessors, they begin to yield to times and to necessity, being resolved that their endeavours are all in vaine, and that they strive against the streame."

These broader issues are untouched in Milton's verses, which deal only, in highly imaginative strains, with the alleged physical decrepitude of nature, the less fruitful theme of Hakewill's first book, and are designed as a moment of poetic ornament in a serious discussion. Even so, however, his juvenile participation in this debate on the side of the moderns, is significant in its consistency both with his humanistic inheritance and with his later attitude in theology, politics, and education. The inferences thus suggested regarding Milton's intellectual attitude are confirmed, moreover, by the position which he consistently adopts in his own academic orations, whenever the subject affords the least opportunity for the expression of his real convictions on vital issues.

In the first Prolusion,[18] dated by Masson in 1628–9, though the subject is a trifling one, Milton plainly alludes to differences in point of view which have thrown him into opposition with the majority of students and tutors. "Etenim qui possim ego vestram sperare benevolentiam, cum in hoc tanto concursu, quot oculis intueor tot ferme aspiciam infesta in me capita; adeo ut Orator venisse videor ad non exorabiles. Tantum potest ad simultates etiam in Scholis aemulatio, vel diversa Studia, vel in eisdem studiis diversa judicia sequentium."[19] The second exercise,[20] presumably somewhat later, embodies a

[18] *Utrum Dies an Nox praestantior sit?*, Mitford, VII. 411 ff.

[19] "For how can I hope for your good will, when, in this so great concourse, as many heads as I behold with my eyes, almost the same number do I see of visages bearing malice against me; so that I seem to have come as an *orator* to persons not *exorable?* Of so much efficacy in producing private grudges is the rivalry even in schools of those who follow different studies, or different methods in the same studies." — Masson, vol. I. 276.

[20] *De Sphaerarum Concentu*, Mitford, VII. 421 ff.

disparagement of Aristotle in comparison with Plato, and the same point of view is represented in the undated Latin verses *De Idea Platonica quemadmodum Aristoteles intellexit*. Here Milton speaks in scorn of the unimaginative mind which cannot conceive the archetypal idea because he cannot see and touch it. With fine irony at the close he declares that if Plato expects his philosophic fancy to be received as truth he must call back the poets whom he has banished from his Republic. The third Prolusion [21] is an argument against scholasticism and a broad defense of the humanistic attitude and of the study of science. In the spirit of Bacon's *Novum Organum*, Milton condemns the perpetual wrangling of the schools as unfruitful either for virtue or true knowledge, and he invites the student to turn his eyes abroad upon the rich world of man and nature, ascending by degrees to the knowledge of himself and of God. His statement shows perfect comprehension of the case against the very debates in which he was himself called on to participate, and it establishes the groundwork for his entire program of future intellectual activity. The *Tractate of Education* is but an application of the method of approach advocated in this early exercise and much of *Paradise Lost* an embodiment of its results. The emphasis on physical science is particularly noteworthy. Milton can hardly be said to have possessed the true Baconian vision of man's mastery of nature by experiment and observation, but he certainly maintained throughout his life a more than ordinary interest in all branches of scientific knowledge, his deepest enthusiasm being naturally reserved for astronomy, with the most modern conceptions in which field he was, as has often been noted, thoroughly familiar.

The documents at which we have been glancing are proof, then, of the early confirmation of Milton's general intellectual point of view. They reveal the true source of all his later radicalism in humanistic culture rather than in the more specific and practical traditions of politics and religion, pointing to Erasmus and not to Luther as his progenitor. They show also the untimely establishment in him of the propagandist attitude.

[21] *Contra Philosophiam Scholasticam, op. cit.*, pp. 425 ff.

He consciously assumes the rôle of spokesman for a cause, playing in the little world of the University a part strikingly analogous with that which he was afterwards to adopt in public affairs. Such activities lie, of course, outside the sphere of poetry. They spring, however, from kindred sources in Milton's consciousness. No student of the poet need be told how impossible it is to separate his general opinions and purposes from his more intimate emotions, or his propagandist utterances now and later from his dominant instinct for self-portraiture and self-justification. The Latin exercises are rich in indications of Milton's early absorption in his own career, and they contain the germs of many elements in his later conception of himself as a being set apart from others and bound to cultivate himself for special uses. In the Latin portion of the exercise composed for the vacation celebration of 1628 [22] he alludes as follows to his college nickname, "the Lady," converting what was intended or thought to be intended as a disparagement into an argument of superiority." A quibusdam audivi nuper Domina. At cur videor illis parum masculus? . . . scilicet qui Scyphos capacissimos nunquam valui pancratice haurire; aut quia manus tenenda stiva non occaluit, aut quia nunquam ad meridianum Solem supinus jacui septennis bubulcus; fortasse demum quod me virum praestiti, eo modo quo illi Ganeones: . . . at videte quam insubide, quam incogitate mihi objecerint id, quod ego jure optimo mihi vertam gloriae. Namque et ipse Demosthenes ab aemulis adversariisque parum vir dictus est. Q. itidem Hortensius omnium Oratorum post M. Tullium, clarissimus, Dionysia Psaltria appellatus est a L. Torquato." [23] That he had already begun to meditate on fame, on the kind of audience,

[22] *In Feriis aestivis Collegii* etc., Mitford, VII. 441 ff.

[23] "By some of you I used lately to be nick-named 'The Lady.' Why seem I to them too little of a man? . . . Is it because I have never been able to quaff huge tankards lustily, or because my hands never grew hard by holding the plough, or because I never, like a seven years' herdsman, laid myself down and snored at midday; in fine, perchance, because I never proved my manhood in the same way as those debauched blackguards? . . . But see how absurdly and unreflectively they have unbraided me with that with which I on the best of grounds will turn to my glory. For Demosthenes himself was also called too little of a man by his rivals

fit though few, to which it was worth while to address himself, and on the need of long preparation for the high tasks to which he felt himself called, is evidenced in the same exercise and elsewhere in the Prolusions.

These thoughts are the materials out of which Milton is to build the ideal structure of his personality, as we have it displayed in self-sufficient grandeur in his later works. As yet the conception is too new and fragmentary to be manageable as a theme of art, but we may find in *Elegy I* an echo, however softened, of the psychological processes which manifest themselves more rawly in the prose. It is thus that he refers to the incident of his banishment from Cambridge:

> Me tenet urbs reflua quam Thamesis alluit unda,
>   Meque nec invitum patria dulcis habet.
> Iam nec arundiferum mihi cura revisere Camum,
>   Nec dudum vetiti me laris angit amor.
> Nuda nec arva placent, umbrasque negantia molles;
>   Quam male Phoebicolis convenit ille locus!
> Nec duri libet usque minas perferre Magistri,
>   Caeteraque ingenio non subeunda meo.
> Si sit hoc exilium, patrios adiisse penates,
>   Et vacuum curis otia grata sequi,
> Non ego vel profugi nomen sortemve recuso,
>   Laetus et exilii conditione fruor.
> O utinam vates nunquam graviora tulisset
>   Ille Tomitano flebilis exul agro;
> Non tunc Ionio quicquam cessisset Homero,
>   Neve foret victo laus tibi prima, Maro.[24]

---

and adversaries. Quintus Hortensius, too, the most renowned of all orators after M. Tullius, was nicknamed 'a Dionysiac singing woman' by Lucius Torquatus." — Masson, I. 292. Milton's tone here is bantering, but one can read between the lines.

[24] "That city which Thames washes with her tidal wave keeps me fast, nor does my pleasant birth-place detain me against my will. I have no wish to go back to reedy Cam; I feel no homesickness for that forbidden college room of mine. The bare fields there, niggard of pleasant shade, do not please me. How ill does that place suit with poets! I have no fancy to endure forever my stern master's threats or those other actions at which my nature rebelled. If this is "exile," to live under my father's roof and be free to use my leisure pleasantly, I will not repudiate either the outcast's name or lot, but will in all happiness enjoy this state of exile. Oh would that Ovid, sad exile in the fields of Thrace, had never suffered

One catches in these lines, in spite of the assumed lightness and well-bred indifference which the cultured but naïve youth wears like a borrowed garment, more than a hint of his real mood of resentment and hurt pride. Any touch of disgrace he may have felt is promptly converted to a judgment of the University as no fit place for poets and to a consciousness of satisfaction in his superior surroundings and pursuits at home. Very interesting as evidence of the kind of mental activity prompted in Milton by such an experience is the allusion to Ovid. There is obviously something here which goes beyond ordinary Renaissance practice of classical illustration. Milton has been meditating on the analogy between his own little exile and the fate of Ovid until he has made a kind of imaginative identification of himself with his Roman predecessor, as later, when the assault was intended to the city he fancied himself a Pindar, striking reverence into the heart of the military conqueror, and, finally, in blindness, found a solace for affliction and an answer to his enemies by remembering:

> Those other two equall'd with me in fate,
> So were I equall'd with them in renown,
> Blind Thamyris and blind Maeonides,
> And Tiresias and Phineus, prophets old.

For Milton the fellowship of the great is at once a refuge and a vindication. The passage in *Elegy I* is the transmutation into poetry of the personal references in the prose oration, the passages in *Paradise Lost* on his blindness are the verse renderings of the replies which he made to Salmasius' tauntings in the *Second Defence*.

But these considerations by no means exhaust the importance of the first elegy as an index to Milton's awakening emotional and imaginative life. In his defensive retreat from the hostility of the real world he takes refuge not alone in his reverence for the past but in a conscious devotion to beauty in all its forms. The disfavour into which he has momentarily fallen, while not

---

a worse lot! Then he would have yielded not a whit even to Ionian Homer, nor would the first praise be thine, Virgil, for he would have vanquished thee."

taken too seriously, has had the effect of throwing him back upon himself and has prompted him to reveal sensations which have hitherto found no place in his poetry. Thus, after greeting Diodati and alluding to the cause of his sojourn in London, he launches into a description of the enjoyments which his leisure affords him. The poem is a less mature and more personal *L'Allegro* and *Il Penseroso* in one. He speaks briefly of his reading, then, at greater length of attendance at the theater. Finally he turns to nature and the spring, reserving for chief place among the objects of his enthusiasm "the maiden bands who go by like flaming stars." On this theme he expatiates with an ardor which belies the artificial medium in which he writes. The lines abound in images full of enticement to the sense of youth.

> Et decus eximium frontis, tremulosque capillos,
> Aurea quae fallax retia tendit Amor;
> Pellacesque genas, ad quas hyacinthina sordet
> Purpura et ipse tui floris, Adoni, rubor! . . .
> Creditur huc geminis venisse invecta columbis
> Alma pharetrigero milite cincta Venus,
> Huic Cnidon, et riguas Simoentis flumine valles,
> Huic Paphon, et roseam posthabitura Cypron.[25]

It was, of course, to be expected that Milton should express himself with decorum and in an established academic mode. Sensuous desire is never with him a simple lyric force. It is from the beginning complicated by ethical and ideal influences and moulded in its expression by literary traditions. As, before, the poets have been Milton's guides in the milder affections of his youth, so now they are his tutors in the more compelling ones. For the present his guide is clearly Ovid, to whom he twice refers in *Elegy I* and whose stylistic example he mainly follows throughout the poems of this group. We might infer from the elegies alone the intense delight with which he has given himself to the study of the *Heroïdes* and the *Amores,* and the stimulating effect

[25] "And exquisite grace of brow, and floating locks, — golden nets which Love casts deceivingly, — inviting cheeks, to which the purple of the hyacinth, yea, even the blush of thy flower, Adonis, is dull! Men say that hither blessed Venus came, escorted by her quivered soldier-boy, drawn by twin doves, willing to love London more than Cnidos, or the vales watered by the stream of Simöis, or Paphos, or rosy Cyprus."

which this study has had on his awakening imagination. Fortunately, however, there is other evidence, for Milton has given in one of his prose works an account of his Ovidian enthusiasm, and indeed of the whole phase of his experience which this enthusiasm initiates, an account at once so coherent and so minutely faithful as to make it an outstanding document in the study of his early literary development.

The passage consists of an elaborate analysis in the *Apology for Smectymnuus* of the formation of his youthful ideals of chastity, written in 1642 in reply to certain defamatory statements of Bishop Hall. Although provoked by a stinging accusation and taking the form of a piece of special pleading, Milton's utterance is obviously much more than a merely improvised defense. It is rather the result of a long process of introspective meditation, now summarized in a review of that part of his early creative work which he recognizes as most essentially individual in its inspiration, and serving, for those who cared more for the writer than for the controversial issue, as a kind of biographia literaria or " Growth of the Poet's Mind." The opening sentences go far toward interpreting the emotional reactions which, as we have seen, find partial expression in *Elegy I.*

I had my time, readers, as others have, who have good learning bestowed upon them, to be sent to those places where, the opinion was, it might soonest be obtained; and as the manner is, was not unstudied in those authors which are most commended. Whereof some were grave orators and historians, whose matter methought I loved indeed, but as my age then was, so I understood them; others were the smooth elegiac poets, whereof the schools are not scarce, whom both for the pleasing sound of their numerous writing, which in imitation I found most easy, and most agreeable to nature's part in me, and for their matter, which what it is there be few who know not, I was so allured to read, that no recreation came to me better welcome. For that it was then those years with me which are excused, though they be least severe, I may be saved the labour to remember ye. Whence having observed them to account it the chief glory of their wit, in that they were able to judge, to praise, and by that could esteem themselves worthiest to love those high perfections, which under one or other name they took to celebrate; I thought to myself by every instinct and presage of nature, which is not wont to be false, that what emboldened them to this task, might with such diligence as they used embolden me; and that what judgment, wit, or elegance was my share, would herein best appear, and best value itself, by how much more wisely, and with more love of virtue I should choose (let rude ears be absent) the object of not unlike praises. For albeit these thoughts to some will seem virtuous and commendable, to others only pardonable, to a third sort perhaps idle; yet the mentioning of them now will end in serious.

Nor blame it, readers, in those years to propose to themselves such a reward, as the noblest dispositions above other things in this life have sometimes preferred: whereof not to be sensible when good and fair in one person meet, argues both a gross and shallow judgment, and withal an ungentle and swainish breast.[26]

We have here indicated a highly important moment in Milton's responsiveness to the stimulus of reading. The grave historians and orators, imperfectly apprehended, have left him moved by a cool and detached enthusiasm only; the smooth and glowing love poetry of the Roman elegists has spoken powerfully to his emotions and has roused in him the desire to exercise on similar themes the poetic talent which he is already conscious of possessing.[27] In a youth nursed in the literary traditions of the Renaissance, and, indeed, in any youth of Milton's temperament, this was entirely natural. The pagan sensuousness and romantic tone of Ovid and his fellows have put them in a quite different category from other classic writers, giving to their appeal an immediacy and force like that of contemporary poetry. It is characteristic of Milton that he should represent his enjoyment of these authors as accompanied by reflection and his creative impulse as guided by a conscious purpose and ideal. The elegists must, he thinks, have accounted it the first glory of their genius that they were able to judge of the excellence which they celebrated in verse. Their ability adequately to judge and praise these excellences was, moreover, the proof of their worthiness to love them. True glory, Milton implies (and

[26] *Prose Works,* Bohn edition, III. 116–117.

[27] Did Milton make his excursions into the seductive region of Ovidian elegy in the regular course of school reading, as he seems to imply, or on his own initiative and privately? The *Metamorphoses* appears in all the school curricula of the time, but I find no mention of any other work of Ovid. Presumably the amatory poems would be ruled out of St. Paul's on moral grounds, and one hardly imagines even a university tutor directing a boy of sixteen to them. Milton does not mention Ovid at all among the authors to be read in his own model school. Probably he takes the *Metamorphoses* for granted.

the idea is one to which he clung throughout his life) comes not from the praises of men but from the well-grounded consciousness of inner worth. This satisfaction he will be able to enjoy in higher degree than the elegists in proportion to the superior wisdom and virtue with which he will make choice of the object of his praise.

Something of all this is clearly matter of later interpretation. In the first elegy there is little, if any, of the devotion to an ideal object implied in the prose statement. The moral reaction is negative rather than dynamic. It is evidenced in the fact that the poet allows himself no indecencies of expression and that he checks himself in his praise of the starry maidens, by announcing that, while Cupid grants him immunity, he will make haste to quit their presence:

> Et vitare procul malefidae infamia Circes
> Atria, divini Molyos usus ope.

The herb moly, again employed in Milton's elaboration of the Circe myth in *Comus,* may be taken to represent the sure guidance of Christian ethics, to which he has hitherto owed his safety amid the strongly felt allurements of the senses. Aside from this Puritan touch (and even this has a kind of precedent in Ovid's declaration that though his verse is corrupt his life is chaste) there is nothing in the poem to suggest that Milton was as yet anything but the enthusiastic though somewhat timid disciple of his Roman predecessor in matter as in manner. The one passage in which he explicitly challenges comparison with Ovid is prompted by patriotism rather than by any philosophically based consciousness of superiority:

> Nec Pompeianas Tarpeia Musa columnas
> Iactet, et Ausoniis plena theatra stolis.
> Gloria virginibus debetur prima Britannis;
> Extera sat tibi foemina posse sequi.[28]

In general, then, *Elegy I* is an expression, on the one hand, of Milton's sensitive self-love, on the other of a new and intense

[28] "Let not the poet who lived by the Tarpeian rock [Ovid] boast the dames of Pompey's porch, nor the theatre full of Roman stoles. To the virgins of Britain first glory is due; suffice it, foreign woman, that thou canst follow them."

delight in beauty, nourished by contact with the most sensuous and romantic of ancient poets and given artistic direction by the typical Renaissance ambition to "overgo" some reputed classic name in his own tongue and upon a kindred theme. These related motives are the basis of an enduring inspiration. We may trace the first of them in a poem of the succeeding year, the epistle to Thomas Young, where warm personal affection, more strongly felt no doubt in the partly hostile environment of the University, is combined with indignation at the harshness of the English church which has compelled so excellent a man to seek his sustenance abroad. Milton's sympathy for Young is a kind of extension of the mood of defensive self-pity which we have seen implied in *Elegy I.* He reminds him that other preachers of the word — Elijah, Paul, Jesus — have been victims of persecution, as he had earlier reminded himself that Ovid, a poet, was driven into exile. Finally he gives a personal application to the motive of Psalm CXXXVI, assuring his friend that the Lord of Hosts who defended Zion will stand at his side amid the clash of battle which surrounds him. Milton writes with an accent of sincerity which leaves no doubt of the hold which the subject has taken on his emotions, but he indulges in no such aesthetic dreaming as in the first elegy and the suppressed excitement which underlies the erotic imagery of the earlier poem is entirely lacking.

It emerges again, however, in *Elegy VII,* Milton's next work, which belongs apparently to the year 1628. Here the poet picks up the theme of *Elegy I* and carries the amatory experience therein initiated to a second stage. In the first poem, as we have seen, he had made declaration of a general susceptibility to the attraction of sex and implied a fear lest, if he remained in London, Cupid might not long grant him immunity. In *Elegy VII* he represents himself as having at length enrolled perforce in the ranks of actual lovers. The deity appears to the poet in the early dawn of a spring morning, boasts of his power over men and gods, and warns him that he too shall feel it. His Muse shall not succor him, nor the serpent of healing Apollo give him aid. There follows the description of an amatory encounter—the mere exchange of glances with one among the maidens toward whom in his suburban walk he rashly allowed his eyes to rove. Her beauty pierces to the heart and the poet becomes a hopeless servant of the God whose power he has defied. In elaborating the episode Milton draws heavily upon the phraseology of ancient erotic verse, and in particular upon the allegorical and mythological love machinery of Ovid. His more immediate model is the *De Neaera* of Buchanan.[29] The Scotch poet, like Milton, represents himself as a rebel against love. The blind boy, in anger, empties his quiver against him and fills his breast with arrows. Finding even this in vain he binds him with the tangles of Neaera's hair and leads him captive as a warning trophy for all scorners of his might. Strongly, however, as Milton's poem smells of the oil of humanism, there can be no mistaking the eager delight with which he gives himself to the spirit of his theme, importing into his verses an enthusiastic glow which is entirely absent from the elegant and pointed couplets of his original. The opening allegory of Cupid and the subsequent description of the poet's woe are academic enough and effectively conceal emotion; the lines, on the other hand, in which he narrates his springtime encounter with a nameless love sound wholly real and individual:

> Et modo qua nostri spatiantur in urbe Quirites,
> Et modo villarum proxima rura placent.
> Turba frequens, facieque simillima turba dearum,
> Splendida per medias itque reditque vias;
> Auctaque luce dies gemino fulgore coruscat.
> Fallor? an et radios hinc quoque Phoebus habet?
> Haec ego non fugi spectacula grata severus,
> Impetus et quo me fert iuvenilis agor;
> Lumina luminibus male providus obvia misi,
> Neve oculos potui continuisse meos.
> Unam forte aliis supereminuisse notabam;
> Principium nostri lux erat illa mali.[30]

[29] *Elegiarum Liber, Poemata,* Amstelaedami, p. 317.

[30] "And now I took my pleasure, sometimes in the city parks, where our citizens promenade, sometimes at neighboring country-places. Crowds of girls, with faces like to the faces of goddesses, came and went radiantly through the walks; the day brightened with a double splendor. Surely, the sun himself stole his beams from their faces. I was not stern

Whether or not these verses recount an actual incident they express real and acute sensations, and the poem as a whole gives evidence of an all but complete surrender to the Ovidian attitude and mood.

An even bolder abandon characterizes *Elegy V,* the next poem in this series, written in the spring of Milton's twenty-first year. The poet greets the season and describes in ecstatic language the sensation of a returning poetic impulse in his breast. The spring it is which has given him his genius and the spring shall be celebrated in his song. What follows is strikingly pagan in tone and luxuriant in imagery. Earth bares her rich breast to the love of Phoebus. Cupid wanders about the world stirring all Earth's children to follow her example. Venus rises with restored youth as from the warm sea. The youths cry " Hymen " throughout the marbled cities. Throngs of golden-girdled maidens go forth yearning for love. At nightfall Sylvanus and the Satyrs wanton in the fields; Pan riots, and Faunus pursues the Oread, who hides in order that she may be found.

In subject and general conception this piece, like *Elegy VII,* depends upon a poem of Buchanan, the *Majae Calendae,* printed in the *Elegiarum Liber.*[31] There are resemblances also in detail. Thus Buchanan as well as Milton alludes to the rejuvenation of Venus, depicts Cupid as furbishing his arrows and rekindling his torch, and describes the rout of all Earth's sons and daughters under the impulse of desire:

> Applauduntque deo pueri, innuptaeque puellae
>   Queis rudis in vacuo pectore flamma calet.
> Plaudit utrique deo quicquid creat humidus aer,
>   Quicquid alit tellus, aequora quicquid alunt.

In Buchanan, however, the love theme is subsidiary and there is nothing to correspond to Milton's description of the effect of the coming of spring on his own inspiration as a poet. The

---

with myself; I did not flee from the gracious spectacle, but let myself be led wherever youthful impulse directed. Rashly I sent my gaze to meet theirs; I could not control my eyes. Then by chance I noted one supreme above the others, and the light of her eyes was the beginning of my ills."

[31] *Poemata,* p. 301.

difference is essential and stamps Milton's work as a directly personal utterance, the fullest expression we have yet encountered of the motives and yearnings which dominated his imagination at this time.

We may pause at this point to consider the significance of the fact that these very intimate reactions should take place under the influence of classical rather than of English poetry and should come to expression in Latin rather than in the poet's mother tongue. It has already been noted that Milton seems in his second academic year to have abandoned for the time being his early experimentation in English verse, presumably as a result of the humanistic tendency to undervalue the vernacular as a source of serious culture. There were additional reasons why he should have employed the learned medium in the poems which we have just considered. The element of Puritanism in his early environment had bred in him a timidity and sense of shame which inhibited his open utterance of any but the most decorous and approved, or in some cases, the most trivial sentiments. To give rein to sensuousness in the vernacular was to range oneself with a group of unacceptable licentious rhymsters. To do so in Latin was to follow the tradition of the honored classics and of the eminently respectable learned moderns, like Buchanan, who had imitated them. Against this somewhat pedantic attitude stood Milton's patriotism and his natural instinct for expression in his mother tongue, and ultimately these forces triumphed over his humanistic predispositions and freed him to pour himself out in English. His feelings on the subject are recorded in the enthusiastic apostrophe to his native language from which quotation has already been made. This piece, an English digression in a Latin vacation exercise, was composed during the Easter term of 1628, a year earlier than the fifth Latin elegy, and it is natural to associate Milton's renewed consciousness of the claims of English verse with the access of creative power which he describes in the latter poem. We may connect it also with more mature and serious meditation on his vocation as a poet, clear evidence of which appears in these pieces for the first time. In *Elegy V* Milton characterizes his poetic insight in terms which manifestly anticipate his later consciousness of the kind of task to which he felt himself called:

> Iam mihi mens liquidi raptatur in ardua caeli,
> Perque vagas nubes corpore liber eo;
> Perque umbras, perque antra feror, penetralia vatum;
> Et mihi fana patent interiora Deum;
> Intuiturque animus toto quid agatur Olympo,
> Nec fugiunt oculos Tartara caeca meos.
> Quid tam grande sonat distento spiritus ore?
> Quid parit haec rabies, quid sacer iste furor? [32]

In the *Vacation Exercise* there is an expansion, in similar terms, of the same idea:

> Yet I had rather, if I were to choose,
> Thy service in some graver subject use,
> Such as may make thee search thy coffers round,
> Before thou clothe my fancy in fit sound;
> Such where the deep transported mind may soar
> Above the wheeling poles, and at Heaven's door
> Look in, and see each blissful deity
> How he before the thunderous throne doth lie,
> Listening to what unshorn Apollo sings
> To the touch of golden wires, while Hebe brings
> Immortal nectar to her kingly sire;
> Then, passing through the spheres of watchful fire,
> And misty regions of wide air next under,
> And hills of snow and lofts of piled thunder,
> May tell at length how green-eyed Neptune raves,
> In Heaven's defiance mustering all his waves;
> Then sing of secret things that came to pass
> When beldam Nature in her cradle was;
> And last of kings and queens and heroes old,
> Such as the wise Demodocus once told
> In solemn songs at King Alcinous' feast,
> While sad Ulysses' soul and all the rest
> Are held with his melodious harmony,
> In willing chains and sweet captivity.

The fruits of Milton's declared intention to return seriously to English composition were delayed for some six months after

[32] Now my spirit is rapt into the skyey steeps, and freed from the flesh I walk through the wandering clouds; through the shades I go, and the caverns, inmost prophetic sanctuaries; and the inner fanes of the gods lie open to me. My soul sees all that comes to pass in Olympus, and the darks of Hades escape not my vision. What lofty song does my soul intend, as it stands with lips apart? what does this madness bring to birth, this sacred fury?

the writing of the *Vacation Exercise*. There exist the English *Song on a May Morning* and the sonnet *To a Nightingale*, both of which I should ascribe to period of the Latin elegies, and, indeed, specifically to the spring of 1629.[33] The first is a purified lyric comment on the theme of *Elegy V*, its contrast with the latter poem in style and mood being due to Milton's momentary reversion to the spirit of Elizabethan song. In the sonnet the opening lines are a direct translation from the Latin, and the conclusion embodies a declaration of the rôle which Milton has consciously adopted in accordance with his own feelings and his devotion to his Roman models:

> Whether the Muse or Love call thee his mate,
> Both them I serve, and of their train am I.

The sonnet is not, however, itself Ovidian in tone. Neither is it, like the song, Elizabethan. It suggests rather the direct influence of Italian models and represents a transition on Milton's part to a new set of foreign poetic allegiances, responding to and helping to determine an important change in literary mood.

Such a transition is duly recorded in Milton's account of himself in the *Apology for Smectymnuus*. The significance of the passage, the first sentence of which has already been quoted, appears to have been overlooked entirely by the poet's biographers and critics:

> For blame it not, readers, in those years to propose to themselves such a reward as the noblest dispositions above other things in this life have sometimes preferred; whereof not to be sensible when good and fair in one person meet argues both a gross and shallow judgment, and withal an ungentle and swainish breast. For by the firm settling of these persuasions, I became, to by best memory, so much a proficient, that if I found those authors anywhere speaking unworthy things of themselves or unchaste of those names which before they had extolled, this effect it wrought on me, from that time forward their art I still applauded, but the men I deplored; and above them all preferred the two famous renowners of Beatrice and Laura, who never write but honor of them to whom they devote their verse, displaying sublime and pure thoughts, without transgression.

[33] The argument, so far as the sonnet is concerned, is given in detail in my article *The Arrangement and Dates of Milton's Sonnets, Modern Philology*, Jan., 1921. The position which I have assigned to the Song is made probable by its relation to *Elegy V*.

Milton associates the change in his literary point of view with his ambition and his personal idealism, making it an inevitable outcome of the resolve to be the highest that his mind perceived. He becomes an adept in rejecting the grosser enticements of the flesh, and his literary taste responds to the conscious exercise of his judgment. Dante and Petrarch are the poetic embodiments of his new aspirations. In these poets, as in the Romans, he finds illustrations of the devotion of genius to the praise of beauty, but he finds them also inflamed by a pure idealism in the light of which the limitations of their predecessors may be judged. The art of the Romans he still, like a good humanist, judges superior, the men themselves far lower in the spiritual scale. His own path is clear. He will continue to rival the pagans in their perfection of outward form, but he will follow the Christians in the purity and elevation of their conceptions. This is the formula for Milton's youthful poetic aspirations. It was later transformed to suit with a more mature idea of his true objects, but it was never abandoned. We may well question, however, whether, in viewing his early romantic yearnings and aesthetic enthusiasms as an aspect of the higher aspirations of the soul, Milton is not reading retrospectively into his experience the ideas of a later time. Such a process is a familiar one in the literary history of the Renaissance. We have its prototype in Dante's spiritual interpretations in the *Vita Nuova* of sonnets many of which were written in a purely mundane mood. The most, then, that we can infer from the passage quoted is that Dante and Petrarch came in turn to supplant Ovid as objects of Milton's literary discipleship. The results of this new allegiance are indicated in the *Sonnet to a Nightingale* and more directly in the Italian poems which immediately follow it in the edition of 1645.

The assumption that these pieces must have been composed in Italy has hitherto obscured their significance in the scheme of Milton's early work. They are to be read as documents in the history of the phase of Milton's emotional and imaginative life which begins when he first enrolls himself as a lover and which definitely ends, as we shall see, before he took up his residence at Horton. I should date them immediately after *Elegy V* and the English Sonnet, i.e., between the spring of 1629 and the winter of 1629–30.[34]

The Italian sequence is, like the first elegy, addressed to Diodati and is ostensibly devoted to the praise of a foreign lady named Emilia,[35] whom Milton has apparently met in London and whose servant he proclaims himself in language of extravagant compliment to be. These poems are manifestly Petrarchan. Milton is still more interested in himself and his verses than he is in the object of his praise. In the second sonnet and the canzone he gracefully elaborates the image of himself endeavoring to transplant the flower of Italian speech into an alien soil surrounded by the ridicule of uncomprehending English youths who bid him pluck the laurels which await him in his mother tongue. His answer is that his lady tells him "This is the language of which Love himself is boastful." In the third sonnet he confesses to Diodati his former scorn of love has yielded. In the last poem in the series he tells that his heart is bold and constant, armed in adamant, secure against the attacks of force or envy, raised above vulgar fears and hopes, eager for every excellence and devoted to the Muses; it is less firm in its susceptibility to love alone. Even such a one, it will be remembered, is Adam,

in all enjoyments else
Superior and unmoved, here only weak
Against the charm of beauty's powerful glance.

Elsewhere he praises the lady's gentle spirit and dark-eyed beauty. She is possessed of more languages than one, and her song draws the moon down from its sphere. In such degree only do the poems express enthusiasm for a feminine embodiment of the good and fair. It was, of course, to be expected that this

[34] This is in accord with the consensus of recent scholarly opinion. See John Smart, *Milton's Sonnets;* also D. H. Stevens, *The Order of Milton's Sonnets, Modern Philology,* April, 1919, and my own study cited above. No error has done more to obscure Milton's early poetical development than the assumption that the Italian poems must have been written during Milton's continental journey.

[35] See Smart's work cited above.

amatory verse should contain nothing inconsistent with the standards of conduct and taste which Milton had set for himself. What we miss is such sublimation of emotional experience as might have resulted if Milton's spirit had really been enkindled at this time by the *Vita Nuova* and the lyric poetry of the *dolce stil,* as he had a little earlier been enkindled by the Roman elegies. But though he mentions Dante it is evidently only Petrarch who really avails him, and the religion of love, which glows in Dante with transcendent fervor, is pale and conventionalized in his successor. This religion in its sincerity is not for Milton. In the Italian sonnets he has, indeed, rid himself of sensuousness, but only by means of a temporary abstraction of his art from his actual emotional experience. The higher mood, when it comes to him at this stage in his development, will be born of an ethical reaction, for Milton is at heart a humanist and a Protestant and his acceptance of the point of view of courtly and romantic love is, after all, a *tour de force.*

For the first clear indication in his creative work of such an ethical reaction we are prepared by the next passage in the prose statement. The change in attitude is again connected with his purpose and ambitions as a poet. The suggestions as to the character of his thoughts on this subject which we have noted in the *Vacation Exercise* and in *Elegy V* are now explicitly confirmed.

> And long it was not after [he continues] when I was confirmed in this opinion, that he who would not be frustrate of his hope to write well hereafter in laudable things, ought himself to be a true poem; that is a composition and pattern of the best and honorablest things; not presuming to sing praises of heroic men, or famous cities, unless he have in himself the experience and practice of all that which is praiseworthy.

Milton's language suggests that the confirmation of his convictions regarding the relation between personal conduct and poetic achievement and the accompanying resolution to devote himself to something higher and more serious than amatory lyrics marks a definite stage in his inner history. We can fix the moment of this change with considerable precision, for its first fruits in his poetry are to be found in the sixth Latin elegy, written at the Christmas season of 1629, some six months later than *Elegy V.*

The poet addresses Diodati, "who, sending the author some verses from the country at Christmas time, asked him to excuse their mediocrity, on the ground that they were composed amid the distractions of the festival season." Milton expostulates at the implication that revelry is not propitious to poetry, citing to the contrary the examples of Ovid, Anacreon, Pindar, and Horace. Bacchus and Erato, Ceres and Venus, are the patrons of elegy, and feasting, wine, and love its proper sources of inspiration. With the epic poet it is different. He must live austerely like an ascetic. His life must be pure. He is like a priest who ministers at the altars of the gods. In conclusion Milton tells what he himself is writing — an ode on the Nativity as a birthday gift to Christ.

The formula here given for the discipline of the epic poet is, allowing for the more exalted language of poetry, so precisely identical with that of the statement in the *Apology* as to make it clear that Milton is in the latter statement looking back to and thinking in terms of his meditation of 1629. We may infer that the Latin utterance represents a definite resolution regarding his life work. It is natural to associate such a resolution with the poet's coming of age on December 9 of the same year. He was apparently in the habit of taking account of himself at various anniversaries of his life, witness the *Sonnet on His Being Arrived to the Age of Twenty-three* and the one to Skinner on the third anniversary of his blindness. The thought that he was now in the technical sense a man may well have prompted him to look upon his earlier performance as belonging to the past, and the coincidence of his birthday with the Christmas season explains the mood in which he took up the subject of the Nativity.

The poem itself, as all critics have recognized, strikes a new note in the poetry of Milton. Belonging in its general tradition to the sober vein to which he had already declared allegiance in the English poems and exhibiting, like them, the influence of the Spenserian school, it quite transcends the earlier poems in elevation and poetic fervor. We feel that here, for the first time, we have the genuine and characteristic reaction of Milton's personality upon a serious religious object. He contemplates the event, not at all with the loving surrender of a Catholic poet to its human sweetness, but with an austere intellectualized emotion stirred in him by the idea of its moral significance. Christ is, for him, not a babe, nor indeed a person at all, but a symbol of purity and truth, that truth which "came once into the world with her divine Master, and was a perfect shape most glorious to look on." The pagan deities are multiform ugliness of error, put to rout by the god-like simplicity of Christ as shadows by the sun. The poet completely identifies himself with his conception and this identification calls forth all his imaginative and expressive powers. However much Milton's precise theological ideas may have changed in later life and his ethical sense become enriched with the content of experience, his attitude retains to the end the form which it assumes in the *Nativity Ode*. The poem is the lyric prelude of *Paradise Lost* and in an exacter sense of *Paradise Regained*.

I have, I think, said enough to suggest that the moment in Milton's literary life represented by *Elegy VI* and the *Nativity* is something more than a passing mood. It remains to consider how consistently he maintained this lofty and severe position.

Obviously we need look for no such complete break with the past as would result from a sudden religious conversion, nor even for the kind of outward change of profession for which not a few of his seventeenth century predecessors and contemporaries in English verse gave precedent. Milton never felt the need of clothing his Muse in a mourning garment. He remains to the end what he had always been, a humanist, and his ultimate exclusive adherence to religious themes is the result of a long development. His work after 1629 is still eclectic in its inspiration and full of variety. The poem on Shakespeare, the two epitaphs on the University Carrier, and the elegy on the Marchioness of Winchester belong to the immediately succeeding years. These works exhibit a fresh range of contact with earlier English verse. Largely abandoning the manner of the Fletchers and definitely rejecting the "new-fangled toys and trimming slight" of the metaphysical school, Milton enrolls himself among the sons of Ben. *On Shakespeare* and the two Hobson poems

(1630 and 1631) are in the vein of seventeenth century epigram. The elegy for the Marchioness (1631) is his first essay in octosyllabic couplets, a measure which carries with it the pure and classic style of the Jonsonian lyric:

> Gentle Lady, may thy grave,
> Peace and quiet ever have!
> After this thy travail sore,
> Sweet rest seize thee ever more.

The spirit of the earlier elegy on a Fair Infant finds an echo in the tender delicacy with which Milton celebrates this gentle mother's death in child-bed, likening her to the biblical Rachel,

> Who, after years of barrenness,
> The highly favored Joseph bore
> To him who served for her before,
> And at her next birth, much like thee,
> Through pangs fled to felicity,

but the poetic mode has changed. A direct suggestion for the poem appears to have come from William Browne's celebrated *Epitaph on the Countess Dowager of Pembroke.*[36] Compare the two openings:

> Under this marble hearse
> Lies the subject of all verse:
> Sidney's sister, Pembroke's mother,

and Milton's

> This rich marble doth inter
> The honored wife of Winchester,
> A viscount's daughter, an earl's heir.

The last lines of Browne's lyric similarly supplied Milton with the conceit upon which he constructed the poem on Shakespeare:

> Marble piles let no man raise
> To her name: for after days
> Some kind woman born as she,
> Reading this, like Niobe
> Shall turn marble, and become
> Both her mourner and her tomb.

[36] The lines, as given in the text, had appeared in the fourth edition of Camden's *Remains* (1629), p. 336. See *Athenaeum,* Aug. 11, 1906, p. 159.

> What needs my Shakespeare for his honored bones,
> The labour of an age in piled stones. . . .
> Then thou, our fancy of itself bereaving
> Dost make us marble with too much conceiving;
> And so sepulchred in such pomp dost lie,
> As kings for such a tomb would wish to die.

These poems, then, give evidence of Milton's continued delight in the pure artistry of verse and of his willingness to give himself even after the earnest declaration of *Elegy VI* to various more or less impersonal aesthetic moods. There are, however, clear indications of a conscious change in the main direction of his literary purposes from this time on. The seven Latin elegies represent, as we have seen, the serious fruit of Milton's early ambition to enter the lists with the great names of literature, the choice of Ovid as a model being dictated by the example of Buchanan, by his own sympathetic taste, and by a sense of the appropriateness of the material to youth. Having attained his goal he promptly abandons it in favor of the higher seriousness of epic poetry. His progress, as Professor Rand points out, is strikingly parallel with that of Virgil, whose poetry passes through various stages from the atmosphere of Alexandria to that of Augustan Rome. Of this parallel Milton himself was fully aware. The idea of it must already have been present in his mind when he wrote the poem *On the Morning of Christ's Nativity,* as a true messianic eclogue, corresponding to the Roman poet's prophecy of the Golden Age which was to follow upon the birth of a son to Pollio and matching that utterance in its already half-epic exaltation. The materials of Milton's future poetry are as yet but vaguely defined, but his mind is plainly set toward the mysteries of Heaven and Hell and the deeds of "pious heroes and leaders part devine." The spell of Petrarch allures him only momentarily from his true path. In taking formal farewell of the elegiac mood he takes farewell of all amatory trifling. At any rate he no longer appears in the rôle of a romantic lover, and a postscript appended to the Latin poems dismisses the whole experience as belonging to a bygone phase.

Haec ego mente olim laeva, studioque supino,
  Nequitiae posui vana trophaea meae.
Scilicet abreptum sic me malus impulit error,
  Indocilisque aetas prava magistra fuit;
Donec Socraticos umbrosa Academia rivos
  Praebuit, admissum dedocuitque iugum.
Protinus, extinctis ex illo tempore flammis,
  Cincta rigent multo pectora nostra gelu;
Unde suis frigus metuit puer ipse sagittis,
  Et Diomedeam vim timet ipsa Venus.[37]

That we do not find Milton turning at once to epic verse is not surprising. For a work designed to rank his name with greater ones than Ovid he naturally felt himself, at the age of twenty-one, unready. Instead, he proposes, apparently, a series of lofty religious poems celebrating the successive events in the life of Christ and the festivals of the Christian calendar. Of these the *Nativity* was triumphantly completed, and a poem *On the Passion* earnestly begun at the Easter season of the following year. His failure to complete this piece illustrates the breakdown of his higher inspiration when the theme found no responsive echo in his own experience. The crucifixion, neither now nor later, had the slightest hold on his emotions. That Milton did not fully recognize the conditions of the successful exercise of his poetic faculty is suggested by the character of the note appended to the *Passion*,[38] and also, perhaps, by the fact that he appears still to have cherished the plan of a series of poems on the events as late as the Horton period, when he wrote the complete but uninspired piece *On the Circumcision* (see below).

[37] These vain trophies of my idleness I set up in time past, in unbalanced mood and with lax endeavor. Vicious error hurried me astray, and my untaught years were an ill mistress to me; until the shady Academe [*i.e., Plato's philosophy*] offered me its Socratic streams, and loosened from my neck the yoke to which I had submitted. At once all these youthful flames became extinct, and since then my breast is rigid with accumulated ice; whence Cupid himself fears freezing for his arrows, and Venus dreads my Diomedean strength.

[38] "This Subject the Author finding to be above the years he had when he wrote it, and nothing satisfied with what was begun, left it unfinished."

We have, I think, in Milton's inability to satisfy with anything like the fullness of success which he had attained in the elegies the ideal which he had set for himself in 1629 the true explanation of his feeling of immaturity and failure confessed in the noble sonnet *On His Being Arrived to the Age of Twenty-three.* Milton did not, when he wrote these lines, "forget the Latin poems," as Moody suggests. He remembered them all too well. Nor could he have been dissatisfied with anything in the mere technique of his achievement in English verse. The idea that he was thinking of Thomas Randolph as one of the spirits more timely happy than himself is patently absurd, for there was nothing in the work of Randolph or any contemporary poet that Milton could have envied. The Roman epic poet Lucan or even Sir Philip Sidney would be a more plausible suggestion, if we must assume that Milton had any particular person in mind. But his sense of a lack of inward ripeness was primarily with reference to his own ideals and it could have been dissipated only by a successful beginning at epic poetry, which he had not, so far as we know, attempted, or by the maintenance through a number of similar works of the level of high seriousness which he had momentarily attained in the poem on the Nativity. The result of his dissatisfaction appears to have been the resolution to wait patiently for his time, withdrawing his energies for the present from serious composition and devoting himself to intellectual, moral, and aesthetic self-cultivation. Not until after his Italian journey, i.e. in 1639–40, did Milton deliberately set forth to vindicate his "inward ripeness" by attempting to realize the next stage in his literary plans.

The intervening years of his residence at Horton I am disposed to regard as scarcely less epochal than the earlier period at the University. Though the foundations of his culture were firmly established and the controlling ideas and motives of his life already operative, his transition to full intellectual maturity had not yet taken place; and the divergent or contradictory elements in his consciousness remained to be fused by the tremendous energy of Milton's mind into philosophic and aesthetic wholeness. Among the all too scanty documents which enable us to trace Milton's spiritual development in the years under discussion the manuscript letter to an unknown friend, written apparently near the beginning of the Horton period, bears emphatic testimony to the strain of moral earnestness which found expression in *Elegy VI* and the sonnet *On His Being Arrived to the Age of Twenty-three.* This elaborate piece of self-analysis in the more explicit medium of prose represents, like Milton's earlier and later vindicatory utterances, the fruits of a process of serious self-examination regarding his way of life. It was his habit, as we have observed, to call upon his powers of expression as a means of confirming himself in a course of action to which his nature and his reason counselled him. The tone of confident assurance which this letter shares with other similar pronouncements is, I am inclined to believe, primarily a form of utterance and may cover real uncertainty and debate.

Such a debate would naturally have preceded Milton's decision to postpone or abandon his proposed entry into the church and settle down for a period of independent study on his father's country estate. The actual literary expression of his purposes and meditations was apparently occasioned by the expostulation of a serious-minded friend, who took it upon himself to be the prompter of the youthful poet's conscience. This friend (whom we may assume to have been a divine) had evidently warned Milton that the hours of the day were passing and had suggested that he was allowing his love of study to become a form of idleness and self-indulgence. In reply, Milton admits that study as a mere gratification of curiosity is not praiseworthy, but he feels assured that this weakness cannot be ascribed to him. The love of learning alone, he says, would not suffice to weigh against the motives which would naturally urge him toward an active life. These motives he analyzes with characteristic thoroughness: they are the need of providing for a family and home; the desire of fame; the consciousness that God demands our employment of the talent which is lodged in us. His real reason, he concludes, viewing the matter quite objectively, is precisely that he may more thoroughly prepare himself to render up a true account. He is, he adds, the more inclined to this course because he has noted a certain belatedness in himself, as recorded in the sonnet written on the occasion of this twenty-third birthday. The sonnet is included in the letter and indeed the prose composition has somewhat the air of an artistic setting for the poetical gem. It is even possible that the expostulating friend is a figment of Milton's imagination. At any rate, what he is primarily doing is giving expression to the recurrent mood of earnestness which had already come to constitute a profound and essential element in his emotional experience.

It is odd but characteristic that Milton should, in this statement, say nothing whatever regarding his literary purposes and ambitions. No reader previously unacquainted with his thoughts on this subject could possibly infer them from the letter, the plain implication of the language being that he intends, when he is ready, to labor in the vineyard as a minister. It is possible, of course, that in the suggestion about a congregation and preaching Milton was maintaining a mental reservation, having already determined to interpret his ministry in terms of the poetic enunciation of divine truth. More probably he had not yet altogether abandoned the plan of entering the church. In any case there is a misleading suppression of a part of his full mind, which we may regard as a characteristic manifestation of Miltonic strategy. The friend is representative of the normal judgment of the world. He is not, therefore, an intimate of the inner shrine of Milton's purposes and, since he presumably holds the common inadequate view of art, would misunderstand and condemn a confession of the important place which poetry occupied in his thought. In his undergraduate days Milton had freely enough proclaimed his interest to the circle of his academic contemporaries. Since he had come to take a more serious view of himself he had reserved his confidences, communicating them privately to the entirely sympathetic Diodati, and now, with an apologia based on the true and elevated conception of poetry, to his father.

The charming Latin epistle *Ad Patrem* was probably written

contemporaneously with the English letter at the beginning of the Horton period, and it should be set beside the latter statement as completing the representation of Milton's point of view at this time. The contrast between the two is striking. In the Latin epistle Milton surrenders himself entirely to his enthusiasm for self-cultivation and creative art. We hear nothing of his intention to enter the church, nothing of the need of rendering account of the " one talent which 'tis death to hide." Milton extolls poetry as a worthy object of highest endeavor, drawing his arguments from the tradition of Renaissance criticism so nobly embodied in Sidney's *Apology for Poetry,* and he appeals to his father on the strength of his own devotion to a sister art to continue to indulge the son in his pursuit of knowledge and in his conception of himself as " a part though the humblest of the gifted throng." That Milton does not directly give expression to his dominant ethical motive while he is hymning his delight in the Muses for their own sakes is an illustration of the characteristic zeal which leads him to suppress one part of his consciousness while another is momentarily engaging his attention. But even here the implications of his idealism are present. He will not mix obscurely with the dull rabble or join forces with the profane. The poetry which he praises is that which chants the exploits of heroes, and chaos, and the broad-laid foundations of the world. The viewpoint is essentially that of *Elegy VI,* though the emphasis has changed with the occasion.

We are now prepared to consider in detail the poetic fruitage of the Horton era. It was probably at the very beginning of the period, before the date of the English letter to a friend, that he composed the famous pair of lyrics, *L'Allegro* and *Il Penseroso.* Indeed, it is quite possible that they go back to some vacation interval in his university life. The uncertainty somewhat disturbs the precision of our study of Milton's early literary career. In any case, however, the poems can hardly belong to the period of the fifth elegy and the *Song on a May Morning.* They resemble these pieces, to be sure, in their enthusiastic expression of Milton's joy in beauty, but they exhibit a conscious particularity in the development of the aesthetic motive which may be taken to imply a later and more complex attitude. It is as if Milton had deliberately set out to imprison the essence of his literary culture without admixture of more personal ideals and to survey systematically the whole range of his aesthetic pleasures. Whether this was done in his last years at the University, along with the poem on Shakespeare and the elegy on the Marchioness of Winchester, or in the first exhilaration of his release from the academic environment, among the fresh delights of Horton, does not much matter.

The true bearing of the companion pieces is best understood by comparison with *Elegy I*. In the Latin poem, as we have seen, Milton combines the recitation of his intellectual and artistic delights with an account of his reaction against the University and a confession of his susceptibility to love. The passage on the theater does not separate comedy from tragedy; the expression of his enthusiasm for nature is not elaborated and passes quickly into a rhapsody on the English maidens. In *L'Allegro* and *Il Penseroso,* taking rather more than a hint from Burton, Milton amuses himself by analyzing his aesthetic reactions and classifying them in two contrasting modes. There is, of course, no question of two individuals. *L'Allegro* and *Il Penseroso* are equally Milton. To interpret the fiction otherwise is to assume that a cultivated lover of music may care only for the scherzo movement of symphonies, or that a nature enthusiast takes pleasure in sombre but not in cheerful landscapes or a trained play-goer in tragedy to the exclusion of comedy. It is to deny, in short, the catholicity of Milton's taste, the very thing that the poems are designed to illustrate and do illustrate.

Equally absurd is Moody's description of the poems as a kind of summing up of two possible attitudes toward life, which Milton, while feeling the appeal of each, must have recognized the practical impossibility of combining, or his suggestion that *Il Penseroso* reflects the advancing shades of Puritanism and, in Milton, the giving way of the exuberance of youth to the sobriety of manhood. In point of fact *Il Penseroso* is quite as much Elizabethan in mood as *L'Allegro* and as little touched with

Puritanism, while the cheerfulness of the latter poem is anything but the exuberance of youth. The two pieces taken together are, indeed, the evidence of a carefully disciplined and completely self-possessed maturity of aesthetic cultivation and of a mind free for the moment from temperamental bias of any sort. The poems are studiously objective, even the effects of his reading being represented as elements in an impersonal experience. The element of sex, moreover, is carefully excluded. The choirs of maidens who usurped the landscape in *Elegy I* are here kept at a becoming distance. The passing reference to neat-handed Phillis, and the "store of ladies whose bright eyes rain influence," with the vaguer surmise of a possibly beauty in a distant tower, are but pleasurable additions to an undisturbed sense of visible and meditated loveliness.

But Milton's sojourn in the realm of purely idyllic beauty could not, given his nature and education, be very long. For him the writing of poems like *L'Allegro* and *Il Penseroso,* however exquisite the result, was in a sense a *tour de force.* We may assume that after a year or so, at most, of aesthetic leisure on his father's estate he would have felt the need of a return to more serious and purposeful endeavor. The English letter, which I have already analyzed and which we may now fit more exactly into its place in the Horton era, reflects such a moment in his thought. The fact that Milton at this time began to set down his compositions in the Cambridge manuscript may also be significant. A little later (c. 1636), as we shall see, he embarked on a more consistent course of study than the discursive and dilletante readings recorded in *L'Allegro* and *Il Penseroso,* and started to accumulate notes toward a philosophy of life in the *Commonplace Book.* In poetry he returns for a brief interval to the sober vein of the *Nativity.*

I have already noted his attempt to continue the devotional strain of that poem in the odes on the Passion and the Circumcision. Both these pieces are undated. The first of them most probably succeeded the *Nativity* at the following Easter season. It is tempting to assume that the poem on the Circumcision came between them on the appropriate occasion in

January, 1629–30. But this is almost certainly not the case. For though the piece is allied in theme to the *Nativity,* in form and style it is closely associated with the verses *At a Solemn Music* and *On Time,* and all three belong to a later date in Milton's literary career. The evidence of the Cambridge manuscript is, I believe, decisive on this point. In that document, *At a Solemn Music,* in three drafts, immediately precedes the *Letter to a Friend,* and the poems *On Time* and *On the Circumcision* follow it. Then comes *Comus,* establishing a *terminus ad quem* in 1634. The letter and the three companion odes are not much earlier; they would, indeed, belong to the same year if Masson's date for *Arcades,* which precedes them in the manuscript, is to be trusted. The poems represent a new experiment in English verse of the more solemn sort. *On Time* has its kinship in idea with the English letter and the sonnet *On His Being Arrived to the Age of Twenty-three,* but in place of the mood of disturbed self-searching reflected in those utterances, it is expressive of deep religious and contemplative joy, the chords of which Milton had already touched in the *Nativity:*

> Then long Eternity shall greet our bliss
> With an individual kiss,
> And joy shall overtake us in a flood;
> When everything that is divinely good,
> And perfectly divine,
> With Truth, and Peace, and Love shall ever shine
> About the supreme throne
> Of him to whose happy-making sight alone
> When once our heavenly-guided soul shall climb,
> Then, all this earthly grossness quit,
> Attired with stars we shall for ever sit,
> Triumphing over Death, and Chance, and Thee, O Time.

Similar imagery and an identical emotion pervade the poem *At a Solemn Music.* Both works are dignified and noble compositions, deeply felt and phrased in beauty. They are more mature in style than the *Nativity,* but come short of it in metrical felicity and in poetic fervor. The more vital forces of Milton's personality are not engaged in them. *Upon the Circumcision* is less fortunate. Milton strives to frame his thoughts to sadness in remembrance of Christ's sacrifice, symbolically suggested according to religious convention by the event which he commemorates, but the Muse withholds her wonted blessing on his endeavor. Only in the opening, where the poet is dealing momentarily with his native theme of the celestial song which attended the birth of Christ, does he achieve real beauty of feeling and expression:

> Ye flaming powers, and winged Warriors bright,
> That erst with music and triumphant song,
> First heard by happy watchful shepherds' ear,
> So sweetly sung your joy the clouds along,
> Through the soft silence of the listening night. . . .

The succeeding lines show, to my judgment, a falling off of inspiration.

With these comparatively slight and experimental pieces Milton apparently abandons any further attempt to express the religious mood in verse. But two poems of any sort, *Comus* and *Lycidas,* were written during the remaining four or more years of the Horton period and both of these were composed for definite occasions at the request of others. At the opening of *Lycidas* Milton alludes to his feeling of unreadiness and to the resolution which he had apparently cherished of waiting for his ultimate inspiration before writing again at all:

> Yet once more, O ye Laurels, and once more,
> Ye Myrtles brown, with ivy never sere,
> I come to pluck your berries harsh and crude,
> And with forced fingers rude
> Shatter your leaves before the mellowing year.
> Bitter constraint and sad occasion dear
> Compels me to disturb your season due.

The occasional character of these poems does not, however, diminish their significance. They are, indeed, the great masterpieces of Milton's youth, springing from the deepest sources of his inspiration. They reveal, moreover, new influences of more far-reaching importance in the moulding of his inner life than the delightful but unserious children of the Muse who had dominated his art in the composition of *L'Allegro, Il Penseroso,* and *Arcades.* The key is again provided by Milton's autobiographical statement in the *Apology for Smectymnuus:*

Next (for hear me out now readers, that I may tel ye whither my younger feet wandered), I betook me to those fables and romances, which recount in solemn cantos the deeds of knighthood founded by our victorious kings, and from hence in renown all over Christendom. There I read it in the oath of every knight that he should defend to the expense of his best blood, if so befell him, the honour and chastity of virgin or matron; from whence even then I learned what a noble virtue chastity must be, to the defence of which so many worthies, by such a dear adventure of themselves, had sworn. And if I found in the story afterward, any of them, by word or deed, breaking that oath, I judged it the same fault of the poet, as that which is attributed to Homer, to have written indecent things of the gods. Only this my mind gave me, that every free and gentle spirit, without that oath, ought to be born a knight, nor needed to expect the gilt spur, or the laying of a sword upon his shoulder to stir him both by his counsel and his arms, to secure and protect the weakness of any attempted chastity. So that even these books, which to many others have been the fuel of wantonness and loose living, I cannot think how, unless by divine indulgence, proved to me so many incitements, as you have heard, to the love and steadfast observation of that virtue which abhors the society of the bordellos.

The interest of this passage as an index to Milton's enthusiasm for the literature of romance and as a revelation of the intense subjective passion with which he read, is obvious. One is reminded of the phrase about "dinging a book a quoit's distance from him" in *Areopagitica*. Considered from the point of view of our detailed analysis of the poet's early literary development the statement bears a more particular significance. The plain implication of the context is that these imaginative wanderings of his youthful feet belong not to an indefinite period, and certainly not to his boyhood, but to the epoch which immediately succeeded his devotion to Dante and Petrarch and his resolution to shape his career toward the highest forms of poetry. In view of the reliability of Milton's account thus far the presumption is in favor of an equal precision in his statement at this point. Let us consider the passage more closely with a view to determining the exact character of the literary reference.

The general terms of the description apply well enough to the *Morte d'Arthur*, a book, certainly, in which the high vows of knighthood are both taken and broken and which has often enough been "fuel of wantonness," but it is not Malory who would have inflamed a young idealist with the love of chastity and it is not his work of which Milton is thinking as marking an epoch in his development as a poet. Much more plausibly it is the romantic poets of the Renaissance — Boiardo and Ariosto among the Italians, and particularly Spenser who would first have come to his attention and first aroused his enthusiasm for their subject matter, leading to a subsequent exploration of the more authentic legends in medieval romance and chronicle. The single phrase " solemn cantos " is sufficient to determine the fact that Milton had the *Faerie Queene* specifically in mind. We may compare the later expression in *Areopagitica,* " our sage and serious Spenser " and the reference in *Il Penseroso,*

> Or if aught else great bards beside
> In *sage and solemn* tune have sung
> Of turneys and enchantments drear
> Where more is meant than meets the ear.

Now the time at which Milton first made the acquaintance of Spenser or the Italians is uncertain. The allusions to Ariosto in the *Commonplace Book* belong between circa 1634 and 1637 and may well represent a first extensive study in this period, following upon the earlier occupation with Dante and Petrarch. The *Faerie Queene* Milton must, one would suppose, have read before. We may, however, safely infer from the quoted passage that, no matter how early he may have felt the interest and charm of Spenser, the influence of his lofty and serious cantos as a powerful stimulus to his emotions was first deeply felt at the point in his development which we have now reached. It is in consonance with such an assumption that there are in Milton no allusions to Spenser and no marked trace of his influence in anything written before the Horton period. In a poet as susceptible of literary influence as Milton has shown himself to be, this would be strange indeed if he had already been profoundly stirred by the enthusiasm which he describes. Striking too is the fact that in his first statements regarding his plans for epic he should give no hint of his later intention to deal with Arthurian material. It seems probable that his purposes were shaped in this direction by his study of the Italians and by his acceptance of Spenser as his English master.

The proof that Milton's statement does actually mark the

moment of a new allegiance and that this moment coincides with the beginning of the Horton period is to be found in the English poems themselves. His adoption at this time of the pastoral mode is in accord with the precedent of Spenser as well as with that of Virgil. The clear allusion to the *Faerie Queene* in *Il Penseroso* I have already quoted. It is, however, when we come to *Comus* that we feel for the first time the full effects of the impregnation of Milton's thought with the poetic idealism of his great Elizabethan predecessor. We are prepared by the terms of Milton's description to find the relation here dynamic and essential. The extraordinary degree to which Spenser actually affected Milton's art I shall consider in a moment. For the present the important thing to observe is that he carried to the *Faerie Queene,* by his own confession, the same highly serious and subjective attitude which he had brought to his earlier reading, finding in his exaltation of chastity something to which his own nature and mood responded with unusual power, and that this response belongs definitely to a phase of his emotional idealism for which he had not yet found a satisfactory expression. If the way of thinking and judging in the passage from the *Apology* seems rather immature for the age of twenty-two or thereabouts, this only harmonizes with our general impression of Milton's temperament and with what he appears to have felt about himself. It remains, of course, quite possible that such ascetic dreamings go back in their origin to an earlier period, for Milton is not fixing a chronology but describing the stages in a development, and we need believe only that these influences and this experience first reached their full fruition in the Horton period. This consideration applies also to Milton's further statement regarding his contact with Platonic philosophy, which it is desirable to quote before undertaking the analysis of *Comus.*

Thus from the laureate fraternity of poets [he goes on], riper years and the ceaseless round of studies led me to the shady spaces of philosophy; but chiefly to the divine volumes of Plato and his equal Xenophon: where if I should tell ye what I learned of chastity and love, I mean of that which is truly so, whose charming cup is only virtue, which she bears in her hand to those who are worthy (the rest are cheated with a thick intoxicating potion, which a certain sorceress, the abuser of love's name carries about) and how the first and chiefest office of love ends in the soul, producing those two happy twins of her divine generation, knowledge and virtue. With such abstracted sublimities as these, it might be worth your listening, readers, as I may one day hope to have ye in a still time, when there shall be no chiding.

The actual beginnings of Milton's study of Plato go back to his school days. The passionate assimilation of the doctrine of love and virtue is evidently the work of his later youth. The dialogue uppermost in his thoughts is the *Symposium*, which he has evidently been studying along with the parallel account in Xenophon's work of the same name in the Horton period, perhaps for the first time. It is significant that he makes his new interest follow and grow out of his reading of poetry. That a poet should be a poet's guide to emotional Platonism is very natural. That Spenser should have been the guide of Milton is particularly so. For the later born poet found in his predecessor not only his own serious love of virtue combined with a fine responsiveness to sensuous beauty, but the embodiment of the Platonic philosophy with which he was already acquainted, touched after the fashion of the Renaissance with the romantic charm of sex. The two influences are henceforth one. They combine in *Comus* to give a quality of poetic inspiration wholly new in Milton's work, a fusion of the ecstacies of sense and spirit which the poet has hitherto been unable to obtain.

The myth of Circe had long been established as a Platonic symbol of the degredation of the soul through sensuality [39] and as such had attracted Milton as early as the first Latin elegy. It had received imaginative transformation and adaptation to the Christian ideal of sexual purity at the hands of Spenser in the second book of the *Faerie Queene*. The reference in *Areopagitica* shows the impression which the allegory of the Bower of Bliss had left on Milton's mind.[40] It seemed to him the prime

[39] For example, in Heraclitus Ponticus, *Allegoriae in Homeri Fabulas de Diis,* a copy of which has come down to us bearing Milton's signature and the date 1637. See Sotheby, *Ramblings*, p. 125.

[40] ". . . which was the reason why our sage and serious poet Spenser, whom I dare be known to think a better teacher than Scotus or Aquinas, describing true temperance under the person of Guion, brings him in with

illustration of the superior power of poetry to enforce a moral truth, a principle on which his own subsequent practice of the art was to take its stand. The appropriateness of the material to the masque was obvious.[41] Very naturally, therefore, he chose the motive as a vehicle for the expression of those inmost thoughts and feelings which had gradually grown clear and dominant in his consciousness. The classical framework of the myth is, as might be expected, adhered to more closely by Milton than by Spenser, or rather he definitely attaches his own invention to it where Spenser transforms the original to the substance of his dream. The embodiment of Platonic thought, moreover, is specific, appearing in particular passages, very strikingly in the famous one on chastity, and in the poem as a whole. Milton has taken evident pains to point the allegory and to make his fiction wear the aspect of a Platonic myth. Take, for example, the following exposition of the symbolism of Circe's cup,

> which as they taste
> (For most do taste through fond intemperate thirst),
> Soon as the potion works, their human countenance,
> The express resemblance of the gods, is changed
> Into some brutish form of wolf or bear,
> Or ounce or tiger, hog, or bearded goat,
> All other parts remaining as they were.
> And they, so perfect is their misery,
> Not once perceive their foul disfigurement,
> But boast themselves more comely than before,
> And all their friends and native home forget.

Incidentally he moralizes, after the fashion of Plato and his followers, the stories of Diana and Minerva, and that of Cupid and Psyche, creating a genealogy analogous to that of Love in the *Symposium.*

All this is the fruit of Milton's conscious classicism. It is, however, to Spenser that *Comus* is most deeply indebted in its poetic essence. In his elaboration of the fiction, as in the quality of his emotion, Milton has been influenced by his master's

---

his palmer through the cave of Mammon and the bower of earthly bliss, that he might see and know, and yet abstain."

[41] The Circe myth had been employed in Browne's *Inner Temple Masque,* presented Jan. 13, 1614.

romantic allegory of chastity in the third book of the *Faerie Queene*. This is clearest, so far as plot incident is concerned, in the parallel between the rescue of Amoret in Book III and the freeing of the Lady at the close of *Comus*. In both works the enchanter is surprised as he stands before his enthralled victim endeavoring to subdue her will to his lust. In Spenser the rescuer (Britomart) strikes him down, but is told that only he can undo the spell which he has worked. She then forces him " his charms back to reverse." In Milton the brothers, after having put Comus to flight, are informed by Thyrsis that they should have secured him as the instrument of the Lady's release.

> Without his rod reversed
> And backward mutters of dissevering power
> We cannot free the Lady that sits here.

The identity of phrase and of idea is quite conclusive of Milton's indebtedness at this point. He undoubtedly received modifying suggestions for the plot from other sources, but nothing so essential as he derived from the *Faerie Queene*. The relationship here is one which extends to the fundamental philosophy and poetic method.

It is not by any means confined to this one episode. Britomart, the central figure in Book III, is Spenser's symbol of what Milton calls the sun-clad power of chastity. The martial conception underlies such passages as *Comus*, 440 ff. The idea that chastity draws down Heaven to its defense, which is the dominant motive in the whole of *Comus*, is set forth by Spenser in the episode of Proteus's rescue of Florimel attacked by the lustful fisherman, with the poet's comment, so much in the spirit of certain passages in *Comus*,

> See how the heavens, of voluntary grace
> And sovereign favour towards chastity
> Doe succor send to her distressed cace.
> So much high God doth innocence embrace.

A more specific suggestion came to Milton from the description of the Garden of Adonis in Canto VI. I have already alluded to his introduction of Cupid and Psyche, with the mention of their allegorical descendants, Youth and Joy, as an instance of his Platonizing mythography. The immediate pattern of Milton's description is Spenser, who introduces as symbols of the Platonic creative principle first Venus and Adonis, then Cupid and Psyche, endowing the last two with a daughter, Pleasure. To the detail of Milton's curious application of this material I shall return in another connection. Enough has been said to confirm the assumption that *Comus* was written under the dominating poetic influence of Spenser, as surely, though not as exclusively, as the Latin elegies were written under the spell of Ovid and the Italian sonnets under that of Petrarch. Imitative, on the other hand, *Comus* certainly is not, for the unique personality of Milton is stamped upon the whole composition and the accent of his poetic idiom is heard everywhere. Milton could thus acknowledge his indebtedness as to a revered and beloved teacher, without feeling that his originality had been subjugated. He evidently considered his relationship to be analogous to that which Spenser had himself maintained toward Chaucer, and as the Elizabethan poet had delighted to express his gratitude to his predecessor under the name of Tityrus, so Milton pays graceful tribute to Spenser as Meliboeus,[41a]

> The soothest shepherd that ere piped in plains.

I am not disposed to attach exaggerated importance to Milton's confession to Dryden in his old age that Spenser was his "original." If the phrase is taken to mean that Spenser, more than any other poet, enabled Milton to interpret his genius to itself and to find a medium for his emotions at a crucial moment in his development, it says no more than truth. It is true also that Milton continued in Spenser's debt throughout his career and that, as Professor Greenlaw has ably shown,[42] the poetic fabric of *Paradise Lost* owes vastly more to the *Faerie Queene* and the *Four Hymns* than is apparent on the surface. Of all this Milton was clearly mindful. His own genius was, however,

[41a] In support of this identification see J. F. Bense, "'Meliboeus old' in Milton's 'Comus,'" *Neophilologus,* I. 62–64.

[42] *Studies in Philology,* XIV. 196–218.

after all, radically different from Spenser's and his culture was too wide and the influences under which it operated too complex to allow him to remain, like the Fletchers, a Spenserian. The idea of poetical sonship, which Milton possibly suggested to Dryden in the conversation about his own poetic origins, was a fiction prompted by gratitude and by the precedent of Spenser's own adoption of the only earlier English poet who was in any sense his equal as the one from whom he had derived his lineage.

With the principle of chastity Milton in *Comus* largely settled his account. The intensity with which he seized upon this virtue as the center and test of his ethical idealism is explained by the strength of his own romantic passion, a passion which is still the chief motive force of his imaginative life. Occasional passages give direct and moving expression to Milton's wider ethical convictions, but it is " the sage and serious doctrine of virginity " that holds the center of his thought and the mood of the poem contrasts strikingly with the glowing but mature enthusiasm of *Paradise Lost*. As a matter of fact *Comus* appears to reflect a partial suppression of the poet's sensuous excitement rather than its supersedence or complete conversion. For Milton this could be no resting-place, however happy the immediate poetic product.

I have said that the poem settled Milton's account with chastity. The subject, indeed, continued to occupy him as late as 1642 when he penned the passage in the *Apology* and, as I believe, until his marriage, but it no longer forced itself upon his creative art. What *Comus* did not do was to end the mood of youthful excitement by giving full imaginative expression to Milton's emotional life. Such an expression demanded not the exaltation of a negative virtue, but some more fervid celebration of the mystery of love, such as he apparently still had in mind when he promised to edify his readers with a representation of these abstracted sublimities at a time when there should be no chiding. A sort of fulfillment of this vague promise is, as we shall see, contained in *Paradise Lost,* but when Milton ultimately came to gather up in the epic the ripe fruit of his experience his attitude had undergone great changes, and the form in which he embodied the mystery of love bore a much modified relation to these promptings of his youth. It is rather to the documents of the later Horton period itself that we should look for the more immediate traces of Milton's idealized passion.

There needs no resort to psychological theory to show that the very restraints which Milton imposed upon himself intensified the sensuous impulses of his nature or to make clear the influence of these impulses on his reflective and imaginative processes. The very fervor with which he seizes upon the doctrines and imagery of the *Symposium* is evidence of his intoxication with something more glowing than purity as an abstract and negative ideal. He is compelled in the revelation of his new experience to repudiate the amatory phase recorded in the elegies, and he does so, not by destroying these children of his more sensuous Muse, but by carefully dating the elegies and appending to them the engaging postscript already quoted.[42a]

But the banishment of the earthly Aphrodite is only one phase of Milton's new philosophical discipleship. In the teaching of his master, friendship, the friendship of the good, is the human motive force and basis of the devotion of the soul to its ultimate divine object. With Platonic love in its romantic form Milton had, as we have seen, already experimented immaturely and unsuccessfully in the Italian sonnets. The tradition, while not without its appeal to him, was essentially foreign to his temperament. It was associated, too, in his own day with things and persons that he condemned, for the doctrine of Platonic love had received a new lease of life at the court of Henrietta Maria, where it had become more than ever a mask of triviality and corruption.[43] In contact now with the pure source which these vagaries had perverted Milton needed no longer dally with a false ideal. He substituted consciously and deliberately the principle of friendship, attaching new meaning to a sentiment which had already played a part in the experience of his boyhood and youth. It is not without significance that the first prose letters to his early acquaintance, Charles Diodati, which Milton cared to preserve and publish, should date from the year 1637

[42a] Above, p. 127.

[43] See Jefferson Fletcher, *The Religion of Beauty in Woman,* pp. 166 ff.

or that the only important poems to be composed between that year and 1641, *Lycidas* and the *Epitaphium Damonis,* should be elegies to the memory of dead friends. The earlier exchange of verse epistles with Diodati had apparently ceased some eight years before, and Milton seems to imply that letters of any sort and even meetings had recently become infrequent. The renewal of the old intimacy was evidently initiated by Milton. "Jam istuc demum plane video te agere," he writes on September 2, 1637, "ut obstinato silentio nos aliquando pervincas; quod si ita est, euga habe tibi istam gloriolam, en scribimus priores."[44] He has, he continues, taken pains to inquire after Diodati's welfare from his brother, and, having been accidentally informed that his friend was in town, he had hastened to his lodgings only to find them vacant. The letter is one of warm importunity, prompted by a desire of closer community of understanding and affection. "Quare," he concludes, "quod sine tuo incommodo fiat, advola ocyus et aliquo in loco te siste, qui locus mitiorem spem praebeat, posse quoquo modo fieri ut aliquoties inter nos saltem visamus, quod utinam nobis non aliter esses vicinus, rusticanus atque es ŭrbicus."[44] Diodati evidently replied to this appeal by a letter in which he wished Milton health six hundred times. The poet in turn, on September 23 of the same year, writes a long letter in which he opens himself without reserve. The document is as remarkable a Miltonic revelation as we have met. It reflects as in a mirror a whole phase of the Renaissance—the attempt of high souls to make the spiritual discipline of Platonic philosophy a reality, to relive an imagined antiquity in a finer way than any humanist who was not also a poet could comprehend. It is the more heroic in that Milton in his generation stands alone as the last of a giant race. His idealism harks back to the days of Ficino and Pico and the Platonic academy of Lorenzo dei Medici.

[44] "I clearly see that you are determined not to be overcome in silence; if this be so, you shall have the palm of victory, for I will write first. . . . Wherefore as soon as you can do it without inconvenience to yourself, I beseech you to take up your quarters where we may at least be able to visit one another; for I hope you would not be a different neighbor to us in the country from what you are in town."

There can be no mistaking the change which has come over his attitude since his earlier verse epistles. His former pleasant companionship, brooded upon in absence, has taken on the character, on his side at least, of a fully developed Platonic relationship. He has, apparently, not had the many letters for which he hoped, but his old regard has suffered not the slightest diminution. "Non enim in Epistolarum ac Salutationum momentis veram amicitiam volo, quae omnia ficta esse possunt; sed altis animi radicibus niti utrinque et sustinere se; coeptamque sinceris, et sanctis rationibus, etiamsi mutua cessarent officia, per omnem tamen vitam suspicione et culpa vacare: ad quem fovendam non tam scripto sit opus, quam viva invicem virtutum recordatione. Nec continuo, ut tu non scripseris, non erit quo illud suppleri officium possit, scribit vicem tuam apud me tua probitas verasque literas intimis sensibus meis exarat, scribit morum simplicitas, et recti amor; scribit ingenium etiam tuum, haudquaquam quotidianum, et majorem in modum te mihi commendat."[45] The contrast between these and earlier expressions

[45] "For I do not think that true friendship consists in the frequency of letters or in professions of regard, which may be counterfeited; but it is so deeply rooted in the heart and affections, as to support itself against the rudest blast; and when it originates in sincerity and virtue, it may remain through life without suspicion and without blame, even when there is no longer any reciprocal interchange of kindness. For the cherishing aliment of such a friendship as this there is not so much need of letters as of a lively recollection of each other's virtues. And though you may not have written there is something that may supply the omission: your probity writes to me in your stead; it is a letter written on the innermost membrane of your heart; the simplicity of your manners, and the rectitude of your principles, serve as correspondents in your place; your genius, which is above the common level, writes, and serves in a still greater degree to endear you to me." . . . But, lest you indulge in an excess of menace, I must inform you, that I cannot help loving those who are like you; for whatever the deity may have bestowed on me in other respects he has certainly inspired me, if any ever were inspired, with a passion for the good and fair. Nor did Ceres, according to the fable, ever seek her daughter Proserpine with such unceasing solicitude, as I have sought this idea of the beautiful in all the forms and appearances of things (for many are the forms of the divine). I am wont day and night to continue my search; and I follow in the way in which you go before. Hence, I feel an irresistible impulse to cultivate the friendship of him who, despising the prejudices and false conceptions of the vulgar, dares to think, to speak, and to be that which the highest wisdom has in every age taught to be

of Milton's regard for Diodati is striking. In 1629 he had addressed him as a pleasant reveller from whose way of life his own more serious aspirations were beginning to withdraw him. Now he hails him as the embodiment of the Platonic good and fair, making their friendship a part of the loftiest meditations of his soul. "Ego enim," he continues, "ne nimis minitere, tui similes impossible est quin amem, nam de caetero quidem quid de me statuerit Deus nescio, illud certe; δεινόν μοι ἔρωτα, εἴπερ τῷ ἄλλῳ τοῦ καλοῦ ἐνέσταξε. Nec tanto Ceres labore, ut in fabulis est, Liberam fertur quaesivisse filiam, quanto ego hanc τοῦ καλοῦ ἰδέαν, veluti pulcherrimam quandam imaginem, per omnes rerum formas et facies: (πολλαὶ γὰρ μορφαὶ τῶν Δαιμονίων) dies noctesque indagare soleo, et quasi certis quibusdam vestigiis ducentem sector Unde fit, ut qui, spretis quae vulgus prava rerum aestimatione opinatur, id sentire et loqui et esse audet; quod summa per omne aevum sapientia optimum esse docuit, illi me protinus, sicubi reperiam, necessitate quadam adjungam."[45] As of old he rounds out his flight with a communication of his own poetic aspirations: "Quid cogitem quaeris; ita me bonus Deus, immortalitatem. Quid agam vero? πτεροφυῶ, et volare meditor: sed tenellis admodum adhuc pennis evehit se noster Pegasus, humile sapiamus."[45]

This letter, then, is Milton's fullest and most direct expression of the philosophic aspect of the Platonic enthusiasm which reached its height toward the close of the Horton period. Such an expression was appropriate to the cooler element of prose. In the exactly contemporary elegy *Lycidas* (it is dated November, 1637, in the Cambridge manuscript) and the somewhat later *Epitaphium Damonis,* where Milton is again the poet, with his singing robes about him, his rapture is loftier and more intense. It is commonly and I think rightly assumed concerning the first of these works that Milton had enjoyed no par-

the best. . . . Do you ask what I am meditating. By the help of Heaven an immortality of fame. But what am I doing? I am letting my wings grow, and preparing to fly; but my Pegasus has not yet feathers enough to soar aloft in the fields of air." — Bohn translation, with modifications.

ticularly close intimacy with Edward King, its subject. The mood is one of reflective melancholy and tender pathos rather than of poignant sorrow, though the latter note is not altogether lacking. There is no direct statement of Platonic doctrine, but the idea of a pure and inspiring friendship, founded in virtue and associating itself with the most elevated self-communion, underlies the whole poem and is in conformity with the present aspect of Milton's experience. The digressions on fame and the clergy, which are really not digressions at all, together with the concluding utterances regarding immortality, are expressions of Milton's deepest thoughts upon the central topic of the aspirations, ideals, and destiny of the poet.

In the *Epitaphium* the accent of personal grief is keener and the reflective element less pronounced. The immediacy of his sense of loss throws Milton back upon the mood of intimacy and affection which had characterized his early association with Diodati and had survived the process of Platonic idealization. The old habit of communicating his poetic plans in Latin to the sympathetic ear of Diodati is pathetically continued in the passage in which Milton describes his attempt at an Arthurian epic. The external conventions of the pastoral are adhered to even more rigidly than in *Lycidas,* but the deep emotion which inspired the poem burns through them at every point.

The culmination of this emotion in the close of the *Epitaphium* involves a moment in Milton's imaginative life which has not yet been introduced into this discussion, the result of an infusion into his consciousness of one element of Christian mysticism. The subject may best be introduced by quoting the final paragraph of Milton's prose apologia:

> Last of all, not in time, but as perfection is last, that care was ever had of me, with my earliest capacity, not to be negligently trained in the precepts of the Christian religion: this that I have hitherto related, hath been to shew, that though Christianity had been but slightly taught me, yet a certain reservedness of natural disposition, and moral discipline, learnt out of the noblest philosophy, was enough to keep me in disdain of far less incontinence than this of the bordello. But having had the doctrine of holy scripture unfolding those chaste and high mysteries, with timeliest care infused, that "the body is for the Lord and the Lord for the body;" thus also I argued to myself, that if unchastity in a woman,

whom St. Paul terms the glory of man, be such a scandal and dishonour, then certainly in a man, who is both the image and glory of God, it must, though commonly not so thought, be much more deflowering and dishonourable; in that he sins both against his own body, which is the perfecter sex, and his own glory, which is in the woman; and, that which is worst, against the image and glory of God, which is in himself. Nor did I slumber over that place expressing such high rewards of ever accompanying the Lamb, with those celestial songs to others inapprehensible, but not to those who were not defiled with women, which doubtless means fornication; for marriage must not be called a defilement.

It is, then, in the precepts of religion that Milton finally grounds his habit of restraint in matters of sex. The careful Christian discipline of his childhood and its fundamental importance in determining his actual conduct might, of course, even without his declaration, have been taken for granted. What primarily interests us in the foregoing passage, however, is its revelation of the intensity with which he seized upon certain New Testament passages and assimilated their doctrine and still more their imagery to the substance of his own poetic thought. We have here a new source of inspiration the results of which may be clearly traced in his creative work. The teaching of St. Paul is for him a "chaste and high mystery" of divine authority, which supersedes, though it is not discordant with, the inspired utterances of Diotima. The Platonic principle of the supremacy of soul has its religious counterpart and intelligible fulfillment in the pronouncement "the body is for the Lord and the Lord for the body." Thus in the passage from *Comus*, "So dear to Heaven is saintly chastity," the framework of Platonic idealism is fitted with a specific ethical and Christian content. The second scriptural passage which Milton "did not slumber over" and which he here adduces as the climax of his meditation, carries us still further. The "place" is Revelation, xiv. 1 ff.: "And I looked, and, lo, a Lamb stood on the mount Sion, and with him an hundred forty and four thousand, having his father's name written in their foreheads. . . . And I heard a voice from Heaven as the voice of many waters and as the voice of a great thunder: and I heard the voice of harpers harping with their harps: And they sung as it were a new song before the throne, and before the four beasts and the elders:

and no man could learn that song but the hundred and forty and four thousand which were redeemed from the earth. These are they which were not defiled with women; for they are virgins. These are they which follow the Lamb whithersoever he goeth."

It would be a great mistake to dismiss Milton's reference as a merely casual employment of Scripture in the usual manner of the seventeenth century controversialist. His avowal of special interest in it falls in with too much that we know to be characteristic of his state of mind in the period now under discussion. We have, for example, indications from other sources that Milton shared, in some degree at least, the predilection of his time for the shadowy semi-religious borderland between philosophy and occultism represented by the Cabala and the Hermetic books.[46] His contact with materials of this sort certainly dates from the Horton period and it is naturally associated with his Platonic studies. Thus the passage in *Il Penseroso* in which he describes his nightly readings is true to the practice of his time in its emphasis on the more dubious Neoplatonic speculations. It is not the authentic spirit of Plato which must be unsphered to reveal

> What worlds or what vast regions hold
> The mortal mind that hath forsook
> Her mansion in this fleshly nook;

and to tell

> Of those demons that are found
> In fire, air, flood, or under ground,
> Whose power hath a true consent
> With planet, or with element,

but the spirits of Hermes, Iamblichus, and Michael Psellus. It was evidently not for nothing that the poet was a coeval of Henry More. There is, to be sure, no reason to suppose that he ever committed himself seriously to the intellectual extravagance of his fellow alumnus and the little group of inspired fanatics who surrounded him. And so often in his experience the imaginative impulses which fundamentally made him a poet encountered in Milton intellectual inhibitions which prevented him from

46 " thrice-great Hermes," *Il Penseroso*, v. 88.

surrendering himself to them without reserve. Though for that separate and limited part of Milton represented by *Il Penseroso* the speculations of Hermes might join with the translunary dreams of Plato and the enchantments drear of Spenser in affording a fascinating realm for curiosity to explore, he could hardly allow in these fantastic writings more than a small residuum of truth to challenge his more sober thought.

With the apocalyptic parts of Scripture the case was different. Even Plato and Spenser must yield precedence to inspired authority, in whose prophetic rapture a more daring and untrammeled expression was the garment of a profounder and more authentic truth. There is evidence enough of the position of importance occupied by the Book of Revelation in his thought. He adduces it in the introduction to *Samson Agonistes* in support of his thesis as to the dignity of drama, referring to the commentary of Paraeus, where the work is analyzed into scenes and choruses. The same point had been made by him over twenty years before in *Reason of Church Government*. We must remember also that it was in Revelation that Milton found the chief scriptural authority for the war of the angels,[47] with mystic and philosophic implications of which he shows himself to be conscious in his own treatment of the theme. Doubtless he was already meditating on those passages during the Horton period and glorying in their majesty and strangeness. His sense of their significance would have deepened with the years, and, in the end, enriched and elaborated by far-brought associations, they became the center of his imaginative activity. The appeal of the symbolic image of the Lamb and the throng of virgins was more immediate and intense. It clearly belongs to the passing phase of emotion which we have associated with Milton's adolescence, now drawing to a close.

The passage did not, of course, stand alone in his thought. It was connected with the general idea of Heavenly love and the mystic marriage of the soul with God, an idea which was deeply interfused with Christian tradition and appears to have enjoyed a special popularity in the religious writing of Milton's

[47] Rev., xii. 3–17.

own day. How profoundly this conception, with its ecstatic biblical expressions, impressed itself on Milton's imagination and how intricately it associated itself with Platonic forms and their Spenserian embodiments may best be understood by a comparative consideration of the three outstanding poems already mentioned as the sole fruit of Milton's creative powers between the years 1634 and 1640, namely, *Comus, Lycidas,* and the *Epitaphium Damonis.*

In the Spirit's Epilogue in *Comus* Milton sings of Paradise. The language is highly esoteric as well as exquisitely poetic, and Milton expressly calls attention in the parenthesis, " List mortals, if your ears be true," to the hidden spiritual meaning. The bliss proposed is that of Heavenly love as the ineffable compensation for a life devoted to the ideal of chastity, the representative and touchstone of all the virtues. In adopting Spenser's image of the Garden of Adonis Milton entirely changes its application, adapting it to his allegory of virtue and its reward, and impregnating the whole with mystical emotion, the rapt ecstacy of apocalyptic vision. The pagan image of the love of a mortal youth for a goddess draws insensibly nearer to the truth in the reversed symbol of the union of the God of love himself with Psyche, the human soul, and if Milton's classic taste prevents him from concluding with an allusion to the Lamb and his eternal bride it is because there is no need.

In the last lines of *Lycidas,* written three years later, the imagery is explicitly Christian:

> So Lycidas sunk low, but mounted high,
> Through the dear might of Him that walked the waves,
> Where, other groves and other streams along,
> With nectar pure his oozy locks he laves,
> And hears the unexpressive nuptial song,
> In the blest kingdoms meek of joy and love.

The nuptial music heard by Lycidas is the new song before the throne of the one hundred and forty and four thousand virgins of Revelation, the " celestial song to others inapprehensible but not to those who were not defiled with women " of Milton's own description.

Finally in the conclusion of the *Epitaphium,* again after an interval of three years, Milton throws off all restraint and concealment of expression (the mask of Latin being in itself a sufficient drapery) and indulges his imagination in a description of the joys of Heavenly love which reaches a point of sensuous intensity far beyond anything we have hitherto encountered in his verse. The first part of the passage is an elaboration of the description in *Comus:*

> Parte alia polus omnipatens, et magnus Olympus:
> Quis putet? hic quoque Amor, pictaeque in nube pharetrae
> Arma corusca, faces, et spicula tincta pyropo;
> Nec tenues animas, pectusque ignobile vulgi,
> Hinc ferit; at circum flammantia lumina torquens,
> Semper in erectum spargit sua tela per orbes
> Impiger, et pronos nunquam collimat ad ictus:
> Hinc mentes ardere sacrae, formaeque deorum.[48]

What follows has its parallel rather in the quoted lines from *Lycidas;* almost every motive, indeed, in the consolation with which Milton brings his lament for Edward King to a close being represented with a greater fervor in the account of the apotheosis of Diodati. It is necessary to give here only the final explicit description of the mystic marriage:

> Quod tibi purpureus pudor, et sine labe iuventus
> Grata fuit, quod nulla tori libata voluptas,
> En! etiam tibi virginei servantur honores!
> Ipse, caput nitidum cinctus rutilante corona,
> Laetaque frondentis gestans umbracula palmae
> Aeternum perages immortales hymenaeos,
> Cantus ubi, choreisque furit lyra mista beatis,
> Festa Sionaeo bacchantur et Orgia thyrso.[49]

[48] "In another place is the mighty stretch of sky where Olympus lies open to view. Yes, and Love is there, too; in clouds his quiver is pictured, his shining arms, his torch, his arrows tipped with fiery bronze. But he does not aim upon our earth at light minds, at the herd of vulgar souls. No; he rolls his flaming eyes and steadfastly sends his arrows upward through the orbs of heaven, never aiming a downward stroke. Under his fire the souls of the blessed burn, and the bodies of the gods."

[49] "Because thy cheek kept its rosy blush and thy youth its stainlessness, because thou knewest not the joy of marriage, lo, for thy virginal spirit virginal honors are reserved. Thy bright head crowned with light, and glad palms in thy hand, thou dost ever act and act again the immortal nuptials, there where singing is, and the lyre mixes madly with the chorals beatific, and the wild orgies rage under the thyrsus of Sion."

It is evident in this astonishing passage that the native sense impulses which first awakened Milton to the beauty of the spring and woman have lost nothing of their power. A part only of his passion has been absorbed in the real experience of friendship; the rest is transmuted into an imaginative and religious rapture which allies him for the moment with the tradition of Catholic Christianity. It does so, to be sure, only outwardly, for there is fundamental disparity between his essentially humanistic attitude and the devout asceticism of the Middle Ages. He belongs by temper and inheritance to the Renaissance. Symbolism in his hands becomes concrete and glowing imagery and the Christian meaning is transfused with the spirit as it is assimilated to the language of Pagan poetry.

With the *Epitaphium Damonis* Milton's early poetic productivity comes to an end. In its last phase it has been the product of the cloistral and contemplative period at Horton, though the mood itself has survived the Italian journey and, as the passage in the *Apology for Smectymnuus* indicates, the beginnings of his active life as a teacher and controversialist. What further fruitage it might have had we cannot tell, but there is little likelihood that the peculiar form of emotional excitement embodied in the *Epitaphium* would have continued long. The whole phase of his experience recapitulated in the *Apology* was essentially youthful and transitory, though Milton's intellectual precocity, his aesthetic discipline, and his almost infallible good taste made its expressions wear a certain deceptive air of maturity. Having served their purpose as the chief inspiration of his Muse when he was still in the main unable to give utterance to his profounder moral and intellectual consciousness, these emotions yielded to time, though not without leaving a permanent impress upon his genius.

Meanwhile Milton's cultural interests were broadening and his purposes in art and life defining themselves more sharply. In abandoning his intention to enter the church he had envisaged another form of public service more congenial to his taste and more consonant with his thirst for an immortality of fame. To fulfill this purpose it was necessary for him to equip himself with understanding of the world of men and affairs, and in particular to gain a sound basis for the formulation of his views on the great issues which were beginning to agitate the public mind of his time. Accordingly we find him embarking about the year 1635 on a course of modern historical study, beginning with the authorities on the later Roman empire, and progressing through the Byzantine writers, the Greek and Latin fathers, the medieval chroniclers of Italy, France, and England, down to the historians of the Reformation and contemporary affairs. Books of public policy and law were included in the program, as were also biography, memoirs, and treatises, ancient and modern, on the art of war. The detail of this reading is recorded in the *Commonplace Book,* where Milton made references to individual passages in his authors and copied out under appropriate headings many excerpts and observations. It is fortunately possible, as I have shown elsewhere,[50] to date many of the entries with considerable exactness, and, in particular, to set apart from the rest the entire body of materials which belong to the Horton period.

This latter group is of the greatest importance as an index to the interests and tendencies which find only scanty echoes in his earlier poetry. A considerable number of the entries reflect the contemporary interest in questions of ecclesiastical custom and in the precedents and authorities regarding them, with a marked predilection for evidence in support of the more liberal Reformation practice. The Puritanism, or more properly the liberalism, of Milton was evidently of very early growth. A note on Constantine's giving the clergy immunity from civil office and one praising the modesty of princes who refuse to meddle in matters of religion show his fundamental convictions regarding the relations of church and state to have been already in process of formation. Even more striking are the political entries, which contain the gist of Milton's whole republicanism. In the earliest stratum a broad interest is manifested in the relation of prince and subject, as in the following: "Ad subditos

[50] See *The Chronology of Milton's Private Studies,* in the *Publications of the Modern Language Association,* XXXVI. 251–313.

suos scribens Constantinus magnus nec alio nomine quam fratres appellat." In a slightly later group of entries (still within the Horton period) the political materials are more obviously related to the issues of the day. Thus the title "Rex" is begun, with entries relative to the deification of the Roman emperors, and that of "Subditus," with two notes giving instances of Papal release of subjects from allegiance to a sovereign. The setting down of the title "Census et Vectigal" is evidently connected with interest in the illegal exactions of Charles. And finally one note is definitely republican: "Severus Sulpitius ait regium nomen semper liberis gentibus fere invisum." Were it not for the unquestionable evidence of the manuscript we should have been inclined, I think, to ascribe this last citation rather to the period of the tract *Of the Tenure of Kings and Magistrates* (1649) than to that of *Lycidas*. To the earlier period, however, it certainly belongs and it is, with the rest, conclusive evidence of the degree to which Milton had matured his thought on public questions before he found himself actually surrounded by the influences which determined his public career. The Horton entries as a whole give definition to Milton's subsequent mention of "many studious and contemplative years altogether spent in the search for civil and religious knowledge" and to his description of himself as having from his youth "studied the distinctions between civil and religious rights."

The convictions thus formed came ultimately to be as intimate an element in Milton's consciousness and as available to him for poetic expression as the introspective activities of which we have been tracing the effects on his creative work. They did so in the degree to which they became associated with his personal life and ideals and with his conception of his function as a poet. Thus the outburst against the clergy in *Lycidas*, the first great passage in which he voices his convictions on an issue of the day, owes its emotional intensity to the fact that it is, in reality, a justification of his decision not to enter the church and a vindication of his idea that he could fulfill an analogous function more effectively in his own way. It is significant that neither in this passage nor in anything else written during his early years does Milton give utterance to the passion for political and intellectual freedom which became one of the supreme inspiring motives of his eloquence. His opinions on the subject were, as we have seen, already fixed, but nothing had yet happened to bring it home to him in the form of personal desire. Later, when he found himself hampered in his own activities by the restraint of a narrow authority and a narrow law, his impersonal convictions were converted into passion and achieved memorable expression in prose and verse. It is not surprising that, looking back from that later viewpoint, he should have forgotten that his feelings had not always been the same, and should have substituted for the mixed motives which kept him out of the church the single determination not to subscribe himself slave.

To say this much is not, of course, to say that the issues to which Milton devoted his life meant nothing to him until they became personal; it is simply to affirm the principle that the gap between mere intellectual and moral sincerity and poetic sincerity is a wide one and that Milton came only gradually into his full imaginative inheritance. The processes by which the infusion of his ethical and political ideals with personal emotion is accomplished, and, conversely, the process by which the promptings of desire are converted into universal truth — these processes are the fundamental facts of Milton's development. The difference between his earlier and later work is due simply to a shift in the center of his experience and to a consequent widening of his grasp of the moral issues which confront mankind. The increasing maturity of his ideas is reflected in the richer and more harmonious conception which he now adopts of his work as a poet — a conception which at length completely reconciles his need of ministering to men as a teacher of the truth with his desire to create beauty and with his passion for fame. Speaking again in the *Reason of Church Government* (1641) of his plans for epic and dramatic poetry, he concludes with the following analysis of the function of the poet-teacher:

These abilities, wheresoever they be found, are the inspired gift of God, rarely bestowed, but yet to some (though most abuse) in every nation; and are of power, beside the office of a pulpit, to inbreed and cherish in a great people the seeds of virtue and public civility, to allay the perturbations of the mind, and set the affections in right tune; to celebrate in glorious and lofty hymns the throne and equipage of God's almightiness, and what he works, and what he suffers to be wrought with high providence in his church; to sing victorious agonies of martyrs and saints, the deeds and triumphs of just and pious nations, doing valiantly through faith against the enemies of Christ; to deplore the general relapse of kingdoms and states from justice and God's true worship. Lastly, whatsoever in religion is holy and sublime, in virtue amiable and grave, whatsoever hath passion or admiration in all the changes of that which is called fortune from without, or the wily subtleties and refluxes of man's thoughts from within; all these things with a solid and treatable smoothness to paint out and describe, teaching over the whole book of sanctity and virtue, through all the instances of example, with such delight to those especially of soft and delicious temper, who will not look upon truth herself, unless they see her elegantly dressed; that whereas the paths of honesty and good life appear now rugged and difficult, though they be indeed easy and pleasant, they will then appear easy and pleasant, though they were rugged and difficult indeed.

Though this passage was written a year before the retrospective discussion in the *Apology,* it better represents Milton's mature aims at the outset of his career of public service, and the form of the ideal which was actually to dominate his creative activity henceforth. The poet no longer speaks privately to the aspirations of the individual, but to the public conscience of mankind. While he still cherishes for himself and for the few who can receive it the esoteric doctrine of chastity and true love, his immediate attention is bent, with all the tremendous energy of his spirit, upon the broader theme of "virtue and public civility," "justice and God's true worship," "the rugged and difficult paths of honesty and true life." He advocates public festivals, "as in those famous governments of old," where, not only in pulpits but at set and solemn panurgies, in theaters and porches, the people may be led, by wise and artful recitations, combining recreation with instruction, to the practice of justice, temperance and fortitude. The function which he here proposes to himself is thus essentially a public one, analogous, on the one hand, to that of the prophets of Israel and on the other to that of the orators of Greece and Rome. In the imagination of such a task Milton's ambitions take the form of a loftier enthusiasm than the desire to rival an Ovid or even a Spenser, and though he is still questioning "what king or knight before the conquest might be chosen in whom to lay the pattern" of a Christian hero, it is easy to see that such a theme will fail to satisfy his present more comprehensive purposes. From the standpoint of the present discussion we may affirm that the emotions of love and friendship have given way to that of patriotism as the dominant motive of Milton's expressive power. His passion for individual perfection henceforth clothes itself in zeal for public righteousness and his vision is more often directed toward outward objects and events.

There is no real break, however, in the continuity of his inner life. Whenever Milton is attacked, as he was by Bishop Hall, he becomes acutely introspective. Affliction also has the natural effect of turning his imagination upon the world of his own moral and religious consciousness. Such utterances as the autobiographical statements in the *Second Defense*, the lyric parts of *Paradise Lost*, and the sonnets are the result. In these expressions we have the full fruit of Milton's mature lyric emotion, so far as it is generated by conscious superiority of personality and moral ideals. The mood is that of the *Sonnet on His Being Arrived to the Age of Twenty-three*, intensified by a sharper sense of the opposition of circumstance and enriched by a profounder religious feeling.

The development of his thought of sex is more complicated. To follow it we must return again to the end of the Horton period when Milton was beginning to regard the chapter of his youth as closed. The change is marked by a turning of his thoughts toward the philosophy of marriage, a direction clearly indicated by certain entries in the *Commonplace Book* which belong to the later Horton period. These entries cite the testimony of various authors regarding the practice of marriage among the apostles and the clergy of the early church. Milton is evidently satisfying himself that marriage is no defilement even for a priest, and, inferentially, that his own not inferior priesthood of poetry does not demand a state of celibacy. One sentence from Justin Martyr is to the effect that the Jews countenanced polygamy "propter varia mysteria sub ea latentia," a curious bit of evidence of Milton's early interest in the vagaries of radical Protestantism. In the *De Doctrina Christiana,* written a whole generation later, he is at pains to show that polygamy is countenanced by Scripture and is not abhorrent to reason. I am not disposed to take this strain in Milton's thought too seriously. It is for him a kind of *a fortiori* directed against the lingering tendency of men like Laud to return to an attitude regarding marriage which did violence at once to Milton's instinct and to his reason, and which he felt to be unscriptural and unprotestant. For him the married state was divinely instituted and without the shadow of a stain. His militant enthusiasm on the subject is recorded poetically in the famous passage in *Paradise Lost:* [51]

> Nor turn'd, I ween,
> Adam from his fair spouse, nor Eve the rites
> Mysterious of connubial love refused:
> Whatever hypocrites austerely talk
> Of purity, and place, and innocence,
> Defaming as impure what God declares
> Pure, and commands to some, leaves free to all.
> Our Maker bids increase; who bids abstain
> But our destroyer, foe to God and Man?
> Hail, wedded Love, mysterious law, true source
> Of human offspring, sole propriety
> In Paradise of all things common else! . . .
> Far be it that I should write thee sin or blame,
> Or think thee unbefitting holiest place.

In Milton's matured philosophy there was, of course, no inconsistency between the praise of purity and the praise of married love. Yet it is apparent that his mood has changed since the publication of *Comus.* His moral sense no longer throws him into opposition with nature; his idealism takes the form of a glorification of the true and humane conception of love as a spiritual and religious companionship, where the satisfaction of the senses has merely an instrumental though a necessary function. Milton thus makes his personal convictions an element in his public message of reform. Such is the motive of the

[51] Book IV, lines 741–759.

divorce pamphlets, and such is the theme of a considerable portion of *Paradise Lost.* In the passage cited Milton not only defends marriage against asceticism and exalts it in both its physical and its spiritual aspects as a divine mystery, but inveighs against mere sensuality, the domination of passion, the subjection of reason to desire. His direct antagonism to the romantic ideal of love here reaches its culmination and he repudiates as false the whole chivalric conception:

> Here Love his golden shafts employs, here lights
> His constant lamp, and waves his purple wings,
> Reigns here and revels: not in the bought smile
> Of harlots, loveless, joyless, unendear'd,
> Casual fruition; nor in court-amours,
> Mix'd dance, or wanton mask, or midnight ball,
> Or serenate, which the starved lover sings
> To his proud fair, best quitted with disdain.[52]

This motive underlies his insistence on the subordination of Eve. The expression "He for God only, she for God in him" exactly reverses the attitude of the medieval and the Petrarchan lover, whose deification of woman, when it is not actually the mask of sensuality, does violence to the facts and is in all cases full of danger. It is this attitude in Adam to which Eve appeals when she has sinned, and in his momentary adoption of it Adam falls. The doctrine is that of *Comus* in its ethical rather than its ascetic aspect. We recognize in Eve the enchantress Circe and the enchanter Comus, but we perceive that what is exacted of Adam is the control of his instinct, not its denial. What survives of the Platonic view of love, now domesticated and happily wedded to the Christian teaching of St. Paul, is to be found in Raphael's words to Adam in Book VIII:

> What higher in her society thou find'st
> Attractive, human, rational, love still;
> In loving thou dost well; in passion not,
> Wherein true love consists not. Love refines
> The thoughts, and heart enlarges; hath his seat
> In Reason, and is judicious; is the scale
> By which to heavenly love thou may'st ascend,
> Not sunk in carnal pleasure; for which cause
> Among the beasts no mate for thee was found.[53]

52 Book IV, lines 763–770.

53 Lines 586–594.

Even here, however, Milton feels it necessary to modify the ascetic implications in the angel's too uncompromising statement. He does so in Adam's half-abashed reply:

> Neither her outside form'd so fair, nor aught
> In procreation common to all kinds
> (Though higher of the genial bed by far,
> And with mysterious reverence, I deem)
> So much delights me as those graceful acts,
> Those thousand decencies, that daily flow
> From all her words and actions, mix'd with love
> And sweet compliance, which declare unfeign'd
> Union of mind, or in us both one soul; [54]

and in the interested inquiry whether angels love and in what fashion. This opens the way for a final statement of the doctrine of paradisiac love. The passage, which ranks as one of the prime curiosities of Milton's angelology, is as follows:

> To whom the Angel, with a smile that glow'd
> Celestial rosy red, love's proper hue,
> Answer'd: "Let it suffice thee that thou know'st
> Us happy, and without love no happiness.
> Whatever pure thou in the body enjoy'st
> (And pure thou were created) we enjoy
> In eminence, and obstacle find none
> Of membrane, joint, or limb, exclusive bars;
> Easier than air with air, if Spirits embrace,
> Total they mix, union of pure with pure
> Desiring; nor restrained conveyance need
> As flesh to mix with flesh, or soul with soul." [55]

The idea here is obviously the same that we have met at the close of *Comus, Lycidas* and the *Epitaphium*. But it now presents itself in different terms. The heavenly marriage, instead of being the "bliss to die with dim descried" of the human Psyche which has preserved herself free from earthly stain, is rather the celestial counterpart of an experience already known on earth, and the rapture which had attached itself to the contemplation of the mystic garden of Adonis is transferred to the lower but more comprehensible mysteries of the Garden of Eden.

[54] Lines 596–604.

[55] Lines 618–629.

With this final integration of his sensuous and ideal experience Milton's poetic evolution may be said to be complete. The sequence of his development, while it could hardly have been predicted with assurance, represents a normal and logical unfolding of his unique and powerful personality from youth to maturity under the influence of literary and philosophic culture. It was not, of course, unaffected by his personal circumstances and the outward events of his career. But these incidents and circumstances, even such intimate and moving ones as his marriage with Mary Powell, his blindness, the death of his second wife, while they were of immense importance in quickening his emotions and in furnishing him with occasions for the exercise of his philosophy and faith, were in no case the factors which determined the main direction of his creative effort. The same may be said of his years of public service. The struggles of the Commonwealth and Milton's share in them are clearly enough reflected in *Paradise Lost,* but there is no sound basis for the supposition that the poem differs in its general intention from what it would have been if Milton had written it in 1642. If, then, we continue to look to the conditions and events of Milton's later life for much of the substance and fiber of his major works, it is in the records of his youth that we must seek the essential bent of his genius and the primary moulding forces of his imagination. The great initial impulses of his nature, as these impulses were stimulated and guided by a succession of ideal influences, remain the all-important motives of his poetic art.

NOTE. — It is pointed out to me by Mr. Harris Fletcher of the University of Michigan that the verse epistle to Thomas Young (*Elegy IV*), dated by Milton "anno aetatis 18" and discussed on page 114 of the present study as presumably belonging to the year 1627, was actually written in March, 1625 (*cf.* Stern, *Milton und seine Zeit,* I. 29–30, and note). It therefore antedates *Elegy I* and suggests that the first stages of the process of self-realization which I have described go back to a period earlier than the beginnings of his University career.

SAMSON AGONISTES AND MILTON IN OLD AGE

SAMSON AGONISTES AND MILTON IN OLD AGE

JAMES HOLLY HANFORD

PARADISE LOST, the "monumentum aere perennius" which Milton had planned in youth but whose execution he perilously delayed till beyond his fiftieth year, stood complete and glorious by the summer of 1665. Before its publication in 1667 its author had probably finished the second masterpiece of his maturity, *Paradise Regained.* The composition of *Samson Agonistes* presumably fell within the immediately succeeding years. The two poems appeared together in 1671. Were these later works really afterthoughts, as Thomas Ellwood's well-known anecdote regarding the first of them suggests? Despite the gentle Quaker's unquestionable candor I cannot think so. At his comment, "Thou hast said much here of Paradise lost, but what hast thou to say of Paradise found?", the poet sat in silence and seemed to meditate. We are under no compulsion to believe that he was struck dumb by the novelty of the idea! There is, to be sure, the later very explicit statement, quoted by Ellwood as made when Milton showed him in London the manuscript of *Paradise Regained:* "This is owing to you, for you put it in my head at Chalfont which before I had not thought of," but is it not quite possible that Ellwood is here innocently twisting some merely polite or even ironical remark of Milton's into conformity with his own self-flattering opinion that he was the "fons et origo" of an epic poem?

However this may be, there is a kind of inevitability in these last two works which makes it difficult to accept the idea that a chance suggestion in any very important way determined either of them. In form and general character, at least, we may regard them as predestinate. The evidence goes back to a passage in the *Reason of Church Government,* written in 1641, where Milton takes the reader into his confidence regarding his literary ambitions. He is in doubt, he tells us, whether to adopt the form of an extended epic like the *Aeneid,* or of the brief epic which he says is illustrated by the Book of Job, or of drama, " in which Sophocles and Euripides reign." Since life and energy endured he did all three, taking thereby a triple bond of fame. *Paradise Lost* is the new *Aeneid,* exhibiting all the recognized technique of the full and perfect epic; *Paradise Regained* is something more unusual, a heroic poem composed entirely of dialogue, save for a narrative introduction and conclusion and a few links. Its formal precedent is obviously the Book of Job, regarded not as a drama but, more strictly, as a modification of the epic type. *Samson Agonistes,* finally, is Hellenic tragedy restored.

With his plan of life endeavor thus beyond expectation fulfilled, it seems unlikely that Milton would ever have considered a further addition to his poetical works. The lengthy list of dramatic subjects in the Cambridge manuscript (which includes a " Samson Agonistes " under the title " Dagonalia " and a kind of " Paradise Regained " under that of " Christus Patiens ") together with the corresponding one of epic themes which Professor Gilbert supposes him to have drawn up at the same time [1] — these lists were not in any sense a program. Milton was not given, like the dreamer Coleridge, to projecting vaguely a host of works which he could never write. The manuscript materials are notes taken in the process of canvassing the whole range of available materials before making a final choice. Had Milton enjoyed twenty more years of life and had there been twenty Ellwoods to urge him on, we should never have had at his hands the suggested epic on the deeds of Alfred, or the drama of " Sodom Burning " or the new Macbeth. To write any one of them would have been to mar the antique symmetry of his achievement.

It is not, however, from the standpoint of outward form alone

[1] *The Cambridge Manuscript and Milton's Plans for Epic, Studies in Philology,* 16 (1919). 172–176.

that Milton had reason to regard his contemplated work as done. The three poems are complementary in theme and in ethical idea. Taken together they constitute a complete and unified embodiment of Milton's Christian humanism, the full working out of the didactic purpose which he had accepted as a responsibility implied in his abandonment of the office of preacher for the more congenial one of poet. Let us, as an approach to the present object of giving sharper definition to the significance of *Samson Agonistes* as a work of the poet's last years, consider first the relation of the two companion epics. This relation is clearly not the mechanical one which their contrasting titles might at first suggest, and which, had *Paradise Regained* been named but never written, we should naturally have inferred from Milton's initial statement of his theme:

> Of man's first disobedience and the fruit
> Of that forbidden tree whose mortal taste
> Brought death into the world and all our woe,
> With loss of Eden till one greater man
> Restore us, and regain the blissful seat,

These lines appear to promise a scheme of salvation, according to the ideas of traditional Christianity, and for such a scheme we do not have to await a second work. It is already amply given in the first. But the truth is that Milton pays little more than lip honor to the theological system which his work bears in its superscription. His deeper interest is to be sought elsewhere. At the close of *Paradise Lost* the Archangel Michael, after revealing to Adam at somewhat wearisome length the history of redemption, instructs him in quiet but thrilling words how he may regain what he has lost and build for himself "a paradise within thee happier far." [2] The program is that of all humanity, for Adam is the representative of man. Mere repentance and the sacrifice of Christ are but the form of salvation. The thing itself involves the coöperating will as manifested in the successful meeting of future trial. It is the work of no vicarious and of no single act, but of patient moral discipline in a world of evil, according to a pattern from above. The

[2] Book XII, lines 574 ff.

actual exhibition of the process is not included in *Paradise Lost.* The unique situation of Adam made it impossible for him to serve as an illustration of the struggles and triumphs which raise man from his degraded state. His story is of a fall. It remained for Milton to embody in another work its counterpart, to set forth in detail the successful encounter of humanity with the manifold forms of evil which present themselves in the complexities of a developed civilization. In this view *Paradise Regained* becomes a necessary sequel of *Paradise Lost.* Its theme, in its ethical as distinct from its theological aspect, is, indeed, already foreshadowed in the earlier poem, where the Christian virtues of faith, hope, love, humility, patience are indicated by the angel for Adam's attainment.[3] Their exemplification is in Christ, who becomes for Milton the second Adam, protagonist of a humanity confronted with choices which the first Adam in the freshness of the world could not have known. This is the key to the development of the temptation scenes in *Paradise Regained.*[4] The first and third temptations are special, having to do with the peculiar character and mission of Christ. The second — the kingdoms of the world and the glory of them — is universal, implying all human moral issues. Milton accordingly elaborates it into a "survey of vice with all its baits and seeming pleasures," for which Christ's calm answers afford the antidote of reason. The critical objection that the temptations, given the nature of Christ, are not tempting, is beside the point. They are such temptations as experience shows to be the characteristic ones of men at large — luxury, wealth, power, fame, the pride of knowledge. By his indifference to these allurements and by his Socratic exposition of their emptiness Christ instructs all men how they may despise them. It is no mere piece of biblical commentary that Milton is composing, nor is it an attempt at portraiture of the historic Christ (though this

[3] *Loc. cit.*

[4] This view of the theme of *Paradise Regained* and the corresponding interpretation of the conflict in *Samson Agonistes* are set forth in a different connection in my article *The Temptation Motive in Milton, Studies in Philology,* XV (1918). 176–194.

motive from time to time appears). It is rather a pictorial map of the moral universe, a representation of the happier inner Paradise of life according to right reason, an image of redemption in the only sense in which Milton in his maturer years could even pretend to understand redemption.

The theme was one which commanded the full resources of a life of meditative study, not in the dubious realms of demonology and Christian myth, but in the sun-clear walks of moral and religious wisdom, in history and political philosophy, in the biography of good men and great, in the exalted teachings of poet and seer, most of all in the gospels taken in their plain historical and moral sense, and such a theme gave Milton the opportunity to be altogether his humanistic self. In *Paradise Lost* he had been committed to a more or less inflexible story and to a traditional system of ideas which his best endeavor could not wholly rationalize or adopt to his own more individual thought, with the result that though his imagination was stimulated to unexampled activity, the work is but an imperfect and distorted image of his philosophical point of view. In *Paradise Regained* he was largely free. It is no wonder that he resented the suggestion that the second work was inferior to the first. Though lacking in color and vivid outward incident, it had even its points of superority. Its drama was of an inward intensity like that of the Book of Job. Its truth was unmixed with the accessory element of fiction. To Milton, in the severity of his age, this was argument of excellence. He knew, moreover, that the poem was more harmonious than *Paradise Lost,* simpler if less sensuous, and woven more close in "matter, form, and style."

It is now possible to consider the less obvious position of *Samson Agonistes* in Milton's poetic scheme. Formally and theologically the poem has no relation at all to its predecessors. For Milton does not, in his interpretation of the Old Testament material, adopt the point of view of the medieval religious drama, which built everything it treated into a single structure, regarding the events and characters of Hebrew history as episodes in an action which proceeded logically from the creation of the angels to the day of judgment. The story of Samson has for him an independent human value, neither implying nor prefiguring the life of Christ. For this very reason it adapts itself more naturally to his purposes, and affords the means of completing his representation of the state of man. The function of Christ we have already seen. He is, besides being the redeemer, the second Adam and the model man. But unlike Adam, Christ is without sin. Hence while he is the pattern and guide of human life, his victory is not, as ours must be, a recovery of something lost. The full account of man in his relation to the forces of good and evil demands another picture — the representation of frail humanity, burdened with the memory of former sin, but now repentant, restored to strength, and wrestling successfully with further trial. To what extent can *Samson Agonistes* be shown to fit this ideal prescription? The question raises some points of interpretation which appear to have been neglected by the numerous critics who, since Samuel Johnson, have discussed the merits of the work as drama.

When Milton, in 1641, first considered the life of the great but erring Hebrew champion as possible literary material and set down five subjects from it in the Cambridge manuscript, he was doubtless prompted chiefly by the coincidence of the story with characteristic themes of ancient drama. Samson was blind through his own guilt like Oedipus. In all other respects he was a Hebraic Herakles — the performer of incredible labors, enthralled by woman, sealing his baffled strength by a final destructive act. Such circumstances meant much in Milton's predisposition to a literary theme. More influential, however, in his final decision in favor of the subject was his perception of the parallel between Samson's sin and that of Adam. The point had already impressed itself upon him when he wrote of Adam's fall in the Ninth Book of *Paradise Lost*,

> So rose the Danite strong,
> Herculean Samson from the harlot lap
> Of Philistean Dalilah, and waked
> Shorn of his strength, they desolate and bare
> Of all their virtue.[5]

[5] Lines 1059–1062.

In the tragedy itself he is concerned with the fallen Samson's recovery of God's lost favor. The process involves his punishment and repentance, and the facing of new trials with a firmness won of experience and faith. It involves also a reward in the consciousness of God's having again accepted him as a worthy instrument of his purposes.

The trial itself is, I believe, the real center of the inward action, providing the play with such vital dramatic conflict as it exhibits. The Chorus and Manoa continually suggest distrust and compromise. They imply, in their attempted consolation, that Samson has been deceived in his belief that he once enjoyed God's special favor and was his chosen vessel. His marriages were not, as he had supposed, of a divine suggestion. God's dealings in sending the angel of his birth and apparently electing him as the champion of Israel, only to desert and leave him impotent, are unintelligible, if not unjust, for all has been turned to the glory of the Philistines. Against this Samson opposes, on the whole, the attitude of faith. He resists the suggestion that God was not really with him in the past. He reiterates the cry that nothing of all his evils has befallen him but justly. He meets the challenge of Manoa's

> Yet Israel still serves with all his tribes,

with the rejoinder that it is they themselves who through their own weakness have neglected God's proposed deliverance. For himself he knows that he has forfeited all hope, but he remains unshaken in the belief that God will not

> Connive, or linger, thus provoked,
> But will arise, and his great name assert.

Throughout the dialogue there are marked similarities to the Book of Job. Manoa and the Chorus have a function analogous to that of the friends who sharpen Job's agony by their mistaken comfort. Samson's resistance of the attempt to shake the convictions of his innermost experience has its counterpart in Job's passionate denial of the imputation of unrighteousness. There is, of course, a formal contrast between the two, in that Samson, unlike Job, is afflicted by a sense of sin, but both are loyal to truth and both maintain their positions against the apparent facts. Both, finally, are rewarded for their consistency by a manifestation of God's approval. With Job it is the voice out of a whirlwind, with Samson the renewal of "rousing motions" of innermost impulse, which have stirred and guided him to great deeds before his fall.

Of these motives there is in the Scriptural account of Samson not the slightest hint. The hero of the Hebrew chronicle is a naïve and semi-humorous märchen figure, whose sluggish intellect is far removed from any capability of spiritual conflict. Milton preserves the traits of his impulsiveness of temper and his original simplicity of spirit, but endows him, after his disillusionment, with extraordinary force of mind and with penetrating insight. The infusion into this mighty champion of old, of the complex emotions of the maturest and most profound creation of Hebrew thought, is the last masterful stroke of Milton's genius. For it, he had, to my knowledge, no precedent in literary tradition.

But if Milton is indebted to Job for the most essential elements in his conception of Samson's character, it is to his own constructive imagination, working within the artistic forms provided by occidental drama, that he owes the development of his theme. In the Book of Job there is little outward action and no clear progression. In *Samson* there are both. The framework of the plot is that of a Greek play. It is simple even to meagerness. Samson is consoled by the Chorus, worried by Dalilah, insulted by Harapha, summoned before the Philistines by an officer. Old Manoa is busy meanwhile with misguided plans for his release, the moment of his success ironically coinciding with that of Samson's death. A messenger relates the catastrophe. The Chorus sings of Samson's fate and triumph.

Within this formal action the spiritual movement is richer than one at first observes. At the opening Samson is a spectacle of tragic misery and debasement. Out of his intense depression there rises higher and higher the note of active pain. At first his utterance concerns chiefly his physical and outward state:

O loss of sight, of thee I most complain!
Blind among enemies! O worse than chains,
Dungeon or beggery, or decrepit age!

The first chorus, unheard by the protagonist, echoes and interprets his lament, with emphasis on the contrast between what once he was, is now. In the ensuing dialogue Samson's attention is diverted from his present wretchedness to its causes and significance. The memory of his fault is more bitter than the punishment wherewith it has been visited.

Ye see, O friends,
How many evils have enclosed me round;
Yet that which once was the worst now least afflicts me,
Blindness, for had I sight, confused with shame,
How could I once look up, or heave the head,
Who, like a foolish pilot, have shipwracked
My vessel trusted to me from above.

The sight of Manoa wakes "another inward grief," and his words are as a goad to Samson's bitter remembrance. His proposal to treat with the Philistine lords serves only to reveal his son's indifference to his outward fate. The scene culminates in a spiritual outburst, expressive no longer of the hero's physical misery and obvious disgrace,

Ensnared, assaulted, overcome, led bound,
Thy foes' derision, captive, poor, and blind,

but of the inner agony of soul which springs from full contemplation of his sins, "and sense of Heaven's desertion." The opening words of the passage clearly indicate the forward movement:

Oh, that torment should not be confined
To the body's wounds and sores,
With maladies innumerable
In heart, head, breast, and reins,
But must secret passage find
To the inmost mind,
There exercise all his fierce accidents,
And on her purest spirits prey,
As on entrails, joints, and limbs,
With answerable pains, but more intense,
Though void of corporal sense! [6]

[6] Lines 606–616.

The conclusion is one of unrelieved despair and marks the darkest moment of Samson's suffering, corresponding precisely to Adam's remorseful misery as he meditates upon his sin:

> Hopeless are all my evils, all remediless.
> This one prayer yet remains, might I be heard,
> No long petition — speedy death,
> The close of all my miseries and the balm.

Henceforth we have recovery. By confronting his own guilt without evasion, and by resisting the temptation to doubt God's ways are just, or to fear for the ultimate triumph of his cause, Samson has won the right to be put to proof a second time. His firmness is subjected first to the insidious approaches of Dalilah, whose visit, however doubtfully motivated in itself, is essential to the idea of the drama. Her plea is specious, but Samson remains unmoved, the significance of his victory being pointed out in the choric comment,

> Yet beauty, though injurious, hath strange power,
> After offence returning, to regain
> Love once possessed, nor can be easily
> Repulsed, without much inward passion felt
> And secret sting of amorous remorse.

He next confronts physical force in the person of Harapha, who collapses, like all brute menace, before the champion's indifference to fear, and the chorus, participating for the moment in Samson's strength, sings the great ode,

> O how comely it is, and how reviving,
> When God into the hands of their deliverer
> Puts invincible might,
> To quell the mighty of the earth, the oppressor,
> The brute and boistrous force of violent men.[7]

They are, of course, like Samson himself, still blind to what is to come, and they go on to sing of patience as the final crown of saints.

The coming of the officer creates a problem. Samson's refusal, at first, to do his bidding illustrates his uncompromising alle-

[7] Lines 1267 ff.

giance to the God of his fathers and his contempt of personal safety. The Chorus suggests the easier way of yielding, pointing out the fact that he has already served the Philistines (with the old implication that he cannot regard himself as a being set apart). Their reasoning is met with a clear distinction between compromise in things indifferent and the surrender of a point of conscience. Then, as if in answer to this final proof of Samson's single devotedness to God's service, comes again the inner prompting, " disposing to something extraordinary my thoughts." He obeys it unhesitatingly and goes forth under divine guidance as of old. He has, in a sense, regained his own lost Paradise, and in his story Milton, by vindicating the power of a free but erring will to maintain itself in obedience and be restored to grace, has again asserted eternal Providence and justified the ways of God to man.

The fact that Samson is an Old Testament figure and achieves his triumph before the time of the Redeemer shows the true place of Christ in Milton's system. The blood of his sacrifice is plainly no necessary instrument of salvation; even his example may be dispensed with by those who enjoy a direct and special relation with the Divine. Yet the Hebrews did have Christ in prophecy, and for the men of later time he is the way. By his present example the path is open, not for chosen heroes alone, but for all, to

> love with fear the only God, to walk
> As in his presence, ever to observe
> His providence, and on him sole depend,
> Merciful over all his works, with good
> Still overcoming evil, and by small
> Accomplishing great things — by things deemed weak
> Subverting worldly-strong, and worldly-wise
> By simply meek; [8]

Such is Milton's final teaching and the ethical goal of his poetic art. The desire expressed in the introduction to Book IX of *Paradise Lost* to sing " the better fortitude of patience and heroic martyrdom," is fulfilled by the portrayal of a divine pattern in *Paradise Regained*. *Samson Agonistes* is its nearest

[8] *P. L.*, XII. 562–569.

possible fulfillment in the life of mortal man. To embody it more completely by representing the humbler trials and victories of daily life would have been incompatible with the tradition of Milton's literary allegiance — incompatible, too, with the memory of the heroic struggle in which he himself had been engaged.

Of this experience and this struggle I have as yet said nothing. How deeply it enters into the bone and sinew of *Samson Agonistes* no one can doubt. That Milton felt the parallel between his own situation and that of Samson and that he in some way identified himself with his hero is obvious and has been emphasized by the biographers. I have myself elsewhere pointed out that in making Samson wrestle with despair Milton was championing his own faith assaulted by inward murmuring and challenged by the apparent failure of his cause.[9] It remains to enquire as to the extent and nature of this personal identification and to analyze more exactly the psychological reactions, conscious and unconscious, which are implied in the composition of the play.

Let us recognize at once that *Samson Agonistes* is a work of art and not a disguised autobiography. To a reader unacquainted with Milton's life the poem would seem as monumentally independent as *Prometheus Bound.* It deserves to be so judged and would, perhaps, stand higher as a masterpiece of art if it had been less often used as an illustration of Milton's personal life and temper. It should not, however, suffer from interpretation in the light of the poet's characteristic moods and thoughts, if we clearly recognize the conditions of their operation in his creative work. His most intimate emotions are invariably sublimated by the imagination and so far depersonalized. The process enables him to project himself with sympathy into characters and situations which have only a partial analogy with his own. So it is with his representations of Comus, or of Satan and Adam in *Paradise Lost.* In other cases, as in those of Dalilah, Eve, or Mammon he is capable, within a limited range, of being as objective as any artist of essentially romantic temper.

In the representation of Samson, Milton has undoubtedly put

[9] *Studies in Philology,* XV. 176–194.

more of himself than in any other of his imaginative creations. The sense of power and dignity, the "plain heroic magnitude of mind," the will toward championship are Milton. So too is the noble self-pity, expressed in the consciousness of deprivation in the loss of sight ("The sun to me is dark, and silent as the moon"), and the feeling of physical helplessness ("In power of others, never in my own"). But all this is heightened and idealized for purposes of art. The tragic gloom and flat despair of Samson, the wretchedness of pain, the distaste of life, are the embodiments of an aesthetic mood which owes quite as much to literature as to personal experience. As a matter of fact the impression left by such direct biographical records as we have of Milton in old age is quite the reverse of this, suggesting the persistence in him to the end of a temper unspoiled by tribulation. The "cheerful godliness" of Wordsworth's sonnet appears to be an entirely appropriate description of the poet's habitual outward mood in the last years of his life.

With regard to his blindness it is worth noting that the most poignant allusions to it were written longest after the event itself. At the actual moment of the catastrophe Milton was silent. His poetical occupation in the immediately succeeding years was the translation of Psalms, a literary and religious discipline. In 1654 he gives expression in prose, not to his sense of irrecoverable loss, but to the consciousness of spiritual compensation in "an interior illumination more precious and more pure."[10] In 1655, on the third anniversary of his loss of sight, he allows himself to consider how his "light is spent ere half his days," and to give voice to the pathos of his condition, only, however, as a preparation for the expression of acquiescence and of the consolations which come from the sense of having sacrificed himself in a noble cause. The utterances in *Paradise Lost* are touched with a deeper pathos, but it is first in *Samson,* where they are no longer directly personal, that they become a tragic cry:

> Dark, dark, dark, amid the blaze of moon,
> Irrecoverably dark, total eclipse,
> Without all hope of day.

[10] *Defensio Secunda, Prose Works* (Bohn), I. 239.

A similar account might be given of the poet's antifeminism. It is entirely absent from the sonnets which belong to the days of his estrangement from Mary Powell. Indeed the two poems written at that time, *To a Virtuous Young Lady* and *To the Lady Margaret Ley,* are sincere though sober tributes to female virtue. The general indictment of the sex begins with Adam's words to Eve in Book X of *Paradise Lost* and reaches a strain of unrelieved bitterness in *Samson Agonistes.*

Such are the facts, as we read them in the chronological consideration of Milton's works. One cannot fail to be struck by the analogy which exists between the processes of the poet's expression of certain phases of his inmost experience in this last epoch of his literary life and the youthful development which we have studied in the preceding essay. The position of *Samson Agonistes* in its relation to the complex of emotions and ideas which centered in the poet's blindness is singularly like that of *Comus* with reference to the conflict of sensuous and ideal impulses in his adolescence. Each represents the culmination of a train of introspective thoughts which may easily be conceived to have been disturbing to Milton's mental equilibrium. In each work he appears to achieve for the first time a full expression of these emotions, and in achieving it to obtain a spiritual mastery of them. The result is one which is always, perhaps, in some degree present in the intenser activity of the creative imagination, and it has received general recognition from the critics and philosophers of literature. The most luminous statement is the following by Croce in his *Aesthetic.*[11] "By elaborating his impressions man frees himself from them. By objectifying them, he removes them from him and makes himself their superior. The liberating and purifying function of art is another aspect and another formula of its character as activity. Activity is the deliverer, just because it drives away passivity. This also explains why it is usual to attribute to artists both the maximum of sensibility and the maximum of insensibility or Olympian serenity. The two characters are compatible, for they do not refer to the same object. The sensibility or passion re-

[11] Chapter 2. Douglas Ainsley's translation, 1922.

lates to the rich material which the artist absorbs into his psychic organism, the insensibility or serenity to the form with which he subdues and dominates the tumult of sensations and passions."

It is scarcely possible to determine the degree to which Milton, in recreating and transforming emotions which in their rawer form made inroads upon his carefully cherished serenity, experienced a similar deliverance. Some light may be gained, however, by a consideration of certain neglected aspects of the play itself, the indications, namely, which the poet has given of what he himself thought of its function as a work of art. These indications refer mainly, to be sure, to what he looked for in its effect upon the reader or spectator, but they are not without application to the artist as well and it seems to me quite clear that Milton must have been guided in his interpretation of the power of tragedy to effect spiritual benefits upon others by what he had himself experienced in creating it.

The question centers in his understanding of the formula for tragedy and its purgative effect as given in the famous Aristotelian definition. The importance of this formula in Milton's thought and the degree to which he must have been conscious of it in constructing his drama are suggested by the fact that he quotes it in Latin on his title page and devotes the first part of his prose preface to its elaboration. His opening statement is as follows: "Tragedy as it was anciently composed hath been ever held the gravest, moralest, and most profitable of all other poems; therefore said by Aristotle to be of power by raising pity and fear, or terror, to purge the mind of those and such like passions, that is to temper and reduce them to just measure with a kind of delight, stirred up by seeing those passions well imitated."

In considering the application of this principle to *Samson Agonistes* we must observe, first of all, that, by representing a clearly marked triumph of the human will over its own weakness, and by the substitution of Providence for blind fate as the power which overrules the action, the play provides material for a different understanding of catharsis from that contemplated by Aristotle, an understanding which falls in with the first part of Milton's description — that tragedy is the gravest, moralest, and most profitable of poetic forms — rather than with the last — that it transforms painful emotions into pleasurable. On a superficial view we might, indeed, be tempted to regard the purgation, as Milton actually worked it out, as a purely ethical and religious process, the result of a consciously didactic purpose by which our faith is strengthened and our sympathy with Samson's pain swallowed up in our exultation in his triumph. It is the function of Manoa's last speech and of the final chorus to emphasize this motive:

> Come, come, no time for lamentation now,
> Nor much more cause; Samson hath quit himself
> Like Samson, and heroicly hath finished
> A life Heroic. . . .
> With God not parted from him as was feared,
> But favouring and assisting to the end.
> . . . .
> All is best, though we oft doubt,
> What the unsearchable dispose
> Of highest wisdom brings about
> And ever best found in the close.

To some critics [12] these quotations have seemed an adequate formula for the poem as a whole, and a mark of the failure of *Samson Agonistes* to embody the genuinely tragic motive of the unsuccessful struggle of man with fate. Such a judgment is obvious and in part correct. It fails, however, to take account of the actuality of the tragic impression which the drama must leave upon every reader who comes to it unhampered by definitions and comparisons. The pain of the earlier scenes is something which cannot be so easily displaced. Sealed as it is with the hero's death, it outlives all consolation, as the tragic suffering of Hamlet outlives the accomplishment of his purpose, the choric benediction of Horatio, and the restoration of a wholesome commonwealth by Fortinbras. The pronouncement "All is best" is of scarcely more avail than the identical formulae which bring Greek plays to their conclusion and from which this

[12] See Paull F. Baum, *Samson Agonistes Again, Publications of the Modern Language Association,* XXXVI (1921). 365 ff.

one is derived. The consolation which is offered of "what can quiet us in a death so noble" is not enough. Samson should have gone on from one glad triumph to another and emerged unscathed. Outward circumstance, the treacheries of others, and his own conspiring fault have brought him low, and have constrained him to wear, however gloriously, the crown of martyrdom. Here surely is tragedy enough. Though Providence is proclaimed, its ways are dark and its face, at times, is hardly to be distinguished from the countenance of Fate herself. The secret is that there remains an irreducible element in the midst of Milton's faith — a sense as keen as Shakespeare's of the reality of suffering which neither the assurance of God's special favors to himself nor his resolute insistence on the final triumph of his righteousness can blot out. The antique strain in Milton's experience and thought stands side by side with the Christian, and the two alternate or combine in their domination of his artistic moods. It is in vain that he repudiates stoicism as a futile refuge and a false philosophy; he is betrayed by the vehemence of his declarations against it, and he instinctively adopts its weapons.

These considerations prepare us to examine the operation in *Samson Agonistes* of catharsis in its strict Aristotelian sense. Milton's effort to demonstrate in his drama the truth of Aristotle's pronouncement is part and parcel of a thoroughgoing conscious classicism, which extends far beyond such matters as the ordering of the incidents and the employment of ancient devices like the messenger. It is shown in a more philosophic and intrinsic way in the subtle turns which the poet gives to the interpretation of his theme in order to bring it more nearly into conformity with the spirit of ancient tragedy. Professor Baum [13] counts it a major defect of *Samson Agonistes* that the hero's tragic fault is undignified and sub-heroic. But observe the means which Milton takes to dignify it. He associates it with the most dignified of all tragic faults — rebellious pride. Intoxicated by success Samson forgets to refer his victories to their source, and so becomes, in Milton's interpretation, an instance of

[13] *Loc. cit.*

classical hybris. Like Shakespeare's Mark Anthony he "struts to his destruction."

> Fearless of danger, like a petty God,
> I walked about, admired of all, and dreaded
> On hostile ground, none daring my assault.
> Then swollen with pride, into the snare I fell
> Of fair fallacious looks, venerial trains.[14]

This is somewhat forced, one must confess, and Milton appears to be aware of it. Witness the shading he is compelled to give to the idea in the following:

> But I
> God's counsel have not kept, his holy secret
> Presumptiously have published, impiously,
> *Weakly at least and shamefully* — a sin
> That Gentiles in their parables condemn
> To their Abyss and horrid pains confined.[15]

The cloak of Prometheus and Tantalus evidently refuses to fit the less majestic Hebrew Titan. The conception of hybris and Ate applies more perfectly to the Philistines and is accordingly invoked in the triumphant semi-chorus beginning in line 1669:

> While their hearts were jocund and sublime,
> Drunk with idolatry, drunk with wine
> And fat regorged of bulls and goats,
> Chaunting their idol, and preferring
> Before our Living Dread, who dwells
> In Silo, his bright sanctuary,
> Among them he a spirit of phrenzy sent,
> Who hurt their minds,
> And urged them on with mad desire
> To call in haste for their destroyer.
> They, only set on sport and play,
> Unweetingly importuned
> Their own destruction to come speedy upon them.
> So fond are mortal men,
> Fallen into wrath divine,
> As their own ruin on themselves to invite,
> Insensate left, or to sense reprobate,
> And with blindness internal struck.

Both passages, however, are illustrative of the degree to which Milton had grasped the central motive of Greek tragedy and

[14] Lines 529–533.

[15] Lines 496–501.

the pains he was at to bring his own material under the ethical, religious, and artistic formulae afforded by it.

A more vital result of his assimilation of the point of view of his ancient models is to be found in the great chorus which follows Samson's deeper expression of despair, in lines 608–650. If anything in Milton or indeed in all modern literature deserves to be called a reproduction of antiquity it is this passage. It is as perfectly representative as Milton could have wished of "Aeschylus, Sophocles, Euripides, the three tragic poets unequalled yet by any, and the best rule to all who endeavor to write Tragedy," and it comes little short of their noblest choral odes in the grandeur and intensity of its tragic feeling. In the majestic rhythms of the opening the Chorus sings of the vanity of consolation in the ears of the afflicted and expostulates with Providence in its uneven course with men. Thoroughly Greek and as thoroughly Miltonic is the centering of attention on the woes, not of the common rout of men who grow up and perish like the summer fly, but on those of heroic mould, "with gifts and graces eminently adorned." The ensuing lines embody the idea of the excess of evil which rains down on the head of the tragic hero according to Aristotle's description in the *Poetics:*

> Nor only dost degrade them, or remit
> To life obscured, which were a fair dismission,
> But throw'st them lower than thou didst exalt them high —
> Unseemly falls in human eye,
> Too grievous for the trespass or omission;
> Oft leav'st them to the hostile sword
> Of heathen and profane, their carcasses
> To dogs and fowls a prey, or else captived,
> Or to the unjust tribunals, under change of times,
> And condemnation of the ungrateful multitude.
> If these they escape, perhaps in poverty
> With sickness and disease thou bow'st them down,
> Painful diseases and deformed,
> In crude old age;
> Though not disordinate, yet causeless suffering
> The punishment of dissolute days. In fine,
> Just or unjust alike seem miserable,
> For oft alike both come to evil end.

The personal note here is too distinct to be mistaken. "Unjust tribunals under change of times," "their carcasses to dogs and fowls a prey" are certainly echoes of the Restoration, with its brutal trials of men like Henry Vane, and the indignities to which the bodies of Cromwell and Ireton were subjected. The parallel and not less wretched fate of poverty and disease is Milton's own. He goes so far as almost to specify the rheumatic ills from which we know him to have suffered — "painful diseases and deformed" — with the bitter reflection that these afflictions, justly the fruit of dissipation, may come also to those who, like himself, have lived in temperance. Nowhere else in his works, not even in the laments of Adam, does Milton permit himself to indulge in so unrelieved an expression of pagan sentiment. He does so under the shield of dramatic objectivity, yet none of his words spring from deeper sources in his consciousness. Here momentarily he faces the world with no other arms than those of pure humanity, giving utterance to a view of life directly opposed to that to which he had subdued his thinking as a whole.

It is in such a mood as this and in such an utterance that Milton must, if ever, have felt, in his own emotional experience, the reality of the Aristotelian catharsis, and the need of it. The question of the means whereby affliction may be soothed is one which had always interested him, and his works contain numerous suggestive utterances on the subject. It is prominent in the discussion of the case of Samson. Thus, contemplating, at this point, his hero's misery, he makes the Chorus tell how useless for the sufferer in his pangs are those wise consolations of philosophy, "writ with studied argument, lenient of grief and anxious thought." It is only, they affirm, by "secret refreshings from above" that the afflicted wretch can be restored. But such refreshings are obviously not always to be commanded. To prepare for their benign influence the mind must first be emptied of its pent-up bitterness, and for such a process tragedy, in the Aristotelian conception, supplies the means. So, one would suppose, might Milton have thought and felt. And if such was his experience it is not surprising that he should have dwelt with such insistence on the rationale of the process in his prose preface.

His initial statement I have already quoted. Pity, fear, and like passions, it implies, are, in their raw state, dangerous and painful. Objectively represented, they are tempered and reduced to just measure by a kind of delight. "Nor is Nature," adds Milton, "wanting in her own effects to make good his assertion; for so, in Physic, things of melancholic hue and quality are used against melancholy, sour against sour, salt to remove salt humours." This passage has often been cited with approval by classical scholars as expressing the soundest modern interpretation of the dark oracle of Aristotle's pronouncement, and there has been discussion of Milton's priority in employing the medical analogy. No one, I think, has called attention to his application of this conception to the analysis of Samson's spiritual ills in an outstanding passage in the play itself. The hero has just expressed his indifference to the efforts proposed in his behalf and his expectation of an early death. Manoa replies:

> Believe not these suggestions, which proceed
> From anguish of the mind, and humours black
> That mingle with thy fancy.[16]

There follows the great lyric outburst of Samson's spiritual woe, which must now be given at greater length.

> O that torment should not be confined
> To the body's wounds and sores,
> With maladies innumerable
> In heart, head, breast, and reins;
> But must secret passage find
> To the inmost mind,
> There exercise all his fierce accidents,
> And on her purest spirits prey,
> As on entrails, joints and limbs,
> With answerable pains, but more intense,
> Though void of corporal sense!
> My griefs not only pain me
> As a lingering disease,
> But, finding no redress, ferment and rage;
> Nor less than wounds immedicable
> Rankle, and fester, and gangrene,
> To black mortification.
> Thoughts, my tormentors, armed with deadly stings,
> Mangle my apprehensive tenderest parts,

[16] Lines 599–601.

Exasperate, exulcerate, and raise
Dire inflammation, which no cooling herb
Or medicinal liquor can assuage,
Nor breath of vernal air from snowy Alp.
Sleep hath forsook and given me o'er
To death's benumbing opium as my only cure;
Thence faintings, swoonings of despair,
And sense of Heaven's desertion.

The idea which Milton here develops with somewhat shocking explicitness is obviously the same as that which underlies his conception of catharsis—the idea, namely, that the passions operate in precisely the manner of bodily poisons, which, when they find no outlet, rage destructively within. Samson is given over to pity and fear, and there is no apparent prospect of relief, no cooling herb or medicinal liquor to purify the "black mortification" of his thoughts. It is quite clear, then, that Milton intends to suggest a kind of Aristotelian diagnosis of Samson's tragic state, parallel to the more obvious religious interpretation which I have previously expounded. But if he partly identified himself with his hero, then such a diagnosis would serve also to that extent to describe his own. As, however, he draws a sharp distinction on the religious side between Samson's spiritual darkness and his own illumination by an inner light, so here he must have been conscious of a difference in the manner of their deliverance from the morbid introspection to which they are equally subject. The intensity of Samson's pain lasts only so long as he remains inactive. His lyric elaboration of his inward woe is immediately followed by the unexpected visits of his foes. His attention is thus distracted from his suffering to a series of situations which confront him and he finally loses himself in glorious though disastrous action.

For Milton, in the impotence of his situation after the Restoration, there can be no such deliverance. He is enrolled perforce among those "whom patience finally must crown." But he has in his possession a recourse without which the way of patience is at times too hard. The purgation which the untutored champion of Israel must find in deeds is available to the man of culture through the activity of the mind and spirit. It offers itself to Milton in a dual form, corresponding to his twofold inheritance from the Reformation and the Renaissance. As the play draws to an end the two motives are subtly balanced and as nearly reconciled as, perhaps, it is within the power of human skill to reconcile them. The champion's final deed and the triumph of God's uncontrollable intent promote in us a sense of exultation and confirm our faith, but the greatness of his suffering and the pathos of his death produce a different effect, making possible the serene dismission of the close:

> His servants he, with new acquist
> Of true experience from this great event,
> With peace and consolation hath dismissed
> And calm of mind, all passion spent.

It is characteristic of the critical self-consciousness which Milton carries with him even in his moments of highest creative inspiration and suggestive also of the vital uses to which he turned aesthetic as well as religious doctrine that the last word of all should be an almost explicit reference to the tragic formula which he had derived from the authority of "the master of those who know."

THE RELIGIOUS THOUGHT OF DONNE IN RELATION TO MEDIEVAL AND LATER TRADITIONS

THE RELIGIOUS THOUGHT OF DONNE IN RELATION TO MEDIEVAL AND LATER TRADITIONS

LOUIS I. BREDVOLD

THE term "metaphysical poetry," consecrated by use since the time of Dryden, has been a fruitful source of misunderstanding of Donne and his followers. It originated at a time when the metaphysical style was regarded as a literary fad or affection, an intellectual gymnastic. Donne, said Dryden, "affects the metaphysics, not only in his satires, but in his amorous verses, where nature should reign; and perplexes the minds of the fair sex with nice speculations of philosophy, when he should engage their hearts, and entertain them with the softnesses of love." Dr. Johnson, in a famous passage, spoke of the *discordia concors* of the metaphysical style as of a mere exhibition of ingenuity. The reader, "though he sometimes admires, is seldom pleased;" and the desire of these poets, Johnson thought, "was only to say what they hoped had never been said before." Dryden and Johnson provided the fundamental ideas and set the tone for succeeding scholarship and criticism down to comparatively recent times. Even so different a critic as Hazlitt praised fervently Johnson's denunciation of the "conceitists."[1] Hallam thought that in the poetry of Donne "it would perhaps be difficult to select three passages that we should care to read again."[2] Masson, indeed, ventured the surmise that "the admiration of his contemporaries was not a mere pretence," but he could nevertheless see in Donne's verses only mental acrobatics.[3] "Metaphysical poetry" suggested only a meaningless preoccupation with the forms of a decayed scholasticism.

[1] Hazlitt, *The Comic Writers,* Lecture III.

[2] Hallam, *Literature of Europe* (2d ed.; London, 1843), II. 31–33.

[3] Masson, *Life of Milton* (Boston, 1859), I. 377.

Since Masson, criticism of Donne and his followers has become much more enlightened and sympathetic, and the studies of them are too numerous to be discussed here. But the most important recent contributions, by Courthope, Palmer, and Grierson, have in common, very significantly, that they attempt to explain the metaphysical style as the result of the manner in which these poets understood and experienced life. They all relate the school of Donne to the general movement of the Renaissance, in its modern conception since Burckhardt,[4] that is, as a disintegration of Medievalism and a liberation of the individual. Palmer thought that Donne belonged to the second phase of the development of this new individualism.

> " A second period of the Renaissance began," he says, " a period of introspection, where each man was prone to insist on the importance of whatever was his own. At the coming of the Stuarts this great change was prepared, and was steadily fostered by their inability to comprehend it. In science, Bacon had already questioned established authority and sent men to nature to observe for themselves. In government, the king's prerogative was speedily questioned, and Parliament became so rebellious that they were often dismissed. A revolution in poetic taste was under way. Spenser's lulling rhythms and bloodless heroes were being displaced by the jolting and passionate realism of Donne. . . . The soul of man took the place of the outer world, while the old delight in daring and difficult tasks appeared in this new sphere as a kind of intellectual audacity and an ardent exploration of mental enigmas. To how many strange theories did this England of the first half of the seventeenth century give rise! To exploit a new doctrine became more exciting than a voyage to the Spanish main."[5]

Courthope insisted that the school of " wit " which developed simultaneously in all the literatures of Europe must be " the result of the operation of similar forces, religious, social and political, and of the influence of some wide-spread literary tradition."[6] Its essential characteristics, paradox, hyperbole, and

[4] On the importance of Burckhardt's work in laying the foundations of modern study of the Renaissance, see Walter Goetz, *Mittelalter und Renaissance, Historische Zeitschrift*, 98 (1907). 30–54, and Émile Gebhart, *La Renaissance Italienne et la Philosophie de l'Histoire, Revue des Deux Mondes*, 72 (1885). 342–379.

[5] *The English Works of George Herbert* (ed. G. H. Palmer; Boston, 1905), I. 98–99, 155–156.

[6] *Pope's Works* (ed. Elwell and Courthope; London, 1889), V. 52–61.

excess of metaphor, he traced to the survival of Medievalism; but they were only the fragments of a decayed age. Many poets of the Renaissance, characterized by "a new kind of Pyrrhonism" represented by Montaigne, "seized upon the rich materials of the old and ruined philosophy to decorate the structures which they built out of their lawless fancy. On such foundations rose the school of metaphysical wit, of which the earliest and most remarkable example is furnished in the poetry of John Donne."[7] Grierson, likewise, explains the metaphysical style as a blending of the "dialectic of the Schools" with the "new temper of the Renaissance."[8]

These three students therefore agree, though with varying emphasis and interpretation, on the fundamental principle that the metaphysical style is an expression of the disintegration of medieval thought under the influence of the new individualism and scepticism of the Renaissance.

Rather surprisingly, a still more recent study seeks to minimize the Renaissance element in Donne.[9] The author, Mary Paton Ramsay, is a disciple of Professor Picavet of Paris, whose special contribution to the history of medieval philosophy has been an emphasis on the strong Plotinian element in it. And it is in the most complete discipleship to M. Picavet that Miss Ramsay has written her study of Donne; she sought to explain by the persistence of this medieval Plotinian tradition "la mentalité du poète lui-même, et celle de sa génération."[10] She therefore ignores the Pyrrhonism, not only in Donne, but in the English Renaissance as a whole. "Nos remarques," she says, "sont limitées à la littérature, mais nous croyons pouvoir affirmer qu'il ne faut pas parler de l'esprit sceptique dans la première partie du [dixseptième] siècle. L'esprit de critique sceptique ne fit vraiment son apparition en Angleterre qu'avec

[7] Courthope, *History of English Poetry* (London, 1911), III. 103–117, 147–148.

[8] *The Poems of John Donne* (Oxford, 1912), II, *Introduction.*

[9] *Les Doctrines Médiévales chez Donne, Le Poète Métaphysicien de l'Angleterre* (Oxford, 1917). I have discussed the methods and results of this study in a review in *The Journal of English and Germanic Philology,* XXI (1922). 347–353.

[10] *Op. cit.,* p. 2.

Hobbes." [11] John Donne was, she believes, a thorough Plotinian, untouched by metaphysical doubts.

> " Chez lui," she says of the poet, " on découvre, en étudiant à fond ses écrits en prose et en vers, un penseur profondément religieux en même temps que fermement convaincu de la valeur de la raison humaine. . . . Dans les hautes régions de la spéculation métaphysique dont les docteurs du moyen âge lui montraient le chemin, il n'y avait pas de place pour les doutes. Des doutes pouvaient tourmenter Donne devant des questions ecclésiastiques mêlées à des conceptions politiques, ou devant son propre coeur conscient de faiblesse et de péché. Mais non quand son esprit s'élève à ces hauteurs. Alors l'idée crée l'expression qui lui convient et nous voyons ce que Donne est capable de produire comme poète." [12]

In other words, the mind of Donne, both as poet and preacher, was seriously and consistently medieval and untouched by the storm and stress of the Renaissance.

We may object at once that this conception of Donne as an exponent of Plotinianism simplifies beyond recognition his complex and enigmatic personality and removes from the story of his inner life that element of dramatic uncertainty and suspense which makes his biography so fascinating. For Donne cannot be explained by any mere systematization of his ideas. His riddle must be read by a sympathetic appreciation of his personality, his greed for knowledge and experience, his difficulties, disappointments and dissatisfactions, and the increasing depth and intensity of his religious feeling; the final study of Donne must be biographical. And yet Donne was obviously a learned man, whose mind had been enriched by many cultural traditions, whose personal feeling and literary expression were conditioned by medieval and Renaissance modes of thought. In another place I have discussed the traditional aspect of Donne's early verse.[13] In this paper I propose to study in a similar way certain aspects of his intellectual and religious experience, his mingled scepticism and mysticism, with the double purpose of tracing his religious development and of re-stating, with special emphasis on some hitherto neglected phases, his relation to

[11] *Ibid.*, pp. 11–12. [12] *Ibid.*, p. 18.

[13] *The Naturalism of Donne in Relation to Some Renaissance Traditions*, in *The Journal of English and Germanic Philology*, Vol. XXII (1923).

medieval thought. The various influences that contributed to his religious experience I shall therefore try to present in their proper biographical, as well as historical, setting.

I

We must, to begin with an effort of the imagination, endeavor to see life as it appeared to the youthful Donne, the law student and courtier in London. He would have been greatly astonished had he heard predicted his future failure at court and his subsequent greatness as a saintly divine. The young man was ambitious for a secular career, and with reason felt himself the master of his fate. He was conscious from the first of very distinguished powers. Educated a Catholic, and anxious to make his way at a Protestant court, he decided to settle for himself the truth about the ecclesiastical question with which he was faced. In his own words, he avoided "any violent and sudden determination till I had, to the measure of my power and judgment, surveyed and digested the whole body of divinity, controverted between our and the Roman Church."[14] This extended study, however, did not lead him to any definite decision, it seems, for some years, although his outward allegiance must have been Protestant. For he soon rose in his profession, saw military service in 1596 with the Earl of Essex, and by 1601 was well on the way to a career. A sensitive, proud, high-bred young man, of great intellectual and personal distinction, he was winning the friendship and confidence of men of prominence in state affairs. After such brilliant prospects, Donne found his career ruined by his secret marriage in 1601.

But Donne had been up to this time something more than an ambitious lawyer and courtier and student of "controverted divinity." Like Bacon, he had taken all knowledge for his province. In a letter, written probably in 1608, he complains that his early study of law was interfered with "by that worst voluptuousness, which is an hydroptic, immoderate desire of

[14] Quoted from *Pseudo-Martyr* (1610), by Gosse, *Life and Letters of John Donne,* I. 25.

human learning and languages — beautiful ornaments to great fortunes; but mine needed an occupation." [15] His restless curiosity in those years led him also into some rather questionable regions of experience and thought, which Walton thought fit to pass over rather lightly in his biography, and which have been largely neglected even by modern scholars. The libertine verse of Donne is no doubt unfit in places for general reading, but as a whole it has a philosophical aspect of such importance that it cannot be ignored in studying the development of the man.[16] In the first place, it is clear from his early verse that Donne was interested in philosophical scepticism, the philosophy of Sextus Empiricus, which had previously so profoundly influenced Montaigne. Whether he studied this recently revived Greek philosophy in Montaigne, or directly in the writings of Sextus Empiricus, or perhaps in both,[17] is not material. Its fascination for him is everywhere evident in his early poems. The cynical *Progresse of the Soule,* written in 1601, closes with an allusion to this mode of thought:

> There's nothing simply good, nor ill alone,
> Of every quality comparison,
> The onely measure is, and judge, opinion.[18]

[15] Gosse, *op. cit.,* I. 191.

[16] I am forced here to use some of the results of my own paper already referred to.

[17] Donne had read Montaigne some time before 1603 or 1604, as appears from a letter in Gosse, *op. cit.,* I. 122. The *Hypotyposes* of Sextus Empiricus had been printed in Greek with a Latin translation, by Henri Estienne, in 1562. This little known publication was in fact, through its influence on Montaigne and others, one of the momentous events in the history of modern thought. It was soon known in England. In 1591 Nashe refers to an English translation, now lost. See Nashe's *Works* (ed. McKerrow), III. 32, and compare also the reference to the "Pironicks," II. 116, and McKerrow's discussion of other borrowings from Sextus, IV. 428 ff. Raleigh's posthumous essay, *Sceptick,* is a fragmentary account of some of the tropes of the Greek sceptics, based directly on Sextus Empiricus, not, as Upham, in his *French Influence in English Literature,* says, on Montaigne. Donne knew the *Hypotyposes* of Sextus as well as the account of Pyrrho in Diogenes Laertius, both of which he quotes in his *Essays in Divinity;* see Jessopp's edition (London, 1855), pp. 67 and 70–71. Compare also a reference to the "sceptic philosophers" in a sermon preached at Whitehall in 1618, in *Works of Donne* (ed. Alford), V. 562.

[18] *Donne's Poetical Works* (ed. H. J. C. Grierson; Oxford, 1912), I. 316.

That this was not merely a passing whim of the young man, must be apparent to the careful reader. For instance, in a letter written in 1613 he remarks: "Except demonstrations," that is, mathematical proofs, "(and perchance there are very few of them) I find nothing without perplexities. I am grown more sensible of it by busying myself a little in the search of the eastern tongues, where a perpetual perplexity in the words cannot choose but cast a perplexity upon the things." [19] The criticism implied is perhaps more one of language than of reason itself, but it indicates a mind disposed to sceptical considerations. And passages will be quoted later from his sermons in which he reflects some of that dissatisfaction with the results of reason which marks philosophical sceptics. To return to the youthful poet, we find him fascinated also by the theory that infinite variety is the law of life, that the universe is in a continual flux. It is illuminating here to compare him in this respect with his contemporary Spenser, who in his last fragments of the *Faerie Queene* has expressed the humanist's sad longing for surcease of change:

> Then gin I thinke on that which Nature sayd,
> Of that same time when no more *Change* shall be,
> But stedfast rest of all things firmely stayd
> Upon the pillours of Eternity,
> That is contrayr to *Mutabilitie:*
> For, all that moueth, doth in *Change* delight:
> But thence-forth all shall rest eternally
> With Him that is the God of Sabbaoth hight:
> O that great Sabbaoth God, graunt me that Sabaoths sight.

But Donne contemplated this mutability without sadness, rather with joy, with eagerness to find therein his own full expression:

> "Change," he said, "is the nursery
> Of musick, joy, life and eternity." [20]

Furthermore, in his early poems he applies this relativist philosophy to the social code which required constancy in love, and especially to the basic doctrine of the *Jus Naturale et Gentium* — the Law of Nature and of Nations. This conception

[19] Gosse, II. 16.

[20] Grierson, I. 83.

of the Law of Nature, ultimately derived from the Stoics, had grown in importance with its constant reiteration through the Middle Ages, until in the Renaissance it was regularly appealed to as the fundamental principle in law, in ethics, in natural theology, — in short, it was the one indisputable philosophical defense of the worthiest and most ideal elements in civilization. The conception of the Law of Nature had thus become the conservative and stabilizing doctrine of Renaissance thought, a bulwark against excessive individualism. It was this ancient and revered doctrine that Donne set himself gaily to disintegrate by means of his corrosive wit, and deride by his extravagant paradox and hyperbole. Still another element in his early poetry is its outspoken and shameless Naturalism — not merely a literary trick, but a code of ethics. He substituted for the Stoic Nature a different nature with its own goddess — Aphrodite Pandemos. All these elements of his thought, namely scepticism, revolt against the Stoic Law of Nature, and libertine Naturalism, are to be found earlier than Donne in Montaigne, and may have been inspired in Donne by a reading of the *Essays*. How seriously he adhered to these professed doctrines is a problem, perhaps insoluble. But they unquestionably fascinated him and left a permanent impress upon his mind. Nevertheless, these sceptical and naturalistic ideas served him not as an abiding place, but as a point of departure in his development. In a very interesting passage of *The Calme*, a passage which need not be taken too literally as autobiography, he suggests three reasons for his joining the Cadiz expedition of 1596:

> Whether a rotten state, and hope of gaine,
> Or to disuse mee from the queasie paine
> Of being belov'd, and loving, or the thirst
> Of honour, or faire death, out pusht mee first,

he will not say, allowing the reader to suppose, if he wishes, that all three motives may have contributed to his decision.[21] This allusion to love as a "queasie paine," in a poem written as early as 1597, is significant in the light of Donne's interest at the same time in the libertine naturalism of the Renaissance. It is a note

[21] Grierson, I. 179.

of restlessness. Avid of experience and knowledge, filled with the Renaissance spirit of sounding the depths of life and truth, Donne was not finding peace in that philosophy of life which gave such contentment to Montaigne. His intellectual and spiritual life — and in this respect he resembles Pascal — began at the point where Montaigne's was concluded. In passing through this stage of naturalistic ethics, Donne attained to a deeper knowledge of himself and his limitations, to an awareness of the need of some transcendental power to save humanity from itself.

> Be more than man, or thou'rt lesse than an Ant,[22]

he wrote in *The First Anniversary* (1611). His experience of the inadequacy of naturalism could not but contribute to the inwardness, the passionate humility, the deep feeling of dependence on some source of spiritual power outside of himself, which marked the saintly divine of later years.

His youthful phases were thus transformed with his more mature experience. Biographers have no doubt been right in crediting much of this transformation to his reversal of fortune and his happy marriage. But it seems probable also that his study of the new astronomy produced something like a crisis in his intellectual and religious development. Donne certainly experienced to a greater degree than most Englishmen of his time the disquieting effect of "Copernicism." Barclay, in his *Icon Animorum* (1614), implies indeed that the followers of Copernicus were numerous in England: "But in Philosophy and the Mathematicks," wrote the satirist, "in Geography and Astronomy, there is no opinion so prodigious and strange, but in that Island was either inuented, or has found many followers, and subtile maintainers, but such as through tedious disputations cannot plainly state the question which they would seeme to vphold: That the Earth is moued round, and not the Heauens: that the Sunne, with the Planets, and all the other Stars are not moued in their globes caelestiall," and the like.[23] Whether or

[22] Grierson, I. 237. The reader may be reminded by this line of the last pages of Montaigne's *Apology of Raymond Sebond.*

[23] Barclay, *The Mirror of Minds* (trans. by Tho. May; London, 1633), pp. 84–85.

not there were many who accepted the new science so early as 1614, there are few traces of it in English writings of the period. Bacon, as is well known, did not understand the mathematical efforts of the Copernicans. Fulke Greville, who took a despondent view of most things in the world, expressed a doubt as to whether the new system could be proved.[24] Donne therefore appears exceptional, both in his eagerness to read the new scientific books and in his readiness to accept their conclusions. In his *Biathanatos,* written probably in 1608, he refers to Kepler's *De Stella Nova in Pede Serpentarii,* published in 1606.[25] Again in 1611, in his *Conclave Ignatii,* he reveals an enthusiastic study of Copernicus and Tycho Brahe and a knowledge of the publications of Galileo and Kepler as recent as that year and the preceding.[26] Donne was following closely the latest research. In the same year, in *The First Anniversary,* he expressed the dejection produced by this new science. Describing the melancholy state of the world, he says that the

> new Philosophy calls all in doubt,
> The Element of fire is quite put out;
> The Sun is lost, and th'Earth, and no mans wit
> Can well direct him where to looke for it.
> And freely men confesse that this world's spent,
> When in the Planets, and the Firmament
> They seeke so many new; they see that this
> Is crumbled out againe to his Atomies.
> 'Tis all in pieces, all cohaerence gone;
> All just supply, and all Relation.[27]

" Copernicism in the mathematics," he writes in a letter in 1615, " hath carried earth farther up, from the stupid centre; and yet not honoured it, nor advantaged it, because for the necessity of appearances, it hath carried heaven so much higher from it." [28] Even towards the end of his life, in a sermon preached in 1626,

[24] In *A Treatise of Human Learning. Works* (ed. Grosart), II. 17.

[25] *Biathanatos* (London, 1644), p. 146. It is interesting to note in this connection that there is in the British Museum a presentation copy of this book given by Kepler to James I.

[26] Gosse, I. 257.

[27] Grierson, I. 237. Cf. letter to Countess of Bedford, I. 196.

[28] Gosse, II. 78–79.

he reproaches his age for the slowness with which the new science is accepted.

"What one thing," he asks, "do we know perfectly? Whether we consider arts, or sciences, the servant knows but according to the proportion of his master's knowledge in that art, and the scholar knows but according to the proportion of his master's knowledge in that science; young men mend not their sight by using old men's spectacles; and yet we look upon nature, but with Aristotle's spectacles, and upon the body of man, but with Galen's, and upon the frame of the world, but with Ptolemy's spectacles." [29]

He makes two pointed uses of this reference to science. In the first place, he manifests the full force of his scepticism regarding traditional philosophical and scientific knowledge.

"Almost all knowledge," he says, "is rather like a child that is embalmed to make mummy, than that is nursed to make a man; rather conserved in the stature of the first age, than grown to be greater; and if there be any addition to knowledge, it is rather a new knowledge, than a greater knowledge; rather a singularity in a desire of proposing something that was not known at all before, than an improving, an advancing, a multiplying of former inceptions; and by that means, no knowledge comes to be perfect. One philosopher thinks he has dived to the bottom, when he says, he knows nothing but this, that he knows nothing; and yet another thinks, that he hath expressed more knowledge than he, in saying, that he knows not so much as that, that he knows nothing." [30]

In the second place, Donne uses the new science here, as in *The First Anniversary,* to illustrate the transitoriness and imperfection of this earth and all it contains:

I need not call in new philosophy, that denies a settledness, an acquiescence in the very body of the earth, but makes the earth to move in that place, where we thought the sun had moved; I need not that help, that the earth itself is in motion, to prove this, that nothing upon earth is permanent; the assertion will stand of itself, till some man assign me some instance, something that a man rely upon and find permanent.[31]

The gaiety of the young philosopher of flux and change has now departed; that mutability is a perplexing spiritual problem was a discovery of the mature Donne, and when he at last acquired a sense of the sadness of this transitoriness, it was the more acute because of the new scientific knowledge which had never troubled Spenser.

[29] Alford, III. 472. [30] *Ibid.,* III. 472. [31] *Ibid.,* III. 483.

II

Having seen in these adventures in the Naturalism, Scepticism and new astronomy of his own day, what freedom of movement and independence of judgment was characteristic of Donne, we may ask what his relation was to some of the central philosophical conceptions of the Middle Ages. In this discussion I shall follow those historians who regard Realism as the typically medieval philosophy, and Nominalism as the first sceptical or liberating reaction of the modern spirit against medievalism.[32] For in medieval thought the possibility of knowledge was regarded as axiomatic; the human mind must be fitted to know reality, and reality must be such that it can be known. " Knowledge," says Dante, at the beginning of the *Convivio*," is the distinguishing perfection of our soul, wherein consists our distinguishing blessedness." And the chief impediment within the soul to this perfection appears " when vice hath such supremacy in her that she giveth herself to pursuing vicious delights, wherein she is deluded to such a point that for their sake she holds all things cheap." Only a debased character, it was thought, could be tormented by doubt, and therefore those who were suspected of questioning the orthodox plan of salvation were significantly called " Epicureans," a term which remained current in that sense from the thirteenth century to the seventeenth.

To appreciate the power which such rigid and intolerant orthodoxy exercised over the medieval mind, we must remember the work medievalism had to do after the barbarian invasions and the Dark Ages, namely to organize anew and institutionalize

[32] See especially Hauréau, a fervent champion of the French Revolution, in his *Histoire de la philosophie scolastique* (1850; revised, 1872–1880); a similar position is taken by Andrew Seth Pringle-Pattison, in his article on Scholasticism in the *Encyclopedia Britannica,* 11th edition. English students of the great Nominalist Occam have not failed to find significance in the fact that he was a countryman of Francis Bacon and Hobbes, a " thinker mentally akin to them," full of sturdy English independence. See T. M. Lindsay, in *British Quarterly Review,* Vol. LVI (July, 1872), and George Croom Robertson, *Philosophical Remains* (London, 1894), p. 37.

civilization. In the intellectual as well as political and ecclesiastical spheres, it had to restore order and authority. On the political side, this contructive effort aimed at a universal empire; on the ecclesiastical side, at a universal church. On the intellectual side it aimed at a counterpart and support of these: a Summa Philosophiae and Summa Theologiae. The Middle Ages required a thorough and dogmatic intellectualism, which Aquinas, the representative medieval philosopher, thought he had achieved. "The prime author and mover of the universe is intelligence," he says in his *Summa contra Gentiles.*[33] "Therefore the last end of the universe must be the good of the intelligence, and that is truth. Truth then must be the final end of the whole universe" (Book I, chap. i). However, for various practical reasons few people are qualified to pursue knowledge and thus achieve their blessedness (Book I, chap. vii); therefore they have to accept on faith as much of it as is necessary to salvation. But to say that the natural dictates of reason are *contrary* to faith, is to accuse God of having given us two contradictory principles, an obviously absurd proposition (Book I, chap. vii). Reason is dependable so far as it can go. We cannot know the essence of God, because "the human understanding cannot go so far of its natural power to grasp His substance, since under the conditions of the present life the knowledge of our understanding commences with sense; and therefore objects beyond sense cannot be grasped by human understanding except so far as knowledge is gathered of them through the senses" (Book I, chap. iii). But although what we now accept on faith cannot give us perfect blessedness, when we shall see God we shall have knowledge itself; for happiness consists in the perfect activity of the human intellect and the end of all "Subsistent intelligences" is to know God (Book III, chaps. i-lxiii). According to the philosophy of Realism, God must be conceived of as the highest universal, *Ens,* Being. The intellectual approach to God was therefore a disciplining and enlightenment of the mind as it ascended the pyramid of universals,

[33] Translation by Joseph Rickaby, S. J., *Of God and His Creatures* (London, 1905).

until at the apex it achieved a mystic comprehension of the Mosaic "I am that I am." [34]

But, as the Nominalists questioned the whole rationalistic philosophy of the Realists, so they also attacked this idea of the identity, in their absolute aspects, of reason and faith. John Duns Scotus, the first great critic of Aquinas, maintained that God is not absolute intelligence, but absolute will. The good is good merely because God wills it. As there is no science which can explain the inexplicable, the world is thus reduced to an indeterminism with no rational principle. Though the full sceptical conclusion of such a philosophy was not clear to the Scotists, it is easy to see in retrospect the development of a cleavage between reason and faith as we recede farther and farther from Aquinas. In the Nominalism of Occam the distinction between reason and faith is made absolute. For Occam, by denying the philosophical value of universals, denied that God could be known, and thoroughly rejected the basis of Natural Theology; all knowledge of God, even of His existence, and all the truths of religion and ethics, had to be accepted on faith.[35] Thus arose the notion of a double truth, a separation of philosophy and theology, in the interests of a less rationalistic religious experience. Such influential followers of Occam as Peter D'Ailly (1350–1425) and John Gerson (1363–1429), both Chancellors of the University of Paris, went beyond Occam both in their scepticism and in their emphasis on faith. Gerson, especially, is known as a mystic. It has frequently been observed that mysticism flourishes best outside of the bounds of dogma; the spirit of rationalism tends to dispel the ecstatic vision. And this lesson of religious wisdom the seventeenth century could learn from the late Middle Ages. It was this tradition of the antagonism

[34] Dante, likewise, found the intellect in this life inadequate to comprehend God, not because of its own weakness, but because it is condemned to use the imagination and thus see through a glass darkly. *Paradiso,* XXXIII. 142: "All' alta fantasia qui mancò possa." The same idea is expressed in other passages of the *Paradiso:* IV. 37–42; X. 46–48; XXIV. 24. See also Edmund G. Gardner, *Dante and the Mystics* (London, 1913), pp. 175–177.

[35] See the summary of his *Centilogium theologicum,* in Erdmann, *History of Philosophy* (London, 1898), I. 511–512.

between faith and reason that made the poet Cowley, even though not a mystic, identify the tree in the garden of Eden, whose forbidden fruit brought all our woe, with the *Arbor Porphyrii,* the medieval "tree of universals" which bore the fruit of Realism:

> That right *Porphyrian Tree* which did true *Logick* shew,
> Each *Leaf* did learned *Notions* give,
> And th' *Apples* were *Demonstrative*. . . .
> The onely *Science* Man by this did get,
> Was but to *know* he nothing *Knew*. . . .[36]

In this railing "against the dogmatists" Cowley shows not a trace of Sextus Empiricus and classical philosophy; the seventeenth century poet is expressing the spirit of medieval Nominalism.

The historical rôle of Nominalism was to emancipate the European mind from medieval rationalism. But a similar service was also performed by some heretical rationalists who, finding the theory of the "double truth" a useful defense when in trouble with the authorities, urged this separation of the jurisdictions of faith and reason. The most notorious case was that of Pomponatius (1462–1525), professor of philosophy at Bologna, whose writings implied a doubt as to the immortality of the soul and the freedom of the will. When accused of heresy, he defended himself on the principle, "I believe as a Christian what I cannot believe as a philosopher."[37] The church of course never accepted officially the theory of the double truth, and the Lateran Council in 1512 condemned the proposition of Pomponatius: "as what is true," it was decreed, "can never contradict what is true, we determine that every proposition which is contrary to the truth of the revealed faith is entirely false."[38]

The Thomistic identity of reason and faith was thus attacked

[36] Abraham Cowley, *The Tree of Knowledge,* in *Poems* (ed. Waller; Cambridge, 1905), p. 45.

[37] In his *Biathanatos,* ed. cit., p. 216, Donne referred to Pomponatius as an "excellent philosopher." But he maintained in a sermon in 1617 that truth in philosophy must be truth in divinity. Alford, V. 470.

[38] Pünjer, *History of the Christian Philosophy of Religion* (Edinburgh, 1887), pp. 50–52.

on various sides, but the Catholic Church, which had already accepted Aquinas as the unique Christian philosopher, established his intellectual tradition as orthodoxy and continued it amid the philosophical turmoil of the late Middle Ages and the Renaissance. Its consistency with this tradition was perhaps most decisively indicated in its rejection of the revived Augustinianism of the sixteenth and seventeenth centuries, especially of the Jansenists.

This brief sketch of some of the main developments of scholastic thought regarding the nature of religious truth should at least serve to emphasize the complexity of the medieval heritage of the Renaissance; when we say that Donne was a student of Scholastic philosophy, we must remember that he read, besides Aquinas, such men as Occam, Gerson, Pomponatius and Raymond of Sebonde. Donne was immensely curious and receptive, and in him we can find the whole ferment of his age in all its variety. On the other hand, it would be an error to suppose, although he frequently refers with scorn to the "doctrines of the schools,"[39] that Donne brushed away with one gesture all medieval philosophy as if it were cobwebs. The intellectual doctrine of Aquinas attracted him profoundly. In his *Essays in Divinity,* written in 1614–15, as he was preparing to enter orders, he places Aquinas beside Augustine, his favorite theologian, calling him, as he addresses himself to God in prayer and contemplation, "another instrument and engine of Thine, whom Thou hadst so enabled that nothing was too mineral nor centric for the search and reach of his wit."[40] Donne studied Aquinas as he studied everything, with ardor, but with critical independence, and with reference to his own experience. We can therefore best estimate his allegiance to Aquinas and other medieval influences by examining the nature of his religious experience. Three aspects of it are especially important in this connection: his indecision as to which was the true church, his conception of the relation between faith and reason, and his Augustinianism.

39 See, for illustrations, Alford, I. 508; V. 517; V. 588–589.

40 *Essays in Divinity,* ed. cit., p. 37.

III

The medieval church, relying on and taking full advantage of the principle of intellectual certainty expressed in the philosophy of Aquinas, was in spirit and ideal statesmanlike. It dealt with intellectual vagrancy by administrative methods. So in the seventeenth century the growing variety among Protestant sects seemed to Bossuet, that statesman of the church, a self-evident proof of the error of all Protestantism. A heretic he defined as a man who has formed an opinion. Many Protestants, it is to be feared, would at that time and even this, have subscribed to Bossuet's definition; nevertheless, the tendency of Protestantism was to place emphasis less and less on the enforcement of established truth, and more and more on the search after truth. The differences and debates of the Protestant theologians contributed largely to the establishment of the new principle of toleration — a principle not without some sceptical implications. "Where there is much desire to learn," Milton said in his *Areopagitica*, "there of necessity will be much arguing, much writing, many opinions; for opinion in good men is but knowledge in the making."

Into the wilderness of opinion Donne had, as we have seen, courageously set out, with a fine youthful — not to say medieval — assurance that he could find the true religion. In his satire, *Kinde pitty chokes my spleene*,[41] written in his youth, he speaks with scorn of those feeble, hesitating spirits who adhere to any sect without studying and thinking the problem through for themselves. Mirreus the Catholic, Crantz the Calvinist, Graius the Anglican, are sketched with a few strong, uncomplimentary strokes. Then there are others:

> Carelesse Phrygius doth abhorre
> All, because all cannot be good, as one
> Knowing some women whores, dares marry none.
> Graccus loves all as one, and thinkes that so
> As women do in divers countries goe
> In divers habits, yet are still one kinde,
> So doth, so is Religion; and this blind-
> nesse too much light breeds.

[41] Grierson, I. 154–158.

He expresses confidence that truth can be found by earnest effort, provided one goes back far enough to the original sources and cultivates an open mind. And one cannot escape the obligation of making a choice:

unmoved thou
Of force must one, and forc'd but one allow;
And the right; aske thy father which is shee,
Let him aske his; though truth and falsehood bee
Neare twins, yet truth a little elder is; [42]
Be busie to seeke her, beleeve mee this,
Hee's not of none, nor worst, that seekes the best.
To adore, or scorne an image, or protest,
May all be bad; doubt wisely; in strange way
To stand inquiring right, is not to stray;
To sleepe, or runne wrong, is.

But unceasing labor is necessary.

On a huge hill,
Cragged, and steep, Truth stands, and hee that will
Reach her, about must, and about must goe;
And what the hills suddenness resists, winne so;
Yet strive so, that before age, deaths twilight,
Thy Soule rest, for none can worke in that night.

But Donne himself discovered that this truth was even more difficult to reach than he had imagined. All sects, he says in a letter dated by Gosse 1607, need to be purged of false doctrines:

I begin to think that as litigious men tired with suits admit any arbitrament, and princes travailed with long and wasteful wars descend to such conditions of peace as they are soon after ashamed to have embraced; so philosophers, and so all sects of Christians, after long disputations and controversies, have allowed many things for positive and dogmatical truths which are not worthy of that dignity; and so many doctrines have grown to be ordinary diet and food of our spirits, and have place in the pap of catechisms, which were admitted but as physic in that present distemper, or accepted in a lazy weariness, when men so they might have something to rely upon, and to excuse themselves from more painful inquisition, never examined what that was.[43]

[42] In a sermon in 1618 Donne says "that is best in matter of religion that was first."—Alford, V. 583; cf. III. 292. The paradox that the newest philosophy is soundest, and the oldest divinity, seems to have been proverbial. See De Mornay, *De la Verité de la Religion Chrestienne* (Leyden, 1651), p. 88; Overbury, *Works* (London, 1890), p. 179; and Francis Osborne, *Works* (8th ed.; London, 1682), p. 92.

[43] Gosse, I. 174.

In a letter impossible to date exactly, Donne expresses a broad tolerance towards all sects as containing some truth:

"You know," he says, "I never fettered nor imprisoned Religion, not straightening it friarly, *ad Religiones factitias* (as the Romans call well their orders of Religion), nor immuring it in a Rome, or a Wittenberg, or a Geneva; they are all virtual beams of one Sun, and wheresoever they find clay hearts, they harden them and moulder them into dust; and they entender and mollify waxen. They are not so contrary as the North and South Poles, and that (?) they are co-natural pieces of one circle. Religion is Christianity, which being too spiritual to be seen by us, doth therefore take an apparent body of good life and works, so salvation requires an honest Christian." [44]

In his toleration, his comprehensive sympathy with opposed sects, and his willingness to simplify and therefore to discard non-essential doctrines, Donne thus anticipated such latitudinarians as Falkland, Hales, Chillingworth and Sir Thomas Browne.[45] In a letter written in 1615, as he stood on the threshold of his career in the church, he suggested that the merits of the various religions or sects within Christianity may not be absolute, and that violent conversions from one to another may be dangerous, irrespective of the relative degrees of ascertainable truth in each:

As some bodies are as wholesomely nourished as ours with acorns, and endure nakedness, both which would be dangerous to us, if we for them should leave our former habits, though theirs were the primitive diet and custom; so are many souls well fed with such forms and dressings of religion, as would distemper and misbecome us, and make us corrupt towards God, if any human circumstance moved it, and in the opinion of men, though none. You shall seldom see a coin, upon which the stamp were removed, though to imprint it better, but it looks awry and squint. And so, for the most part, do minds which have received divers impressions.[46]

In the same letter, referring to Protestantism and Catholicism, he says: "I will not, nor need to you, compare the religions. The channels of God's mercies run through both fields; and they

[44] Gosse, I. 226.

[45] The untrustworthy gossip, John Aubrey, has recorded that Falkland and Hales were the first Socinians in England, and that Chillingworth in his youth much delighted in Sextus Empiricus. *Brief Lives* (Oxford, 1898), I. 150, 173, 279. Whether authentic or not, the remark concerning Chillingworth indicates that the sceptical trend of latitudinarianism was evident at that time.

[46] Gosse, II. 78.

are sister teats of His graces, yet both diseased and infected, but not both alike."

Evidently Donne could at best make a compromise in deciding upon allegiance to any one church. He insisted nevertheless upon the necessity of the visible church and of the ecclesiastical element in religion. He was in no sense a dissenter. He realized the religious value of rituals and symbols, as making a deeper appeal than merely to the understanding.[47] "He that undervalues outward things," he said in a sermon in 1621, "in the religious service of God, though he begin at ceremonial and ritual things, will quickly come to call sacraments but outward things, and sermons, and public prayers, but outward things, in contempt."[48] Donne was opposed to extreme individualism in religious experience; the individual must find his religion in the church. "I see not this mystery," he said in another sermon, "by the eye of nature, of learning, of state, of mine own private sense; but I see it by the eye of the church, by the light of faith, that is true; but yet organically, instrumentally, by the eye of the church."[49] Since an ecclesiastical organization, even though at its best it is so imperfect, is so essential, it is wise and right to be loyal to that church which has served us. "It is an irreverent unthankfulness, to think worse of that church, which hath bred us, and fed us, and led us thus far towards God, than of a foreign church, though reformed too, and in a good degree."[50] And yet, these imperfect churches could not satisfy Donne; he longed for the true church, the truly Catholic and universal church. "The church loves the name of Catholic," he said in a sermon at the Hague, "and it is a glorious, and an harmonious name; love thou those things wherein she is Catholic, and wherein she is harmonious, that is . . . those universal, and fundamental doctrines, which in all Christian ages, and in all Christian churches, have been agreed by all to be necessary to salvation; and then thou art a true Catholic."[51]

[47] Alford, VI. 19 ff. and 42–43; V. 66 ff.

[48] *Ibid.*, V. 67.

[49] *Ibid.*, V. 419. Cf. III. 344.

[50] *Ibid.*, IV. 485.

[51] *Ibid.*, III. 273. Cf. *Essays in Divinity*, ed. cit., pp. 130–132.

It seems clear therefore that Donne's allegiance to the Church of England was of a compromising and pragmatic nature; as Grierson has said, it "never made the appeal to Donne's heart and imagination it did to George Herbert." [52] He never found the one true church he had been seeking for. Even in the *Holy Sonnets,* written after 1617, when he was eminent as an Anglican divine, he was still searching, now no longer in "controverted theology," but in prayer, for a church to which he could give undivided, uncritical allegiance:

> Show me deare Christ, thy Spouse, so bright and cleare.[53]

Thus this man of unusual intellectual passion and power, whose desire for truth was deep and imperative, saw it always eluding his grasp; always a seeker after truth, but pursuing it in vain, he suffered painful dejection and disillusionment. He lived always intellectually tormented. Doubt was not to him, as it had been to Montaigne, a soft pillow on which to rest his head, but pain and restlessness, search and endless labor.

IV

Donne had, however, in the meantime found a new source of spiritual insight and comfort. It seems probable, as Courthope says,[54] that his happy marriage had a redeeming influence upon him and inspired his nobler love poems. But he had a religious awakening also. In one of his love poems, *A Valediction,* occurs a striking statement that "all Divinity is love and wonder," [55] an idea which Donne repeated years later in *The First Anniversary:*

> The world containes
> Princes for armes, and Counsellors for braines,
> Lawyers for tongues, Divines for hearts, and more,
> The Rich for stomackes, and for backes, the Poore;

[52] Grierson, II. 236.

[53] *Ibid.,* I. 330. This sonnet was omitted, for obvious reasons, in seventeenth century editions, and was first printed by Gosse, II. 371.

[54] *History of English Poetry,* III. 156.

[55] Grierson, I. 30. Compare Carlyle's sentence in *The Hero as Divinity:* "Worship is transcendent wonder; wonder for which there is now no limit or measure; that is worship."

The Officers for hands, Merchants for feet,
By which, remote and distant Countries meet.
But those fine spirits which do tune, and set
This Organ, are those peeces which beget
Wonder and love; and these were shee.[56]

The thought had been impressed upon his mind that the soul of the world is not knowable to reason, that the true theology appeals in some other way; in some personal experience or crisis he had acquired an insight into a mystery not explained by "controverted divinity" and become a mystic. From that time reason began to lose its preëminence, his spiritual life gained in power and intensity, and his prayer became

Looke to mee faith, and looke to my faith, God.

The relation between reason and faith, we have seen, was one of the crucial problems in medieval thought. Aquinas had given it an intellectualistic solution, affirming that reason and faith are identical in their absolute aspects, and that faith is therefore provisional. In the seventeenth century Malebranche, in his fusion of Cartesianism with the Catholic tradition, went even farther than Aquinas and declared an emphatic preference for reason: "La raison doit toujours être la maîtresse; Dieu même le suit. L'Intelligence est préférable à la Foi: car la Foi passera, mais l'Intelligence subsistera éternellement."[57] Such a conclusion is natural if one premises that the universe is knowable and the blessedness of man consists in the perfect knowledge of it. Donne, on the contrary, always gives reason the subordinate place. He begins a verse letter to the Countess of Bedford, some time between 1608 and 1614, with the statement:

Reason is our Soules left hand, Faith her right,
By these we reach divinity.

But he would,

not to encrease, but to expresse
My faith, as I beleeve, so understand.[58]

[56] Grierson, I. 246. Cf. "All love is wonder," in *The Anagram,* I. 81.
[57] Malebranche, *Traité de Morale.*
[58] Grierson, I. 189. Cf. *Essays in Divinity,* ed. cit., p. 142.

He labored always to understand. "No one may doubt," he wrote in a letter in 1612, "but that that religion is certainly best which is reasonablest." [59] And in his *Elegy on Prince Henry* (1613), he almost identifies the spheres of reason and faith:

Looke to mee faith, and looke to my faith, God;
For both my centers feele this period.
Of waight one center, one of greatnesse is;
And Reason is that center, Faith is this;
For into'our reason flow, and there do end
All, that this naturall world doth comprehend:
Quotidian things, and equidistant hence,
Shut in, for man, in one circumference.
But for th'enormous greatnesses, which are
So disproportion'd, and so angulare,
As is Gods essence, place and providence,
Where, how, when, what soules do, departed hence,
These things (eccentrique else) on faith do strike;
Yet neither all, nor upon all, alike.
For reason, put to'her best extension,
Almost meetes faith, and makes both centers one.[60]

The reason, too, is a valuable defender of the faith against rationalistic attacks. "It is not enough for you," Donne said in a sermon in 1623, "to rest in imaginary faith, and easiness in believing, except you know also what, and why, and how you come to that belief. Implicit believers, ignorant believers, the adversary may swallow; but the understanding believer, he must chaw, and pick bones, before he come to assimilate him, and make him like himself." [61]

Reason, Donne gladly admitted, has its place in religion, but subordinate to faith. Faith goes beyond it both in power and authority. "Rectified reason," he said in a sermon, "is religion." [62] Again, "Mysteries of religion are not the less believed and embraced by faith, because they are presented, and induced, and apprehended by reason." [63] Natural theology, too, has its place, but is inadequate. "The invisible God was presented in visible things, and thou mightest, and wouldest not see him: but this is only such a knowledge of God as philosophers, moral

[59] Gosse, II. 8.
[60] Grierson, I. 267.
[61] Alford, I. 314. Cf. V. 571, 576, 582 ff., and VI. 24.
[62] *Ibid.*, III. 286.
[63] *Ibid.*, V. 453.

and natural men may have, and yet be very far from making this knowledge any means of salvation."[64] Religion is therefore of a distinctly supra-rational origin. "Grace does not grow out of nature; for nature in the highest exaltation and rectifying thereof cannot produce grace. . . . Nature, and natural reason do not produce grace, but yet grace can take root in no other thing but in the nature and reason of man."[65] Natural reason can at best point in the direction of faith. "The light of faith, in the highest exaltation that can be had, in the elect, here, is not that very beatifical vision, which we shall have in heaven, but it bears witness of that light. The light of nature, in the highest exaltation is not faith, but it bears witness of it."[66]

Not only did Donne regard reason as inadequate, but he was also troubled by a consciousness of a contradiction between reason and faith. In his *Litany,* written about 1609 or 1610, he had already formulated for himself the prayer:

> Let not my minde be blinder by more light
> Nor Faith, by Reason added, lose her sight.[67]

"The Scriptures," he said in the sermon preached at the Hague, "will be out of thy reach, and out of thy use, if thou cast and scatter them upon reason, upon philosophy, upon morality, to try how the Scriptures will fit them, and believe them but so far as they agree with thy reason; but draw the Scripture to thine own heart, and to thine own actions, and thou shalt find it made for that."[68] The unreasonableness of Christianity he could celebrate as its glory, the seal of its divine character. Was it easy to believe, he asks,

> that from that man, that worm, and no man, ingloriously traduced as a conjurer, ingloriously apprehended as a thief, ingloriously executed as a traitor; they should look for glory, and all glory, and everlasting glory? And from that melancholic man, who was never seen to laugh in all his

[64] *Ibid.,* VI. 36. Cf. I. 297; V. 517–518, 574, and 582 ff.

[65] *Ibid.,* VI. 44.

[66] *Ibid.,* V. 66.

[67] Grierson, I. 340. Cf. Alford, III. 261.

[68] Alford, III. 302. Compare V. 64, where Donne defines the light of faith as "not only a knowing, but an applying, an appropriating of all to thy benefit."

life, and *whose soul was heavy unto death;* they should look for joy, and all joy, and everlasting joy: and for salvation, and everlasting salvation from him, who could not save himself from ignominy, from the torment, from the death of the cross? If any state, if any convocation, if any wise man had been to make a religion, a gospel; would he not have proposed a more probable, a more credible gospel, to man's reason, than this? [69]

Among the numerous passages on this subject, perhaps the most emphatic occurs in a sermon preached on Christmas Day, 1621, on the text, "He was not that Light, but was sent to bear witness of that Light" (John, i. 8.).

"In all philosophy," he said, "there is not so dark a thing as light; as the sun, which is *fons lucis naturalis,* the beginning of natural light, is the most evident thing to be seen, and yet the hardest to be looked upon, so is natural light to our reason and understanding. Nothing clearer, for it is clearness itself, nothing darker, it is enwrapped in so many scruples. Nothing nearer, for it is around about us, nothing more remote, for we know neither entrance, nor limits of it. Nothing more easy, for a child discerns it, nothing more hard, for no man understands it. It is apprehensible by sense, and not comprehensible by reason. If we wink, we cannot choose but see it, if we stare, we know it never the better. No man is yet got so near to the knowledge of the qualities of light, as to know whether light itself be a quality, or a substance. If then this natural light be so dark to our natural reason, if we shall offer to pierce so far into the light of this text, the essential light Christ Jesus, (in his nature, or but in his offices) or the supernatural light of faith and grace, . . . if we search farther into these points, than the Scripture hath opened us a way, how shall we hope to unentangle, or extricate themselves? They had a precious composition for lamps, amongst the ancients, reserved especially for tombs, which kept light for many hundreds of years; we have had in our age experience, in some casual openings of ancient vaults, of finding such lights, as were kindled, (as appeared by their inscriptions) fifteen or sixteen hundred years before; but, as soon as that light comes to our light, it vanishes. So this eternal, and this supernatural light, Christ and faith, enlightens, warms, purges, and does all the profitable offices of fire, and light, if we keep it in the right sphere, in the proper place, (that is, if we consist in points necessary to salvation, and revealed in the Scriptures) but when we bring this light to the common light of reason, to our inferences, and consequences, it may be in danger to vanish itself, and perchance extinguish our reason too; we may search so far, and reason so long of faith and grace, as that we may lose not only them, but even our reason too, and sooner become mad than good." [70]

These illustrations of Donne's wrestling with the problem of reason and faith afford an insight into some of those contradic-

[69] *Ibid.*, V. 430–431.

[70] *Ibid.*, V. 55.

tory impulses which make his life and character seem so paradoxical. He began with an almost Thomistic confidence in reason; he labored to *know*. But though he rightly felt himself more successful in this effort than most men about him, he was forced to confess that knowledge is difficult and uncertain even to the best minds, and that much philosophizing is often a vanity of the spirit. This defeat of the reason was, however, a spiritual gain. Unconvinced by "controverted divinity," Donne discovered in his own experience another divinity of "love and wonder." Not indeed by any sudden revelation of his spiritual powers, but through years of privation, disappointment, doubt, years of the "agony and exercise of sense and spirit," [71] did the student, lawyer and courtier yield his life and soul fully to the guidance of faith. One need only compare Donne with his contemporaries, Sir John Davies and Lord Herbert of Cherbury, to realize how largely he had been liberated from the inhibitions of rationalism. The darkening of the understanding, Donne has said himself, is one of those afflictions by which God turns the soul to himself. "Those helps," he said in a sermon, "which are

deduced from philosophy and natural reason, are strong enough against afflictions of this world, as long as we can use them, as long as these helps of reason and learning are alive, and awake, and actuated in us, they are able to sustain us from sinking under the afflictions of this world, for, they have sustained many a Plato, and a Socrates, and Seneca in such cases. But when part of the affliction shall be, that God worketh upon the spirit itself, and damps that, that he casts a sooty cloud upon the understanding, and darkens that, that he doth *exuere hominem,* divest, strip the man of the man, *eximere hominem,* take the man out of the man, and withdraw and frustrate his natural understanding so, as that, to this purpose, he is no man, yet even in this case, God may mend thee, in marring thee, he may build thee up in dejecting thee, he may infuse another, *ego vir,* another manhood into thee, and though thou canst not say *ego vir, I am that moral man,* safe in my natural reason and philosophy, that is spent, yet *Ego vir,* I am that Christian man, who have seen this affliction in the cause thereof, so far off, as in my sin in Adam, and the remedy of this affliction, so far off, as in the death of Christ Jesus, I am the man, that cannot repine, nor murmur, since I am the cause; I am the man that cannot despair, since Christ is the remedy.[72]

[71] Donne's own words; see Gosse, I. 190.
[72] Alford, V. 320.

V

The relation of the religious experience of Donne, in its essential nature and not merely its incidental aspects, to the main currents of religious thought in his age and to the main traditions within Christianity, involves necessarily a discussion of his Augustinianism. For not only was he peculiarly the disciple of Augustine,[73] but the influence of the Bishop of Hippo was highly important in the development of thought in the sixteenth and seventeenth centuries. The nature and extent of this influence must here be indicated as briefly as possible.

Even externally, the career of Augustine has striking resemblances to that of Donne. His personal distinction, his secular ambition, his extensive experience with the argumentative aspect of religion, his mature conversion, can all be paralleled in the life of Donne. But more striking, and certainly more important, is the similarity in the religious experience of the two men, in their assimilation and rejection of philosophical thought, in the fundamental needs of their personalities and in the direction in which these guided their religious development. Augustine, it is true, passed more definitely through his first two stages, his study of scepticism in the New Academics, and his adherence to Platonism. The influence of the first was sufficient to make him a keen and profound critic of the theory of knowledge, and to force his attention back upon his own nature as the only source of certainty. "Noli foras ire, in teipsum redi; in interiore homine habitat veritas."[74] In searching within himself he discovered, long before Descartes, the basic fact of his own self-consciousness and its significance in the search for certain knowledge.[75]

[73] Miss Ramsay has frequently noted this fact, although she missed its significance. *Op. cit.*, pp. 179, 181–182, 220, 225, 252–253, 257, etc.

[74] *De Vera Religione,* 72. Quoted by W. Cunningham, *S. Austin and his Place in the History of Christian Thought* (London, 1886), p. 22, n. 1.

[75] Augustine's anticipation of Descartes has often been pointed out. Already Bossuet, in a letter to Bishop Huet, declared that the "choses utiles" said by Descartes were already familiar to him in Plato, Augustine, Anselm and Aquinas. See quotation by Brunetière, *Études Critiques* (Paris, 1896), 5. 48–49.

Spiritual realities are within us, but they are the manifestations of Eternal Being. The knowledge of oneself leads to a knowledge of God. For a time an ardent student of Platonism, Augustine acquired a belief in a rational and intelligible order in the universe through an apprehension of which we might ascend to its source in God. This Platonic phase of Augustine explains the statement so often made that he was "the father of scholasticism in virtue of his dialectic mind." [76] "Here are the ideas," says one authority, "which were developed in the splendid structure of the scholastic philosophy and which in another form reappeared in the *Théodicée* of Leibnitz, and the *Analogy* of Butler." [77]

But Augustine developed beyond Platonism and its rational Logos, and became also the father of mysticism. In his introspection he discovered desires that Platonism could not satisfy, and inclinations that it could not correct. "Thou didst set me face to face with myself," he says in a meditative passage, "that I might behold how foul I was, and how crooked and sordid, bespotted and ulcerous." [78] The weakness of his own will, his sense of sin, and a perception of his own personality, these discoveries in his own nature showed him the necessity of a redemption beyond the power of Platonic ideas. The doctrine of grace, which became in later centuries known as the distinctive doctrine of Augustinianism, is an expression of Augustine's feeling of the utter helplessness of human nature to accomplish its own salvation. In humility of spirit he felt a supreme need for a personal God, not merely a Plotinian Universal Reason. He read in the Platonists, he says in a well-known passage in his *Confessions*, the doctrine of the Logos: In the beginning was the Word, and the Word was with God, and the Word was God. But that "the Word was made flesh, and dwelt among us," he did not read there.[79] The Word become flesh and living

[76] Schaff, Philip, *History of the Christian Church* (5th ed.; New York, 1899), III. 1018.

[77] Cunningham, *op. cit.*, p. 35.

[78] *Confessions*, VIII. vii. 16. I quote from the translation by Marcus Dods (Edinburgh, 1876).

[79] *Ibid.*, VII. ix. 13–14.

among us, bearing for us our miseries and frailties and sins, giving us the inexpressible consolation and comfort of a personal love and sacrifice for us, such was the religion of Augustine. He desired, not primarily to *know* God, but to rest his soul in the bosom of God, in the bosom of Christ, who was God become humanity and therefore full of the sympathy he craved. "I know not," he says, "how any rational demonstration of God could satisfy me; for I do not believe that I know anything as I desire to know God." [80] Though not a philosophical sceptic, Augustine was nevertheless ready to discard not only Platonism, but all philosophy and knowledge if it hindered in any way his devotion to the Christian religion. "For unhappy is the man who knoweth all those things, but knoweth Thee not; but happy is he who knoweth Thee, though these he may not know." [81]

The complex personality of Augustine thus stimulated down through the ages two divergent types of religious thought, the intellectualistic and the mystic. Although revered as the founder of the idealistic philosophy of the Catholic church, Augustine also attracted certain disciples in the Middle Ages and the Reformation primarily by his mysticism and piety. He was widely read among the Nominalists and the medieval mystics, who had in common at least an aversion to the intellectualism of Thomas Aquinas. He stimulated their tendency towards a spiritual mode of thought, based on a very distinct dualism of mind and body; he confirmed their belief that the moral life depends more on the will of man than on his intellect; and he taught them the art of observing the processes of the inner life, on which especially the mystics concentrated their attention.[82] In medieval England, Thomas Bradwardine felt his inspiration.[83] Such early reformers on the Continent as Huss and Wessel cultivated Augustine more than any other religious

[80] Quoted by R. L. Ottley, *Studies in the Confessions of St. Augustine* (London, 1919), p. 89.

[81] *Confessions,* V. iv.

[82] Siebeck, *Die Anfänge der neueren Psychologie in der Scholastik,* in *Zeitschrift für Philosophie und phil. Kritik,* 93 (1888). 188–191.

[83] Cunningham, *op. cit.,* pp. 153–154 and 178.

writer except Paul. "It may very well be said," declares Harnack, "that there never would have been a Reformation had there not been first a revival of Augustinianism." [84] Luther and Melancthon, Zwingli and Calvin were moulded by Augustine more than by any other church teacher. Thus, although Augustine was one of the saints and accepted authorities in the Catholic church, the Augustinianism of the sixteenth and seventeenth centuries became anti-Catholic in spirit, continuing and intensifying the medieval opposition to Thomism. Nourisson, himself a Catholic, admitted this antinomy and tried to resolve it: 'On ne saurait le méconnaître, de l'Augustinianisme corrompu, mais enfin de l'Augustinianisme procède le Protestantisme. Car, sans parler de Wiclif et de Huss. . . . Luther et Calvin ne font guère autre chose, dans leurs principaux ouvrages, que cultiver des semences d'Augustinianisme." [85] Within the Catholic church there were only two important Augustinian developments of a pietistic or anti-intellectual kind, and both were declared heretical; the first was led by Michael Bajus, at Louvain, whose Augustinian doctrines were condemned by Pius V in 1567; the second was of course Jansenism, whose greatest representative was Pascal.

To this tradition Donne belongs as a religious teacher and mystic; true to this tradition, he was dissatisfied with the impersonal and intellectual conception of God, desiring a personal God in which his heart, not his mind, might find rest. He repeats Augustine's criticism of Platonism: to think, he says, "that we can come to this by our own strength, without God's inward working a belief, or to think that we can believe out of Plato, where we may find a God, but without a Christ, or come to be good men out of Plutarch or Seneca, without a church or sacraments, to pursue the truth itself by any other way than he hath laid open to us, this is pride, and the pride of the angels." [86] The consciousness of his sin and weakness and misery he fostered and desired as essential to religious insight and religious longing.

[84] Harnack, *History of Dogma* (London, 1899), VII. 17.

[85] Nourisson, *La philosophie de saint Augustin* (2me ed.; Paris, 1866), II. 176.

[86] Alford, III. 47. Cf. V. 424–425.

"Man's infirmity requires spectacles; and affliction does that office." [87] Humility is the beginning of wisdom; it is "the seed, and kernel, and soul of all virtues." [88] "We are not worthy as to profess our unworthiness; it is a degree of spiritual exaltation, to be sensible of our lowness; . . . even humility itself is a pride, if we think it to be our own." [89] Donne is of the Augustinian tradition also in his insistence on the helplessness of man and the necessity of grace. "Miserable man!" he says. "A toad is a bag of poison, and a spider is a blister of poison, and yet a toad and a spider cannot poison themselves; man hath a drachm of poison, original sin, in an invisible corner, we know not where, and he cannot choose but poison himself and all his actions with that; we are so far from being able to begin without grace, as then when we have first grace, we cannot proceed to the use of that, without more." [90] Therefore Donne did not look to philosophy to illuminate the path of life with such confidence as, for instance, Spenser; the pure in heart, he said, get by their purity "this main purchase, that which all the books of all the philosophers could never teach them so much as what it was, that is true blessedness." [91] Donne learned in the school of affliction and anguish, which he so often refers to as the best school for the soul, that he needed another blessedness than truth and knowledge. And therefore the humiliation of the intellect, too, was necessary, lest the feeble light of the reason make us blind to the greater light of faith. In a sermon preached in 1624, on the conversion of St. Paul, he speaks of the light which struck Paul blind:

"This blindness of which we speak," he says, "which is a sober and temperate abstinence from the immoderate study, and curious knowledges of this world, this holy simplicity of the soul, is not a darkness, a dimness, a stupidity of the understanding, contracted by living in a corner, it is not an idle retiring into a monastery, or into a village, or a country solitude, it is not a lazy affectation of ignorance; not darkness, but a greater light,

[87] *Ibid.,* IV. 565.

[88] *Ibid.,* V. 571. Cf. 600 ff.

[89] *Ibid.,* V. 555.

[90] *Ibid.,* V. 577. Cf. VI. 108–109. For a criticism of Catholic doctrine, see VI. 48.

[91] *Ibid.,* I. 191.

must make us blind. . . . There are birds, that when their eyes are sealed, still soar up, and up, till they have spent all their strength. Men blinded with the lights of this world, soar still into higher places, or higher knowledges, or higher opinions; but the light of heaven humbles us, and lays flat that soul, which the leaven of this world had puffed and swelled up."[92]

Donne's religious experience, then, was a mystical one, and though he sought always to make it reasonable and even comprehensible, he had to recognize that his spiritual life was beyond the power of reason and weakened by a rationalistic mode of thought. He belonged to the anti-intellectual tradition of Augustine. And it is perhaps partly due to Donne's influence on the religious and poetical development of Herbert and Vaughan, that we find in them also, a recognition of this dualism of faith and reason. Herbert was hardly a mystic; but in a poem called *Divinitie* he says:

> As men, for fear the starres should sleep and nod,
> And trip at night, have spheres suppli'd;
> As if a starre were duller then a clod,
> Which knows his way without a guide:
>
> Just so the other heav'n they also serve,
> Divinities transcendent skie:
> Which with the edge of wit they cut and carve.
> Reason triumphs, and faith lies by. . . .
>
> Then burn thy Epicycles, foolish man;
> Break all thy spheres, and save thy head.
> Faith needs no staffe of flesh, but stoutly can
> To heav'n alone both go and leade.[93]

And Vaughan, in a poem with the sceptical title *Vanity of Spirit*, has explained how his repeated attempts to know the secrets of the world and of himself had failed, one after another, until, his intellect exhausted, he gave himself up to the mystical experience which can be complete only in another world.

> Quite spent with thoughts, I left my cell, and lay
> Where a shrill spring tun'd to the early day.
> I begg'd here long, and groan'd to know
> Who gave the clouds so brave a bow,

[92] *Ibid.*, II. 307–308.
[93] *The English Works of George Herbert* (ed. Palmer), III. 97.

Who bent the spheres, and circled in
Corruption with this glorious ring;
What is His name, and how I might
Descry some part of His great light.
I summon'd Nature; pierc'd through all her store;
Broke up some seals, which none had touch'd before
Her womb, her bosom, and her head,
Where all her secrets lay abed,
I rifled quite; and having past
Through all the creatures, came at last
To search myself, where I did find
Traces, and sounds of a strange kind.
Here of this mighty spring I found some drills,
With echoes beaten from th' eternal hills.
Weak beams and fires flash'd to my sight,
Like a young East, or moonshine night,
Which show'd me in a nook cast by
A piece of much antiquity,
And hieroglyphics quite dismember'd
And broken letters scarce remember'd.
I took them up, and — much joy'd — went about
T' unite those pieces, hoping to find out
The mystery; but this ne'er done,
That little light I had was gone.
It griev'd me much. At last, said I,
" Since in these veils my eclips'd eye
May not approach Thee — for at night
Who can have commerce with the light? —
I'll disapparel, and to buy
But one half-glance, most gladly die." [94]

As has been said earlier, Donne resembles Pascal in that his development began at the place where Montaigne's ended. Such a comparison between Donne and Pascal must be made with reservations, but it is helpful in indicating the position of Donne in relation to the seventeenth century. Profoundly influenced by the philosophical scepticism which had been popularized by Montaigne, Pascal built upon this philosophical scepticism an apologia for the Christian religion. This development was not so singular as it is generally thought to have been.[95] It has not

[94] Vaughan, Henry, *Poems* (ed. Chambers), I. 57. Passages from Augustine's *Confessions,* especially Book X, would furnish an excellent commentary on this poem.

[95] Edouard Droz has discussed the similarity, in this respect, of Pascal to Lactantius and Augustine. *Le Scepticisme de Pascal* (Paris, 1886), pp. 282–296.

been sufficiently noticed that a parallel development appeared in England at the same time and even earlier. Sir Thomas Browne, in his *Religio Medici* (1642), anticipated Pascal. Glanville appeared as an apologist for Christianity as well as for science in his *Vanity of Dogmatizing* (1661) and *Scepsis Scientifica* (1665). In Dryden's poems on religion we find the same paradox of moderate Pyrrhonism as the basis of submission to faith. Donne was the earliest of these seventeenth century religious Pyrrhonists in England, and because he came early his scepticism is less obvious and daring. But all his experience, his youthful interest in the relativist thought typified by Montaigne, his search for the true church, his wrestling with scholastic divinity, his gradually deepening religious insight, had all directed him towards the conclusion of Pascal, that philosophical dogmatism is a danger to the religious life, that the heart has its reasons of which the reason knows nothing. Pascal's thought is a fusion of the scepticism of Montaigne and the Augustinianism of the Jansenists. Donne had studied the same scepticism, in Sextus Empiricus and probably in Montaigne, and cultivated Augustine as his favorite religious teacher. He thus knew intimately the two traditions which converged also in Pascal.

VI

Unlike Pascal, however, Donne wrote in the "metaphysical style." Since this phrase, so well established, is yet so conducive to misinterpretations of Donne, it is necessary in a survey of the relation of Donne to medieval and modern traditions of thought, to discuss the significance of his style. I do not intend here to give any complete account, from either the historical or the esthetic point of view, of the "conceit" in Renaissance poetry and prose; its origins were too remote and the explanation of its popularity is too complex. My one purpose is to glance briefly at Donne's use of it, to see in what way the "conceit" was made expressive of his idiosyncracies, and thus not only to appreciate better the sincerity of his mode of expression, but also to formulate a definite conception of what is medieval and what is modern in his style, both in prose and poetry.

The "conceit," everyone knows, was common in English poetry before Donne. He appropriated it and gave it that peculiar quality and power which was his own, but which influenced his admiring successors to the extent of forming a poetical school. Professor Alden has given a definition of the "conceit," based on an analysis of it in Sidney and Shakespeare: "A conceit is the elaboration of a verbal or an imaginative figure, or the substitution of a logical for an imaginative figure, with so considerable a use of an intellectual process as to take precedence, at least for the moment, of the normal poetic process."[96] This definition expresses admirably also that dualism of Donne's nature which heightened the disharmony between his intellect and that poetic and mystical experience out of which his poetry and prose were made. His constant return upon himself, his study of his own feelings and emotions, and his attempts to state them in intellectual terms, all this introspection and analysis is as apparent in his sermons as in his verse. It is especially marked in Donne because of the imperfect harmony between the intellectual and poetic sides of his nature. Schelling coined an illuminating phrase when he said that "no one, excepting Shakespeare . . . has done so much to develop intellectualized emotion in the Elizabethan lyric as John Donne."[97]

This intellectuality, or "wit," as it was then called, of Donne's poetry and prose appears also in other forms than the "conceit"; it is sometimes paradox, sometimes hyperbole, sometimes a plain and straightforward reasoning about his subject. But in its most characteristic form it is a symbolism, a rendering of spiritual or emotional experience in terms apprehensible, not to sense or imagination primarily, but to the intellect. We may quote one of his most daring, yet successful, conceits in his early verse, the familiar one of the compass. It expresses a transcendental conception of the unity of two souls in love:

[96] Alden, Raymon Macdonald, *The Lyrical Conceit of the Elizabethans*, in *Studies in Philology*, XIV (1917). 137.

[97] Schelling, *A Book of Elizabethan Lyrics* (Boston, 1895), *Introduction*, xxiii.

But we by a love, so much refin'd,
  That our selves know not what it is,
Inter-assured of the mind,
  Care lesse, eyes, lips, and hands to misse.

Our two soules therefore, which are one,
  Though I must goe, endure not yet
A breach, but an expansion,
  Like gold to ayery thinnesse beate.

If they be two, they are two so,
  As stiffe twin compasses are two,
Thy soule the fixt foot, makes no show
  To move, but doth, if th'other doe.

And though it in the center sit,
  Yet when the other far doth rome,
It leanes, and hearkens after it,
  And growes erect, as that comes home.

Such wilt thou be to mee, who must
  Like th'other foot, obliquely runne;
Thy firmnes makes my circle just,
  And makes me end, where I begunne.[98]

By using the " conceit," an intellectual and impersonal mode of expression, to communicate his most intensely personal, inward and mystical feelings, Donne gave it imaginative and poetic power. The concepts of the intellect became the symbols of inexpressible spiritual experience. The recent editor of Donne's prose, Mr. Logan Pearsall Smith, after reading and re-reading his volumes of sermons, speaks of this mysticism, this " something baffling which still eludes our last analysis. Reading these old hortatory and dogmatic pages, the thought suggests itself that Donne is often saying something else, something poignant and personal, and yet, in the end, incommunicable to us." [99] Only long reading, perhaps, can give us the full sense of this incommunicable feeling beneath some of the apparently arid discussions in the sermons. In his labor to express it he draws upon all life and all knowledge, upon the most homely matters of daily experience as well as upon the distinctions of the Scholastic

[98] Grierson, I. 50.

[99] Smith, Logan Pearsall, *Donne's Sermons* (Oxford, 1920), *Introd.*, p. xxxv.

philosophy. It is a great error to represent Donne's mind as always preoccupied with the subtleties of medieval thought. He was really preoccupied with the subtleties of his own soul. Donne preached out of his own experience, as he startled his contemporaries, and all his understanding readers since, by the sincerity of his poetry written out of his own experience. No one has looked more directly upon the realities of life, no one has had his vision of reality less impeded by tradition, than Donne. But in the expression of even the most subtle, evanescent or mystical phases of his experience, he puts it into intellectual terms, into "conceits." There is a truth, in spite of its perverse and unsympathetic statement, in the comment of Macdonald: "The central thought of Dr. Donne is nearly sure to be just: the subordinate thoughts by means of which he unfolds it are often grotesque, and so wildly associated as to remind one of the lawlessness of a dream, wherein mere suggestion without choice or fitness rules the sequence."[100]

To illustrate this symbolical value of the "conceit" in Donne's sermons I shall quote first a passage in which the "conceits" are called "images," and in which there is no borrowing from medieval philosophy; the real subject is transcendental, but is evoked by a succession of not unfamilar metaphors and symbols:

> No image, but the image of God, can fit our soul; every other seal is too narrow, too shallow for it. The magistrate is sealed with the *Lion;* the *Wolf* will not fit that seal: the magistrate hath a *power* in his hand, but not *oppression.* Princes are sealed with the *Crown:* the *Mitre* will not fit that seal. Powerfully, and graciously they protect the Church, and are supreme heads of the Church; but they minister not the Sacraments of the Church: they give preferments; but they give not the capacitie of preferments: they give order who shall have, but they have not Orders by which they are enabled to have that they have. Men of inferior and laborious callings in the world are sealed with the *Crosse;* a *Rose,* or a *bunch of Grapes* will not answer that seal: ease and plentie in age must not be looked for without crosses, and labour, and industrie in youth. All men, Prince, and people; Clergie, and Magistrate, are sealed with the image of God, with a conformitie to him; and worldly seals will not answer that, nor fill up that seal. We should wonder to see a mother in the midst of many sweet children, passing her time in making babies and puppets for her own delight. We should wonder to see a man, whose chambers and galleries were full of curious masterpieces, thrust in a village fayre, to look

[100] Macdonald, George, *England's Antiphon* (N.Y., n.d.), p. 114.

upon sixpenie pictures, & three-farthing prints. We have all the image of God at home; and we all make babies, fancies of honour in our ambitions. The masterpiece is our own, in our own bosome; and we thrust in countrey fayres, that is, we endure the distempers of any unseasonable weather, in night-journeys and watchings; we endure the oppositions, and scorns, and triumphs of a rivall, and competitour, that seeks with us, and shares with us. We endure the guiltinesse and reproach of having deceived the trust which a confident friend reposes in us, and solicit his wife or daughter. We endure the decay of fortune of bodie, of soul, of honour, to possesse lovers pictures, pictures that are not originals, not made by that hand of God, Nature; but artificiall beauties: and for that bodie we give a soul; and for that drug, which might have been bought where they bought it, for a shilling, we give an estate. The image of God is more worth then all substances; and we give it for colours, for dreams, for shadows.[101]

We may compare the method of this passage, which seems to the modern reader comparatively simple and natural, with another, in which Donne uses in a similar manner symbols which are antiquated to us; the image is based on the medieval belief that the circle is a symbol of God, because it is the most perfect geometrical figure:

One of the most convenient Hieroglyphicks of God, is a Circle; and a Circle is endlesse; whom God loves, hee loves to the end: and not onely to their own end, to their death, but to his end, and his end is, that he might love them still. His hailestones, and his thunderbolts, and his showres of bloud (emblemes and instruments of his Judgements) fall downe in a direct line, and affect and strike some one person, or place: His Sun, and Moone, and Starres, (Emblemes and Instruments of his Blessings) move circularly, and communicate themselves to all. His Church is his chariot; in that, he moves more gloriously, then in the Sun; as much more, as his begotten Son exceeds his created Sun, and his Son of glory, and of his right hand, the Sun of the firmament; and this Church, his chariot, moves in that communicable motion, circularly; It began in the East, it came to us, and is passing now, shining out now, in the farthest West.[102]

Donne's experience in the second passage is as comprehensible to us as that in the first, but the imagery gives it a medieval flavor. Even so, however, Donne uses the image of the circle here exclusively as an image, and not as a philosophical concept.[103]

101 *Donne's Sermons* (ed. Smith), p. 153.

102 *Ibid.*, p. 134. For parallel uses of the circle see Donne's *Devotions upon Emergent Occasions* (ed. Sparrow; Cambridge, 1923), note, page 152.

103 The medieval respect for the circle had Aristotle for authority. In

In conclusion I shall quote two characteristic passages from his *Divine Poems,* both illustrating his feeling of dependence on God for forgiveness, strength and blessedness. We know how deep that feeling was in Donne, and we cannot doubt the sincerity of even such "conceited" verse as the beginning of *The Litanie:*

> Father of Heaven, and him, by whom
> It, and us for it, and all else, for us
>   Thou madest, and govern'st ever, come
> And re-create mee, now growne ruinous:
>   My heart is by dejection, clay,
>   And by selfe-murder, red.
> From this red earth, O Father, purge away
> All vicious tinctures, that new fashioned
> I may rise up from death, before I'am dead.[104]

In the concluding stanzas of his *Hymne to God, my God, in my sicknesse,* the "conceit" is raised almost to the sublime by its intensity:

> We thinke that *Paradise* and *Calvarie,*
>   *Christs* Crosse, and *Adams* tree, stood in one place;
> Looke Lord, and finde both *Adams* met in me;
>   As the first *Adams* sweat surrounds my face,
>   May the last *Adams* blood my soule embrace.
>
> So, in his purple wrapp'd receive mee Lord,
>   By these his thornes give me his other Crowne;
> And as to others soules I preach'd thy word,
>   Be this my Text, my Sermon to mine owne,
>   Therfore that he may raise the Lord throws down.[105]

---

his *Metaphysics,* Book XII, Chap. viii, he had said that the stars and planets must be eternal essences, for they move in perfect circles, and a body which moves in a perfect circle must be eternal and unresting. The medieval mind, believing that the world is to be explained by forms and essences, had a profound faith in a priori reasoning, not only in philosophy, but in science. Kepler, as he worked over his calculations on the paths of the planets, was forced, though reluctantly, to abandon these perfect circles for ellipses. The circle lost its mysterious significance, and the world its beautiful order. As Donne said, in the poem quoted above:

> 'Tis all in pieces, all cohaerence gone;
> All just supply, and all Relation.

[104] Grierson, I. 338.
[105] *Ibid.,* I. 368.

The style of Donne, then, was an expression of his mind. If the term "metaphysical" be understood to signify a poet expounding medieval philosophy, or indeed any philosophy, it is not applicable to Donne; he expounded no system, he was not a philosophical poet in the sense that Lucretius was, or Sir John Davies, his contemporary. If by the epithet we mean only that Donne used, in his "conceits," some of the terms and distinctions of medieval thought, it may be admitted to be partially applicable, though misleading in its emphasis. Donne took his imagery wherever he found it — from Renaissance science, from daily life, or from the Church Fathers or the disquisitions of the Schools. He used the imagery understood by the educated men of his time. But his purpose was to express his inner self, his moods, whims, emotions, aspirations, in their infinite complexity and subtlety. He was a "psychological" poet in the sense that he found his poetical material in his own experience; his poetry, like his preaching, is introspective. The genuineness of his poetic and religious nature shines through the crabbed verse and the tortured "conceits." It is true that Donne was one of the most intellectual of writers. His mind was made of the toughest fibre, and there is the same toughness in his style. But he is a great writer because he expresses with such intensity, thoughts and experiences that are poetical and human.

GNOSIS AND THE QUESTION OF THOUGHT IN VEDĀNTA

STUDIES IN PHILOSOPHY AND RELIGION

1. FREUND, E.R. *Franz Rosenzweig's Philosophy of Existence: An Analysis of* The Star of Redemption. 1979. ISBN 90 247 2091 5.
2. OLSON, A.M. *Transcendence and Hermeneutics: An Interpretation of the Philosophy of Karl Jaspers*. 1979. ISBN 90 247 2092 3.
3. VERDU, A. *The Philosophy of Buddhism*. 1981. ISBN 90 247 2224 1.
4. OLIVER, H.H. *A Relational Metaphysic*. 1981. ISBN 90 247 2457 0.
5. ARAPURA, J.G. *Gnosis and the Question of Thought in Vedānta*. 1986. ISBN 90 247 3061 9.
6. HOROSZ, W. and CLEMENTS, T. *Religion and Human Purpose*. 1986. ISBN 90 247 3000 7.
7. SIA, S. *God in Process Thought*. 1985. ISBN 90 247 3103 8.
8. KOBLER, J.F. *Vatican II and Phenomenology*. 1985. ISBN 90 247 3193 3.

GNOSIS AND THE QUESTION OF THOUGHT IN VEDĀNTA

Dialogue with the Foundations

JOHN G. ARAPURA

McMaster University, Hamilton
Ontario L85 4K1, Canada

1986 **MARTINUS NIJHOFF PUBLISHERS**
a member of the KLUWER ACADEMIC PUBLISHERS GROUP
DORDRECHT / BOSTON / LANCASTER

Distributors

for the United States and Canada: Kluwer Academic Publishers, 190 Old Derby Street, Hingham, MA 02043, USA
for the UK and Ireland: Kluwer Academic Publishers, MTP Press Limited, Falcon House, Queen Square, Lancaster LA1 1RN, UK
for all other countries: Kluwer Academic Publishers Group, Distribution Center, P.O. Box 322, 3300 AH Dordrecht, The Netherlands

Library of Congress Cataloging in Publication Data

Arapura, John G. (John Geeverghese), 1920-
Gnosis and the question of thought in Vedānta.

(Studies in philosophy and religion ; 5)
Bibliography: p.
1. Vedanta. 2. Thought and thinking. I. Title.
II. Series: Studies in philosophy and religion
(Martinus Nijhoff Publishers) ; v. 5.
B132.V3A735 1984 181'.48 84-16564
ISBN 90-247-3061-9

ISBN 90-247-3061-9 (this volume)
ISBN 90-247-2346-9 (series)

PRINTED IN THE NETHERLANDS

TABLE OF CONTENTS

Preface 1

Introduction: Gnosis and the scope of philosophizing in Vedānta 5
That which philosophy and philosophizing are about and the thought which pertains to it 9
I. Thought as approached from human consciousness as the ground 10
II. Thought as approached from the correspondence of being to being as the ground 15
III. Thought as approached from gnosis as the ground 19

Chapter I: Gnosis and philosophical thought in the *Ṛg Veda* 29
The text of the *Ṛg Veda* 29
The Veda and the Vedas; the Veda meaning idea 31
Ṛg Vedic Mantras 36
Vāk and the Vedic telling 47
The continuing currency of thought through concrete speculation 52

Chapter II: Gnosis and philosophical thought in the Upanisads 57
The texts of the Upaniṣads 57
The meaning of the word *upaniṣad* 59
The Upaniṣads as the culmination of Vedic Relation 61
The Centrality of *Brahman/Ātman* in the Upanisads 65
Description of *Brahman/Ātman* 75
Gnosis and thought 78

Chapter III: Gnosis and philosophical thought in the *Bhagavadgītā* 93
Commentary on the *Bhagavadgītā* 96
The *Gītā* and *Brahma-vidyā* 103
The philosophy of the *Gītā*: the fundamental outlook 107
The teaching about the two observances expanded into a comprehensive horizon 114
The conclusion 131

Chapter IV: Gnosis and philosophical thought in the *Brahma Sūtra* 135
The arrangement of the text 136
The circle of gnosis philosophy 139

A preliminary statement based on the first four *Sūtras* 144
Cause the primordial question 154
The unfolding of the system in the main body of the Bhāsya 166

Notes and additional references 201

PREFACE

It would probably be generally admitted that Vedānta is the apex of the Indian (or Eastern) religious philosophies. Yet today it commands so little attention, in part, no doubt, because the modern mood in scholarship refuses anchoring and centering of thought.

The present work seeks to address modern thought though not in the modern mood. It is nevertheless motivated by the belief that there are times when the timeless is most timely.

It is possible that the sources of a tradition such as Vedānta, if approached properly, will yield something which can be brought within the ambience of the contemporary philosophical quest, at least of its still largely unmanifest undercurrents. The present work is intended to be an act, imperfect as it is, in that direction. That marks the difference of this project, called *Gnosis and the Question of Thought in Vedānta*, from customary studies in Indology.

The term "gnosis" as employed in this context is a translation of its cognate Sanskrit term *jñāna*, the latter, however, having a much wider range of meaning than the former, especially in view of the latter's appropriation for a specific usage by the Gnostic traditions of both the East and the West. In the general expression of Vedānta too the Gnostic understanding of *jñāna* has undoubtedly persisted especially in the so-called *jñāna-mārga*, or "way of gnosis", made popular from early medieval times on. However, in this present work we seek to return to the original meaning of *jñāna* (or gnosis, as we shall refer to it, using the Greek-Western cognate) – inasmuch as it prevails in the foundational texts of Vedānta, with which we shall hold dialogue. Accordingly, we see gnosis as ground of philosophical thought. This character of gnosis has, as often as not, remained hidden behind a veil. The task that is set before us, as understood in this present work, is to become witnesses of gnosis disclosing itself as the ground of thought, that is, of thought as such, to become witnesses of a great tradition opening its hand and letting us see that distinctively human thing it has been holding. In the past, Vedānta like other Eastern traditions has been approached from the customary standpoints of mystical contemplation, scholastic disputations and life-wisdoms. While none of these standpoints is called into question, it is maintained by us that the other standpoint – of thought as such – must not remain under eclipse, inasmuch as it alone makes philosophy.

That thought is inexchangeable with anything else, even with contemplation, not to say with methods of disputations or with psycho-metaphysical techniques, that it is without another to take its place, that while it is the sum of our questions and of answers to those questions, the sum of both our doubts and beliefs, of both our inability and ability to know, it is nonetheless something more is the truth to which that paramount phenomenon which we call philosophy has testified again and again. The same testimony also tells us that thought is also much more than any expression it has ever been given. It is the clarity with which we hear this that sends us to a tradition which silently promises to show us the highest ground from which thought may arise, without at the same time distorting the fact that what arises from that ground is still what opens itself to us as thought rather than something else.

It is for the sake of investigating the possibility, and with it the nature, of thought that may arise out of the ground which is gnosis that the fundamental texts of Vedānta have been approached. A word may be said about the unmistakable similarity between this investigation and Martin Heidegger's probing dialogue with the Greek sources of Western philosophy: in fact the latter has served as an inspiring model for our task. However, there is also a point of departure – one among several – for while Heidegger seizes thought in its historicality, with a view to letting thought unfold its destiny in its concealment in the present, no such effort is made in respect of thought that has its ground in gnosis, for there we are outside historicality altogether vis-à-vis thought. And yet it is recognized that the kind of dialogue which Heidegger held with the sources that lie in Greek antiquity has shown us the way of productively holding a dialogue with Vedāntic foundations. And, moreover, we come to know that despite the difference on account of historicality, in the thought that has its ground in gnosis (Vedānta) there is nevertheless an unfolding that has absolute and compelling significance for the present.

Now about the word "present", let it be said, lest there by any false anticipation, that it is used in this context merely in a general sense, marking our universal situation in respect of both thought and existence, without having any intention of saying anything about the present, presentness and thought and their relation to one another which are so much a part of Heidegger's investigations, even when they have to do with the Greek sources. Neither Vedānta nor any other Eastern tradition had any part in bringing us to the standpoint that underlies the word "present", the decisiveness and inescapability of which, however, are what have acted as our impetus to turn to a tradition such as Vedānta in order to see how its gnosis serves as the ground of thought, and how it may respond to the present. We add that insofar as Vedānta (or any other non-Western tradition) had no part in delivering us to where we are, both in thought and in existence, it will have to speak essentially from the outside. And that freedom it has is not bad, as long as it is not accompanied by the claim of possessing an ability to deliver us *from* the present – and such claims are invariably attended by total misunderstanding of what the present entails for both good and bad and of what lies behind the present. However, Vedānta's adherence to gnosis and its implications of the eternal extended to thought has an absolute and compelling significance for the present, that is, in the general sense of where we are both in thought and existence. And moreover, another side of Vedānta – its kinship with the Greek tradition in respect of Logos (*Vāk*) – will show its surprising ability to be apprehended by Western thought, which is so profoundly shaped by the Greek Logos. This side of Vedānta has invariably been missed in the past because of the predisposition on the part of writers to see it within the general context of what is called vaguely Eastern Philosophy. An effort is being made in this work to redress this, as it will be evident. Vedāntic Logos is not Greek but it has deep affinities and dissimilarities with the Greek, which are what make it an alternative and at the same time a complement.

It is clear that the task envisaged in this work is to take a first, essential step in showing how gnosis as enshrined in Vedānta is ground of thought à la philosophy, undertaken through a dialogue with the foundational texts and them only. Further steps may indeed by taken once this one holds, and upon its basis deeper dialogue with the West is also possible. Strangely enough, an earlier book by the author, *Religion as Anxiety and Tranquility*: *An*

Essay in Comparative Phenomenology of the Spirit, will also be a beneficiary, in retrospect.

Lastly, in respect of acknowledging what the author owes and to whom, the people to be mentioned are: his wife, Protima, whose gift of entering with deep understanding into the author's mind is an abiding source of strength to him; Mrs. Ross (Grace) Gordon, the senior secretary of his department, who has painstakingly and with perceptive care brought the manuscript up to a fit state – not to omit the many students whom he has had the privilege to teach and to guide over the years.

Now, there is the matter of acknowledging material quoted from other books. However, by far the vast majority of quotations are from ancient or medieval Indian texts which, like all such things, are the possession of the world; as for the translations of those, they are my own. In addition, there are just a very few citations from modern Western philosophical works. Accordingly, passages from:

What is called Thinking? By Martin Heidegger, English translation by J. Glenn Gray, Copyright C, 1968, New York, Harper Row, Publishers, Inc., reprinted by permission;

What is Philosophy? By Martin Heidegger, translation by W. Kluback and J.T. Wilde, Copyright 1958 and reprinted with the permission of Twayne Publishers, a division of G.K. Hall & Co., Boston;

On the Geneology of Morals, by Friedrich Nietzche, translated by Walter Kaufmann and R.J. Hollingdale, Copyright, 1969, reprinted with the permission of Random House, Inc., New York.

A Clarification with Regard to Capital or Small First Letters of Some Terms

The reader will, no doubt, observe such a variation especially in the case of certain Sanskrit terms. The explanation is that when the thing itself is mentioned, that is, wherever warranted, the first letter will be in capitals, whereas when it is the term that is mentioned the first letter will be small. Any other kind of such variation is explained in the text itself, wherever it occurs.

INTRODUCTION

GNOSIS AND THE SCOPE OF PHILOSOPHIZING IN VEDĀNTA

What follows is an account of Vedānta, undertaken with a view to exploring the nature of philosophical thought in that tradition, and simultaneously of exploring the scope of philosophizing it offers. It is needful and it is useful for us to philosophize, particularly in our spiritually dangerous times. And we can philosophize fruitfully only by turning to the store-houses of wisdom preserved in our great traditions. We must indeed think for ourselves but when we do so in the most genuine way, that is, free from egoism and conceit and most of all without being hindered by that most binding shackle of all, namely, the assumption that the thinking that we do is somehow ours while we do the thinking *for* all, it will become clear to us that we are not alone in this and that we are not left without witnesses to what we strive after.

We turn to these store-houses of wisdom, paying heed in equal measure to their own character and to their vogue in the traditions of man, on the one hand, and, on the other, to the way we turn to them. There then takes place an interplay between these two, and that is what will decisively enable us to seize these store-houses of wisdom as philosophy.

In the pages to follow what we aim to show is precisely such an interplay *vis-à-vis* the Vedāntic tradition. That which comes into a philosophizing purview and which we can seize as such is philosophy. Is Vedānta philosophy? Or more generally, is there such a thing as Eastern philosophy? Although for more than a century, that is since the West's introduction into Eastern wisdoms, scholars have been writing books on Vedāntic and other Eastern "philosophies", these questions have been hanging in the background. Surely, orientalist scholars could not have been expected to await an answer to these, and so they have freely and uninhibitedly exercised their privilege in speaking of the systems of Eastern wisdom as "philosophy". However, great modern philosophers of the West – not just scholars – like G.W.F. Hegel and Martin Heidegger,[1] by telling us that philosophy is only Western, have forced us to think the matter over again and more carefully. In trying to demonstrate that there are some Eastern traditions which can claim the name philosophy we are not laying that claim on their behalf in the precise respects in which these great philosophers have denied it to them but in a more special manner, that is to say, by trying to show that these traditions have properties which make it possible, and even necessary, for us to seize them as philosophy. Heidegger in his well-known lecture published under the title *What is Philosophy*? (*Was ist das – die Philosophie*?) undertakes a penetrating investigation of the genesis and career of philosophy. Within the strict limits of that masterly investigation there is decidedly no room left for any such thing as a non-Western "philosophy". To quote:

> The word *philosophia* tells us that philosophy is something which, first of all, determines the existence of the Greek world. Not only that – *philosophia* also determines the innermost basic features of our Western-European history. The often heard expression 'Western-European philosophy' is, in truth, a tautology.[2]

But the question today is, ought we not to surpass these limits and grasp other traditions and by philosophizing and – insofar as they enable us to do so – bring them into a philosophizing purview through an interplay? The question can also be turned around: ought we not to do this in order to be able to philosophize in a new and unlimited way? [Heidegger's definition of the verb 'to philosophize' is apt: it means "to enter *into* philosophy, to tarry it in, to conduct ourselves in its manner."][3]

The task that we are about to undertake has these questions as its background, although its aim is not just furnishing an answer to them. Our undertaking here will be only in respect of Vedānta but we will give an account of it in terms of the question of its scope of philosophizing. Hence it is obvious that ours is going to be different from all other accounts in not being either historical or merely expository, or apologetical for that matter. Rather, it will be a hermeneutical one. But what actually do we mean by "hermeneutics"? Basically, it is the same as what we mean by interplay, but one in which the interpreted subject-matter, what the interpreter brings with him and the means of interpretation all fuse into one single, homogeneous philosophical activity. The means of interpretation must be called by the name "dialogue".

We, therefore, must undertake our task by means of a dialogue with the Vedānta tradition. The dialogue will have to be with the texts and with the thinkers, actually with the thinking of the thinkers. Does not all this sound, at least initially, rather rhetorical? Can we really *talk* with the texts and with the thinkers of the past? In order to answer these questions we must first of all grasp the nature of the talk involved here. Let us begin with a kind of talk we make in our everyday life for an approach to the understanding of this other talk. Thus, if we look deeply enough into what transpires in our ordinary life, we can easily see that we do commune with Nature, with beings in our environment and with symbols of reality, both far and near. Actually, it is this communion, despite all its interruptions and hindrances, that makes us persons, by letting personhood surface to the region of our conscious life. At the next level, that is, if we are to understand Nature, our environment and the symbols of reality far and near, we must look upon them as events to be grasped so that by grasping them we visualize a sphere of Meaning (or at least meanings and patterns). We can go to further levels from here but from then on the everyday experience itself becomes the ground for perception at greater depth. One has several choices here, as one may turn to art, poetry, science or history, and in all these hermeneutics is necessary. The artist, the poet, the scientist and the historian choose different events (e.g., the physical, psychic, psychophysical, chemical, biochemical, astronomical, human or historical) with which to commune, and choose different modes of communion. They are all, however, pushed over into another dimension where thought must transcend the given framework of ordinary human interaction and discourse. The dimension is transpersonal, which is what in the last resort ensures the possibility of all *personal* communication.

In philosophy, the dialogue with text and thinkers of the past is philosophical dialogue. The texts as well as what the thinkers have spoken (or thought) are the events with which we have to commune. As Heidegger states, "This mutual talking of what always anew peculiarly concerns philosophers as being the Same, that is talking, *legein* in the sense of *dialegesthai* (conversing) is talking as dialogue."[4] Further, "it is one thing to determine and describe the opinions of philosophers. It is an entirely different thing to talk through with them, and that means that of which they speak".[5] In philosophy there is this peculiarity: the events which constitute the texts and the thought of the thinkers (together forming the subject-matter), with which dialogue is to take place, are not the reality that philosophy and philosophizing essentially are all about. In speaking with the texts and the thinkers we can only speak of that of which they themselves speak and not *with* it – and as a matter of fact neither could they. So then, in taking this route of dialogue with them, i.e., with the events of the texts and of the thinkers' thinking, we will be observing an attitude of circumspection towards that which philosophy and philosophizing are all about (be it predicated on "Being" or "Ultimate Reality").

For the dialogue with the Vedānta tradition the texts chosen will have to be the central ones, which are, in the universal verdict of the tradition itself, the *Ṛg Veda*, the Upaniṣads, the *Bhagavad-gītā* and the *Brahma Sūtra*, the last three together in a special way being called the *prasthāna-traya*, or triple foundation. These texts present certain events, which we must correctly describe as knowledge-events, and are accordingly not to be taken as either temporal or personal. The responses to the demand for hermeneutics of these knowledge-events were already made primordially within the texts themselves and in later epochs by the thinkers who are called *ācaryas*, through whose thinking the events have passed to us so that they may be seized as philosophy by being brought into the philosophizing purview in our day.

What is the philosophizing purview that we have in mind? We may put it initially as that which is a genuine outcome of the knowledge-events of the Vedānta texts and of the thinking of the Vedānta thinkers which can address itself to us as thought, and no more and no less. The above statement (which is, however, not yet a description) will show that what we are setting about to do is different from the two customary expressions of Vedānta, i.e., as an elaborate and intricate logico-metaphysical structure and as a profound mysticism.

In order, however, to obviate any misunderstanding, let us affirm in the clearest terms possible that the value and validity of these two above-mentioned expressions are by no means called into question. On the contrary, we proceed on the assumption that they are absolutely integral to Vedānta (as also to other, allied traditions). Further, we must also take note of the striking fact that these two expressions in most Asian traditions are not only inter-related but lean on each other, enhancing each other. And as for Vedānta especially, the precision and subtlety of its categories in both respects are utterly stunning even as sheer feats of conceptual and analytical virtuosity and speculative power. Traditionally, however, it is the mysticism of Vedānta (and of other Eastern systems) which has held the imagination of the West – and that is still true. The logico-metaphysical structure has also engaged the attention of many notable and astute scholars of the West. These two expressions still merit the highest consideration.

In our present treatise we not only do not avoid the logico-metaphysical structure and the mysticism of Vedānta but actually observe them and treat them as the irremovable and essential background of what we strive for, and draw inspiration from them. It is only that the exploration of the nature of philosophizing is not considered the same as speaking about either of them separately or together.

THAT WHICH PHILOSOPHY AND PHILOSOPHYZING ARE ABOUT AND THE THOUGHT WICH PERTAINS TO IT

A few pages back we spoke of an attitude of circumspection towards that which philosophy and philosophizing are all about, and we observed in parenthesis that it may be predicated on "Being" or "Ultimate Reality". In fact, it can be just as legitimately predicated on other terms, for instance, "the Good". But the demonstration of such possibilities brings no profit. However, this circumspection is not something we learn naturally but only in the context of dialogue with philosophical traditions or with traditions that can be seized as philosophical in the actual philosophizing. Nor has this circumspection anything to do with agnosticism and scepticism, they being its very opposite. For in fact, rather than denying the prospect of thought attaining what it sets out to attain, it reinforces it by making the task hopeful. Therefore, dialogue with traditions conduces to the deepening and maturing of philosophical thought.

Before we proceed any further we must re-capitulate the sense of what was just stated above by clearly defining philosophical thought as that thought which pertains to what philosophy and philosophizing are about (predicated on such terms as "Being" and "Ultimate Reality"). And then we can see that there are three ways in which the task of philosophical thought, as defined above, is approached. And the three approaches, far from being exclusive of one another, may actually support one another and must eventually be seen as belonging together. The dialogue with the traditions will enable us to perceive them all distinctly. Hence we may speak of philosophical thought in the following three ways: (I) as approached from human consciousness as the ground; (II) as approached from the correspondence of being to Being (or Ultimate Reality) as the ground; and (III) as approached from (what for the want of a more appropriate word we shall call) gnosis as the ground. Let us try to analyse these three below.

I. THOUGHT AS APPROACHED FROM HUMAN CONSCIOUSNESS AS THE GROUND

Our own consciousness is what every one of us has access to and what has potential access to everyone and everything. There is a primordial operation of consciousness as a consequence of its interaction with what it encounters as reality, first of all the world itself, both in its determinate and indeterminate aspects. In this interaction consciousness clearly engages with itself as well. In this way all reality becomes phenomena in the primary sense, namely, of their own shining (the word phenomenon, Greek *phainomenon*, having derived from the stem *pha* – Sanskrit cognate *bhā* –, to shine) and showing themselves. But the primary sense right away ushers in a secondary sense, namely, that of seeming, because in showing itself reality does not show itself *as* itself. Therefore, it is seen as though through a veil that conceals it from consciousness, that is to say, it becomes an "appearance". And the more consciousness encounters it the more impenetrable becomes the veil of appearance which sets it off from the underlying reality.[6]

Here consciousness finds itself pushed over into a new dimension of encounter with reality, and that we know as wonder. Although wonder is a universal experience, sometimes and in certain cases it becomes a shock that puts consciousness on the road to thinking. It is that kind of wonder carrying a shock with it that the Greeks called *thaumasein* or astonishment (or amazement). We are told by both Plato and Aristotle that astonishment is the origin *(ārchē)* of philosophy. Plato writes: "For this is especially the *pathos* of a philosopher, to be astonished, for there is no other origin of philosophy than this", (*Theatetus* 155d).[7] And likewise Aristotle: "For through astonishment men have begun to philosophize both in our times and in the beginning", (*Metaphysics* A2, 982b, 125q).[8] Martin Heidegger explains Plato's and Aristotle's statements to the effect that astonishment is not to be treated as just the beginning of philosophy in a mere historical sense but that it is its perpetual origin all the way. Thus he clarifies:

> It would be very superficial and, above all, very un-Greek, if Plato and Aristotle are only determining that astonishment is cause (*Ursache*) of philosophizing. If they were of this opinion, that would mean that at some time or other men were astonished. Impelled by this astonishment, they began to philosophize. As soon as philosophy was in progress, astonishment became superfluous as a propelling force so that it disappeared. It could disappear since it was only an impetus. However, astonishment is *ārchē* – it pervades every step of philosophy.[9]

Now, if this powerful shock of wonder, i.e., astonishment, attends us every step of the way as it stimulates thought pertaining to what philosophy and philosophizing are about, we must try to see how this thought operates. Here we will outline it in the following manner. This is only a description of the way we think even when we do not know that we think. And hence it is not a prescription. We can only call that thinking thinking in the philosophical sense when it becomes aware of itself. And we will also notice that the natural prospect of thinking has no end as it is always at its painful beginning. But the prospect of achieving self-conscious clarity as to what natural thinking is is also a process that automatically advances it. And this too is made possible by wonder called astonishment, which also characterizes our own natural thinking. Thus we see some natural paths of thought, three of which (the main ones) will be outlined below.

Firstly, *thought as the penetration of the hidden depths of reality*.
In respect of this, thought incorporates both intuition and imagination. The problematic posed by the reality (i.e., *Ultimate* Reality) of all that appears to consciousness is the reason for thought's attempt to penetrate to what is hidden. It is not the absence of intuition into such reality as comes before consciousness but its very presence that sets thought on this path, for the intuition

itself brings the problem. Whatever is intuited as essence is such only in a doubtful sense and the abstractions (concepts) drawn from intuitions add to the doubtfulness. Therefore, the mind spontaneously and freely goes to work to fill the gap with imagination. As Edmand Husserl observes, "conceptual construction certainly takes place spontaneously and free fancy likewise, and what is spontaneously produced is of course a product of the mind."[10] Imagination itself is not reliable because it is fancy, but what is imagined may either be a mere creature of that fancy or it may be a still hidden reality which while refusing to yield itself to intuition may yet be doing so, although falsely through fancy. But in either case, that is, whether what is imagined is a mere product of fancy or a reality which only reveals itself through it, the shock of wonder, namely astonishment, continues to urge thought to go further. This is another and deeper than usual sense in which astonishment must be said to pervade every step of philosophy.

However, in the very interest of thought going further in penetrating reality, there is need to secure the intuitions (or concepts) to some solid base. That entails two corollaries: (a) shifting of the intuitions as between true and false; (b) structuring of those that are determined as true through the use of proportional relations. As to the first, the true intuitions are those that will bear the light of repeated examination as possibilities under all conceivable conditions and will stand up without being falsified in the respects in which they are supposed to be true. They are the ones that have the potentiality to be principles in the service of coherent theoretical explanations which can be erected on them. It is here that the ideal laws of identity, non-contradiction and excluded middle present themselves. As to the second i.e., structuring of true intuitions through the use of proportional relations, the supreme forms of it are analogy, the assignment of right properties to right substances, and lastly, the deduction of general properties from the combination of two or more individual properties (or rather sets of properties) and in that way the induction of unintuited substances. The same proportional relations are used in communication, i.e., in the transaction that takes place between speaking and understanding as well as in the transference of knowledge gained through intuition.

In both these corollaries i.e., shifting of intuitions as true from false, and the structuring of the true through proportional relations, a deeper *ratio*, or Reason, is involved as they are not found to be self-grounded. And this deeper *ratio*, or Reason, is common to both.

Secondly, *thought as the act of boundary-making for coping with the boundless.*

This takes place at the terminus of intuition and even of imagination. This is the free flight in which thought has nowhere forward to go and hence recoils to where it started from. Even imagined realities are only landmarks which the mind can set up with its freely constructed images. So like a free-flying bird, the mind returns because there is nothing upon which to light, and merely reports the immensity of what has driven it back home. But whenever thought returns, like the homing pigeon, where it started from becomes the boundary. This behaviour of thought is simply acting in obedience to the intrinsic need of the mind to sustain itself. But it does report about the ungraspable immensity beyond the boundary, and in fact doing so is the real gain achieved by its return. Ultimate Reality is, therefore, not something about which anything definite can be reported except that it always lies beyond any boundary that thought can reach. The boundary itself is that, to use the description of the *Taittirīya Upaniṣad*, "whence speech, along with mind, returns without reaching (what is still beyond the boundary)".[11] What thought reports (through speech) is merely what is at the edge of the immensity seen from our side, i.e., at the boundary from which it recoils. But insofar as the boundary is of thought's own making and as such it calls it ultimate, it acts as a positive and firm ground that informs it with the power to find its way back as well as to report that there is a beyond. This ground is Reason which is invoked in both the sifting of intuitions and in the structuring of them, as already discussed above.

Thirdly, *thought as the penetration of the otherness inherent in phenomena.*

This is really complementary to the first path of thought we described, i.e., thought as the penetration of the hidden depths of reality, but it is approached from a different angle. Some phenomena have a built in otherness, while others do not. However, in naming all phenomena by their particularities there is a direct negation of otherness. Hence when we say 'here', the "here" means not "there" or anywhere else, and vice-versa. Likewise in respect of 'this' and 'that'; 'now' and 'then', etc., etc. But such is not the case with phenomena like time, life and being, and contrariwise, eternity, death and non-being.

Time and eternity are, by definition, opposites of each other. But time cannot be thought without that inherent otherness, i.e., eternity, nor can eternity be thought without and apart from time. But even so, paradoxically enough, in thinking either of them it is necessary to contrast it with an inherent other, which by definition is its opposite, however in the same respect. The inherence of eternity in time is revealed by the fact that time's beginning and end cannot be contemplated or conceived, which means that its otherness is the governing condition of its being thought and that, however, is manifestly absent. Therefore it is evident that the absence of something in something else (in the same respect) is not antithetical to its inherence as a notion. But then before we lay it down like this, we should consider some theoretical ways in which time has been approached either with an eye to eternity or without it. In none of these ways what we speak of as the inherent otherness between time and eternity that governs our thinking and the necessity to think them together seem to be recognized. Thus one view of time depicts it as pure momentariness with no reference to eternity. Another view is based on duration, with which we are supposed to wrest time's essence and thereby recover its own essential being. According to yet another view, time and eternity intersect in some higher mystical or metaphysical experience, which is therefore called "eternal now". There are many more. No doubt, each has its own strength. But we are not talking about solutions but about the problem itself. But the problem persists not only in respect of time and eternity but also in respect of life and death, being and non-being, and of many other pairs. Now, because there are these problems and also precisely because there are no real solutions to any one of them, there are *many* different solutions. And therefore, the natural paths of thought keep on moving forward, never coming to an end.

Now, over against this approach to what philosophy and philosophizing are about (with its natural paths), proceeding as it does from human consciousness as the ground, we must outline the other two approaches (i.e., from the correspondence of being to Being, and from gnosis respectively', which are marked out by the definiteness of their understanding of the subject-matter.

II. THOUGHT AS APPROACHED FROM THE CORRESPONDENCE OF BEING TO BEING AS THE GROUND

This approach is a definite path, and it has been most clearly adumbrated in the writings of Martin Heidegger. [Heidegger has to be taken most seriously because he writes not on his behalf only but on that of the whole tradition coming down from the Greeks. Besides, he tells us that this is what is to be understood by *philosophy*.]

Raising the question "What is philosophy?" he observes [marking the definiteness of the path] : "the first thing for us to do is to lead the question to a *clearly directed path,*[12] so that we do not flounder around in either convenient or haphazard conceptions of philosophy."[13] "[This] tradition which bears the Greek name *philosophia*, and which is labelled for us with the historical word *philosophia*, reveals the direction of a path on which we ask, 'What is philosophy?' "[14] "We must then ourselves, through our thinking, go to meet philosophy on the path it is travelling. Our speaking must co-respond to that which addresses the philosophers. If this co-responding is successful to us then in the true sense of the word, we respond to the question, 'What is philosophy?' "[15] Then, explaining the identity of meaning between "to respond" (German, *ent-sprechen* and "to answer to" (German, *antworten*), he adds, "The answer is not a reply (*n'est pas une response*), the answer is rather the co-respondence (*la correspondance*) which responds to the Being of being".[16]

> In such a correspondence we listen from the very outset to that which philosophy has already said to us, *philosophy*, that is, *philosophia* understood in the Greek sense. That is why we attain correspondence, that is, an answer to our question, only when we remain in conversation with that to which the tradition of philosophy delivers us, that is, liberates us. We find the answer to the question, "What is Philosophy?", not through conversing with that which has been handed down to us as the Being of being.[17]

This path is not a break with philosophy in its history but is an adoption and transformation of what has been handed down to us, in other words, destruction (*Destruktion*, perhaps meaning destructuring.) "Destruction means to open our ears, to make ourselves free for what speaks to us in tradition as the Being of being. By listening to this interpellation we attain the correspondence."[18]

The wide-ranging scope of philosophy is already trimmed to the dimensions of the conduit pipe of the correspondence of being to Being. The natural paths of thought as characterizing that wide-ranging scope of philosophy is exhibited in Heidegger's exposition in "the unfolding attitude specifically adopted by us" towards the natural correspondence of being to Being that constitutes our nature.

> **Are we, humans, not always already in such a correspondence with the Being of being, and, what is more, not only *de facto* but by virtue of our nature? Does not this correspondence constitute the fundamental trait of our nature? This is indeed the case. [But] although we do remain always and everywhere in correspondence to the Being of being, we nevertheless, rarely pay attention to the appeal of Being. The correspondence to the Being of being does, to be sure, always remain our abode. But only at times does it become an unfolding attitude specifically adopted by us. Only when this happens do we really correspond to that which concerns philosophy which is on the way towards the Being of being.[19]**

The achieving of such correspondence through philosophical thinking is what Heidegger calls attunement (*Gestimmtheit* or disposition),[20] or tuned correspondence (*gestimmte Entsprechen*).[21] Philosophy being understood thus, there is no chance of surrendering thinking to "the accidental changes and vacillations of sentiments." "It is rather a question of pointing out that every precision of language is grounded in a disposition (*Disposition*) of correspondence, I say, in heeding the appeal."[22] This "essential disposition of correspondence" (*die wesenhafte Gestimmtheit des Entsprechens* = essential attunement of correspondence), Heidegger wants to show, is not a modern invention. So he writes, "The Greek thinkers, Plato and Aristotle, already drew attention to the fact that philosophy and philosophizing belong in the dimension of man which we call tuning (in the sense of tuning and attunement)."[23]

The astonishment (*thaumasein*) which is the *ārchē* of philosophy is here shown to be something distinct from what the word appears to us ordinarily [and hence distinct from what is appropriated by the natural paths of thought such as we have demonstrated to proceed from the ground of human consciousness]. Accordingly, "Astonishment is the tuning within which the Greek philosophers were granted the correspondence to the Being of being."[24]

At this point we must go back to where Heidegger has already explained to us the very meaning of philosophy, it having to do in its genesis with the *sophon*, which Heraclitus had expressed as "One (is) all" (*Hen panta*). It is explained that "All" stands for the whole, the totality of beings, while "one" stands for Being. "The *sophon* says all being is in Being. To put it more pointedly – being *is* Being".[25] The verb *is* (which, however, is only implicit in Heraclitus' own formula) is only transitive and means approximately "gathered together" (*versammelt*). "Being gathers being together insofar as it is being. Being is the gathering together – *Logos*."[26] "[And yet it is] just this fact that being is gathered together in Being, that in the appearance of Being being appears that astonished the Greeks and them alone. Being [small b] – that became the most astonishing thing for the Greeks."[27]

The *sophon* exhibits this unity or correspondence between being and Being. From the *sophon* apparently Heraclitus coined the phrase *aner philosophos* (*hos philei to sophon*, he who loves the *sophon*). The word *philein* (loving) expresses the *harmonia* between Being and being, and that is its distinctive feature in the Heraclitean sense. And this is the correspondence. In the speaking of the *Logos* this correspondence is expressed, and speaking in the way of the *Logos* (that is, *homolegein*) is the speaking of the *sophon*-loving man. [Heidegger further shows that philosophy (*philosophia*) came in the efforts (of Socrates and Plato) to "rescue and protect the astonishing thing" from others' attacks. The *harmonia* became a yearning (*orexis*) and a striving for the *sophon*. "And the striving is determined by *Eros*."]

The whole of Western philosophy (which for Heidegger is the whole of philosophy) is the continuation of what the Greeks called *epistēmē theoretikē* (speculative knowledge), that is to say, a kind of competence or skill (*epistēmē tis*), which is capable of being on the lookout for this very *harmonia* (in different ways at different epochs) and of seizing it in its glance and of holding it.[28] Heidegger would not deny that philosophy has changed in the more than two thousand years of its history. He observes: "At the same time we ought not, however, to overlook the fact that philosophy from Aristotle to Nietzsche, precisely because of these changes throughout their course, has remained the same. For transformations are the warranty for the kinship in the same."[29]

It is significant that Heidegger, who is probably the greatest philosophical student of the history of Western philosophy, has not only exposed the main thrust of that history (as different ways of tuning being to Being in different epochs), but has also acted as its greatest critic (both constructive and destructive), pointing to a possibility of thinking beyond it, which may also have been there before it took to the course it did. But the way towards that goal lies through philosophy. For no doubt, the criticism of philosophy with a view to finding a path of thought beyond it (and behind it) is also a philosophizing act, for one must still speak the language of what one must overcome.[30] The course on which Western philosophy had been destined to travel right up to the present, producing as one of its logical products modern technology itself with its calculative thinking, Heidegger argues, was set by Plato. So from Plato to Aristotle, to the Middle Ages, to Descartes, to German idealism, and further to Nietzsche, on the one hand, and to technology, on the other, the path has been the same. What persists through all these, he shows, is the self-giving of Being in different ways. The path, he considers fate-laden (*geschicklich*, different from *geschichtlich*, or historical). So he demonstrates how Western philosophy has been travelling along a fateful path. Now, although it was Plato who gave a decisive orientation to this path, it was in a sense already there even from Anaximander onwards. Heidegger speaks of the "fate-enmeshed formulations" along the path such as "*physis, logos, hen, idea, energeia*, substantiality, objectivity, subjectivity, Will, Will to power, Will to Will."[31]

The decisive direction of this path is in the understanding of truth. In its Greek origin *a-letheia* (truth) meant the self-unconcealment of Being through all the concealments (i.e., of beings). Plato, Heidegger argues, subjected truth to *idea* (related to the infinitive *idein*, to see or view). Truth thus became a matter of correct view, wherein was laid the ground for the secondary notion of truth as *adequatio rei ad intellectum*. This, he shows, is the beginning of metaphysics, which is a man-centred approach to Being. And thus thought in philosophy, although it still remains – and always has – the tuning of being to Being, in its fateful course it became – and has remained – something that man does in respect of Being rather than what Being does in respect of man. [This is the ground of his criticism against humanism.]

Thought has remained bound by this not-yet challenged ordinance, which has hitherto precluded a deeper way of tuning being to Being. Heidegger shows an approach to thinking wherein that deeper way unfolds itself. Hence Heidegger's approach to thought has been described as an overcoming of metaphysics or more broadly as philosophical overcoming of philosophy (i.e., as understood in its fate-laden sense prevailing hitherto in the West). All the critical work of Heidegger *vis-à-vis* the history of Western philosophy has been most beautifully characterized by H.G. Gadamer thus: "Heidegger attempted to take the step backward and in so doing take the step forward as well, a step which will allow modern civilization to realize the limits of Greek thought, of *alētheia* and its formative power." And then Gadamer adds this (for us) significant statement: "It may be that by virtue of this a dialogue has become possible with philosophical traditions which have developed outside these limits if they learn to free themselves from any tendency to parallel Western thought."[32]

III. THOUGHT AS APPROACHED FROM GNOSIS AS THE GROUND

We have discussed two of the three grounds from which to approach thought. A third remains, namely gnosis. Fundamentally, it is akin to the second, i.e., the tuning of being to Being, in that it cannot be discussed abstractly but only in terms of some concrete spiritual history. The second ground as we have seen, is known to us only in the concrete spiritual phenomenon of Western philosophy, which by definition is philosophy as such. The spiritual history where we are able to encounter gnosis is somewhat wider in its distribution and occurrence. But while it has disappeared from most of the traditions of the world, it is still remarkably preserved in Vedānta as well as in traditions that have kinship with it. And it is undoubtedly in Vedānta, in view of its unequivocal clarity in the matter, that we can seek in gnosis a distinct ground of the thought which it is possible to seize as philosophy, although doing so, no doubt, is problematical.

The difficulty in treating gnosis as having anything to do with philosophical thought does not come from the first ground we have dealt with (and the natural paths of thought that emerge from it) as it can, in this respect, be simply neutral. But the correspondence of being to Being, and gnosis are both definite and distinct grounds, each in its own way. To put them together is a problem. While from the one whichever way we move we are always in thought in the sense of philosophy, the picture is far from clear in respect of the other. Does gnosis really generate thought in the philosophically seizable sense? That is the question.

The answer to this question can be "yes", if we resolve to understand gnosis as that which is the ground of thought, that is to say, within the framework of the universally applicable ontological question as to thought, i.e. thought in respect of its pure being, rather than outside it. There is, for sure, a tautologous ring to this statement but that will cease when we realize that the question always outruns any framework we can advance, confining thought to its philosophical manifestation such as is evident in our own procedure here, till *it comes to rest in what we may describe as the disposition of Being (or Ultimate Reality) itself*, a disposition which is towards us. *Whether we should call this disposition thought or something else, of which thought itself is an extension, is a moot question*. However, in those traditions which regard it as something else it is called gnosis, and thought itself must then be taken as extension of gnosis and also as receptivity to it, rather than extension of Being as such and receptivity to Being.

The difference must seem trivial and merely verbal till we realize that in gnosis there is no concealment in its unconcealment as there would be in thought that understands itself as direct receptivity to Being. But gnosis appears, and in its appearing the possibility of thought comes to pass – of all thought. Now that we are talking about concealment and unconcealment we have reached the point at which we must consider darkness and light, which are the most fundamental notions in philosophy, although not universally recognized.

In the ordinary, everyday thinking, even as technical philosophy, darkness and light are merely sequential conditions which qualify our knowledge of specific objects of inquiry. Through various kinds of reasoning, experiment, etc., our state of darkness pertaining to objects is replaced by a state of their illumination. As is the scope of the objects in question so is the scope of darkness and light. But if objects themselves are to be viewed as ultimate, the laws affecting the natural paths of thought that we described (i.e., as penetration of the hidden depths of reality, boundary-making for the boundless and penetration of the otherness inherent in phenomena) will all apply.

In deeper thinking, where Being itself is what is thought, it is no longer the simple sequentiality of darkness and light but a profound relatedness between them that is most significantly at work.

And there is no question but that this is what makes philosophical thought profound, insofar as it has always got to do with Being. And this has been well demonstrated by the history of Western philosophy, especially where the question of Being has stirred it from the depth.

In gnosis, by contrast, there is neither sequentiality of darkness and light nor their relatedness, for there is only light. This is what distinguishes gnosis. *The light that is gnosis is the pure effulgence of Ultimate Reality.*

Gnosis, nevertheless, provokes thought. However, far from replacing or rendering irrelevant all other kinds of thinking, it acts as the ground for reviewing them in its own light. It provides a background of illumination in which to place all our previous questions while enabling us to see why there should have been questions at all, why Being itself is such as it is and not otherwise, that is to say, why it generates thinking (and wonder itself).

Gnosis enables thought always to move *in* knowledge, and for this movement there is no limit at all. Thought, therefore, is nothing but realization. *Realization is the limitless possibility of gnosis that is given over to thought.* The possibility is limitless because it is grounded in the truth that the *Real is the Real*, such self-identity being the only abiding warranty for thought. It also counterposits the ceaseless, epochal shifting of the ground of thought, especially of the profound thought which through the inter-relatedness of darkness and light seeks Being. Therefore, in the limitless scope of thought's moving *in* knowledge there is no place or need for shifting the ground.

Gnosis places thought right inside the truth that the Real is the Real, and is oriented in the direction of realizing that it is so, and hence of realizing that thought's own being is dependent on it. Obversely, if it were not for thought to realize it, there would not be the proposition that the Real is the Real.

However, the proposition that the Real is the Real can be stated in two fundamentally different ways. One way to do so is to give it the form "x = x", *x* standing for any entity or any number, but there is nothing in it to *realize* by thought. It is simply a law – that of identity – that arises in the sifting of the intuitions as between true and false [such as we discussed in the context of a corollary to one of the natural paths of thought, i.e., the penetration of the hidden depths of reality]. The law of identity clearly serves an important need in logic but it arises not because anybody seriously questions the self-identity of things and numbers – not at all. Now we move on to the second way of saying, the Real is the Real, which is the way grounded in gnosis. Here this proposition describes thought's project in motion. *Realization* is the name given to that project and it belongs with the *Real* in the first occurrence of the word in the proposition as well as in the second. But there is a distance between the two occurrences and that distance is the challenge that gnosis places before thought, bestowing upon it also its grace, whereby thought is enabled to move *in* knowledge, and, as we have said, there is no limit for this movement.

This movement of thought, viz., realization, is undoubtedly a creative one, but not in the sense of production. Nothing is produced and not the least knowledge. The Real is there already; the self-effulgence of the Real, viz., gnosis is, therefore, there already. What is there thus is called *self-obtained* (*svataḥ-siddha*), not something *to be obtained (sādhya)* as the result of production. That is the highest creative movement of thought which is not production and is not burdened by considerations of it, and hence in the most genuine sense free.

Creativity of thought is the playing out of the meaning of the proposition, the Real is the Real, in all the highways of thought, including those that are natural and those that have been opened especially by the philosophy grounded in the tuning of being to Being. Thus it does not disclaim anything, neither analogy nor predication nor presupposition, and not the least correspondence of being to Being, and yet it is not ruled by anything because the Real is criterionless.

By playing out the meaning of the proposition that the Real is the Real, all things become lucid and the *why* and *wherefore* of such baffling mysteries as agnosis (*ajñāna*), both universal and individual, sorrow (*duḥkha*) etc., became self-explicated. They come to be grasped as belonging to the purposiveness implicit in the proposition that the Real is the Real. And as there is no other execution of its purpose than the playing out of its meaning, thought is lifted above the realm of becoming and history, without, nevertheless, its losing touch with them.

This, then, is the way thought is approached from gnosis as the ground, and the Vedānta tradition offers the paramount example of it. There is, however, no reason to believe that this approach is the exclusive perogative of that tradition or that it would have been impossible without it. But it has its distinctiveness, which is that it has given us a body of texts followed by a whole tradition of reflective thinking based on those texts. Vedānta above all is *mīmāṁsā*, that is to say, a system of well-guided, thoughtful reflections upon the texts, or a scheme of exegesis, on the basis of which it is possible to play out the meaning of the essence of the texts, i.e., that the Real is the Real. That the Real is the Real is the outcome of learning about the Real from the texts. And how do we learn this from the texts and from nothing else in place of it, and how is it that we do not learn this in the same manner from other sources? These questions are answered by the nature of the texts insofar as they beckon us to turn to them for knowledge. The texts themselves are not something which could have been produced if they were not already there on their own. They are, however, something to which we can turn because they are already there on their own.

That the Real has a name is also what we learn from the texts. The name is *brahman* and it is both the fullness of meaning and the start of the explication thereof at one and the same time. [But the name is not a particular name, for there is not a particular person or a particular being that answers to it.] The word '*real*' (like its Sanskrit equivalent *sat* or *satya*) is not a name, as it is simply thought's word like many other words. It is not different from "goodness'", "happiness", "love", etc., which are not names but only verbal designations for what is *to be known, to be had*. They are thought's words. Although a name, *brahman* is not like other names, and further it belongs with gnosis. It is a peculiar name, drawn out of the Vedic religious history and cannot have full meaning outside its context. Such a name is a camouflage for the sake of discouraging those who approach it indifferently. [By contrast, that which has subsequently been used as a synonym for the name *brahman*, viz., *ātman* is not a name, but a word, generally like *soul*, which thought drew out of human experience. In this respect it is not different in its origin from such a word as '*real*'. As a matter of fact, insofar as *Brahman* became identified with *ātman* (*Ātman*), we must understand that identity as the original, and still Vedic, way of saying that the Real is the Real.]

Nevertheless, for thought's sake *brahman* has to be translated as Reality or Being, for then only can we have the proposition that the Real is the Real, which sets thought on its way. But translation itself, far from giving up the fullness of meaning that the name carries, is but the first step towards realization. In fact the translation is both provocation of thought and, obversely, responsiveness to the thought provoked – both carried out in the texts themselves *ab origine*.

So in order to round off this Introduction we must return to what was stated at the beginning as the nature of the work that is set forth in these pages: a dialogue with the texts and the thinkers who have spoken (or thought) in the tradition of the texts. To quote a statement made then: "The texts as well as what the thinkers have spoken (or thought) are the events with which we have to commune." Also: "In speaking with the texts and the thinkers we can only speak of that which they themselves have spoken and not *with* it – and as a matter of fact neither could they." This pertains to what we have described as observing "an attitude of circumspection towards that which philosophy and philosophizing are all about (be it predicated on "Being" or "Ultimate Reality".)

Now, in respect of giving an account of Vedānta as philosophy we have begun to discover how it can be seized as philosophy by being brought into the philosophizing purview. In this respect there is no question but that ways have to be found for Vedānta itself to come into the purview of all that can be called philosophy, not only by coming into their proximity but also by both stirring, and being stirred by, them.

It is Vedānta's consistent and clear-cut exposition of gnosis as the ground of thought that makes it peculiarly relevant for philosophy, in view of the fact that that ground has been completely eclipsed and lost sight of in modern times, thanks to the radical turns that philosophy has taken especially since Kant. But this historical situation is only peripheral to advancing that which is timeless. However, it is also the timeliness of the timeless that calls for Vedānta to be seized as philosophy, for which there is only one way, namely that of letting its depths be searched anew as ground of thought in an age in which such a search is most needful and most useful. The seizing of Vedānta will serve as a catalyst for all that is akin to it to collect around it.

Hence we propose to search for the nature of philosophical thought in Vedānta in the following pages. Our search will be restricted to a particular block of time and philosophical events, from the *Ṛg Veda* to Śankara's writings, through the Upaniṣads, the *Bhagavadgītā* and the *Brahma-Sūtra*. Why this block and this only? The reason is that it represents a complete line as far as the foundation-laying career and the formation of the Vedāntic philosophy of gnosis are concerned. The texts themselves are a mixture of gnosis expressed through language and of human thought already provoked by gnosis. But the human thought in the texts by no means stands apart from gnosis, which is the reason why from the beginning the texts include the hermeneutics of gnosis. However, while thought by its very nature changes, gnosis does not, because it is above the transitional modes that govern the relation among yesterday, today and tomorrow. Therefore, thought which has its ground in gnosis manifests this changelessness through its very changes, and does not seek to make either yesterday or today or tomorrow the absolute point from which to view all processes.

Śankara himself is the great culminating point of this gnosis tradition. The post-Śankara scholars of the Śankara line, no doubt, developed fine points of argument and speculation with incredible skill. And this development is not at all superfluous as it embodies Vedānta's scholasticism, and there has been such a rich harvest to be reaped from what has been sown even in this respect between the *Ṛg Veda* and Śankara. And there has been gnosis mysticism too going on side by side, often in the same scholastic tradition, no doubt undergirded by Yoga methods. But now in our undertaking we search for the nature of the philosophical thought in a different way from the scholastic tradition, in respect of the ground that stretches from the *Ṛg Veda* to Śankara, such as we have already described.

It has already been implicitly clear – if someone should raise such a question – why we have not included non-Śankarite, Vedāntic writers, who came after Śankara, like Rāmānuja, Madhva, Vallabha and Nimbarka? The answer will be implicit in the very fact that we have restricted ourselves to searching for the nature of philosophical thought by pursuing the line which culminates in Śankara as far as the tradition is concerned, in what Śankara himself defines in a breathtakingly simple way as "the vision of the truth (or thatness) of the Ultimate Essence in which is no distinction of knowledge, known and knower" (*jñāna-jñeya-jñātṛ-bhedarahitam paramārtha-tattva darśanam*)[33]. That which issues in this vision must be seized as philosophy in the philosophizing purview which opens itself before us. [In Indian writings today the Sanskrit word for vision, i.e., *darśana*, which is like *theorea* in meaning, is used as a translation for 'philosophy'.] In this practice, however, only the intention is good, and the practice is also justifiable because there is no other word. However, vision is not philosophy, for only that which is seized in thought is justly entitled to be called philosophy. On the other hand, insofar as the vision can be seized as philosophy it is philosophy, in the sense that in being seized it becomes philosophy, that is to say, becomes capable of being thought and needing to be thought.

In the following pages we will take up the four basic texts (and the thought of Śankara, which is really an extension and culmination of the texts themselves) as the complete line of the gnosis philosophy of Vedānta. We will consider how gnosis provokes and directs thought and how gnosis and the vision it goes in hand with can be seized as philosophy. This is the task to which we are addressing ourselves.

One final word must be said about the essential religious character of the tradition, as otherwise the picture will not be complete. The texts are, above all else, religious both in their origin and primary use. When it is said that their origin is religious it is meant that the unavoidable historical and human agencies through which they have come do not constitute their essence, as they are rather extraneous to religion. When it is said that their primary use is religious it is meant that they serve the ends of the ultimate liberation of the soul. That this is such cannot be doubted. But insofar as gnosis is looked upon as the way to liberation a predisposition to regard thought as merely transitional is generated, undercutting the realization of the inner destiny of thought itself as the very extension of gnosis, which is what is being attempted to be shown here in this work.

It is not at all warrantable to deny the essential religious character of these texts, origin and primary use included. But without in any way denying it, we recognize the fact that thought extends its domain so as to embrace what is essentially religious both in origin and primary usage. This is as much an ordinance of religion as of thought (insofar as it still recognizes its ground in gnosis) and therein the twain are no longer separate. The ordinance really comes from gnosis. Here even the question of liberation becomes no longer detachable from the wholeness to which gnosis summons thought and, reversely, thought becomes no longer detachable from the question of liberation. Here all artificiality must come to an end, for what is to be realized is *that* the Real is the Real in all possible ways, which is philosophy's manner of putting us in a position to realize the Real *as* the Real – and nothing more may be asked of philosophy than that it put us in such a position.

CHAPTER I

GNOSIS AND PHILOSOPHICAL THOUGHT IN THE ṚG VEDA

THE TEXT OF THE *ṚG VEDA*

[For our hermeneutics of the *Ṛg Veda* we have found some of the ways in which Heidegger approaches the pre-Socratic Greeks to be useful. Yet the significant difference between what Heidegger seeks – and seems to find – and the Vedāntic tradition requires us to put gnosis rather than Being itself as the ground of thought. The use of gnosis clearly also safe-guards that which is essential to thought in respect of Ultimate Reality.]

Gnosis unveiled in the tradition of Vedānta had its beginnings in the Vedas. That is the apparent reason why the word *vedānta*, meaning end, consummation or essence, of the Veda, came to be coined. It is this connection that makes an encounter with the core of all the Vedas, i.e., the *Ṛg Veda*, necessary.

Undoubtedly, the *Ṛg Veda* can be approached, and has been approached, in modern as well as ancient times from perspectives other than that of Vedānta. But it is clear that in a study such as ours which has taken Vedānta as the standpoint for its perspective there is no place for any other approach. And besides, it is not the case that Vedānta stands as a sentinel forbidding another kind of entry into the Vedas, for those who are impelled to enter them through other gates may indeed do so. However, if it becomes clear that the Vedas had been preparing for the Vedāntic gnosis to be fully spoken, along with the essence of that gnosis, i.e., *Braham*, then the choice of this path will have been automatically justified.

The objectives in inquiring about an ancient and remote text can obviously be various. For us, however, there is only one objective, namely, that of raising the question of thought, in the sense of the thought that has to do with the investigation of Ultimate Reality. There again, whether or not we already understand such thought to be approached from the ground of gnosis makes all the difference. In the light of the Vedāntic tradition that is the only understanding possible. Therefore, our hermeneutics of the *Ṛg Veda* is also intrinsically the hermeneutics of the approach to thought from the ground of gnosis. And accordingly, it cannot be a wide ranging study of the text of the *Ṛg Veda* (as also of the subsequent texts) for all kinds of purposes and for the satisfaction of all kinds of curiosities, legitimate as they all may be in their own way. Between what is outlined here and existing studies on the *Ṛg Veda*, there is no significant point of contact and so we join no debate with them. When we study the text we unceasingly ask ourselves questions about gnosis itself and about thought approached from gnosis as the ground.

It is because the text and our thought have the same common ground of gnosis that hermeneutics is possible. And through hermeneutics we come to recognize this common ground. It is, therefore, a means of discovery. That is how we are enabled to know what the text says and that is the way we know our own thinking and hear the text speak to us from within ourselves.

Ultimate Reality always remains the supreme subject-matter of philosophical thought, and the study of the text is undertaken as a circumspect way of thinking about it, that is to say, both as guiding and as being guided by such thinking. The Vedāntic tradition with its definite understanding of thought takes control of our thinking by letting it express itself in terms of gnosis.

Vedānta places such thought in an already flowing stream, which, according to it, begins with the Vedas. It understands itself as the essence of that stream. The critical examination of this self-understanding is important enough but is, nevertheless, peripheral to a greater undertaking of thought, namely, that of bringing it to the orbit of the question of Ultimate Reality in terms of the gnosis that Vedānta sets forth.

The objective of seizing the Vedic text as philosophy has to be achieved by a continuing dialogue with it. In fact, such a dialogue has gone on from the end sections of the *Ṛg Veda* and the other Vedas themselves, i.e., the Upaniṣads, which in turn became the texts to be seized as philosophical by the thinkers who came in the period subsequent to the Vedas but standing in their stream. The continuity of this dialogue is interminable and we too are placed in the stream. It is correct to say of the Vedas that they not only manifest the common ground that our thinking has with them, i.e., gnosis, but are also beginnings of all Indian investigations in the historical sense. Our concern with the Vedas, however, is not in the respect that they are historical beginnings but in the respect that they hold the *origin*, which is the common ground our thinking has with them.

There is much speaking in the Vedas, no doubt, but their essence consists as much in what they say as in what they withhold. The Upaniṣads and the subsequent Vedāntic tradition as dialogues with the Vedas brought out what was said as well as what was significantly not said. The statements that Heidegger makes with respect to the dialogue with the texts which hold the origin of Western thought is entirely applicable here.

> Every interpretation is a dialogue with the work, and with the saying (i.e., the original). However, every dialogue becomes halting and fruitless if it confines itself obdurately to nothing but what is directly said – rather than the speakers involve with each other in *that* realm and abode about which they are speaking, and lead each other to it. Such involvement is the soul of dialogue. It leads the speakers into the unspoken.[1]

Our task, then, calls for us to have dialogue with the *Ṛg Veda* in this comprehensive sense. However, what is not said is not separable from what is said as they are not distinct from each other. To *see* what is not spoken, by hearing the words spoken, is the essential understanding of meaning. And to *show* through speaking is the essence of communication. That is how the Vedas work.

THE VEDA AND THE VEDAS: THE VEDA MEANING IDEA

First, let us look at the word *veda* and find out what it means. The word is cognate with *vidyā*, another noun from the common root, *vid*. However, the same word-sound, *vid*, functions as five different roots, from which come five different verbs with their own meanings or rather meaning-clusters and, accordingly, with distinct conjugations and also derivations. These are *vid*, to know or to see; *vid*, to happen or to be in existence; *vid*, to get or obtain, or to find, or to feel; *vid*, to discuss or consider; *vid*, to feel, to tell, to dwell.[2] [This situation of the same word-sound functioning as different roots for words of different meanings is a common feature of Sanskrit.] The *Dhātupāṭha* xxiv, 56 gives *vid*, to know, as the first root, from which in conjugation arises the verb *vetti*, meaning he, she or it knows. The other roots, however, do not at all seem unrelated to *vid*, to know. Heidegger shows some parallels in Greek, for instance λέγειν, which means at one time "to lay" and at another "to tell". Even though the situation in Greek vis-à-vis λέγειν is as complex as similar situations in Sanskrit, Heidegger's remark is illuminating: "We ask: what is it that takes place when λέγειν means both 'to lay' and 'to tell'? Is it only by accident that these meanings come together under the common roof of the same word-sound? Or is there something else? Could it be that that which is the essence of telling, that which is called λέγειν has come to light as a laying"?[3] Surely, we cannot but wonder whether such seemingly diverse meanings as to know, to see, to happen, to be in existence, to consider, to feel, to tell, and to dwell, are not bound together at some great depth, from which different roots (like roots of plants and trees) issue forth, the depth being that which gives rise to all language, i.e., consciousness. Now to speak of the root *vid*, to know or to see, it is clearly related to Greek *εiδεiν*, Latin *videre*, German *wissen* and old English *wot*.

As for the text, it is correct to say, surprising as it may seem, that there is no such book as *the* Veda in the accurate sense of that word, for there are only particular books like *Ṛg Veda, Yajur Veda, Sāma Veda* and *Atharva Veda*. At the same time Veda is a name for all the Vedas as well as their parts. That the Veda (singular, not collective, usage) is eternal (*nitya*) and not composed by man or god (i.e., *apauruṣeya*) is an accepted belief in the Vedic-Vedāntic tradition. That characterization does not unequivocally apply to the actual books. What it really points to is *the* Veda in the sense of the IDEA (all letters capital, in order to distinguish it from *idea* in the sense of form). The equation, Veda = IDEA, is also well justified by the cognate roots *vid* and *ειδειν*, from which the two words respectively come. This Veda or IDEA may be taken in the sense of gnosis, meaning the disposition towards us of Ultimate Reality.

The Veda is, however, also the word or *Logos* (*Vāk*, or *Śabda*) and the Veda being eternal the word too is eternal. Thus Śankara, in re-affirming the insights of his pre-cursors, Jaimini and Bādarāyaṇa, that the Veda is eternal, states that the word of the Veda too must be taken as eternal, insofar as it is the origin of all things: "And thus, it is because the world consisting of conditioned forms such as the gods have proceeded from the word of the Veda that the word of the Veda also should be understood as eternal".[4] And he cites support from the earliest (i.e., Mantra) portion of the *Ṛg Veda*, 10.71.3: "They achieved through holy sacrifice perfect progress in the understanding of *Vāk*."[5] The Veda, the IDEA, is eternal – but eternal in the sense that it belongs with the Absolute which houses the cosmic becoming, *not in the sense of belonging with the Absolute which is still beyond that.*

In sequel to the afore-mentioned statement, Śankara moves from speaking of the Veda in the singular to speaking of the Vedas in the plural. There, appealing to earlier texts, he observes: "The seers with the permission of the Self-born (*svayambhu*) through their *self-energizing intellectual penance* (*tapas*) obtained the *Vedas along with the epics* (*Vedān setihāsān*) at the end of the previous epoch". This most significant transition from the singular to the plural is invariably missed by scholars and translators. The truth is, it is the IDEA which houses the archetypal forms that serves as the basis for the recurrent production of the cosmos at the beginning of each cyle. And it would be absurd to imagine that it is the actual, individual Vedas, namely, the *Ṛg Veda*, etc., which serve as that basis.

In the mythological works, the eternal Veda, the IDEA, was depicted in terms of a notion that is appropriate for them, that is to say, as a praeter-historical entity, conforming to an *ab-original* vision of time. Accordingly, these works speak of an entity which actually existed in the mythological past. We call it *praeter-historical* because its existence is conceived in the model of things of history, yet not historical in the concrete sense. And we cannot very well call it *pre-historical* as that would bring it within the scope of actual history. The *Viṣṇu Purāṇa* and the *Matsya Purāṇa*, both much later in composition than the Vedas (i.e., the *Ṛg Veda*, etc.), speak of such a praeter-historical Veda, which branched out into the four collected texts or *Saṁhitās*, accompanied eventually by a drastic reduction in size. The original is said to have been perfect unlike the ones which have come in history, i.e., our Vedas, which are described as very imperfect. No doubt, this account reflects the general view of the Purāṇic mythologies, according to which the golden age lay in some praeter-historical antiquity, history itself being a degeneration or winding down to an inevitable catastrophic anticlimax, while all along the road of time there lie the scattered wreckages of original unities and perfections. As in everything else, divine intervention takes place here in order to salvage the broken fragments of the original text for such preservation of *dharma* and of man as is possible. According to the *Viṣṇu Purāṇa* that one Veda of the golden past was a "vast tree, which soon branched out into an extensive forest".[6] It is said to have had one hundred thousand stanzas, arranged into four collections by Vyāsa (literally, the arranger).

Of the Vedas which has existed in history, and exist today, only the first three – *Ṛg Veda, Yajur Veda* and *Sāma Veda* – were originally recognized. The *Atharva Veda* was reckoned as Veda somewhat later in time. The Vedic texts themselves speak of the Vedas (plural) as having been born, along with the rest of creation. Thus, out of the sacrifice and dismembering of the primoridial cosmic person, or *Puruṣa*, by the gods, it is stated in the *Ṛg Veda* (10.90.9), there arose, along with the celestial bodies, terrestrial creatures and social classes, the *Ṛg Veda, Sāma Veda, Metres* (*Chandas*) and *Yajur Veda*. This is echoed in the *Upaniṣads* also. For instance, the *Bṛhadāraṇyaka Upaniṣad* at its very outset, meditating on the symbol of the horse-sacrifice, uses the same model as in the above *Ṛg Vedic* passage, but substituting *Vāk* for sacrifice (*Yajña*) and *Ātman* (Self) for *Puruṣa* (primeval person). The issuing forth of the three Vedas along with other texts is also described here. Though they are not the same as the IDEA or Veda in the transcendent sense, they are, it is maintained, earthly manifestations of its *logos*.

References to the Veda always must be understood in the often equivocal way they are made. That which is spoken of in the metaphysical sense and those that are described as books or compositions are nevertheless connected by virtue of the metaphysical relation between what is transcendent and its earthly manifestation. Of the latter we must and can speak in terms of the religious history of the Vedic people, but without ever confusing them with the transcendent Veda.

Now to turn to the Vedas of the Vedic religious history, that is the *Ṛg Veda*, etc., they were originally priestly manuals. First there were three, and then four, classes of priests performing diverse functions in a common sacerdotal religion. Sāyaṇa and Yāska quote the *Ṛg Vedic* verse (10.71.11):

ṛcām tvaḥ poṣamāste pupuṣvān gāyatram tvo gāyate śakvariṣu brahmā tvo vadati jātavidyām yajñasya mātrām vimimīti u tvaḥ.

(One brings together the verses. Another sings the *gāyatra* in *śakvarī* metres; another, i.e. Brāhman, narrates the wisdom pertaining to the origins of things; and yet another determines the rules of sacrificial rites.) The four classes are *Hotṛ, Udgātṛ, Brāhman* and *Adhvaryu*. Paul Deussen's account[7] of the functions of the four classes of priests follows the traditional information and his description of the priests (*ṛtvij*) and their relation to the four Vedas is, therefore, well founded. The complete collection of the verses (*ṛcā*) is the *Ṛg Veda* or more correctly *Ṛg Veda Saṁhitā*. The ordered selection of the same, rendered into melody, along with some extra melodies, constituting a psalter, became the *Sāma Veda Saṁhitā*. Likewise, a different anthology of the same verses, cemented together with sentences appropriate for different liturgical acts, formed the *Yajur Veda Saṁhitā*. For simplicity's sake we name the three collections or *Saṁhitās* as *the Book of (sacred) Verses, the Book of Psalms* and *the Book of Rites*. But the core in all the three is always the verses, that is to say the *Ṛg Veda*. We may assume that the narration of the origins of things, though special, is embedded in the *Ṛg Veda Saṁhitā* and never became a separate collection. That means there was no special *Saṁhitā* assigned to the Brahman priest.

The *Atharva Veda*, is a completely different story. It had an independent origin and was later added to the list of the Vedas as the fourth. Although portions of it are deeply speculative, much of its contents are charms and spells (*atharva-angīrasa*), for which reason it was held at a great distance from the original three. It was not admitted for sacred rites. That fact is stated exactly so: *atharva vedastu yajña-anupayuktaḥ, śānti-pauṣṭika-abhicārādi karma-pratipādakatvena atyanta-vilakṣaṇa eva*.

At this point we must take into consideration the division of the four Vedas into sequential parts. Although the parts are four, i.e., Mantras, Brāhmaṇas, Āraṇyakas and Upaniṣads, the traditional authorities usually comprehend the latter three under the general designation of *Brāhmaṇa*. Thus, the *Āpastamba-Yajña-paribhāṣā Sūtra* states: "*mantra-brāhmaṇayor veda nāmadheyam*" (the Mantras and Brāhmaṇas are together called *Veda*).[8] [However, it must be noted that this formal division is not always maintained, for instance, one of the Upaniṣads, the *Īśā*, is not appended to any brāhmaṇa but is part of one of the two variants of the *Yajurvedic* Mantra corpus, namely the *Vājasaneyī Saṁhitā*.]

Now, we adopt the traditional, and very justified, view that the

Ṛg Vedic Mantras are pre-eminent. Therefore, we must restrict ourselves to them, and we shall concentrate on them.

ṚG VEDIC MANTRAS

The *Ṛg Veda* is the Veda of *ṛks*. Sāyaṇa, following Yāska, says "*ṛk* is parise" (*ṛk arcanī iti*). The word *ṛk* expresses the same meaning as the word *arcanī* (*arcanī ityamūm ṛkśabda ācaṣṭe*). The word *ṛk* may be translated "(sacred) verse". There are 10,473 *ṛks* comprehended by 1,017 *sūktas* or hymns, arranged into 10 *maṇḍalas* or books.[9] The word *mantra*, according to Yāska, comes from *manana*, to think, (*mananāt mantra*).[10] The precise meaning of this word is thinking, in the same sense of being mindful of, or taking to heart. The praise of the gods (i.e., *devastuti*) is the way of mindfulness of, or taking to heart, something which is at once said by the praise and at the same time left unsaid. That something is seen by the *ṛṣis*, who, therefore, are the seers. The Mantras are the contents, which overflow the containers, namely, the *ṛks* and the hymns (*sūktas*) which they constitute. Hence the Mantras, as Sāyaṇa says, were seen by the *ṛṣis*, not made, *ṛṣiṇā dṛṣṭam na tu kṛtam*. And, therefore, the *ṛṣis* are seers of the Mantras, *ṛṣayo mantra-draṣṭāraḥ*. As to the puzzling notion of "seeing" the Mantras, a modern explanation is available in one of the passing statements that Heidegger makes: "Can we see something told?" Then he answers, "We can provided what is told is more than just the sound of words, provided the seeing is more than just the seeing with the eyes of the body. Accordingly, the transposition of the leap of such a vision does not happen by itself. Leap and vision require long, slow preparation, especially if we have to transpose ourselves to *that* word, which is not just one word among many."[11] Sāyaṇa explains: "Because by virtue of the energy from the infinitely withdrawn transcendental brooding (*tapasā*) they see the Mantras, a *ṛṣi* is so called –that is the definition", and adds, "One should understand the word *ṛṣi* to mean the seer of the Mantras by supernal knowledge, and that is the reason why it is said in the tradition that the *ṛṣis* are the seers of the Mantras."[12]

The Mantras are the corpus of the overflowing contents of *ṛks*, of what is both said and not said by them, and, therefore, phenomenally embody the transcendent Veda, or IDEA, which in being *seen*, spontaneously and of its own accord extends itself into the sphere of human thought but at the same time protects itself and its votary, the thinker, from the all too common vicissitudes of human thought. [It is because of this protection that the Mantras are also called by the name *chandas*, from the root *chad*, to protect or cover, – *chādanāt chandas* – according to the etymologists like Yāska.] The Mantras, therefore, are the source of the wisdom, in which is the mindfulness, or taking to heart, of that which extends itself into thought and which thought welcomes and receives.

The Mantras are what are put into words by the seers in a mode of language which is most appropriate for them as what were seen. That mode of language combines the essence of all other modes of speech and yet negates them, insofar as it is the union of saying and not saying. This is called *stuti*, eulogy or praise, and is held to be identical in meaning with the word *mantra* itself[13] insofar as the latter can be taken as a mode of speech. The characteristic of this kind of speaking is that there is no interval between it and the seeing, for the two are the same. On the other hand, their unity pervades the highest kind of awareness to which man has access. It is the essential language of man inasmuch as he is that being which is destined to be more than man and inasmuch as he is already open to that possibility. By the same token, it is this kind of speaking that makes that possibility come home to him. In it is housed man's ability to think that which deserves to be thought, and it bears witness to that ability. Also, whichever way we go about it, the gaining of true language is the indispensable condition that ensures the prospect of thinking, but it remains always a prospect, and only a prospect. And as far for the language of *stuti*, or eulogy, it is an indictment upon other modes of speech – and therefore of other things which put forth their claim to be thought. Yet, insofar as it is always a prospect it permits and even generates other modes of speech, i.e., placed between the two boundaries, one of them being the objectifying kind of speech where language functions as a system of representational signs and symbols of reality, or in other words, truths in the propositional sense, i.e., awaiting conformation, and the other being ecstatic utterances struggling to express ineffable experiences.

Outwardly, *mantras* are sung in praise of the deities. For instance, mark these passages: "May we (or, let us), O ye gods, recite that *mantra* fearless and felicity-conferring", (*tamidvocema vidadheṣu śambhuvam mantram devā anehasam*).[14] [The expression *tamidvocema*, may we or let us recite, in 1.41.6 (and occurring also in 1.174.1 and 2.35.2) conveys no sense of obligation as it rather signifies a self-impelling activity (of speaking)]. "Offer a *mantra* that is not mean but well-arranged and exquisite", (*mantram akharvam sudhitam śupeśasam dadhāta yajñiyeṣu*).[15] Sometimes the gods themselves are the singers. "Now Bṛhaspati utters the *mantra* of praise, wherein the gods Indra, Varuṇa, Mitra and Aryamān have made their abode", (*pranūnam bṛhaspati mantram vadati ukthyam yasmin indra varuṇa mitra aryamā devā okāṃṣi cakrire*).[16] It is also to be noted that *mantra* as the supreme form of speech is also the dwelling place of the deities. Further, it is that on which people must (or, actually do) set their thoughts as it is the light by which to walk: "the people have set their thoughts on this thy (i.e., the god's), *mantra", (mantra ye vāram naryā atakṣan*)[17]; "By hearing the *mantra* we walk", (*mantra śrutyām carāmasi*).[18]

Now, the primordial association between *stuti* and thinking, although it may seem strange and unlikely, is worth pausing over a little. We could never have known that possibility had not Heidegger shown how in the West *thinking* and thanking had a deep connection. That connection was found out by following the scent of language. We discover that the same way of scenting language (*Vāk*) is possible in respect of the Vedas too and our nose can lead us to where the connection lies. And we come to know that in this respect *mantra* is thinking and that *stuti*, in spite of the inane sound of the word by which we translate it (i.e., praise, or eulogy), is thanking. It is simply amazing that two traditions, which have followed quite different paths, have so much in common where some profound matters are involved. Heidegger asks: "What is it that is named with the words 'think', 'thinking', 'thought'? Towards what sphere of the spoken word do they direct us? A thought – where is it, where does it go"? And then he explicates, "The Old English *thencan*, to think, and *thancian*, to thank, are closely related; the Old English noun for thought is *thanc* or *thonc* – a grateful thought, and the expression of such a thought; today it survives in the plural *thanks*. The '*thanc*', that which is thought, the thought, implies the thanks."[19] Heidegger grants that the assonances between 'thinking' and 'thanking' are perhaps superficial and contrived – at least might seem to be so at first sight. But the impression will change when we move into what we call "memory" and try to understand it as the real connection:

> [But] the word 'the *thanc*' does not mean only what we call a man's disposition or heart, and whose essential nature we can hardly fathom. Both memory and thanks move and have their being in the *thanc*. 'Memory' initially did not at all mean the power to recall. The word designates the whole disposition in the sense of a steadfast, intimate concentration upon the things that essentially speak to us in every thoughtful meditation. Originally, 'memory' means as much as devotion: a constant concentrated abiding with something – not just with something that has passed, but in the same way with what is present and with what may come.[20]

All this is quite illuminating for the understanding of the Vedas. The sanskrit word *smaraṇa*, from *smar* to remember, is even today used in the above sense of memory. [It is distinguishable from *smṛti*, an objectified form of account retained as an aid to thinking, used officially as designation for certain classes of post-Vedic scriptures.] Heidegger further remarks: "Our attempt to indicate what the words 'thinking', 'thought' and 'memory' say might serve to point at least vaguely towards the realm of speech from whose unspoken sphere those words initially speak. Those words bring to light situations whose essential unity of nature our eyes cannot yet pierce."[21] Again, "pure thanks is rather that we simply think – think what is really and solely given, what is there to be thought".[22] [However, a caution with respect to following through the application of Heidegger's exposition to the Vedas and all that comes from the Vedas, must be pronounced. Thus where, as Heidegger continues on, he develops the idea of "original thanking" as "the thanks owed for being" we feel it is appropriate to substitute *gnosis* for *being*, which would certainly be the case in the discipline of Vedānta.]

In the *Vedas* we notice that *mantra* is what calls thinking. The thinking that is thus called is realized in a unique and exemplary manner in the Upaniṣads. The call is provocation, or more properly *in-vocation*, of thought. In fact, the call of the *mantra* is invocation of the wisdom which it itself is. The *Ṛg Veda* says: "With *mantra* we in-voke, from within, Agni the wise one" (*mantrair agnim kaviḥ achā vadāmi*).[23] This usage has doubtless been at the root of the coined word *ā-mantraṇa*, from *ā-mantṛ*, to *invite, invoke*, call, call forth or address, occurring already in the *Atharva*

Veda, some Brahmaṇas and later in the *Mahābhārata*, etc. The verbal forms of it are found in the Upaniṣads. One occurrence in the *Bṛhadāraṇyaka Upaniṣad* (2.1.15) is most striking in that it is an address made to a sleeping person, suggesting awakening from sleep as symbolic of the objective of *āmantraṇa* (address), and thus demonstrating what it means to think. Ajātaśatru and Gārgya, two great thinkers, are the principals in an anecdote which says: "The two together came to a person who was asleep. They address him (*tam āmantrayām cakre*) by these names: 'O great King, dweller in the white region (*bṛhan puṇḍara-vāsaḥ rājann iti*)'. He did not wake up till Ajātaśatru rubbed him with his hand." [A slightly altered version of this appears in *Kauṣītaki Upaniṣad* (4.19)]. The verb *āmantṛ* is also used in the sense of calling out, asking a question. Satyakāma (a name, which literally means desirer of truth) called out asking (*āmantrayām cakre*) his mother: "I would become a student of sacred knowledge, of what family am I?" (*Chāndogya Upaniṣad*, 4.4.1).

Heidegger's discussion of the Greek *κελέύειν*, to call, can throw much light on the word *āmantṛ* as well. He points to the sense in which a verbal form of that Greek infinitive is found in the older Greek version of the New Testament passage, Matthew 8.18: "Idōn de ho Iēsous ochlon peri auton ekeleusen apelthein eis to peran – Seeing a large crowd around him he (Jesus) called to them to go to the other side." Upon this Heidegger comments: "[And] the old word "to call" means not so much a command as a letting-reach, that therefore the call has an assonance of helpfulness and compliance, is shown by the fact that the same word in Sanskrit still means to 'invite'".[24] This is indeed a most arresting observation, although it is not clear what word in Sanskrit Heidegger had in mind. But we know that the most appropriate ones would be *āmantṛ, hve* and *āhve*, all of which are very old and all of which correspond to the Greek *κελεύειν*.

The word *mantra* also passed into some of the later sectarian traditions in a conspicuous way. It went through a rather tangential development in the Tāntric tradition, where it acquired the meaning of evoking or invoking some hidden, spiritual (or occult) power by employing cryptic formulas and esoteric techniques. Sir John Woodroffe, an eminent Western authority on Tāntrism writes: "The subject (of *Mantra*) is of such importance in the Tantras that their other name is Mantra Śāstra (Science of Mantra). But what is Mantra? Commonly orientalists and others describe Mantra as 'Prayer', 'Formulas of Worship', 'Mystic Syllable' and so forth. These are but the superficialities of those who do not know the subject."[25] He argues in a manner consistent with that tradition that the practice of *mantra* has to do with the hidden spiritual power (*śakti*) behind the cosmos, and is a technique for the realization of the unity with the cosmos, and finally with the Reality behind it. Accordingly, the derivation of the word in the tāntric tradition is from the first syllable of the two words *manana*, meditation, and *trāṇa*, liberation.[26] However, it is not possible to find support for such techniques in the Vedic Mantras. The sectarian tradition of gnosis, like all sectarian traditions, is a deviation from thought. This we can see when we understand that the call to thought that the Mantras are leads us to what they are the telling of. Here we are, no doubt, confronted by so-called Vedic mythology, which scholars as a rule assume centres around the gods named in the Vedas.

The telling by the Mantras (i.e. Vedic telling) is, in fact, itself the myth. The gods are merely accessories to the telling. As for myth, the telling, we can learn from Heiddegger again, who writes: "Myth means the telling word. For the Greeks to tell means to lay bare and to make appear – both the appearance and that which has its essence in the appearance, its epiphany. *Mythos* is what has its essence in the telling – what is apparent in the unconcealedness of its appeal. The *mythos* is that appeal of foremost and radical concern to human beings which make man think of what appears, what is in being."[27]

The purpose of the telling, of the *mythos*, is to point to its essence, i.e., gnosis. Accordingly, the telling itself invites, calls forth, thought and there is nothing esoteric or occult in it, and there is no tale. This is the essential character of Vedic myth. This is the line that divides the Vedas from all mythological literature, even of India, as they are all accounts of the transactions of men and gods, reflecting their folly or wisdom and their final encounter with a transcendent law as well as the mystery of fate.

As for the gods of the Vedas, *telling is the region of their dwelling*. The *Bṛhaddevatā*, an ancient commentary, (ii. 88) states: "He who tells the sentence, therein occurs the Seer – *ṛṣi*; he who is told by the sentence, therein occurs the deity," (*saṁvedaṣvāha vākyam yaḥ sa tu tasmin bhavedṛṣi, yastenocyeta vākyena devatā tatra sā bhavet*). The elementary constituent in the telling is the name (*nāma*). [Name here has nothing to do with the devotional repetition of the divine names familiar in many religions.] What then is name, ontologically? According to the *Amarakośa* (Dictionary of Synonyms),[28] name means the following things: *ākhyā*, or that primary constitution of a thing by which it is cognized in its objective existence; *āhvā*, or that particular sound-form by which a particular being is addressed; *abhidhāna*, or naming; *nāmadheya*, or mere name (nominal entity). Unless the name depends on the reality of the named, it will be a mere name. If the name moves away from the original reality that appears in the sense of its own self-shining, i.e., as *phenomenon*, it tends to stand for that which has its essence only in the appearance. Hence the *Chāndogya Upaniṣad* (6.4.1,2,3, and 4) speaks in a refrain with respect to all modifications which have their essence only in the appearance: "They have their origin in the logos; they are mere names", (*vācārambhaṇaṁ vikāro nāmadheyam*). If the name does not stand for that which has its essence in the mere appearance, then it is a legitimate accessory in the telling. The semantic tradition says *artho abhidheya*, i.e., the name is the essence or meaning, insofar as we seek to locate a reality in the essence or meaning underlying name. [The *Amaraṭīkā*, which contains this clue gives three other definitions for meaning. They are *vastu*, or real property; *prayojana*, or use; *nivṛtti*, or deliverance.]

The gods as named have a Nature basis. But this is not the same as to say that they are so-called personifications of "the powers of Nature". That the gods have a Nature basis or a lived-world basis is clearly assumed by Yāska, Sāyaṇa and other traditional interpreters. That is as it should be because man establishes his relation to the world by means of special, worshipping relations to the many guardians of Nature who regulate his world, these being the Sun, Moon, Sky, Earth, Wind, etc.. There never was, even at the stage of the presumed infancy of man's religious and intellectual history, any actual personification of the powers of Nature. What personification there was is merely due to the situation of language insofar as man used it purposively. There is no ground for calling these named guardians of the world "powers of Nature", because the concept "nature" itself could never dwell in the same language as that in which the gods dwell.

Names of gods are their meaning or essence, which no concept as such can represent. They are, no doubt, symbols but not *representational* symbols. That is the reason why Yāska, the etymologist, suggests several alternative derivations – only so-called because they are *intentionally* mere sound-derivations – for each of the names of the deities. They are not meant to be derivations in the modern philologist's sense, and to attempt something like that in respect of those names which have their location in the region of the telling only would have been quite absurd. Actually, they are just sound-play, which alone they can be in the ontology of myth. Yāska gives a variety of these in the seventh chapter of his *Nirukta*. Let us pick out just two of them for illustration. Thus the word *indra* comes from *irā dṛ*, "he gives food", or *irā dhā*, also "he gives food", or *irā dhāraya*, "he holds food", or *indu dru*, "he runs for the sake of Soma", or *indu ram*, "he delights in Soma", or *idam dṛś*, "he sees this", or from *ind*, to be powerful. The word *mitra* comes from *trāyate*, "he saves", or from *pra-miti*, "he destroys", or from *dravate*, "he measures things together", or from *mid*, "to be fat". The pattern is adopted for all the names of the gods, Varuṇa, Agni, *et al.*

Now, insofar as Vedic Mantras are the telling of which the myth is the essence, it is natural to think of the *logos*, for no telling can ignore it. It is noteworthy that when we approach the subject in the manner warranted by the Western tradition in terms of *mythos* and *logos* separately and hence look for corresponding terms in Sanskrit, we find that there are no separate terms for the two. On the other hand, the same word, *vāk*, serves for both, and unless we have made the approach from the Western standpoint we would not even notice that there is a distinction. In the Greek tradition, the two words are there but, as Heidegger makes it clear, they nonetheless mean the same. "*Logos* says the same (as *mythos*); *mythos* and *logos* are not, as historians of philosophy claim, placed in opposition by philosophy as such; on the contrary, the early Greek thinkers (Parmanides, *Fragment* 8) are precisely the ones to use *mythos* and *logos* in the same sense. *Mythos* and *logos* became separated only at the point where neither of them can keep its original nature."[29] Heidegger, continuing on, shows how the two words got separated and points out also the consequence of their separation. "In Plato's works this separation has actually taken place. Historians and philologists by virtue of a prejudice which modern rationalism adopted from Platonism, imagine that *mythos* was destroyed by *logos*." And then he adds, "But nothing religious is ever destroyed by logic; it is destroyed only by the God's withdrawal".

The *Ṛg Veda* has many things to say about *Vāk* and it says it in different ways. As for the origin of the word *vāk*, it is from *vac*

(*Dhātupāṭha* xxiv. 55), which means to speak, tell, declare, mention, proclaim, describe, etc. [Because there are two variant ways of verbal conjugation, a slight distinction is drawn between *vac* root 1 and *vac* root 2, but that is of no significant consequence as far as the noun *vāk* is concerned, nor in fact for the meanings of conjugated verbal forms either for that matter, for the most part.] It is noteworthy that another word, *vad*, closely akin to *vac*, includes "tell", and "lay" or "lay down" in its range of meanings, which clearly remind us of the two different senses in which the Greek *legein* was originally used, as Heidegger shows to be the case. The noun that comes from *vad*, i.e., *vāda*, unlike *vāk*, is already charged with connotations of conceptually ordered propositions, and later of speaking with conceptual backing and logical connectives in situations of argument. But *vāk* is simply speaking as such, speaking of *reality as it is* (*yathā bhūtam*), and entails no conceptual-logical elaboration.

The noun *vāk*, feminine in gender, means voice, speech, language. Originally it included the meaning of sound also. In later literature *vāk* was occasionally employed for statement, or assertion. In the *Ṛg Veda*, however, vāk is used, as a rule, in the sense of speaking especially associated with itself. Therefore, it is as though where the Veda is not told – a condition which the *Ṛg Veda* neither envisages nor conceives – *Vāk* is neither spoken nor heard. And yet insofar as the Veda is told the groundedness of all language in the Vedic *Vāk* is posed. On the contrary, the *Ṛg Veda* does not tell us how to think of language apart from this groundedness, that is to say, as belonging to Nature or even human nature so as at some propitious point to link it to the Vedic *Vāk*. Therefore, the implication is strictly one way, and insofar as we fancy other alternatives to this one way of implication we will surely receive the answer "no".

The Veda, the text, speaks from the perspectives of the way *Vāk* itself wants to speak and does speak. And because of this there can be no way of distinguishing between the way the Veda speaks and the way *Vāk* itself speaks. And even when the Vedas (in plural) speak of *Vāk* they show forth this perspective as an announcement of the ground not only of *Vāk's* own speaking but of *what* they are speaking. The foremost thing they say is about gnosis and this task cannot be performed except by the telling *Vāk*, the *mytho-logos*, itself, which then is both the speaker and the spoken. For that reason what the Vedic texts do is to introduce *Vāk* in different ways.

There are, basically, three different ways of speaking of *Vāk* in the *Ṛg Veda*: (1) as a goddess; (2) in the symbolism of the cow; (3) in direct apposition to gnosis. Let us look at them briefly.

There is a *sūkta* (10.125) which is completely devoted to the goddess *Vāk*. In it the goddess describes herself. [It is also, simultaneously, a hymn sung by a *ṛṣi* in her praise. Thus the speaker is also the spoken – a pattern found throughout the text.] She is co-traveller with the Rudras, Vāsus and the Ādityas, holder aloft of Varuṇa, Indra and the Aśvins; sustainer and nourisher of Tvaṣṭar; queen; gatherer of treasures; one through whose *Māyā* everyone sees, breathes and hears; the sole speaker of welcoming words to the gods and men as they come to the feast; the bender of Indra's bow, etc. She pervades heaven and earth, extends over all creation, touching even heaven with her forehead, and holds together all beings by breathing the strong breath.

In several places in the *Ṛg veda*, the symbol of the cows stands for *Vāk*, most importantly in 1.61, 62 and 164; 9.26, 97 and 101; and 10.67 and 68. The special connection of Indra and Bṛhaspati to *Vāk* (symbolised by the cows) is noteworthy. Their epic battle with the demons who had stolen the cows and kept them bound and hidden in a cave are well-known to those who at least know the lore of the *Ṛg Veda* (as narrated in 1.62; 10.67 and 68). Bṛhaspati the god, too, is a symbol for *Vāk* in the sense that the seeker is also the sought, in the sense that *Vāk's* being brought to light is interchangeable with *Vāk* bringing everything to light, it being light itself: "Bṛhaspati calls out in thunderous voice to the cows", (*Bṛhaspatiḥ abhikanikradat gāh*).[30] "The cows too call out to him in a thousand streams", (*taṁ gāvo abhyanūṣata sahasradhārām akṣitaṁ*).[31] "Bṛhaspati brings them out from the dark into the light", (*Bṛhaspatiḥ tamasi jyotiricchannudusrā ākarvi hi tisra avāḥ*).[32] Bṛhaspati stands for thought as it calls out to *Vāk* and also hears the call of *Vāk*. Thought's calling out to *Vāk* is as much the work of *Vāk* as its own calling forth thought.

It is only insofar as *Vāk* enters the scene does thought discover gnosis as its ground. And only insofar as thought's own questions as well as its responses are heard in the way *Vāk* itself speaks can they be connected with gnosis. Thus, let us take the following questions and answers, (1.164.34 and 35):

Questions: I ask thee about the ultimate end (limit) of the earth;
Thee I ask, where is the navel of the world?; I ask thee of the

stallion's fecond seed; Thee I ask about the ultimate abode of *Vāk*. (*pṛcchāmi tvā param antaṁ pṛthivyāḥ*; *pṛcchāmi yatra bhuvanasya nābhiḥ*; *pṛcchāmi tvā vṛṣṇaḥ aśvasya retaḥ*; *pṛcchāmi vācaḥ paramaṁ vi'omaḥ*).

Answers: The earth's end (limit) is *this* altar;
The world's navel is *this* sacrifice (*yajñaḥ*); The stallion's fecund seed is *this* Soma; The ultimate abode of speech is *this Brahman*. (*iyaṁ vediḥ paraḥ antaḥ pṛthivyāḥ ayaṁ yajñaḥ bhuvanasya nābhiḥ ayaṁ somaḥ vṛṣṇaḥ aśvasya retaḥ*; *brahmā ayaṁ vācaḥ paramaṁ vi'omaḥ*).

The next but one verse articulates the pathos of ignorance and darkness of the one who thought on ultimate things and then declares how in that ignorant, bewildered state he received a part of *ṛta*, or True-Order, due to the approach of *ṛta's* first born, (*yadā mā ā agan prathamajāḥ ṛtasya āt it vācaḥ aśnuve bhāgam asyaḥ*). "The first-born of True-Order" (*prathamajāḥ ṛtasya*) is *Vāk*, i.e., *logos*, in that it is the pre-eminent procession out of True-Order insofar as it itself approaches thought. Thought *receives* a part of *Vāk*. The term for part, i.e., *bhāgaḥ*, is not used in the sense of divided part or division as *Vāk* cannot be divided. To receive a part of *Vāk* is in the proper sense to participate in it, that is, in the sense of the Greek *μετέχειν*, from which comes *μέθεξις*, a word originally used by Plato to express the participation of the forms (*ἰδέα* or *εἰδος*) in the Real itself.

Here a new vision of thought is pre-figured, however dimly. According to it, thought, i.e. in the sense in which it is envisaged and not in any neutral sense, is what participates in *Vāk*. By virtue of such participation it discovers its ground in gnosis, and that discovery itself is part and parcel of the conduct according to the way gnosis itself behaves. And this accord itself is made possible by the grace of *Vāk*, which works simultaneously as that through which gnosis appears and as that which enables thought to discover itself. Within this vision of thought is enclosed another truth which will unravel itself as we move further along, namely, that thought discovering itself and thinking are the same.

VĀK AND THE *VEDIC* TELLING CLIMAXING IN THE HYMN ON GNOSIS

Here we return to what we have called Vedic telling and to the "how" of *Vāk's* communication, or making possible the appearing, through the telling, of gnosis (*jñāna*) – the telling being simultaneously an enabling address to thought. In this way the basis for the accord between gnosis and thought is put forward, primarily in the shape of the understanding of meaning, or *artha jñāna*, so central a concern for the Vedas, a concern that exists within the telling itself. The possibility of understanding meaning comes to pass then the possibility of thought itself comes to pass, that is to say, in accordance with the way gnosis itself behaves. Looked at from the opposite end, however, it is also the case that gnosis appears only insofar as the possibility of thought comes to pass. This is what would be, outside of the grace of *Vāk*, a vicious circle, a catch 22 in colloquial slang. But this is exactly what the grace of *Vāk* breaks down. And only with the breaking down of the impossible vicious circle – which continues to be demonstrated throughout the movement of gnosis philosophy – is there both the appearing of gnosis and the enabling of thought.

The understanding of meaning is the shape the accord between the way in which gnosis behaves and the way in which thought conducts itself takes in the Veda. [This also shows the hermeneutical beginning as well as the ultimate hermeneutical character of gnosis philosophy, as we shall see all the way.] The climactic articulation of the issue of understanding meaning is found in the Hymn on Gnosis, or *jñāna-sūkta* (*Ṛg Veda*, 10.71), which is also where the Vedic telling itself reaches its climax. According to traditional Vedic interpretation, in this hymn the sage Bṛhaspati addresses himself having been astonished by encountering a group of very young children, who were found to be miraculously in possession of that understanding which even great sages had been hard put to achieve.[33]

The hymn begins with the preface,

Verse 1: *bṛhaspate prathamaṁ vāco agraṁ*; *yat prairata nāmadheyaṁ dadhānāḥ*; *yadeṣāṁ śreṣṭhaṁ yadaripramāsīt*; *preṇā tadeṣāṁ nihitaṁ guhāviḥ*.

Translation: O Bṛhaspati, from the first to the last of *Vāk* (is thus): (At the first stage is) address by giving that which is mere name; (At the last stage) the utterance of Vedic *Vāk* in its most excellent form (*śreṣṭham*); Blemishless (*aripram*), hidden in a cave (*nihitamguhā*), shining (*āviḥ*), accessible by grace (*preṇā*).

Following this preface, the subsequent verses are devoted to showing how gnosis is served by the understanding of the meaning of Vedic words:

Verse 2: *saktum iva tita unā punaṁto*; *yatra dhīrā manasā vācam akrata*; *atrā sakhāyaḥ sakhyāni jānate*; *bhadraiṣāṁ lakṣmī nihitādhi vāci.*

Translation: As they sift grain in a cribble,
The wise ones in their mind (cleanse) the words; (Then) the assembled friends (*sakhāyaḥ*) (i.e., the Vedic circle) understand (*jānate*) the meaning to be known; In their (the wise ones') telling or utterance (*vāci*) is holy grace (*bhadreṣām lakṣmiḥ*).

The words, "in their telling is holy grace" carry the assurance that the telling of the wise ones brings meaning with it, and that it would be neither devoid of meaning nor contrary to meaning.[34]

Verse 3: *yajñena vācaḥ pádavīyam āyan*; *tām anvavindan ṛṣiṣu praviṣṭāṁ*; *tām ābhṛtyā vyadadhu purutrā*; *tāṁ śaptarebhā abhi saṁ navaṁte.*

Translation: They (the children) achieved through *yajña* perfect progress in the understanding of *Vāk*; They achieved that which is possible only for great seers; Having brought it forth they spread it widely; (Then) the seven singers set it to song.

Setting it to song is to ensure its perpetuation through time, making sure that it endures: which is what is meant by *tām saptarebhā abhi saṁ navaṁte.*

Verse 4: *uta tvaḥ paśyan na dadarśa vācam*; *uta tvaḥ śṛṇvan na śṛṇoti enām*; *tvasmai tanvaṁ vi sasre*; *jāyeva patya uśatī suvāsāḥ.*

Translation: (In the telling) one though seeing does not see *Vāk;*

Another though hearing does not hear it; But for yet another it shines by itself; Even as a loving, well-adorned bride shows herself to her groom (of her own pleasure).

Verse 5: *uta tvaṁ sakhye sthirapītam āhur*; *nainam hinvaṁtyapi vājineṣu*; *adhenvā carati māyayaiṣa*; *vācaṁ śuśruvāṅ aphalāmapuṣpām.*

Translation: Among friends (i.e., the Vedic circle), of one they say he is settled in gnosis; For it (i.e., gnosis) is not set aside from understanding of Vedic words; One who sets it aside is labouring under an illusion (*māyayā*); And the *Vāk* he hears (i.e., in the telling) bears neither fruit nor blossom.

Verse 6: *yasti tyāja sacividaṁ sakhāyaṁ*; *na tasya vācyapi bhāgo asti*; *yadīṁ śṛṇoti alakaṁ śṛṇoti*; *nahi praveda sukṛtasya paṁthām.*

Translation: Who rejects a friend knows a freind; He has no part (i.e. does not participate) also in *Vāk*; He hears but in vain he hears; And he knows not the path of virtue.

Commentators who know the tradition make it clear that understanding of the words of the Veda is an act of friendship, rather a reciprocation, because the Veda confers its friendship upon those who hear it being told. Hence the Veda is called *sacivid* (meaning *sakhivid*), that is, knower of friends. The knowing of friends means a certain gratitude on the part of the Veda itself to those who help it by understanding it, thus enabling it to abide in the world. The help is the reciprocation of friendship. And further, as Verse 5, lines 1 and 2 make it clear, understanding of the Veda is inseparable from gnosis. Therefore, friendship with the Veda (i.e., friendship as reciprocated) is really the basis of an extraordinary relationship with gnosis itself. The friendship with the Veda now looms before us as the ground of philosophical thought. The possibility of philosophical thought resides in this friendship, which is really, as we have seen, a reciprocated friendship, that is, in other words, not a self-initiated relation on the part of thought but rather a responding one. In these terms philosophy is where thought conducts itself in the way gnosis itself behaves towards thought, which is essentially through *Vāk*. Hence we see quite clearly how and why in the tradition which flows from the Veda philosophical thought is what is approached from the ground of gnosis. And we get a different account of what we may call by the name philosophy. And we also have here a new dimension for thinking itself inasmuch as it is the Veda's own gratitude which is the foundational *thanks* because *Vāk* itself has preceded it as the language of *stuti*, or praise.

Verse 7: *akṣaṇvaṁtaḥ karṇavaṁtaḥ sakhāyo*; *mano javeṣvasamā babhūvuḥ*; *ādaghnāsa upakakṣāsa u tve*; *hṛdā iva snātvā u tve dadṛśre.*

Translation: Friends (of the Veda) possessed of eyes and ears differ in their understanding; Some stand as if in water level (of understanding) up to the mouth; Others stand in water level that reaches the breast and armpit (only); And yet others immerse themselves in water deep enough to dive in.

Verse 8: *hṛdā taṣṭeṣu manaso javeṣu*; *yadbrāhmaṇā saṁyajaṁte sakhāyaḥ*; *atrāha tvam vijahur vedyābhiḥ*; *ohabrahmāṇo vicaraṁtyu tve.*

Translation: When friends who are knowers of *Brahman* In their heart consider profound verses, There some of them are cast aside, While others go far in their deep thinking.

Verse 9: *ime ye nārvāṅgna paraścaraṁti*; *na brāhmaṇāso na sute karāsaḥ*; *ta ete vācam abhipadya pāpayā*; *siṁstantraṁ tanvate aprajajñayaḥ.*

Translation: They (i.e., the former) move not in the path of the virtuous (i.e., in the transcendent); They are not knowers of *Brahman*, nor do they conduct themselves in virtue (i.e., in accord with the way of gnosis); Uttering *Vāk* sinfully, They adopt the craft of the plough and are devoid of the benefit of gnosis.

In this verse those who do not understand *Vāk* are condemmed. It says that these false friends of the Veda are not really knowers of *Brahman* as they only outwardly associate with those who are, that their thinking is mere plodding, altogether unaware of what gnosis is. Their model is the craft of the plough even in their professed freindship with the Veda, and hence they are really devoid of the benefit of gnosis.

Verse 10: *sarve naṁdaṁti yaśasāgatena*; *sabhā sāhena sakhyā sakhāyaḥ*; *kilbiṣasprt pituṣaṇirhi eṣām*; *araṁ hito bhavati vājināya.*

Translation: All assembled friends rejoice on account of the friend who has come (i.e., Soma, the exhilerating friend); Skilful and able to resolve doubts of the assembled; He is their perfector and nourisher; And he disposes himself as the food in the sacred vessel, fit for eating.

Verse 11: *ṛcāṁ tvaḥ poṣamāste pupuṣvān*; *gāyatraṁ tvo gāyatī śakvarīṣu*; *brahmā tvo vadati jātavidyāṁ*; *yajñasya mātrāṁ vi mimīta u tvaḥ.*

Translation: One (i.e., Hotṛ) brings together the verses and recites; Another (i.e., Udgātṛ) sings the *gāyatra* in *śakvarī* metres; Another (i.e., Brāhman) narrates the wisdom pertaining to things that exist; And yet another determines the rules of the sacrificial rite.

This verse simply describes the four divisions in the Vedic telling, assigned formally to four classes of Vedic priest-tellers. Every narration in the Vedas must be seen in the light of the supreme *jñana-sūkta*, or Gnosis Hymn, which has just been explicated. Indeed, the tradition regards this hymn as foundational to the understanding of the *Ṛg Veda* (and other Vedas too) as a whole.

This hymn is where the Indian tradition of gnosis-philosophy actually begins. Does gnosis appear here and in similar references to it in the Veda? The answer is that it does but only to the degree in which dialogue with the hymn – and with the Veda – is successful, that is to say, if carried out on its own terms. If successful, then in the appearing of gnosis thought comes to pass, the possibility of which will have been always held in *Vāk's* telling, but depending also on our observing what is most essential in such thought, namely *the inviolable compact of adoration – of what is worth adoring – and questioning* both together in the same, like two sides of a coin. And thought coming to pass is gnosis releasing itself.

THE CONTINUING CURRENCY OF THOUGHT THROUGH CONCRETE SPECULATION

The thought which is the extension of gnosis holds within it the original astonishment, or the shock of wonder, such being the response to gnosis itself. It is for this reason that it is the compact of adoration and questioning.

However, thought generated this wise is not dissociated from thought in the general sense of what has its ground in human consciousness. With regard to the latter we observed in our Introduction: "There is a primordial operation of human consciousness as a consequence of its interaction with what it encounters as reality, first of all the world itself in both its determinate and indeterminate aspects." We also showed how this latter thought betakes itself to its natural paths, i.e., the penetration of hidden depths of reality, boundary-making for coping with the boundless, and penetration of otherness inherent in phenomena. Now, far from staying at a distance from its stream, the thought grounded on gnosis joins it and seeks to direct it to its own trajectory.

We have, however, no actual model for this operation in the Veda itself. But we have something else that is quite helpful, which is *Vāk's* own further telling, nevertheless harking back to the narration that relates gnosis, of a kind of wisdom concerning existing things. We learn that *Vāk* is not an idle teller of tales, for whatever it tells comes within the orbit of gnosis.

Such telling constitutes the *science of reflection upon things that exist*, which are then, we might say, speculations, cosmogonic in general character. In that manner we are justified in seeing the possibility of thought (as grounded in gnosis) continuing its prevalence through these concrete modes which raise problems in the way thought grounded in human consciousness does. Even so, we will notice that the compact of adoration and questioning is not broken. These speculations cover a fairly large range of "problems" which are posed to human consciousness by what it encounters as reality, priority being given to the very mystery of the world's existence comprehending human consciousness itself in that it is part thereof.

It is in this way that a *science of reflection upon things that exist* comes into being in the *Ṛg Veda*, which is called by a name that means exactly that, i.e., *jāta-vidyā*, mentioned in the Hymn on Gnosis (last verse, line 3) as already a subject of narration by the Brāhman, the third among the four divisions of Vedic priests. The term *jāta-vidyā* acquires, according to the *Nirukta*, 1.8, the specific meaning of wisdom pertaining to the origin of the world. The narration of this takes the form of cosmogonic accounts, which are necessarily circular in that they are themselves understood as being part of the cosmos whose origin is thereby accounted for. The last fact merely reinforces the primordial nature of *Vāk*, which does the telling, albeit now from within the cosmos.

There are several such important accounts, narrated from different perspectives. A few of the best known are the following:

1. The *Puruṣa hymn* (*Ṛg Veda*, 10.90), describing the sacrifice, by the gods, of Puruṣa, the primeval, infinite Personal Being, out of whose dismembered body the cosmos and everything in it, including human beings as well as the Vedas, originated.
2. The *Viśva-karmā hymn* (*Ṛg Veda*, 10.82), according to which the world was made by a primordial architect, Viśvakarmā.
3. The *Prajāpati hymn* (*Ṛg Veda*, 10.121), which celebrates the birth of the Unknown God Prajāpati (Father of beings), who as *Hiraṇya-garbha* (the Golden Germ) himself arose in the beginning and then made the universe.

These above hymns are essentially cosmogonic in their speculative thrust. But there is another which, although cosmogonic, stands out as being of a different character, with greater metaphysical possibilities. This is what is known as the *Nāsadīya hymn*, so called on account of its very first word, *nāsat* (that which is not).

It begins with an indeterminate "then" (*tadānīm*) when "there was" neither "that which is" nor "that which is not" (*nāsadāsīnno sadāsīt*). What it is concerned with is the "then", which is an abyss unmarked by that which is not we perceive in death (*mṛtyu*) as well as by that which is we perceive in the deathless state (*amṛtam*). Out of this Void "the One came into being by the power of heat, or penance" (*tapasaḥ tad mahinā ajāyata ekam*) – and everything else came into being through the "desire" (*kāma*) which entered the One. And desire itself was the seed of all things, itself the first-fruit of the "mind" (*manasaḥ*).

Despite this profound account it is a wistful song. It is, no doubt, true that "the wise who have searched in their own hearts with wisdom could find out the bonds of what is in what is not" (*sato bandhum asati niravindan hṛdi pratiṣyā kavayo manīṣā*). This kind of searching in the heart is similar to what we have characterized as "the primordial operation of human consciousness as a consequence of its interaction with what it encounters as reality in both its determinate and indeterminate aspects", except that, as becomes a hymn of this kind, this reflective operation is held as successful in making a conclusive discovery, the thinkers being paradigmatic "wise ones" – and the wisdom is also the practical one of adjusting life to death. Nonetheless, the hymn ends wistfully in respect of our ever finding anyone who really knows and can tell the answers to a series of questions which are asked at the end, held to be beyond the ken of even the wise who, searching in their hearts, have arrived at positive conclusions as to "how" things that exist relate to, or arise from, the background of their having not existed previously and having to pass out of existence again.

The questions asked now are different, deeper. "Who here knows and who here can tell *whence, wherefore, wither, why* has this creation come into being? (*ko addhvā veda ka iha pra vocat ājātākuta iyam visṛṣṭiḥ*?). This question is repeated several times with slight variations. The key word in these is *kuta*, which translators render as "whence?" That is where the force of the questions are lost. The word has a variety of meanings, and not only in later literature, such as "whither?", "whence?" and not the least "why?", "wherefore?", "for what cause?", and "to what end?". At least the *Ṛg Vedic* usage here is indeterminate such that the sense "why?" "wherefore?", or "to what end?" is powerfully operative, especially read in the proper philosophical context. That is all the more evident because of the "why?" questions pertaining to the world, that is, "why is there a world?", "why is the world such as it is and not otherwise?", "but what does it mean for us that there is a world?", and so on in a progressive and even dialectical manner. These are but forms of the great question of Being. It is to such unavoidable questions for which no one is known to have an answer that the hymn refers when it says: "The embodied principles (the deities) we appeal to in thinking out answers to these questions are posterior to, i.e., part of, the world; then who knows from what cause/for what reason it has arisen?" (*arvāg devā asya visarjanena adha kaḥ veda yataḥ ābabhūva*?). To put it in today's language, not even the greatest philosophers, scientists or even saints have answers to these questions, and it would be vain to expect anyone to have any. That all men are alike, equally helpless before these questions is the final truth of the world.

The wistfulness of the hymn expressed in these questions is, however, only a pointer to gnosis, which far from stifling these questions, actually takes them up into its own ground. But thought as it stands upon the ground of gnosis takes them unto itself, putting them into its own trajectory. In that way, not having answers to certain questions will no longer be a source of distress or defeat or perplexity, as that will be perceived as their very essence and their reason for being, causing them to be meditated upon under gnosis. In this way, questioning's compact with adoration will also be preserved without breach.

CHAPTER II

GNOSIS AND PHILOSOPHICAL THOUGHT IN THE UPANIṢADS

[The Upaniṣads speak essentially of Ultimate Reality (under the name *Brahman*) whose disposition is gnosis. Everything else radiates from this centre. The most definitive speaking of *Brahman* – and of gnosis – is heard in the Upaniṣads.]

THE TEXTS OF THE UPANIṢADS

The Upaniṣads are appended to the second great division of the Vedas, namely, the Brāhmaṇas, as the last portion of the Vedic corpus. They constitute the principal foundation (*prasthāna*) of Vedānta. They are the foundation of all of Indian philosophy.

There are a large number of ancient religio-philosophical texts which bear the name *upaniṣad*. Their total number is variously estimated in different places. The *Muktikā Upaniṣad*, a relatively recent treatise (although called an *upaniṣad*) speaks of 108, while some other sources mention the number of 200. But the vast majority of these do not belong to the Vedic class and, therefore, are not Upaniṣads in the proper sense: they are usually later, sectarian works given the august title *upaniṣad* in an honorary manner. The Upaniṣads proper, on the contrary, are those which belong to the Vedic corpus and their number ranges from 11 to 17. We must first of all take the 11 as forming the core, employing as criterion of judgement the fact that the great Vedānta philosopher of a later day, Śankara, commented on them. These are the *Īśā, Kena, Kaṭha, Praśna, Muṇḍaka, Māṇḍūkya, Aitareya, Taittirīya, Bṛhadāraṇyaka, Chāndogya*, and *Śvetāśvatara*. To this list is usually added the *Kauṣītakī* and *Maitrāyaṇīya* (or *Maitrī*) to make up the thirteen principal Upaniṣads, a canon which has found favour with most scholars of the present day. Then there are the

Mahānārāyaṇa, Jābāla and *Paiṅgala*, to which Śankara himself refers (along with the *Kauṣītakī*) in his great work on the *Brahma Sūtra*. The list of the principal Upaniṣads can be further stretched out by adding another two or three, based on the fact that another great Vedānta commentator, Rāmānuja, refers to them, also as Upaniṣads. However, although it may seem arbitrary, to confine ourselves to the nowadays universally accepted thirteen has some definite practical advantages for a study that does not purport to be either exhaustive or thorough in the matter of canon.

The style and contents of the principal Upaniṣads are such as to permit us to assign them to three successive periods. Accordingly, the following grouping can be plausibly made:

1. The early prose Upaniṣads: The *Bṛhadāraṇyaka, Chāndogya, Aitareya, Taittirīya, Kauṣītaki* and *Kena*.
2. The middle period metrical Upaniṣads: the *Kaṭha, Īśā, Śvetāśvatara, Muṇḍaka* (and *Mahānārāyaṇa*, if this last were to be included).
3. The later prose Upaniṣads: the *Praśna, Maitrāyaṇīya* and *Māṇḍūkya*.

The Upaniṣads vary greatly in length. The two longest are the *Bṛhadāraṇyaka* and *Chāndogya*, while the two shortest are the *Īśā* and *Māṇḍūkya*. From the following observations alone we will get an idea of how much the size varies: the *Bṛadāraṇyaka*, consists of a total, distributed through 6 chapters, of 438 passages, some of which in number of words are individually long enough to accomodate the entire eighteen verses of the *Īśā* or the entire twelve of the *Māṇḍūkya*. The other nine range in between these two extremes.

Clearly, length itself is a small consideration. But, for reasons of their diverse contents as well as of their acknowledged antiquity and originality the *Bṛhadāraṇyaka* and *Chāndogya* have been traditionally accorded the primacy of place among all the Upaniṣads. Some of the material in them are also found in the others, a fact which suggests borrowing on the part of the latter.

Every one of the Upaniṣads is also marked by a certain completeness, most probably owing to the fact that all of them were kept alive in different localities or circles as texts for teaching, until in course of time they were brought together so as to constitute a distinct division of the Vedic literature. From that time onwards, whenever it was, we have had the extant texts grouped together as today.

THE MEANING OF THE WORD UPANIṢAD

Now, what does the word *upaniṣad* literally mean? It is either a deliberate coinage (less likely) or an accidential formation (more likely) from *upa* + *ni* + *sad*, meaning (translating backwards) sitting down devotedly near by, referring most probably to some private sessions at which the proximity, primarily between the teacher and the pupils, assumed both intimacy and confidentiality. Similar substantives with quite contrary meanings have come from the verb *sad*, combined with appropriate suffixes. Thus we have *pariṣad* and *samsad*, both carrying the connotation of *public* assembly. But the Indian tradition has generally tended to explain the origin of the word *upaniṣad* from the point of view of its philosophical meaning. Thus Śankara gives several parallel explanations (probably purported to be derivations as well). In the *Kena Upaniṣad* he defines it as that which destroys (*sādayati, vināśayati*) the ignorance of the nature of 'I' and 'mine' consciousness by moving a person to the Ultimate Reality (i.e., *Brahman*) by the signs of identity (with it).[1] The same derivation is presented in the introduction to the *Commentary on the Īśā Upaniṣad*. In his Introduction to the *Commentary on the Taittirīya* he equates *upaniṣad* with *vidyā* (gnosis), "because, for those who practise it [such things as] conception, birth, old age, etc., are removed (*niśādanāt*) or destroyed, that is to say, insofar as they will be brought near (*upanigamayitṛtvāt*) to the Ultimate Reality (i.e., *Brahman*) in which their highest good rests."[2] In this context he adds, "the books are also called *upāniṣad* on account of the above meaning" (*tadarthatvāt grantho'pi upaniṣad*).[3] In other places too he defines the word as denoting certain books.[4] Clearly, that is close to our modern use of the word.

The word *upaniṣad* appears in the Upaniṣads themselves, obviously not in the sense of books or literary compositions but in the sense of some profound teaching, or *ādeśa*, carrying the association of both secrecy and sacredness. Secrecy is conveyed by certain terms which the Upaniṣads use, in contexts, as synonyms for *upaniṣad*: these terms are *rahasyam* (secret), *guhyam* (hidden in the cave), *guhyatamam* (most hidden in the cave), etc..

As we think of the secret in this respect, the sense of sacredness is inalienable, for somehow at their depth the two are related. The confidentiality involved in secrecy is not a worldly notion. Also, a distinctive character of the secret that is sacred by definition, and vice-versa, is that, in a paradoxical manner of speaking, the truth concerned is for everyone. Observing secrecy appears to be, in a real sense a way of publicly witnessing to a vital character of sacred truth, namely, its universality and accessibility to all in principle. That character is safe-guarded, not denied, by keeping the sacred truth out of profane, public view. Let us refer to a concrete incident recorded in the *Bṛhadaraṇyaka Upaniṣad*, 3.2.13: "Then Yājñavalkya said, Arthabhāga, my dear, take my hand. We two alone shall know of this; this is not for us (to speak of) in public". Then Yājñavalkya took him aside and whispered into his ears.

The rules about imparting the sacred-secret teaching came under a strict code of instruction. Only a very few were reckoned to have the requisite qualification (or eligibility) to receive such teaching, consequent upon a devout commitment to gnosis to be observed for life, which is translated as the ability to enter with understanding into the teaching and to abide in it. These conditions naturally restricted the choice, in the highly stylized and ritually controlled social system of the times, to the best and most faithful of a teacher's circle of pupils, to those properly initiated, with a conventional preference for a teacher's eldest son, assuming that that son is also a devout seeker of wisdom.[5]

The word *upaniṣad* was used in the Upaniṣads as a designation for certain mystical teachings, which were often conveyed in the form of cryptic formulas. Thus, at the end of the *Kena Upaniṣad* we come across the expression *tadvanam* (literally, 'dearest of all'), put forward, as a symbol for meditation and contemplation, by the teacher who was discussing Ultimate Reality. The teacher further says, upon the pupil's request, that this word is the *upaniṣad* (*iti upaniṣad*).[6] Likewise, the famous formula in *Bṛhadāraṇyaka Upaniṣad*, 2.1.20, *satyasya systam* (literally "truth of truth") is called *upaniṣad*. In yet another place (following *Taittirīya Upaniṣad*, 3.10.5), after expounding the eternal truth in the form of a mystical chant, the speaker concludes the text with the words "he who knows thus, this is the *upaniṣad* (*ya evam veda ity upaniṣad*"). There are also several similar other expressions, the most important of which is *tajjalān* – clearly a made up one – upon which one is asked to meditate.[7] The expression *tajjalān* (*Chān-dogya Upaniṣad*, 3.14.1) means that which is the source, the subsistence and the goal of all things.

It is clear that these cryptic formulas and the teachings which they helped to focus were the heart of a whole, wise-spread tradition of wisdom pertaining to Ultimate Reality and to man's liberation from the bondage of ignorance and ill. In course of time the majority of these diverse records of wisdom produced in different Brāhmaṇas and later, perhaps somewhat before the times when the *Bhagavadgītā* and the *Brahma Sūtra* were composed, came to be reckoned together as forming a distinct group of texts of the Vedic classification.

THE UPANIṢADS AS THE CULMINATION OF VEDIC RELATION

Doubtless, it must have taken several centuries for the Upaniṣads as we have them to be formed. However, we can notice reflections in sundry places on the question of the relation between the Upaniṣads, some already formed and some being formed, and the Vedas. In this way, the status of the Upaniṣads is being determined as Vedānta. Thought on that question was already beginning to move forward even in the earlier phases of the texts. The expression "the [transcendent] person in the Upaniṣadic sense (*aupaniṣadam puruṣam*)" occurs in *Bṛhadāraṇyaka*, 3.9.26, which beyond a doubt is a very early passage. Yājñavalkya asked Śākalya about this person in the manner of a fateful test, which the latter failed – and istantly his head fell off (symbolically speaking) as a result. In *Chāndogya*, 3.5.1-4 we find a compelling account of the place of the Upaniṣadic teachings in relation to the Vedas. The Vedas are called the hidden teachings (*guhyā ādeśā*) and described as essences and the Upaniṣadic teachings as the essences of the essences (*rasānām rasāḥ*). The Vedas are described as nectars and these teachings as their nectars (*vedā hy amṛtaḥ teṣām etany amṛtāni*). In *Kena*, 4.7 and 8 the category of *upaniṣad* is employed in the sense of the supreme teaching as that which alone is competent to make *Brahman* known, while the Vedas are regarded as stepping-stones to the Upaniṣadic wisdom:

(The pupil): 'Sir tell (me) the *upaniṣad*'. (The teacher): 'The *upaniṣad* has been told, we have told thee the *upaniṣad* pertaining to *Brahman*'. Ascetic contemplation (*tapaḥ*), self-control (*damaḥ*) work (*karma*) are its support (*pratiṣṭhā*), the Vedas are all (its) members and truth (*satyam*) its resting place (*āyatanam*)'.

The colophonic expression 'this is the *upaniṣad*' (*iti upaniṣad*) at the end of several important statements about *Brahman* actually conveys the sense of a higher source of wisdom than the Vedas, that is to say, in respect of the knowledge of *Brahman*. Evidently, this expression is purposely inserted in crucial places, after certain tellings.

The term *vedānta* is also found used in the Upaniṣadic texts themselves in some places as an official designation for the Upaniṣads, and it is most significant that it should appear in them. We meet with it in *Śvetāśvatara*, 6.22, in connection with a particular teaching which is described as "the highest secret in Vedānta, revealed in a former epoch" (*vedānte paramaṁ guhyam pūrvakalpe pracoditam*). We can only wonder whether the designation is used in reference to those early and mighty Upaniṣads, the *Bṛhadāraṇyaka* and *Chāndogya*, which were probably already looked upon as not only works of high antiquity (as far as the Upaniṣads go) but also as documents of immense spiritual authority. The *Śvetāśvatara* is usually placed among the middle period metrical Upaniṣads. The *Muṇḍaka*, which also belongs to the same period, refers (in 3.2.5,6) to "*ṛṣis* who are satisfied with gnosis" (*ṛṣayaḥ jñāna tṛptāḥ*) and to "ascetics who have properly ascertained the meaning of Vedānta knowledge" (*vedānta-vijñāna suniścitārthāḥ yatayaḥ*). It is quite likely, in view of this reference, that the Upaniṣadic sages of old like Yājñavalkya, Uddālaka and Janaka, serve as models, as they must have already been elevated in the tradition to the status of *ṛṣis*, the difference being that they are not seers of the Mantras, like the Vedic *ṛṣis*, but seers of *Brahman* or *Ātman*.

The Upaniṣads are considered of higher importance than the Vedas (i.e., Mantras) because of that which they are the seeing and hearing – and telling – of, namely *Brahman/Ātman*. This seems to be clearly implied in the famous statement of Yājñavalkya in the *Bṛhadāraṇyaka*, "It is the *Ātman* which is to be seen, heard, thought of and reflected on", (*ātmā vā are draṣṭavyaḥ śrotavyo mantavyo nididhyāsanavyaḥ*).[8] Without any doubt, this judgement of comparison is implied in the discipleship of Nārada, a great knower of the Vedas (i.e., Mantras) and its subsidiary sciences, to Sanatkumāra, a paradigmatic Upaniṣadic figure, for the sake of *Ātman*-gnosis. In his self-introduction Nārada begins by saying, "Venerable Sir, I know the *Ṛg Veda*, the *Yajur Veda*, the *Sāma Veda*, the *Atharvaṇa* as the fourth (Veda) ... etc. But Venerable Sir, I am only a knower of the Mantras (*mantravid evā'smi*), not a knower of *Ātman* (*na ātmavid*)".[9]

"Revelation" in respect of the Upaniṣads means removing the veil that obscures the ground of thought. The ground is gnosis and the removal of the veil is accomplished by *Vāk*. This revelation, this act of *Vāk*, is that by which thought comes to its own. There is no higher revelation than that by which thought comes to its own. In such a revelation thought is not extraneous to gnosis, nor gnosis extraneous to thought. We may single out this fact as the unique character of the Upaniṣads. In the Mantras thought has been struggling to come to its own, and in the Upaniṣads it is finally here. Therefore, there is actually no conflict between the Mantras and the Upaniṣads in spite of the sounds of certain statements *in* the Upaniṣads, which, however, are not Upaniṣadic, that is to say Vedāntic, statements. The sound of these things we hear in the Upaniṣads simply point to the fact that in the Mantras thought has been struggling to come to its own, and that it is finally here.

The word 'finally' is an interpretation of *anta* in *vedānta*, and it is not to be understood in the historical sense insofar as it swallows up history altogether, removing it from the ground of thought. Its meaning is simply ontological because, it having already come, a situation wherein it does not yet exist or one in which it no longer exists is not conceivable except outside the ontological framework, which is the same as the framework of gnosis.

The predicament of philosophical thought as distinguished from any other, i.e., scientific, technological, aesthetic or ordinary, is that it must stake itself on the notion of Ultimate Reality even to the extent of negating what it cannot affirm in knowledge or, may be, of finding a way of comporting itself with ultimate seriousness towards that which lies before it in the spirit of resolute scepsis. Ultimate Reality must come in somehow. In the Upaniṣads, Ultimate Reality is approached through gnosis, as thought itself is seen to proceed from the ground of gnosis. When one says gnosis, in that same breath one says Ultimate Reality and when one says Ultimate Reality, in that same breath one says gnosis.

Gnosis is to be understood as the disposition of Ultimate Reality, a disposition which is towards us. And thought is the extension of gnosis. It is on account of this that philosophy is to be defined as thought conducting itself in accordance with the way gnosis itself behaves. Here thought comes to its own, removing all possibilities of an extraneous relation between itself and gnosis. There is also entailed here the gathering of all other thought that has to do with the question of Ultimate Reality, putting such thought on a new trajectory. Thus, the Upaniṣads present to all philosophy which comes from them the perennial possibility of going into every human sphere of thought in order to gather and orient towards gnosis everything that has to do with the question of Ultimate Reality. The exhibition of that possibility constitutes the body of the Upaniṣadic "philosophy" which radiates from, and in turn focuses on, its core, namely, *Brahma-vidyā* or *Ātma-vidyā*, the term *vidyā* having to be understood as man's intellectual and spiritual appropriation of gnosis.

In the Upaniṣads, thought that is approached from gnosis as the ground is found in its paradigmatic form. Now, we may well ask: how does it act as the ground for receiving – and also for gathering – all other kinds of thinking and how does it provide the background of illumination in which to place all our questions? For the reviewing – as well as gathering – of all other thinking and placing all questions that have to do with Ultimate Reality in an illuminated background is essential for the discourse which forms the body of the Upaniṣadic philosophy to be produced. That is how *Brahma-vidyā* or *Ātma-vidyā* expands itself to the dimensions of coherent philosophical discourse, entailing all kinds of discursive thinking and dialectical arguments, which are known, in that same meaning, by the name *vāda* – and there is a proliferation of such *vādas* in Vedānta.

Gnosis extending itself as thought means, reversely, drawing gnosis into the realm of what always comes to our purview as thought, i.e., having to do with the question of Ultimate Reality so that a great conjunction is effectuated. What is thus called thought may be traced to Being, as its extension (Parmanides), and its essential character may be interpreted as questioning, openness, placing oneself in the draft of Being, etc. (Heidegger). [Other possible understandings are also not to be precluded.]

THE CENTRALITY OF BRAHMAN/ĀTMAN IN THE UPANIṢADS

In the Upaniṣads *Brahman/Ātman* is Ultimate Reality. There philosophy is essentially the laying of the foundation for coherent discourse about Ultimate Reality as *Brahman/Ātman*, which is approached from gnosis as the ground. Coherence is achieved through drawing gnosis into the realm of what comes to our purview as thought, whereby thought also comes to its own. And consequently any lingering signs that gnosis and thought are extraneous to each other is done away with, which is an accomplishment integral to the very purpose of *Vāk*. The revelation of *Brahman/Ātman* is that wherein thought is fully restored as the extension of gnosis, thereby abolishing any appearance of a gulf between them.

To begin with, it will be useful to discuss the words *brahman* and *ātman* in their independent histories, each carrying its own meanings. Although from the point of view of Upaniṣadic revelation as well as philosophy, such a historical tracing of their career is totally irrelevant, it is nevertheless valid, insofar as transformation of words and ideas is the vehicle of revelation through texts. And also, because revelation does not entail the introduction of new words, such an undertaking is entirely legitimate.

Both *brahman* and *ātman* began as obscure ideas in the Mantras and soon acquired greater significance. The word *brahman* had already been there in the Mantras. What it means in most occurrences in the Mantras is a moot question. Whatever else it may have meant eventually, it is incontrovertible that at first it most commonly stood for prayer, that is to say, a special use of words within the telling of the Mantras that already connotes a proximity and closeness to Ultimate Reality and destined to be its linguistic surrogate. Here are some of the references to that effect: "Prayers (*brahman*) for praise have Ghṛtamadas made ready";[10] "Maghavan, he gives prayer (*brahman*) praise, laud and soma".[11] There is in one place the occurrence of the strange phrase "the prayer that carries (or accepts) prayer", (*brahmāṇaṁ brahmavāhasam*).[12] Here in this above and similar occurrences is something very close to the notion of prayer carrying itself or even praying to itself, which would be quite consistent with the meaning of *Vāk*, associated also with the intrinsic potency of ritual, an idea already not too far off in the horizon. In fact, this is expressed in the conception of

Bṛhaspati the god, as Brāhmaṇaspati, the Lord of prayer. This Lord of prayer is also called prayer as in the expression, *brahmāṇam ca bṛhaspatim,*[13] which means literally that.

Prayer as *Vāk* that is intimately associated with ritual is the commonest meaning of *brahman* in the Mantras. But it is already the word with the highest destiny and in such places as in the Hymn on Gnosis, already gives more than a portent of it. Śankara traces the word from *bṛh*, to grow, and accordingly ascribes to it the sense of "growth", of that which expresses itself in speech and in Nature as force. Max Müller adopts that etymology.[14] Paul Deussen perceives it as the human will in its striving towards the divine, whereby the person in the act of prayer returns to the timeless, spaceless, impersonal self of his, which is God.[15] A.B. Keith, while agreeing that the word normally means prayer, nevertheless adds that it can also mean spell and that, furthermore, in many passages it must be taken as "holy power".[16] Heinrich Zimmer accepts the classical Indian derivation (assumed also by Max Müller) from *bṛh*, to grow, but he goes further forward to demonstrate that the verb means, as clearly expressed in the formation *bṛhmyati*, to "increase, strengthen, fortify" and that, therefore, it definitely has the denotation of power assigned by Keith. He particularly cites the Vedic noun *barhaṇa*, from the same root, denoting "power", "strength", corresponding, as he thinks, exactly to a term current in the later tradition, i.e., *śakti.*[17]

Now, there is much to be said for the view that these different meanings proposed need not be taken as exclusive of one another. In fact, each of them can be legitimately ascribed to the term in some occurrence or other. Zimmer's intuition does seem to be able to reconcile different derivations, but then we must stress the following two points: (1) the meaning of *brahman* as prayer, ritual prayer, must be deemed basal and permanent and other meanings can only be added to it; (2) it is perhaps extravagant to imply that the denotation of power is somehow culminative, even for the Upaniṣads.

It is true that the notion of *brahman* blazes for us the trail from the Mantras to the Upaniṣads through the Brāhmaṇas. But if we read only the passages of the Mantras where this occurs or even the Brāhmaṇas alone, without the posterior developments of the Upaniṣads, we certainly would not get the impression that it is of paramount importance in either of them. No doubt, the notion appears quite prominently in the Brāhmaṇas, as it tends to become the supreme principle but is still far from what it is destined to become in the Upaniṣads. The main pre-occupation of the Brāhmaṇas is surely *yajña* (sacrificial rite) as Sāyaṇa quite rightly informs us.[18] Conspicuous as the notion of *brahman* is in them, it is consistently depicted as the highest potency of the sacrificial rite. Concerning this, Keith quite rightly states: "The sacrifice clearly occupied the minds of the priests to the practical exclusion of all else, and their theories were in large measure devoted to the consideration of its relation to the universe, to the gods and to men."[19] And he further observes,

> This theory is the most characteristic and independent part of the Brāhmaṇas: in the speculations as to the unity of the universe and the God in whom that unity finds expression, the Brāhmaṇas are only inheritors of the speculation of the Rigveda, but in the doctrine of the sacrifice they express a theory which may have been held in germ at least in the age of the Rigveda, but which is not expressed there and which doubtless in considerable measure is a new creation.[20]

In the development of a dominant philosophy of *yajña*, which tends to treat sacrifice as a power unto itself, although in conjunction with *Vāk* and even within the framework of the Ultimately Real, the *Atharva Vedic* hymns as well as the special orientation of the *Yajur Veda* made decisive contributions. For this reason it is all too essential to recognize that were we to pursue the development of all aspects of Vedic religion and philosophy we would have been obliged to study these Vedas as well. But this is not what we presently intend to do. So it is enough for us to be confined to the main stream.

In the Brāhmaṇas *Brahman* was mainly thought of as the intrinsic potency of *yajña*, or sacrifice, and this gave a tremendous impetus to the study of correct rules and interpretation of *yajña*. The *Śatapatha* and *Aitareya*, the two most important among the Brāhmaṇas, clearly show the extent to which the notion of *Brahman* dominated the sacrifice. The *Śatapatha* has this striking passage:

> They said to *Brahman* 'we will lay thee down (or set thee up) here'. What will therefore accrue to me? 'Thou shalt be the highest of us' – 'so be it!' They accordingly lay the *Brahman* down here, whence people say that *Brahman* is the highest of the Gods. Now by this fourth layer [of the altar, obviously] these two, heaven and earth, are upheld and the fourth layer is

> the *Brahman*, whence people say that heaven and earth are upheld by *Brahman.*[21]

It is said that in the beginning the gods were mortal, that they became immortal only when they came in possession of *Brahman.*[22] There is nothing greater than *Brahman* "and he who knows that, being himself the greatest, becomes the highest among his own people. This *Brahman* has nothing before it and nothing after it."[23] The Brāhmaṇas attain to the conception of the self-originated *Brahman* (*Brahman Svayaṁbhu*).[24] In all these developments the idea of the bond (*bandhutā*, or *nidāna*) between the ritual and eternal model played a vital role. The *Śatapatha Brāhmaṇa* commends meditation on *Brahman* in order to understand sacrifice.[25]

The *ātman* notion, likewise, had its origin in the Mantras. As in the case of the word *brahman*, so with respect to *ātman* also some consideration of etymology is in order. Customarily, scholars have assumed that the word derived from the root *an*, to breathe, or *at*, to move, or *av*, to blow, and hence to be cognate with the Greek *atmos* and *autmen*. Contrary to this, Deussen suggests[26] that from the beginning the term was highly abstract, derived from the roots *a*, as in *aham* (I) and *ta* (this), so that it meant 'this I', that is, one's own self. Reaffirming the traditional etymology over against Deussen's, Keith cites *Ṛg Veda* passages in support, where the meaning according to him, is obviously wind.[27] But oddly enough, Keith's references really do not prove the derivation from the traditional roots. The word *ātman* occurs in association with *vāta*, etc., meaning wind. Expressions like *ātmā devānām* (the *ātman* of the gods)[28] do not really tell us that *ātman is* wind. In fact, they do not give us any clue to the meaning of the word. However, there is no reason why a notion like this could not have been both abstract and concrete at the same time. Perhaps we must give up the belief that in respect of man's fundamental notions these are mutually exclusive. This situation of the interplay between our abstract conception and concrete perception has to be taken back to that very mythic point which we call the origin of a notion. And we call it mythic point as we cannot really put our finger on something and say "this is the actual point". In the order of the operation of our consciousness, can we really say that abstraction came after concrete perception? Is not perception already controlled by abstraction, and in fact vice-versa as well? Why should wind or breath have suggested the ideas of spirit and self, or conversely, why should such ideas ever have been identified with wind or spirit? It only suggests to us that the power of abstraction had been quite non-temporally co-existent with the faculties of perception, and reminds us that we are not looking for the mystery of their interplay where we ought to look, to wit, in consciousness. It is to the great credit of the Indian philosophies of language, which already had their beginning in the *Ṛg Veda*, that they provided us with a framework in which to investigate the origins of notions in a structure which identifies eternal language with eternal consciousness. [This is not the same as the theories of the origin of names propounded by etymologists like Yāska.] But we must forego consideration of these matters now.

In the *Ṛg Veda* itself there are passages where *ātman* is used in the sense of the self of a being as when it is said of the Sun (*sūrya*) that he is the self (soul) of what moves and moves not,[29] or when Soma (the god of exhilaration) is called the self (soul) of sacrifice,[30] the primeval self (soul) of sacrifice.[31] Then we have the possible reflexive use of the word as the expression "on account of the All *itself*" (*sarvasmāt ātmanaḥ*).[32]

However, in the *Ṛg Veda* we find no instance where the word is used in the sense either of man's soul or self or that of the universal soul, the latter of which comes to be one of the leading characteristics of the Upaniṣads. But these senses indirectly arrive in some places in the Brāhmaṇas, for instance, in the *Śatapatha* in a few places where the real essence of man is set over against the principle of breath by which a person's psycho-physical being is revealed.[33] It is called the "undefined breath",[34] and as the "eleventh breath" in which the ten vital airs (of life) are established.[35] In one place, the heart of the victim of sacrifice is regarded as its *ātman* which is, however, connected with the sacrificial rite through the act of breathing into the victim.[36] There it is also called mind (*manas*). Elsewhere, we read the *ātman* of the sacrificial food, as being full of joy (*ānanda*), even as the gods are full of joy, and on him, therefore, we are asked to meditate.[37] [Henceforth we shall refer to this word used in the sense of the universal Self as *Ātman*, and in all other senses including that of the individual soul as *ātman*. Where the distinction is either not clear or not applicable we will continue to write *Ātman.*]

In another place the *Śatapatha Brāhmaṇa* calls for meditation on the *Ātman*; there we are given the completest and most advanced description of it anywhere in the Brāhmaṇas,

> Let him meditate on the *Ātman* which is made of intelligence, possessing a body of life-breath, with a form of light and with an ethereal nature, which is able to change its shape at will and swift as thought, consisting of all sweet odours and tastes, which holds sway over all the regions and pervades the whole universe, which is silent and indifferent – like a grain of rice, or like a grain of barley, or like a grain of millet or the smallest granule of a millet grain, so is the golden Puruṣa in the heart; like a smokeless light, it is greater than the sky, greater than space, greater than the earth, greater than all beings – that *Ātman* of life-breath is my *ātman* (self); upon passing away from hence I shall attain to that *Ātman.*[38]

The *ātman* notion moves towards a convergence with the *brahman* notion in what may chronologically be the last passages of the Brāhmaṇas as in the *Taittirīya Brāhmaṇa*, 10.6.3.

The Revelation of Identity: a Clarification

The Brāhmaṇas lead to two notions, *Brahman* and *ātman* (*Ātman*) towards a convergence, the logical outcome of which is their identification, which becomes fully expressed in the Upaniṣads. But the matter of the identification of the two is a little more complex than is ostensively assumed by students of the Upaniṣads. In order to perceive that complexity we must take account of the two-fold definition of the idea of *ātman* (*Ātman*) still prevailing in the Upaniṣads. In contrast, *Brahman* is given a consistently univocal meaning as the infinite, all-encompassing, eternal, one only Being, that is, as far as the Upaniṣads are concerned.

In the first place, we can easily see the many passages where *Ātman* is treated as synonymous with *Brahman* and defined identically. In the second place, we can see equally clearly many other passages where *ātman* is treated as the individual self (or soul) synonymous with *jīva*. A few examples will be given below from the two greatest Upaniṣads.

1. *For Ātman as identical with Brahman*

Bṛhadāraṇyaka, 1.4.1-17: Here we have four parallel accounts of the origin of all things; two of these trace all things to *Brahman* and the other two to *Ātman*. We have the following prologic statements in each case: "In the beginning *Ātman* alone was this (world), in the manner of a person", 1.4.1.; "In the beginning, *Brahman* indeed was this (world)", 1.4.10,11; "In the beginning, *Ātman* indeed was this (world)," 1.4.17.

Bṛhadāraṇyaka, 2.4.5, and 4.5.6: "*Ātman* should be seen, heard, etc.", (*ātmā va are draṣṭavyaḥ śrotavyaḥ* etc.).

Bṛhadāraṇyaka, 2.5.1-14: Here "this shining immortal person" (*tejomayo'mṛtamayaḥ puruṣaḥ*) is defined in 14 different contexts as this *Ātman*, this *immortal, this Brahman* and *this all.*

Bṛhadāraṇyaka, 3.4.1: "Explain to me the *Brahman* who is immediately present and directly perceived, who is the *Ātman* in all things", (*yat sākṣād aparokṣād brahma, ya ātmā sarvāntaraḥ, tam me vyācakṣveti*). Bṛhadāraṇyaka, 3.4.2 continues to explain this *Ātman* as "the seer of seeing", "hearer of hearing", "thinker of thinking", and "understander of understanding".

Bṛhadāraṇyaka, 3.7.2-23: The recurring formula is: "He who dwells in the earth, yet is within the earth, whom the earth does not know, whose body the earth is, who controls the earth from within, he is your *Ātman*, the inner controller, the immortal" This formula is repeated twenty times, each time substituting "earth" with a different category.

Chāndogya, 7.25.2: "Now the instruction about *Ātman* (*āthāta ātmādeśa*), *Ātman* is below, *Ātman* is above, *Ātman* is behind, *Ātman* is in front, *Ātman* is to south, *Ātman* is to the north, *Ātman* indeed is all this."

Chāndogya, 7.26.1: "All this is of *Ātman*", (*ātmata eva idaṁ sarvam iti.*)

2. *For ātman as the individual self*

Bṛhadāranyaka, 3.9.26: "On what are you and (your) *ātman* i.e., self, supported (*kasmin nu tvaṁ cātmā ca pratiṣṭhitau*).

Bṛhadāraṇyaka, 4.4.1: [This is the beginning of the great discourse on death which is itself described as the] "*ātman's* getting to the absence of strength", (*ātmā abalyam nyetya*).

3. *For the word used in both senses*

There are very many other examples as well for both usages as described above. But the passages where the word is used in both senses is quite illuminating. For instance, in *Bṛhadāranyaka*, 2.5.15, we have this: "In this *Ātman* are all beings ... and all *ātmans* held together", (*asminn ātmani sarvāṇi bhūtani ... sarva eta ātmanaḥ samarpitāḥ*).

Now we return to the complexity of the matter of the identification of *Brahman* and *Ātman*. In the examples given for the reference to *Brahman* and *Ātman* as identical, what we see is simply identical or homogeneous definition of the two. The two are already pre-supposed to be synonymous or interchangeable. But the philosophical *act* of identification is different. It pertains to the new identification of the individual *ātman* (*jīva*), or self, with the Supreme *Ātman* (or *Brahman*). Śankara clearly explains this: "The term *ātman*, without any qualifying prefix has the denotation restricted to the individual self, like the word 'cow' and the like: hence thou art that Being, O Śvetaketu."[39] The culminating statement expressing this philosophical act of identification occurs nine times in the famous dialogue of Uddālaka with his son. (*Chāndogya*, 6.8.7 – 6.16.3). Here the father repeats the words "that is the truth, that is the *Ātman*, That art thou, O Śvetaketu", (*tat satyam, sa ātmā, tat tvam asi, śvetaketo*). In this context, which is a discussion on death, *Ātman* is synonymous with *Brahman*, while the "thou" of Śvetaketu, stands for his individual *ātman* or self. The same declaration is made in other words "That individual soul (*ātman*) (subject to mortality) is *Brahman*" (*sa vā ayam ātmā brahma*), *Bṛhadāraṇyaka*, 4.4.5. This is clear because the context is the discourse on death, as described above.

This fairly lengthy detour we have found necessary because there is, concerning this matter, some confusion among modern scholars, especially in the light of the convergence of the two nations, *Brahman* and *Ātman*, already taking place in the latest portions of the Brāhmaṇas. This convergence could mean the possibility of identical or homogeneous definition of the two. Here their equation is already pre-supposed and each simply serves as a synonym for the other. The subject of the new declaration, the revolutionary philosophical act, is not the equation of these two already known as two "First Principles", but the equation of these two taken synonymously as but *the* (one) "First Principle", or Ultimate Reality, and the transitory, mortal, finite, individual self anxious for knowledge and spiritual emancipation. To be fair, this identification itself was vaguely anticipated in a meditational mood in the *Śatapatha Brāhmaṇa*, 10.6.32, but that surely does not yet have the force of the identity announced in the Upsaniṣads. In any case, it does not make any difference as nobody has a right to insist that the knowledge must appear only in the texts known as the Upaniṣads. Further, is it not true that sometimes one hears the rumblings before one hears the roar of the thunder itself?

With no recognition of the need for apprehending the distinction outlined above, Deussen, writes: "If for our present purpose we hold fast to this distinction of the Brahman as the cosmical principle of the universe, the ātman as the psychical, the fundamental thought of the entire Upanishad philosophy may be expressed by the simple equation: Brahman = Ātman." Let us call this equation *A*.

Deussen continues:

> That is to say – the Brahman, the power which presents itself to us materialized in all existing things which creates, sustains, preserves, and receives back into itself again all worlds, this eternal infinite divine power is identical with the ātman, with that which after stripping off everything external, we discover in ourselves as our real, most essential being, our individual self, the soul. The identity of the Brahman and the Ātman, of God and the soul, is the fundamental thought of the entire doctrine of the Upanishads.[40]

Let us call this equation *B*.

Modern writers on the Upaniṣads, first Deussen, and following his lead all the others, Keith, Radhakrishnan, Ranade, Hiriyanna, *et. al.*, make it appear that equation A and B are one and the same. As we have argued, the first is already pre-supposed. The Upaniṣads, do not declare it, for that would be carrying no stirring message. On the other hand, the declaration made to one existing individual, who is aware of his finitude and mortality, that he, his self, is one with *Brahman/Ātman* is the message so far not heard, ever, at any time. Śankara makes this point crystal clear in his *Commentary on the Brahma Sūtra*, as he writes:

> The statement 'that thou art' is [made] because of its being the instruction pertaining to the *Brahman*-bond of the embodied person. This instruction as to the *Brahman-Ātman*-hood of the embodied person is given as self-established fact, not as something to be accomplished by effort. Hence, it is this *Brahman*-Ātman-hood of the *jīva*-self which is understood to be based on the scripture, that serves to obliterate the natural notion of a man, about the *jīva*-self which is understood to be based on the scripture, that serves to obliterate the natural notion of a man about the *jīva*-self being of the nature of the body, even as the understanding of rope as the rope obliterates the notion of a snake.[41]

This declaration does not have the character of equating two "First Principles", because it – like all the similar ones – is made in the context of the existing individual's anguished quest for liberation (*mokṣa-vyāpāra*). This would be entirely in accord with Śankara's definition of *upaniṣad* itself as the *vidyā* which destroys (for those who practise it) such things as birth, old age, etc., and brings (them) near to Ultimate Reality.

The declaration of identity brings to us a new knowledge. The emphasis on the "new" should not be taken to mean that the knowledge is historically unprecedented, although incidentally that is also the case. It really means that it is qualitatively novel. As Śankara says, it is self-accomplished or come by itself (*svayam prasiddham*), not something to be accomplished (*na ... prasādhyam*) by us. This gives a new ground for thought, something on the basis of which thought grasps itself in an unprecedented way. The coming to view of this ground is an astonishing fact which forces thought to review its previous foundations including even postulated *a prioris* and presuppositions. Nevertheless, gnosis puts itself at the disposal of thought, both to answer the questions which we have not asked and would never have thought to ask, apart from its arousing power, and to provide new orientations to answers to the questions we have previously asked, those of an existential character as well as those we have clothed with notions in our mind, especially the ones pertaining to "First principles" themselves, and most of all to take into gnosis questions that have no answers.

DESCRIPTION OF BRAHMAN-ĀTMAN

The entire purpose of the Upaniṣads is to reveal *Brahman* and to make thought able to receive what is revealed. As we have said, that revelation takes place by virtue of the movement of gnosis for our benefit. This is a boon. The Upaniṣads say: "He is to be attained only by those to whom he (*Ātman*) grants the boon. To such a one *Ātman* reveals his own nature."[42]

There are many revelatory statements in the Upaniṣads. Through all of them *Brahman*-gnosis is presented as the novel (*anadhigata*) truth. However, there is here a fundamental problem, i.e., in regard to the diversity of the descriptions and what seems to be their divergent emphases. Some of them appear to favour the idea that *Brahman* is quality-less (*nirguṇa*) and beyond personality, while the others to favour the idea that *Brahman* is full of qualities (*saguṇa*) and hence personal. The paradigmatic statement of the first kind is that *Brahman* is "Not this, Not this" (*Bṛhadāraṇyaka*, 2.3.6; 4.4.22; etc.). The following are the examples of descriptions of the second kind: "This shining, immortal person, *tejomayaḥ amṛtamaya puruṣaḥ* (*Bṛhadāraṇyaka*, 2.5.1); Omnipresent God, *devaḥ pradiṣo nu sarvaḥ*, (*Śvetāśvatara*, 2.16); rewarder, *vāmāniḥ* (*Chāndogya*, 4.15.3); etc. In course of time, in the eyes of some theologians this difference between the so-called *saguṇa* and *nirguṇa* descriptions appeared to be of enormous importance. But Śankara, undoubtedly in the spirit of the Upaniṣads themselves, seeks to overcome this distinction. In one place he observes: "It is not possible to say that the Upaniṣads endorse the view that there is a divergence in types of descriptions of *Brahman*. The difference exists merely for the purpose of facilitating different meditations (*upāsana*), and in truth there is no difference – that is the purport".[43] The solution is this: despite the apparent divergence in the descriptions, they are, in respect of the novel truth revealed, utterly homogeneous. An inconsequential problem must not occupy our minds. For it is not error to depict *Brahman* in ways which are natural to the religious mind, and there is no reason to believe that the purport of the *nirguṇa* description is to prevent *Brahman* from being worshipped as God. On the contrary, there is all the more reason for worshipping *Brahman* as God. That such is not the case is a sheer misunderstanding perpetrated by some modern writers. But we must press on and be led to where the Upaniṣads really lead us.

Everything that is said in the Upaniṣads is to be re-ordered from the viewpoint of the following two summit descriptions.

1. *"Not this, Not this" (neti, neti)*

For this we turn to *Bṛhadāraṇyaka*, 2.3.1-6. From stanza 1 to the middle of stanza 6 a brief account of the principles which hold the mind, particularly the religious mind, as it contemplates Ultimate Reality as *Brahman* is given. Stanza 1 enunciates the two forms of *Brahman*, the imaged and the unimaged. The imaged, symbolized by the sun, clearly are the concrete, perpetually grasped entities, (stanza 2), while the unimaged, symbolized by air and ether (*ākāśa*) are the abstract, conceptually grasped entities leading up to the transcedent principles, or, in the technical language, *adhidaivatam*, which literally in the Sanskrit idiom means what pertains to the gods (stanza 3).

The big switch from this type of description to the other takes place in the middle of stanza 6. "Now, therefore, the instruction (pertaining to *Brahman*) 'Not this, Not this', for there is nothing higher than this. Now (its) designation is 'the truth of truth'."[44] The words 'now, therefore' (*atha ato*) are variously used in philosophical texts, but here they indicate a radical switch of themes, which amounts to the surpassing and sometimes even rejection of what was maintained up to that point. This is a stylistic convention found in the Upaniṣads themselves. [The various uses of the term 'now' (*atha*) are discussed in the *Śloka-Vārtika*, 1.1.22-24]. With regard to the significance of this statement Śankara writes:

> How is it, then, that through these two terms 'Not this, Not this' it is sought to describe the truth of truth? It is said: by means of the expurgation of all limiting adjuncts the terms refer to something that has no particularities, whether of name, action, differentiation, species or quality, as the function of language is in respect of them. But *Brahman* has none of these particularities. Hence it cannot be described as such and such, as we can say 'here goes a white cow with horn'. *Braham* is described (at the lower level) by the super-imposition of name and form, and of action, by such expressions as '*Brahman* that is consciousness and bliss', 'what is of the stuff of consciousness' and even by the very words *brahman* and *ātman*. Nevertheless, when we have to describe *Brahman* as it really is, that is, freed from all adjuncts of particularities, then it cannot be described by any means whatsoever. At that point there is only one course left, viz., to describe it as 'Not this, Not this', in other words, through pure negation.[45]

2. *"That Thou art", tat tvam asi*

As with the declaration "Not this, Not this", so with the declaration "That Thou art". The entire 6th chapter of the *Chāndogya Upaniṣad* is an account of how the climactic knowledge of non-duality is imparted to a young man by his teacher (and father) after taking him through the shattering experience of shedding his sense of duality. The young man, Śvetaketu, was well learned in the Vedas and hence had truly imbibed and understood their religious principles. Yet he had not received that instruction "by which the unheard becomes heard, and the unthought thought, the ununderstood understood, (*yena aśrutam śrutam bhavati, amataṁ mataṁ bhavati, avijñātam vijñātaṁ bhavati*)". Śvetaketu is one who had completely lived up to the knowledge of the Mantras. But in the great encounter he confessed, "Surely, those holy men (i.e., his teachers) did not know this, for if they had known it how could they not have told it to me", (*na vai nūnam bhagavantas tad etad avediṣuḥ yadd hi etad avediṣyan katham me nāvakṣyan iti*)? Immediately, Śvetaketu was led into a lengthy and penetrating dialogue on Being (*sat*), and of the origin and repose of beings in Being, (*imāḥ sarvāḥ prajāḥ sadāyatanāḥ satpratiṣṭhāḥ*). Then comes the culminating declaration repeated nine times (6.8.7-6.16.3): "That which is the subtle essence, in which all this has its self, that is the Truth, that is the *Ātman* (Self), That Thou art, O Śvetaketu, so it is", (*raso aṇimā aitad ātmyam idaṁ sarvam, tat satyam, sa ātmā, tat tvam asi, śvetaketo iti*). Śankara writes: "This self is known as Being and it is through the Self that this whole world is imbued with self-hood."[46] The discourse has been leading up to this grand climax. Here the presupposition about Being itself was clarified, as it was laid down as the first step in the teacher's leading Śvetaketu to this culminating declaration. Now the pupil knows what was meant when it was stated (6.2.1): "In the beginning, my dear, this was Being alone, one only without a second", (*sad eva idam agra āsīt ekam eva advitīyam*).

The two declarations, i.e., "Not this, Noth this" and "That Thou art" complement each other. In the one the reality of *Brahman* is asserted negatively, that is, by the exclusion of all notions and pre-suppositions, while in the other it is asserted positively as Being, i.e., understood in an umprecedented way, and as Self. These two are the two summits of the description of *Brahman*. They govern and permeate all others.

In the paradigmatic statements "Not this, Not this", "That Thou art" and many others, *Brahman* is shown to be simply what it is. The revelation takes place through *Vāk*. The knowledge is stored in *Vāk*, in whose keeping it is, and *Vāk* alone reveals it. "*Vāk* is the sole resting place of all Vedas", (*sarveṣāṁ vedānāṁ vāgekāyanam*), says the *Bṛhadāraṇyaka Upaniṣad* (2.4.11).

Now, there is a secondary use of the word *Vāk* in the Upaniṣads, namely as man's language which is the instrument of his thought about Ultimate Reality. In that sense it is described as the companion of the eye and the mind. Ultimate Reality, or *Brahman*, accordingly, is not accessible to man's independent thought, i.e., his eye, his mind and language. Hence it is said "thither the eye goes not, nor language nor mind", (*na tatra cakṣur gacchati na vāggacchati no manaḥ*), *Kena*, 1.3. "Not grasped by the eye or language", (*na cakṣuṣā gṛhyate nāpi vācā*), *Muṇḍaka*, 3.1.8. It is "that whence language returns along with mind without attaining it, (*yato vāco nivartante aprāpya manasā saha*), *Taittirīya*, 2.4.1. This kind of purely human language is held to be distinct from *Vāk* which by its own speaking brings gnosis.

But by taking this position on language and thought, the Upaniṣads do not require that we abandon them. On the contrary, the Upaniṣads only show that language and thought themselves are objects to be grasped, i.e., from the ground of gnosis, rather than they serving as independent means for grasping Ultimate Reality. Hence it is said "That which is not revealed by (human) language but that which illuminates (human) language itself: that verily know thou to be *Brahman*; this (i.e., language) is not what they think this (to be)", (*yad vācā na abhyuditam yena vāg abhyudyate tad eva brahma tvaṁ viddhi nedam yad idam upāsate*), *Kena*, 1.5.

GNOSIS AND THOUGHT

So gnosis is the beginning, not only goal, of all investigations pertaining to Ultimate Reality – if by Ultimate Reality we mean that of which gnosis is the disposition, i.e., *Brahman*. No doubt, through our own thought and our own speculative and other employments of language we can quite conceivably construct views of Ultimate Reality. Or by critical thought and analytical employment of language we can equally conceivably demolish all views of Ultimate Reality. The basic issue in all this is how to relate the known and the unknown with each other. Philosophers have always pitted the known against the unknown, or contrariwise, the unknown against the known, or even juggled the two in the quest for what the Ultimately Real is. But the Upaniṣads put *Brahman* entirely outside this framework of the use of language and thought which point philosophy in these directions. Hence, *Kena Upaniṣad*, 1.4, says, "Other indeed is it to the known and other too is it to the Unknown", (*anyad eva tad viditād atho aviditād adhi*).

The mutual otherness between the known and the unknown is what both critical and speculative philosophers have to work with. Critical philosophers reject philosophical appropriation of the transcendent as they think that such appropriation is an illusion and that it obliterates their mutual otherness, but would institute an enduring dividing line, although the founder of Critical Philosophy, Kant, himself however would summon us to view the unknown that is beyond the limit of what we can hope to know by Pure Reason with ultimate, fundamentally religious, concern. On the other hand, the master of speculative philosophy, Hegel, would overcome the mutual otherness between the known and the unknown by dialectics. However, for the Upaniṣads, the otherness is not what is mutual between the two, but an absolute fact that puts both on the same plane. Also, this absolute otherness of the Wholly Other, i.e., *Brahman*, is both preserved and dissolved in the immediacy of gnosis. The primary assignment that thought assumes for itself is to follow the ways of such utter immediacy, because gnosis puts itself at the disposal of thought.

The questions that one raises by thought, all summed up in the underlying question of all, i.e., that of Being, can receive an answer in gnosis. Hence gnosis always immediately shows forth that of which it is itself the disposition, i.e., *Brahman*, as Being (*sat*), which is the answer to the sum of all the questions that thought has carried as its great burden. The *Praśna Upaniṣad*, 3.2, describes such questions as *atipraśnāḥ*, i.e., as those that are beyond the range of asking, and suggests that only "those whom *Brahman* loves" (*brahmiṣṭāḥ*) are able to receive an answer.

In the light of the Upaniṣads we come to know that there are two ways to approach "Being", that is, (1) as the sum of all questions and (2) as the answer to the sum of all questions. In the first approach we seek a ground upon which and due to which our questions *are* questions. And insofar as that ground itself is not answer we are moved to put it in *epochē* by asking the question as to Being, in the forms of "What is Being?" and "Why Being?". No doubt, the shock of wonder which has provoked the questions helps thought to contain it by means of the *epochē*, and that is necessary as otherwise thought must become paralysed.

What is raised in thought and whose form thought assumes must be answered in thought and thought itself, and if not answered must still be held, but the prospect for that comes only when thought goes beyond what had been till then apprehended as its ground, i.e., Being according to the first approach, in other words, as the sum and source of the questions. That is where gnosis enters the picture as the disposition of Ultimate Reality, offering a different ground to thought, i.e., the thought that answers, as well as holds the questions, including the ones without answers. And Ultimate Reality as Being in the sense of what it essentially is according to the first appraoch, i.e., as the sum and source of all questions, is now restored to a new light. And the thought that works as the answer and as the power to hold the questions is seen as the extension of gnosis, which is what is differently expressed by us as "the disposition of Ultimate Reality".

We may ask "how is this so?" But when asking it we must not forget that it too is a question. When we realize that gnosis is henceforth to be the ground of thought in the sense of extension of gnosis we will be enabled to ask it and also all the others in the manner of review, of gathering, under gnosis.

In the Upaniṣads there are several discussions on Being, or *sat*, but always from the ground of gnosis. The most notable statement, however, is in *Chāndogya*, 6.2.1-2:

> In the beginning this was Being alone, one only without a second. Some say that in the beginning this was non-Being alone, one only without a second. From that non-Being Being arose. But how indeed, dear one, could it be so, said he, how could Being be generated by non-Being? Being itself was this in the beginning, one only without a second.[47]

In the Upaniṣadic tradition 'gnosis', or *jñāna*, has always reference to *Brahman*, often implicitly. But equally often it is also made explicit by the expression '*brahman*-gnosis' or *brahma-jñāna*, thereby eliminating any possible ambiguity of meaning. However, that other expression, *brahma-vidyā*, which means the spiritual and intellectual appropriation of *Brahman*-gnosis, has come to be the more commonly used one. But these are not by any means really different from each other in what they entail for the philosophical discipline. Rather, it is the case that what is only implicit in the one is brought out explicitly and into clearer visibility by the other – that is how they function.

The term *brahma-vidyā* expresses both the *theōrea* and the *praxis* underlying the gnosis which has sole reference to *Brahman*, and hence is applicable to the conduct of thought. So this term gives testimony to the fact that thought can conduct itself in accordance with the way gnosis itself behaves, that is, inasmuch as its sole reference is to *Brahman*.

A brief account of the meaning of the word *vidyā* is in order, although here we are concerned with it as it forms a compound with the word *brahman*. It should be noted that *vidyā* has a wide range of meanings, including even such things as certain kinds of practical skills and knowledge of certain crafts. Archery too, accordingly, is considered a great *vidyā*. So also are medicine, architecture and all the other pursuits which require specialized training and skills. But we also find the word used in the sense of higher, spiritual pursuits. The Upaniṣads use it in that sense and recognize several specific ones such as *agni-vidyā, prāṇa-vidyā, ṣāṇḍilya-vidyā, aumkāra-vidyā*, etc. But the Upaniṣads also recognize such a thing as *avidyā* or agnosis, indicating the eclipse of gnosis. Thus *Chāndogya*, 1.1.10 has it, "*vidyā* and *avidyā* are different from each other", *nānā tu vidyā ca avidyā ca*. It is said that *vidyā* is the means to immortality, *vidyayā vindate amṛtam*, (*Kena*, 2.4). The three Vedas (*Ṛk, Yajus* and *Sāma*) are themselves regarded as *vidyās* (*Chāndogya*, 1.4.2).

But even with respect to the Vedas a tension exists between two views: one which understands them as manuals of ritual activity, or *karma*, and the other which understands them as *vidyā*. And indeed *vidyā* is held to be infinitely the more excellent of the two. Hence *Bṛhadāraṇyaka*, 1.5.16 states, "By *karma* one obtains the world of the fathers (lower heaven), by *vidyā* one obtains the world of the gods", (*karmaṇā pitṛ-lokaḥ vidyayā deva-lokaḥ*). The significance of "the world of the gods" consists in its contrast with the "world of the fathers", and hence it is a symbolic expression for that which is co-ordinate with *vidyā*, i.e., *mokṣa*, or transcendent freedom. Therefore, it is added in the context, "the world of the gods is indeed the best of the worlds: therefore they praise *vidyā*" (*deva-loko vai lokānāṁ śreṣṭhaḥ tasmāt vidyāṁ praśaṁsanti*).

As in the Greek tradition so also in the Upaniṣads there is not a hint of opposition or even separation of *theōrea* and *praxis*. Further, as in the Greek thought, *theorea* was understood as the highest form of *praxis*, and besides, *theōrea* is its own *praxis*. As for words that may be seen as more or less equivalent to the two Greek terms we have in the Upaniṣadic tradition the concrete terms *darśana* or even *sāṁkhya* (for *theōrea*) and *sādhana* or even *yoga* (for *praxis*). But in order to avoid confusion it may be borne in mind that *sāṁkhya* and *yoga* later become names for specific philosophical schools, while, on the other hand, *darśana* began to convey increasingly the meaning of school or "system" of philosophy in general and *sādhana* came to be used more to mean the *modus operandi* of any religio-philosophical school whereby it seeks to realize those things it has set forth as spiritual goals.

As is quite clear by now, the Upaniṣads use the word *vidyā* philosophically. But they further specify the philosophical scope of *vidyā* as *Brahma-vidyā*, which is uniformly extolled, often directly but sometimes indirectly, i.e., as the remote and ultimate implication of the different kinds of *vidyās* or wisdom-pursuits. In one place (*Maitrī*, 2.3), *Brahma-vidyā* is simply set forth as "the wisdom of all the Upaniṣads", (*brahma-vidyā sarvopaniṣad vidyā vā*). Elsewhere (*Muṇḍaka*, 1.1.1), it is called "the foundation of all *vidyās*", (*brahma-vidyā sarva-vidyā-pratiṣṭhā*)." According to the Upaniṣads, philosophy is fundamentally the *theorea* and *praxis* ("theory" and "practice") of *Brahma-vidyā*. No doubt, it is Śankara who brings home this point later on in his commentaries with incredible rigour and consistency. For instance he observes, defining *Brahma-vidyā* thus: "It is being understood by the very use of the word *upaniṣad* that it signifies *Brahma-vidyā*."[48]

Now *Brahma-vidyā* principally applies to three things which most concern man's thought about Ultimate Reality, not just in the Upaniṣads but universally. These three things are Ultimate Reality itself, the world and our own selves. A later Vedāntic formula announces the result of thinking on them thus: "*Brahman* (the Ultimate Reality) is the Truth, the world is a fictional (although powerful) creation, and one's own self is *Brahman* itself and is nothing else" (*brahma satyam jagan mithyā jīvo brahmai'va nāparaḥ*). The Upaniṣads clearly live up to the declared interest in these, as their paramount concern. No doubt, *Brahman/Ātman* is their absolutely dominant theme, but the wisdom pertaining to it, i.e., *Brahma-vidyā*, is held as most relevant to thinking about the world and about our own empirical selves. It is questions about these two which appear first when we think about Ultimate Reality along with the question of Ultimate Reality itself. In the natural dispensation of thought they give rise to metaphysics of the world and metaphysics of the human self, or "psychology". And *Brahma-vidyā*, insofar as it is that whereby gnosis gathers and places in a new trajectory all thought that has to do with Ultimate Reality, allows full scope to the realization of that natural dispensation. That is how the metaphysical developments within Vedānta have occurred, and their foundations are in the Upaniṣads themselves. But these developments as such are not intrinsic or essential parts of *Brahma-vidyā*.

Brahma-vidyā is that wisdom which knows that *Brahman* is Ultimate Reality. In itself it is beyond metaphysics. But insofar as man's thought cannot avoid its own potentiality for metaphysics, *Brahma-vidyā* offers itself as a ground for the expression and development of that potentiality, in which sense it is held as that whereupon metaphysical thought may find a new beginning. *Brahman* being perceived already, we may reflect on it metaphysically, that, is in relation to the world and in relation to the individual self. The Upaniṣads have already led the way in both these respects.

But here the absolute difference between the world and the individual self is something to be noted as being of crucial importance. In the great divide expressed in the above-mentioned formula the individual self is already on the side of, being one with, *Brahman*. The word for the world is *jagat*, from a root which means 'to move'. Therefore, it stands for what is essentially transitory, unstable and in a state of passage. The word for the individual self is *jīva*, from a root which means "to breathe". Therefore, it stands for what is living, in fact life itself. The living being and life are considered eternally real because in the great divide they are on the side of, being one with, *Brahman*, and are to be freed from bondage to what is merely transitory, unstable and in a state of passage.

The world, *jagat*, which by its very definition exhibits characteristics that are opposite in nature to that of *Brahman*, also produces the illusion that it is the ground of our being and of our knowing. For one thing, the world is based on desire, and is what encourages us to hope but is nevertheless always the frustration of desire and the wasting of hope; it is a promise which it is unable to fulfill. And for another, it is the region of fear and anxiety. If it gives us the illusion that it is the ground of our being and of our knowing it also indeed threatens us with the loss of being and shuts off from our view the region of knowing with a thick veil. For all these reasons, it calls for reflection as to what it is, why it is there and whether it is what it seems to be.

It is indeed possible to reflect upon the world with *Brahma-vidyā* or without it, and no doubt the results would be radically different. But reflection with *Brahma-vidyā* includes the gathering and the vicarious re-capitulation, through imagination, of the other way of reflection as well, which no doubt, it consciously transcends. According to this, the conclusion is reached: *Brahman* is what we know but do not know that we know, while the world is what we do not know but assume that we know. From this point reflection on the world with *Brahma-vidyā* continues without abating – which is the model that prevails in Vedānta.

Reflection upon the world with *Brahma-vidyā* will bring two results, one of which will tell us that the world has its ground on what exceeds it, and the other will tell us that it *is not* what it appears to be, that is, it is *Māyā*. These two results must be taken as complementary to each other in the Upaniṣads' explanation of the world.

As to the first result, i.e., that the world is grounded on what exceeds it, the Upaniṣads tell us that the ultimate ground must be unravelled progressively. The matter is presented in a graphic dialogue between Gārgī and Yājñavalkya (*Bṛhadāraṇyaka*, 3.6.1). Gārgi beings: "As all this here is woven, like warp and woof, on water, on what, pray, is water woven, warp and woof". Answer: "On air, O Gārgī". The question continues with principle after principle (*devatā* in Śankara's terminology) replacing water and air till the world of Brahmāḥ (the creator god) is advanced as the ground. But from the fact that the questioning still continues it is clear that even the world of Brahmāḥ is not really to be regarded as the final ground. At this point the dialogue abruptly ends with both Yājñavalkya and Gārgī agreeing to be silent. Nevertheless, one section later (*Bṛhadāraṇyaka*, 3.8), the dialogue between them is resumed in a different vein, and here Yājñavalkya dramatically introduces the concept of *Akṣara*, translated 'imperishable'. Gārgī asks: "That O Yājñavalkya, of which they say it is above the heaven, below the earth, between these two, the heaven and the earth, that which the people call the past, the present and the future, across what is that woven warp and woof?" Yājñavalkya proposes space as the answer. But the question continues: "across what is space woven like warp and woof?" In response, Yājñavalkya declares:

> That, O Gārgī, the knowers of *Brahman* call the imperishable. It is neither gross nor fine, neither short nor long, neither glowing red nor adhesive, neither shadow nor darkness, neither air nor space, unattached, without taste, without smell, without eyes, without ears, without voice, without mind, without radiance, without breath, without mouth, without measure, having no within and without. It eats nothing and nothing eats it... Verily, at the command of that imperishable, O Gārgī, the sun and the moon stand in their appointed stations. At the command of that imperishable, O Gārgī, heaven and earth stand in their appointed stations. At the command of that imperishable, O Gārgī, moments, hours, days and nights, months, seasons, and years stand in their appointed stations. At the command of

that imperishable, O Gārgī, some rivers flow to the east from the snow-capped mountains and others to the west in whatsoever direction.

Yājñavalkya concludes with the final declaration "On this imperishable, O Gārgī is space woven, warp and woof," (*etasmin nu khalu akṣare, gārgi, ākāśa otaś ca protaś ca*).

A note may be added before we continue with the discussion of the concept of the imperishable. Now, the word *akṣara* translated 'imperishable' in this context and in a few more in the Upaniṣads is used essentially in the adjectival sense, with *Brahman* as that which *akṣara* qualifies either explicitly or implicitly. The complete term, therefore, is *akṣara-brahman*, as in *Kaṭha*, 1.3.2. However, the word *akṣara* is also used as a noun in the Upaniṣads, and indeed in the entire tradition, in another sense, that of letter, or syllable. The two must not be confused, although often they are. This latter usage is prevalent in the *Chāndogya Upaniṣad* as it is very much concerned with language – and no doubt in several others too – but the former usage (as the imperishable) is not found in that Upaniṣad at all. Now, while we must not confuse between the two usages, it is also useful to know that in a notable place in another of the Upaniṣads they are brought together. In *Muṇḍaka Upaniṣad*, 2.2-4, we have an interesting instance. Stanza 2 begins with a description of the *Akṣara-Brahman* along the lines of Yājñavalkya's statement as quoted above, as what is "subtler than the subtle, in which are centred all the worlds, etc." It is identified with life, language and mind (*sa prāṇaḥ tad u vāṅmanaḥ*). Then follows a discussion of the famous *Aum* symbol of language. "Taking as the bow the great Upaniṣadic weapon one should place in it the arrow sharpened by meditation. Drawing it with a mind engaged in the contemplation of that, dear one, know that *Akṣara* (i.e., *Akṣara Brahman*) as the target." At this point there takes place an exposition of *Aum*.

However, there cannot be much doubt that the meaning "imperishable" is the original one and the meaning "letter" or "syllable" was later attached to the word. *Akṣara* is the opposite of *kṣara*, perishable, rather synonymous with *jagat*. The letter *a* as in *akṣara* is often used for negation. But negation itself is a multi-faceted device of language and logic, and accordingly, can signify many different things, as elaborately discussed in the *Vṛttis* on the *Vākyapadīya*, nos. 249-315. In this case here, it definitely signifies 'what is beyond', 'what exceeds'. As *kṣara* is to have the denotation of the physical, *akṣara* could conceivably have some shades of the meaning of "metaphysics". But as we have said, *akṣara* to be meaningful must be followed by *Brahman* as what it is governed by. Now, "metaphysics", though not to be strictly so called here, is the outcome of reflecting on *jagat* under the horizon of *Brahma-vidyā*. Whenever this word *akṣara* occurs it should be known that *Brahman* as the metaphysical ground of the world is indicated. It is precisely for this reason that it is said in the *Muṇḍaka Upaniṣad* (1.1.7) that the world is born of *Akṣara* (*akṣarāt sambhavati iha viśvam*). But by the word 'metaphysical' in the Upaniṣadic context we should not understand what is *per se* beyond the physical (*ta meta ta physica*), as in the origin of 'metaphysics' or the physical exceeding the physical after the fashion of what has been put forward as meaning by Heidegger, but rather as what is beyond, or what exceeds, the physical as the ground of the physical (*kṣara*). Clearly, the reason for metaphysics to be is the physical, for which, to begin with, it is the explanation. Therefore, to arrive at the imperishable, which is the highest principle in explanation of the ground of the world, is the first result of reflecting upon the world with *Brahma-vidyā*. But as Śankara insists, one does not come by such a principle through mere logical reflection upon the world but through having had the foundation of *Brahma-vidyā* beforehand, "as it always comes on its own accord (*āgamena*)."[49] The discursive doctrine (*vāda*) of *Akṣara* or, more properly, *Akṣara-Brahman* is, therefore, the first way of metaphysics for the Upaniṣads, in the sense that it is the first result of the reflection upon the world with *Brahma-vidyā*, "metaphysics" having to be understood as the explanation of the physical world in the light of a reality which not only exceeds it but is its ground.

The second way of metaphysics, that is, the doctrine of *Māyā*, is of the same importance as the first, and the two, as we have observed, must be taken as complementary to each other. No doubt, the discursive doctrine of *Māyā*, or *Māyā-vāda*, is the more radical of the two and, in fact, is a unique way of metaphysics, having no counter-part in any other tradition of philosophy. *Māyā-vāda* was fully developed and completely spelt out a long time after the Upaniṣads, by Śankara. It is commonly understood – rather misunderstood – to be a doctrine which holds the world to be illusory. It may be pointed out that this misunderstanding is nothing new, as in fact Rāmānuja, another great commentator of the Vedānta tradition, coming only three centuries after Śankara, himself thought of *Māyā-vāda* to be a doctrine of illusion, and as such severely criticized it. However, if only modern supporters of Rāmānuja knew what he really says about the world they would then be wary because he actually says that the world is eternally existent, being eternally a part, (as body, or *śarīra*), of, *Brahman*. No realist or empiricist theologian would go that far. On the other hand, *Māyā-vāda* would go as far as realists and empiricists would want to go in their affirmation of the reality of the world – and none of them would treat it as eternal, as in fact the notion of eternity itself is in their thinking under oblivion.

As to the existence in seed form of the doctrine of *Māyā* in the Upaniṣads, whether one sees it there or not will depend on one's view of *Brahman*. A view which emphasizes the totally non-dual character of *Brahman* will incline one to see the doctrine of *Māyā* in seed form in the Upaniṣads – and this has been historically found to be the case. On the contrary, any other view of *Brahman* will make one averse to seeing it in the Upaniṣads – and this too has been historically found to be the case.

Clearly then, a rigorous non-dualism of the type of Śankara's has consistently put forth the doctrine of *Māyā* as a corollary to its view of *Brahman*, that is, as the only logically possible explanation according to it of the world and of human experience. The doctrine of *Māyā* simply lays down that what seems different from *Brahman* and seems to stand on its own is not in reality so but that it merely presents a distorted picture of *Brahman* itself. [On the contrary, all those who oppose *Māyā-vāda*, Rāmānuja, the Kashmir Śaivites and others, hold that the world gives a true but imperfect picture of *Brahman*.] Thus the *Bṛhadāraṇyaka* (4.4.19) tells us: "There is no multiplicity here. He obtains death after death who sees it as if it (i.e., Reality) were many", (*naiha nānāsti kiṁcana mṛtyoḥ sa mṛtyum āpnoti ya iha nāneva paśyati*). This statement has traditionally been considered a bulwark of *Māyā-vāda*. The word *māyā* appears by itself or in compound with some other word in a few places in the Upaniṣads, the most important occurrence being in *Śvetāśvatara*, 4.10: "Know Nature to be *Māyā*", (*māyām tu prakṛtim vidddhi*). *Māṇḍukya*, 7 describes the highest state of consciousness (*turīya*) as "that into which the world is resolved", (*prapañcopaśamam*). In *Maitrī*, 6.24 there is that powerful metaphor of the world as a circle of sparks produced by the rotation of the fire-wheel (*alāta-cakram*), hence as a brilliant "appearance" of *Brahman* but only an appearance. This metaphor is expanded later in *Gauḍupāda's Māṇḍūkya Kārikā*, 4.47-52.

The question as to why we see multiplicity (duality) when it is not there is raised in some places very seriously, and that becomes a very important metaphysical problem. As a solution there arises the idea of *ajñāna*, or *avidyā* (agnosis), which pervades the whole world as well as our consciousness. *Avidyā* is depicted as the root "evil" to be overcome. However, it is understood as the very seeing of duality. It is stated in *Maitrī*, 7.9: "Those who are wrapped up amid *Avidyā* imagining themselves to be alone wise and learned wander obdurately and deludely (through the transmigratory cycle) like blind men led by the blind", (*avidyāyām antare veṣṭyamānāḥ, svayam dhīrāḥ panḍitam manyamānāḥ dandramyāmānāḥ pariyanti mūḍhā andhenai'va nīyamānā yathā 'ndhāḥ*). Here again, we can perceive the latter "metaphysical" or discursive doctrine of *Avidyā*only in its sparse and bare seeds in the Upaniṣads although there are many descriptions particularly pertaining to gnosis, which contain it as an implication.

In the tradition which has flowed out of the Upaniṣads, i.e., Vedānta, the doctrines of *Māyā* and *Avidyā* go hand in hand. They are so complementary to each other that they are hardly distinguishable. But these doctrines along with all other "metaphysical" doctrines, which are only explanations, have been put forward by those who sought to interpret and systematize the teachings of the Upaniṣads, chiefly Śankara himself, not as if these doctrines bring home some truth of their own but merely as ancillary to the one all-absorbing concern of all, i.e., *Brahma-vidyā*, both the *theorea* and the *praxis*.

But it must not be thought that *Brahma-vidyā* is either negative or even indifferent towards all other philosophical pursuits. The Upaniṣads would only comprehend all these in *Brahma-vidyā* rather than exclude any. Accordingly, the world and human experience are taken with the utmost seriousness, and, based on *Brahma-vidyā*, are sought to be explained fully and adequately.

So then, the doctrines of *Akṣara-Brahman* and *Māyā* are the results of reflection upon the transitory world (*jagat*) with *Brahma-vidyā*, and are the two ways of "metaphysics" pointed to by the Upaniṣads. It may also be added that it is the fate of the former to have been absorbed into the latter in the Vedānta tradition, but there is no reason why it should be assumed that the former has lost its vogue altogether.

Now let us turn to the Upaniṣads' reflection upon *jīva* (the empirical self). It is important to perceive that while *jīva* in its phenomenal condition shares the transitoriness and perishability of *jagat*, in its real essence it is stable and eternal because it is one with *Brahman*. Reflection on *jīva* with *Brahma-vidyā* confirms the revelation of its identity with *Brahman*, and all the sense of its separateness and of its being part of the *jagat* is destroyed. How the sense of separateness of the *jīva*-hood of the *jīva* has come to be is also to be accounted for by the very principles by which we account for the world. In other words, the sense of separateness of the *jīva* is part of *jagat* while in its essence *jīva* is identical with *Brahman*.

Phenomenally, *jīva* is part of *jagat*. But that part of *jagat* which houses *jīva* in its separateness and individuality is altogether distinct from the rest because it touches the truth of *jīva's* identity with *Brahman*. Therefore, it has an unique status. It carries with it the illusion of being the reality of man's self-hood, his very subjectivity, as distinguished from all other things which are merely objects.

The Upaniṣads view the problem of our understanding of the nature of *jīva*, its essential identity with *Brahman* and its apparent separateness, embracing its individuality, not excluding its empirical constitution, as very important for the "theory" and "practice" of *Brahma-vidyā*. In this respect this understanding goes hand in hand with the understanding of *Māyā* and *Avidyā*. This is the supremely important matter of self-knowledge and a paramount concern of the Upanisads. That matter can in no way be doubted.

In the theme of self-knowledge both the truth of *jīva's* identity with *Brahman* and the fact of its apparent separateness are indicated. Weighing these two things properly is one of the implications of *Brahma-vidyā*. In a striking way it is the co-existence of both these that makes philosophy so exciting and challenging an experience according to the Upaniṣads. There is an on-going dialectic between these two poles, which grips the person engaged in philosophy in the way of the Upaniṣads. An important aspect of this dialectic is grasping the equivocal use of both the word *ātman* and the word *vijñāna* (understanding). The following celebrated passage bears witness to that:

> For where there is duality as it were, there one smells another, there one

sees another, there one hears another, there one speaks to another, there one thinks of another, there one understands another. Where everything has became the *Ātman* (Self, self), then by what and whom should one smell, then by what and whom should one see, then by what and whom should one hear, then by what and to whom should one speak, then by what and of whom should one think, then by what and whom should one understand? By what should one understand that by which all this is understood?[50]

The word *ātman* is used in the sense of the supreme *Ātman*, or *Brahman*, and in the sense of *jīva*. Later, the word *vijñāna* (understanding) is used in two senses, i.e., that of what is already an absolute possession of the knower and that of what is not yet so.

What is called by some scholars "psychology" in the Upaniṣads must be viewed in the light of this dialectic. No doubt, the Upaniṣads give much information on the subject of the *psychē* (to be taken in its original sense of soul rather than mind), but it would be a mistake to assume that they give the information for its own sake or in order to lay the foundation for "psychology" as such. For, as in all cases the ruling interest is the "theory" and "practice" of *Brahma-vidyā*.

Nevertheless, as *Brahma-vidyā* is taken with a gravity beyond compare everything that serves it must be characterized by a befitting rigour. Besides, as one's own *psychē* is the abiding field of one's cognitive and volitional activity and that which always simulates the thinking self, an almost infinite penetration and precision are brought to bear upon the investigation of it.

There are a number of different ways in which the task of comprehending the *psychē* is pursued in the Upaniṣads. One of the most impressive is through the simile of the chariot (*Kaṭha* 1.3.3-11). The body is the chariot (*ratha*), the *ātman* the Lord of the chariot (*rathin*), the intellect (*buddhi*) the chariot-driver (*sārathi*), the senses (*indriyāṇi*) the horses, and the mind (*manas*) the reign (*pragraha*). *Jīva* is defined in this simile as the *ātman* bound to the mind and the senses (*ātmendriya mano-yukta*) and it is called the experiencer (*bhoktā*). The purpose of this simile is to inculcate the same self-knowledge so central an aim in all the Upaniṣads, from a specific angle. Hence it begins with the admonition, "know the self as the Lord of the chariot" (*ātmānaṁ rathinaṁ viddhi*). Further, in self-knowing, the intellect (*buddhi*) plays the dynamic role. It is the intellect that has the power, by virtue of *Brahma-vidyā*, to convert itself into that special agency called understanding (*vijñāna*) so that an individual becomes one for whom understanding is the chariot-driver (*vijñāna-sārathi*).[51]

The *Taittirīya Upaniṣad* (2.1-5) contains another interesting account of the make-up of the *psychē*, where man is described as being converged by five progressively interior sheaths (*kośas*: *anna-rasa-maya* (that of nutrion), *prāṇa-maya* (that of vital breath), *mano-maya* (that of mind), *vijñāna-maya* (that of understanding) and *ānanda-maya* (that of bliss). This is obviously an attempt to set forth the empirical human self (*jīva*) in a comprehensive way, in terms of all the possible levels of his existence. The innermost sheath is that of bliss, for it is said: "This indeed has the modality of a person. According to that, one's personal modality is one with the modality of a person", (*sa vā are puruṣa-vidha eva, tasya puruṣa-vidhatām, anvayaṁ puruṣa-vidhaḥ*).[52] [It may be borne in mind that even bliss is only a sheath. For this reason Śankara argues that our real self (what is one with *Brahman*) is interior to it too.]

The *Māṇḍukya Upaniṣad* gives us yet another account of "psychology" in terms of the four successive quarters, or levels, of consciousness: the waking state (*vaiśvānara*), dream state (*taijasa*), deep sleep (*prājña*) and the "fourth" state (*turīya*). Each of these is analysed for itself. However, it is the fourth that completes all the others, and the real character of the soul is manifested only in it. It is described thus:

> (It) is not that which cognizes things internal, not that which cognizes things external, it is not what cognizes both of them, not a mass of cognition, not cognitive, not non-cognitive, not seen, not to be empirically dealt with, not graspable, not possessed of distinguishing marks, not thinkable, not nameable. (It is) the essence of the knowledge of the one *Ātman*, that into which the world is resolved, peaceful, benign, non-dual. Such they think is the fourth (*cathurtha, turīya*). He is the *Ātman*. It is he who should be known.[53]

These above described passages are the most striking expressions of the nature of the *jīva* in the Upaniṣads. Clearly, they are reflections upon that stable entity, which we empirically know as ourselves and which counterposits *jagat*, the transitory actuality of the world, and the reflection in both cases is undertaken with *Brahma-vidyā*, in the "theory" and "practice" of which they constitute important ways, although it is not possible to argue that they themselves make up *Brahma-vidyā*. In a sense there need be no possible limit to the number of such ways. The Upaniṣads themselves put forth many suggestions, and in principle no possible way is precluded as long as it directly contributes to the "theory" and "practice" of *Brahma-vidyā.*

CHAPTER III

GNOSIS AND PHILOSOPHICAL THOUGHT IN THE BHAGAVADGĪTĀ

[The *Bhagavadgītā* is one text in the Vedānta tradition that has suffered from there having been too many interpretations on it rather than too few. It is Śankara who first claimed this text for the Vedānta's gnosis tradition of philosophical thought, and his interpretation has been challenged over the centuries, including our own. In the present chapter we seek to claim it again for the gnosis tradition and to show that, while it touches life in the raw, thereby serving as a Vedānta text in a unique way with an appeal to all conditions of men, it nevertheless does not fail in its central mission *vis-à-vis* philosophical thought grounded in gnosis.]

The *Bhagavadgītā*, or the *Gīta* for short, is one of the most truly amazing philosophical poems in world literature. Literally translated, the title means the *Song of the Blessed One*. The poem is a dialogue between Kṛṣṇa, venerated in epic, mythology and popular piety as a divine personage in human form, an *avatāra* (descent) of God (hence called *Bhagavān*, or the Blessed One), and Arjuna his human kinsman and pupil, supposedly taking place in the battlefield of Kurukṣetra. What we are about to enter into is a dialogue with this dialogue.

The *Gītā* has held the greatest fascination for religious minds, traditionally in the land of its origin and more recently all over the world. Its narration is captivating and its teaching re-assuring and comforting without being either sentimental or unduly stern. It gives back to every man his soul, his intelligence, his self-reliance and initiative, and for that reason alone those who wish to enter into the religious quest in a philosophical way would find it immensely attractive. Besides, its freedom and catholicity of spirit strikes a sympathetic cord in those modern men who are even vaguely interested in things of the spirit.

The poem forms part of the gigantic epic, the *Mahābhārata*, inserted into it as an episode of one of its books, the *Bhīṣmaparvan*. The poem is short, consisting of only 700 stanzas, arranged into

18 chapters, equal to chapters 25-42 of the *Bhīṣmaparvan* of the epic (and chapters 23-40 of the newly brought out Critical Edition by the Bhandarkar Research Institute, Poona). Although a philosophical poem, the *Gītā* is set in the context of the great Bhārata war which is the subject of the epic, or perhaps fitted into it by some literary device. Therefore, the battlefield of Kurukṣetra where Arjuna the commander of the Pāṇḍavas (who are on one side of the context, the Kauravas being on the other), leads his army, accompanied by Kṛṣṇa his advisor, figures in the narrative as the venue of the dialogue as also the scene of the impending battle. However, the likelihood of an intense philosophical discussion taking place as the armies are preparing for a final and decisive assault need not be raised lest we be deflected from the principal course of trying to understand the teaching. None of the traditional interpreters were deterred by that issue, and there is wisdom in following their example.

In the division of authoritative Indian religious texts, the *Gītā* is included in the secondary class called *smṛti* (those that are remembered), because it is officially part of an epic, while the primary class, *śruti* (those that are primevally "heard" by the ancient seers) contains only the Vedas, in which are included the Upaniṣads. Yet the *Gītā* is elevated above all the other *smṛti* texts, and given honour and authority equal to *śruti* itself.

Each of the 18 chapters of the *Gītā* ends with a colophon, (probably added later) which calls the poem an upaniṣad, and this designation clearly reflects the position accorded it in the tradition. How interesting that it should be put officially under the *smṛti* class and yet be regarded in actuality as tantamount to an upaniṣad! This represents an important phenomenon as far as religious texts go. It bespeaks the fact that in part the *Gītā* is closer to our way of thinking. The man Arjuna raises questions from a historical, human situation somewhat as we would today, and in that sense it is a product of the historical human mind, determining the style of thinking and the manner of the discourse of the text. It touches life in the raw. And yet the content and the event of the teaching make it like an upaniṣad and hence is in essence not a product of the historical human mind. Śankara, the author of the oldest of the existing commentaries, goes so far as to describe the *Gītā* as "the quintessence of all the Upaniṣadic (Vedic) teachings".[1] Other traditional commentators have tacitly accepted this estimate.

Now, as to the modern problem of assigning to the *Bhagavadgītā* either a purely religious or a philosophical character, opinions can be expressed on either side. S. Radhakrishnan, in his book on the *Bhagavadgītā* starts out by saying that it is "more a religious classic than a philosophical treatise". However, such a distinction is hardly feasible from within the text itself. No doubt, it is a religious classic. But we must not understand by "religious" here something exclusive or categorically distinguishable from philosophy. The *Gītā* is religious because "religion" is the foundation of all things great in this world. It would have been absurd for a text which speaks for that which is the greatest to disregard religion, in view of the fact that there can only be artificial, and hence inauthentic, reasons for doing so. "Religion", with all its admitted defects, in the *Gītā's* understanding at least, has always been associated with the quest for that which is the greatest. Therefore, the disregard of it can only come from some deep-rooted lack of reality in one's thinking. "Religion" is not something introduced, as it were from outside, into a spiritual enterprise that has to do with what is great as it is rather intrinsic to such a thing. Understood in this way, the *Gītā* is undoubtedly a religious classic. In terms of our thought on profound questions it is not necessary or even desirable to go on at a tangent and treat religion as a phenomenon in itself (which it also is in other respects) as we only need to take it as an acid test to determine the reality of our thought. The thing that mars our thinking is always some lack of reality in it – the more deep-rooted the worse – and the fundamental problem is how to resist it and bring reality back into our thinking. Ancient philosophical traditions such as Vedānta and Platonism are aware of it. Vedānta tries to deal with it as ethical qualifications for a student, but the word "ethical" must be understood as having to do with reality in our thinking, which is the same as maintaining an attitude of truthfulness towards reality. This attitude may be considered like the prevenience of gnosis, as pre-dawn light, and its basis ultimately is in Reality itself rather than in purely human thought.

COMMENTARIES ON THE BHAGAVADGĪTĀ

In view of the immense intellectual and emotional appeal of the *Gītā* it is but natural that there should be a prolificity of literature pertaining to it. For that reason, it would be appropriate to make a brief survey of the important studies on this text. Not only are there several classical commentaries in Sanskrit but there are also books written on it in the regional languages of India as well as in modern European languages, especially English. Most of the books in the Indian regional languages, however, are usually personal expressions of piety, although an occasional work has turned out to be philosophically challenging as in the case of the *Gītārahasya* of Bal Gangadhar Tilak (originally written in Marāṭhi).

The commentary by Śankara is the oldest of the existing ones. We know that there were other commentaries before his time and that there were a large number of different interpretations prevalent in his day. These facts we gather most of all from a single observation that Śankara himself makes in justification of his attempt to write a commentary. He writes: "Even though the meanings of words and sentences (of the *Gītā*) have been explained by many (writers), to the people of the world it appears to teach absolutely contradictory doctrines. Hence I am setting about to write a succinct exposition (of it) in order to determine its meaning."[2]

In his interpretation of the *Gītā, Śankara* adopted the approach of his own gnosis (*jñāna*) philosophy, more thoroughly and systematically expressed in his commentaries on other Vedānta texts, i.e., the *Brahma Sūtra* and the principal Upaniṣads. As far as we know it is he who first accepted the *Gītā*, along with the *Brahma Sūtra* and the Upaniṣads, as one of "the three foundations" (*prasthāna traya*) of Vedānta, a practice followed by all the traditional exponents ever since.

The next important commentary was written by Rāmānuja, although in fact he followed the main line of interpretation given by a great predecessor, Yāmuna. Rāmānuja was basically a theologian of personalist Vedāntic theism. As in his commentary of the *Brahma-Sūtra* and his single volume exposition of the Upaniṣads as a whole (*Vedārthasaṁgraha*), so in his interpretation of the *Gītā* he unequivocally adopted the devotional standpoint consistent with his own personalist theism. It is clear that on the surface at least the *Gītā*, as also one of the Upaniṣads, the *Śvetāśvatara*, gives support to it. In fact Rāmānuja considers the theistic theme the *Gītā* already expressed in a *Śvetāśvatara* passage (5.1), which runs as follows: "In the imperishable *Brahman*, transcendent and infinite, there lie hidden the two, namely gnosis and agnosis. Of these (the one, namely) agnosis is perishable, while (the other, namely) gnosis is immortal. (But) he who rules over gnosis and agnosis is another".[3] In Rāmānuja's theology this "another" who is above gnosis (simplified and assigned to the realm of the Spirit *à la* the Sāṁkhyan dualism) and agnosis (likewise simplified and assigned to the realm of Matter) owns and rules over them even as a person's spirit owns and rules over his soul and body. The foundation of the entire structure of this theology is the application of this simple but none-too-simplistic analogue. Some modern Christian scholars of Eastern religions appear to feel a very close kinship with Rāmānuja's version of Vedānta while they turn away with a sense of horror from Śankara's. Superficially viewed, this will appear to be justified. Rāmānuja outlines his position as not only the better but the truer alternative to Śankara's, which is characterized as rigorously non-dualistic in ontology, gnosis-centred with respect to the path to liberation and dominated by the theory of *Māyā* (illusion, as often mistakenly understood) in regard to the status of the world. The main thrust of Rāmānuja's arguments is rebuttal of what he takes to be Śankara's doctrines. Accordingly, he elevates devotion (*bhakti*) directed to the personal God (Viṣṇu, Nārāyaṇa, Kṛṣṇa), rather than gnosis as such as the path to liberation (*mokṣa-mārga*).

For some reason the mind of traditional scholars, with the exception of Śankara himself, seems to have revolved around the problem of paths to liberation, and the *Gītā* served as the preeminent single text on which the proponents of the different so-called paths could rest their case. However, it is actually a matter of foisting the phenomenon of the three-fold thematic division of the paths, or *mārgas*, on the *Gītā*. And it is not unlikely that the whole concept of *mārga* was due to Buddhist inspiration. [The word *mārga*, however, is from the verb *mṛg*, to hunt, and from *mṛga*, deer. It is, accordingly, a word which expresses a hunting imagery, and originally meant hunting trail or deer path.] The *Gītā* itself speaks of gnosis, devotion, action and many other things like meditation (*dhyāna*), renunciation (*saṁnyāsa*), etc., and the colophons describe each of the 18 chapters as a particular *yoga*. The example for thematization of the *mārgas* was first set by

Rāmānuja who even favoured the division of the 18 chapters of the *Gītā* into three arbitrary groups of six chapters (*ṣaṭaka*) each, under gnosis (*jñāna*), devotion (*bhakti*) and action (*karma*). Preoccupation with the three paths became general ever since, and up to this day no interpreter has been able to break away from it. However, it is true that Śankara (*à propos Gītā*, 9.3), refers to devotion as one of the various paths (*mārgabheda*), but purely to warn against what is its opposite, namely the path of the mortal world (*mṛtyu-saṁsāra-vartma*), the path leading to perdition (*naraka-tiryagāti-prāpti-mārga*). It is true that the three paths express something essential in the Indian religious phenomenon and would have commanded attention even without the catalytic agency of the *Bhagavadgītā*. But they can hardly occupy an intrinsic place in philosophy even when philosophy takes the question of liberation seriously.

Like Rāmānuja, a number of medieval commentators, Madhva, Nimbarka, Vallabha, Śrīdhara, *et al.*, favoured a devotion-centered interpretation, while a few like Madhusūdana Saraswatī and Jñāneśwar tried their hand at skillfully combining the path of devotion with the path of gnosis, however the concept of path still predominating. Their writings, particularly those of the last two, are very rich in mysticism but are not productive for philosophical thought.

As for the path of action (*karma-mārga*), in the medieval times it was for the most part subsumed under devotion. But before and during Śankara's own time there were interpretations that advocated a combination of gnosis and action (technically called *jñāna-karma-samuccaya*). And actually, it is in our century that a would-be traditionalist has come forward in the person of Bal Gangadhar Tilak to advocate an interpretation strongly favouring the path of action. In all these the path concept dominated, with very little interest in thought as such.

Tilak wrote a gigantic tome called *Śrīmad Bhagavadgītā-rahasya* (the *Secret of the Bhagavadgītā*) subtitled *Karma-yoga-śāstra* (the *Teaching of the Path of Action*), in Marathi, soon translated also into Hindi and English. Actually, it is a revival of the ancient approach of *jñāna-karma-samuccaya* in a modern setting where action is presented as an ethico-political programme rather than as ritualistic works which was the case with the ancient *karma*-philosophy. Nevertheless, Tilak bases his interpretation on the traditional *karma*-philosophy of Pūrva-mīmāṁsā against which

Śankara had directed his powerful critique.

Further, Tilak introduces an element that is entirely foreign to the Pūrva-mīmāṁsā goal of salvation through ritualistic works, but he does so by employing some of the principles of textual interpretation of that school. That element is the goal of secular freedom attained through secular action. The Mīmāṁsā principles of interpretation are seven, of which those of commencement (*upakrama*) and conclusion (*upasaṁhāra*) are considered the most important.[4] Accordingly, Tilak finds that the *Gītā* starts out by posing the problem of the duty of fighting a just war and ends with a clear perception of the nature of that duty. He seems to be persuaded that the power conflict in which Arjuna as a just warrior is involved must be taken as decisive in seeking the meaning of the *Gītā*. No doubt, the description of an ultimately important crisis situation confronting the man Arjuna permeates the text. That no one can deny. Traditional commentators of earlier times were not, however, troubled by this question and so did not attempt to answer it. Also, some modern writers on the *Gītā* like Mahatma Gandhi, not willing to follow Tilak's lead, sought to interpret the war allegorically as an internal, spiritual conflict. An important tradition of interpretation in favour of such an approach has come into being.

Yet another alternative presents itself to us and that seems to make more sense than the others, and hence is preferable. According to that, the human crisis situation must be taken as real and not as a mere allegorical expression of a spiritual conflict, but one that is only triggered by the actuality of battle and is by no means co-extensive with it. The destiny of the battle and its resolution have nothing any more to do with the crisis once it has been triggered into being, as it becomes a philosophical matter that cannot be restrained from moving towards gnosis. In this manner we can think of it as being typical of all problematics which find their way into thought. Do not historical and personal happenings, even bodily happenings, bring in their train deeper problems wrapped up in them? But those problems continue to challenge us even after the happenings might have been resolved not only in actuality, but even in potentiality. Seen in this light, Arjuna appears definitely to be a representative thinker, not only a confused man of action paralysed by despondency, and he is occupied with the problematics to which his particular involvement in a fratricidal war has painfully awakened him, in other words, having been touched by life in the raw. Being thus occupied, he is led, seemingly unwittingly, but in fact quite deliberately, into the deepest philosophical questions. Let us hold in abeyance the elaboration of this approach till we reach the appropriate juncture. In the meantime, let us briefly survey some of the more notable modern studies on the *Gītā*.

The most remarkable book on the *Gītā* written in modern times is *Essays on the Gītā* by Sri Aurobindo. Aurobindo is a great mystic thinker, who through his many well-known writings, has worked out a complete thesophy, including a scheme of mystical life and practice without any comparable parallel in our day. The scheme is known by the name "Integral Yoga". The *Essays on the Gītā* is one of the clearest and most eloquent expressions of this powerful theosophy.

In the metaphysical part of the theosophy Aurobindo divides up Reality into different levels, correlated to levels of consciousness. Fundamentally, he believes that the *Gītā* is a synthesis of Vedānta, Sāṁkhya and Yoga, which he equates with knowledge, works and devotion. He observes: "Such is the analysis, not confining itself to the apparent cosmic process but penetrating into the occult secrets of superconscious Nature, *uttamam rahasyam*, by which the Gītā founds its synthesis of Vedānta, Sankhya and Yoga, its synthesis of knowledge, works and devotion."[5] Clearly, Sri Aurobindo has not escaped the conventional thematization of the *Gītā* teaching into the three paths, which he deals with at length in Book I, Ch. VI.

Aurobindo's interpretation of the *Gītā* is a most important modern testament of a dynamic mysticism and can be matched only by his own *magnum opus, The Life Divine*. He sees the *Gītā* as the manual of an integral programme of Yoga as much for the soul's ascent as for the World Spirit's descent for the sake of the transformation of the cosmos. This programme is seen as the grammar of ascent of an internal-external spiritual epic, with an enormous emphasis laid on self-culture at all (both normally recognizable and not so recognizable) levels of human existence, both individual and corporate. But the question is whether such a programme, however powerful the spiritual epic it unfolds and however stupendous the scheme of its self-culture, adds up to that which we strain after, i.e., thought, although theosophy it is. No doubt, those who are already believers would consider it to be the greatest philosophy or even to be higher than philosophy. For us the question can be answered only on the basis of what thought is in this theosophical programme. Thought in this programme, we see, is taken as a complexly integrated psycho-metaphysical activity, based on the combining of the psycho-material realm of *Prakṛti* (Matter) and the spiritual realm of *Puruṣa* (Spirit). Insofar as Aurobindo creates a monism which combines these two, thought is but the language of the self-unfolding and self-realizing movement of the Spirit, in its passage to the supra-mental level. Thought, accordingly, is nothing but a stage of the development of the spiritual epic and as such the programme itself cannot be approached from any of the grounds from which thought is approached, and hence essentially remains outside thought, except in its instrumental role, which is purely transitional.

The idea that the *Gītā* is a work that has synthesized the many elements of Hindu, nay mankind's, religious beliefs, forging a universally relevant religious philosophy, has gripped several Indian thinkers of modern times. Among them S. Radhakrishnan is worthy of special mention. His study of the *Bhagavadgītā* is a work of great merit. He observes:

> The different elements which, at the period of the composition of *Gītā*, were competing with each other within the Hindu system, are brought together and integrated into a comprehensive synthesis, free and large, subtle and profound. The teacher refines and reconciles the different currents of thought, the Vedic cult of sacrifice, the Upaniṣad teaching of the transcendent Brahman, the Bhāgavata theism, and tender piety, the Sāmkhya dualism and the Yoga meditation.[6]

Accordingly, Radhakrishnan presents the *Gītā* as a book of universal spiritual value. So he writes:

> The suggestions set forth in the *Gītā* about the meaning and value of existence, the sense of eternal values and the way in which ultimate mysteries are illumined by the light of reason and moral intuition provide the basis for agreement in mind and spirit so very essential for keeping together the world which has become materially one by the universal acceptance of the externals of civilization.[7]

Radhakrishnan, too, considers his philosophy to be one of "integral experience", but somewhat differently from Sri Aurobindo's, insofar as he does not envisage any stupendous scheme for lifting human consciousness and human existence to a higher level from the present through creative guidance of the evolutionary-involutionary process. Rather, he is content to discover and utilize the highest common factors of all the religious traditions of mankind, and he believes that the *Gītā* is precisely the text that can help us do so. Further, as a true representative of the post-Rāmānuja Indian religious tradition he assumes that the *Gītā* thematizes the three paths to salvation and argues that the secret of integral experience consists in grasping the synthesis which that text itself has already accomplished.

Apart from scholars who wrote from within the tradition, there are also indologists and scholars of religion who have written books on the *Gītā*. These range from pure indologists concerned only with historical and literary questions, like Franklin Edgerton to Rudolf Otto, a Lutheran religious philosopher, and R.C. Zaehner, an English Roman Catholic historian of religion and writer on mysticism. Otto wrote a highly analytic work translated as *The Original Gītā*, where he sought to show that the nucleus of the text was the famous vision recorded in the eleventh chapter around which the other parts later grew. Zaehner in his extremely articulate book on the *Gītā* shows impatience with the Indian commentators, ancient and modern (with the exception of Rāmānuja), because he believes that they mixed up what they thought with what the *Gītā* thought, and shows equal impatience with the Germans like Otto who are obsessed in characteristic fashion with some *Ur-Gītā*. Zaehner, on the contrary, counts himself among those who are "primarily interested in the actual content of the *Gītā*"[8] that is to say "in what the *Gītā* actually said, not in what others said or what they said in pristine times *not* said".[9] One could only wish that things were as simple as this!

Zaehner studied the book from the point of his dominant, even obsessive, interest in the mystical phenomenon as well as personalist theology. He denounces Śankara's Commentary (and Śankara's whole philosopy) because he considers it to be faulty mysticism insofar as it elevates to the level of highest reality the non-dual, supra-personal (or impersonal) *Brahman*. As for the *Gītā* he has come to the conclusion that it is a supreme text-book of good mysticism. So he observes:

> As I grew increasingly familiar with the text of this wonderful book, it became even more insistently clear to me that here was a text the whole purpose of which seemed to me to demonstrate that love of a personal God, so far from being only a convenient preparation for the grand unitary

> experience or spiritual 'liberation' (the *mokṣa* or *mukti* of the Upaniṣads and the *Vimutti* of the Buddhists) was also the crown of this experience itself, which without it must remain imperfect.[10]

Zeahner believes that in this mysticism the personal God is Kṛṣṇa himself rather than the impersonal *Brahman*. Hence he adds, marking his agreement with the French scholar Etienne Lamotte, the author of *Notes sur la Gītā*:

> Contrary to what one might suppose, the return of the soul into *brahman* is not yet the final stage (terme definitif) or at least the exact expression of perfect deliverance. Krishna, who has supplanted *brahman* both in theodicy and cosmology now surpasses it in eschatology too: it is union with Krishna, the Bhagavat, which is the Ultimate and final stage of deliverance.[11]

While denouncing Śankara, Zaehner speaks approvingly of Rāmānuja who probably comes nearest to the mind of the author of the Gītā." Clearly, this affinity that Zaehner feels towards Rāmānuja is well-grounded as far as the personal divine is concerned. But it has to be recognized that the latter still remains a non-dualist Vedāntin although of a qualified kind. The complexity of that would be quite beyond the range of the simplistic theism so belligerently expressed by Zaehner.

THE *GĪTĀ* AND *BRAHMA-VIDYĀ*

The fact that the oldest known commentators of the tradition unanimously agreed that in respect of the teaching the *Bhagavadgītā* is entirely in accord with the Upaniṣads and that that teaching must be taken as *Brahma-vidyā* has to be treated with some respect, and not just owing to the incidental colophic description at the end of each chapter which declares it to be such. We have already quoted Śankara's remark about the *Gītā* being the quintessence of the Upaniṣadic (Vedic) teaching. Also, in a medieval work, the *Vaiṣṇavīya Tantrasāra*, there is a passage likening the Upaniṣads to the cow, Arjuna to the calf, Kṛṣṇa to the milkman and the *Gītā* to the milk,[12] although it is possible that this metaphor may simply be reflecting an estimate which had already been well established.

However, there is no evidence at all to show that the *Gītā* has any historical links with the Upaniṣads as we know them, other than in respect of the identity of the teaching. Kṛṣṇa nowhere refers to any of the teachers of the Upaniṣads except incidentally to the sage-king Janaka, mentioned in *Bṛhadāraṇyaka Upaniṣad*, and in a different way referred to in the Epic *Rāmāyaṇa* as the father of *Sītā*, the wife of the divine warrior-king Rāmā. At the beginning of the fourth chapter of the *Gītā* Kṛṣṇa makes out that the teaching he, as the timeless teacher-God, had himself originally given to Vivasvān, who handed it to Manu and thus down through posterity till it somehow disappeared from the earth. Even the lineage of personages mentioned there, through whom the teaching had been transmitted, has nothing to do with any of the lines of succession described in the Upaniṣads. Thus in the *Bṛhadāraṇyaka Upaniṣad* (2.6.1-3; 4.6.1-3 and 6.5.1-4), with slight variations in the names of the individuals in the succession, the teaching is ultimately traced to Brahmāḥ the creator-God of mythology and popular belief. Likewise, again, in the *Chāndogya Upaniṣad* (3.11.4 and 8.15.1) Brahmāḥ figures as the original source of the teaching. In the *Gītā* Kṛṣṇa wholly supplants Brahmāḥ in this capacity. The traditional commentators paid scant attention to the teacher or the lineage of transmission as, it seems, it is the teaching and not either of these that decides what is to be taken as *Brahma-vidyā*, which they regard as the essence of the *Gītā*.

The Gītā as an Upaniṣad for the Man Facing a Crisis, Touched by Life in the Raw

One of the most remarkable features of the *Bhagavadgītā* is that the occasion for its utterance is an unusual human crisis that a man faces, well described in the first chapter and at the beginning of the second and echoed throughout. It would appear that such an occasion was worked into the text as a literary context so as to fit the *Gītā* into the epic *Mahābhārata* as an episode of the war. That does not contradict the fact that the occasion may well have been provided by some actual human situation, that of an impending, disastrous conflict. The human situation brought wrapped up within it seeds of thought which could not be cast aside as soon as a resolution was found for the critical human situation, even if that were possible.

According to the graphic description of the situation, Arjuna, the legendary warrior and the exemplary upholder of the celebrated *Kṣatriya* kinghtly code which was the bulwark of *dharma*, has drawn up his army in the field of the Kurus where he is to commence the last and decisive battle against the Kauravas, who also happen to be his kinsmen. He surveys the enemy ranks and espies many who are his own clan elders and former teachers whom fate has now called him to annihilate. He is stricken with anguish and falls into a mood of colossal despondency at the thought that he is to be the channel through which much terrible death and destruction are to be visited upon the community. So he begins to reason that is is better for him to give up his own claim to the kingdom, rightful though it be, and if necessary even court death as a consequence. The tragedy he would like to avoid is not only physical but also moral as he sees it, and by avoiding it he would spare himself unbearable remorse in future.

Arjuna figures in the epic as the archetypal noble man (*ārya*), the highest embodiment of *Kṣatriya* manhood and the upholder and defender of justice (*dharma*). His character essence as defined by the knightly code is valour and compassion. In the *Gītā* description of Arjuna's anguish in the battlefield we have in all the world's literature the finest expression of the inward sufferings of the noble warrior. Arjuna came to the battlefield for the purpose of defending with his sword that foundation of social and cosmic justice called *dharma*. Yet he now fears that the defence of *dharma* in the manner in which fate has thrust upon him would, paradoxically enough, mortally wound and disrupt *dharma*. The quandary is, how can one avoid destroying that for the ostensible defence of which one is to fight a battle, or what is graver and subtler, how can one avoid confusing justice with the ends of one's own selfish desire for gain and the motive of vainglory, even though one may rationalize them? Hence he exclaims: "Alas, what a great evil have we resolved to do in striving to slay our foes through our greedy desire for the joys of (possessing) the kingdom!"[13] He is willing to give the victory to the enemy at the risk of his own life, and hence throws away his famous bow, *Gāṇḍīva*, formerly given him by the warrior-god Indra himself.

Arjuna the exemplary warrior noble man is facing the ultimate moral crisis and describes himself as "one whose mind is terribly confused as to what is morally right" (*dharma-sammūḍha-cetaḥ*).[14] In fact the noble man's morality itself is in crisis, which is the result of drawing together all the contradictions inherent in it.

It is interesting, incidentally, to contrast this "noble man's morality" with what Nietzsche calls "slave morality". It is the former that is peculiarly susceptible to such a crisis, while the latter is not at all so susceptible and hence holds a ferocious strength within itself. Nietzsche tells us that slave morality is rooted in *ressentiment*, that is to say, the secretly nourished reaction of the weak against the strong, which when the opportunity is ripe breaks out in bitterness and hostility, not just against the strong but by extension against the wider world. Is it not for this reason that ideologies based on *ressentiment*, being free from contradictions which afflict the noble man's morality, are relatively more successful in the world in the short run at least? Certainly Arjuna is not a candidate for success in any ideological conflict, any more than, given his sensitivity, he is likely to win a dynamic war of succession. The noble man is doomed from within himself because he embodies the inner ethical contradictions of a just war, while the enemy devoid of those contradictions has an ideological advantage which is the same as the very having of ideology. Nevertheless, Arjuna is being steadied at the level of the noble warrior's existence and is admonished not to give the victory to the potential ideologue's "slave morality". Comparing slave morality with noble morality Nietzsche has this to say:

> While every noble morality develops from a triumphant affirmation of itself, slave morality from the outset says No to what is "outside", what is "different" and this No is its creative deed. This inversion of the value-positing eye – the need to direct one's view outward instead of back to oneself – is the essence of *ressentiment*: in order to exist slave morality always first needs a hostile external world; it needs physiologically speaking hostile external stimuli in order to act at all – its action fundamentally is reaction.[15]

However, we see Arjuna as a different kind of noble man who is not content to ask for the sources of free action undetermined from outside in a way that becomes his character, but as one who is cast into a mood of thought, a mood which expresses itself immediately as a negative urge to escape all that he sees as action. Such escape from action appears to him as the only resolution to the conflict-ridden actuality of the situation that he is confronted with. But the range of the problematics that have been stirred up in him is by no means controlled by that contemplated resolution. For, the choice at the lower level, i.e., whether to act in accordance with the knightly code, of which he is the embodiment, or not to act at all, still remains. And that has to be resolved according to its own inherent law and has nothing at all to do with philosophy. That choice still confronts him and will keep on doing so all the way even when he is engaged in the highest quest. Kṛṣṇa addresses him at that level too, speaking as if he himself has assumed the actuality of Arjuna the warrior. The traditional commentators like Śankara have warned us against viewing that part of Kṛṣṇa's exhortations – appealing to Arjuna's duty to fight the war – as having anything to do with the teaching.

THE PHILOSOPHY OF THE *GĪTĀ*: THE FUNDAMENTAL OUTLOOK

The *Gītā* takes off from the initial description of Arjuna's crisis in a vertical manner, abruptly and expeditiously as it were. We have already hinted at the fact that Arjuna's crisis awakened him to thought, on the surface about his own predicament vis-à-vis *dharma* but in fact going much deeper, in a way unknown to himself. By giving words to his grief on account of human mortality Arjuna, Kṛṣṇa tells him, is speaking wise words: "grieving for those who need not be grieved for thou speaketh wise words", (*aśocyān anvaśocas tvaṁ prajñā vādāṁs ca bhāṣase*), *Gītā*, 2.11a. However, Arjuna has so far spoken nothing that can be directly construed as wisdom. It would, therefore, seem that the expression of grief, which is the deepest actuality of human existence, is itself something that has to do with wisdom, inasmuch as it touches the question of Ultimate Reality, self-descrepant though the manner be. Over against this, Kṛṣṇa sets up the non-self-descrepant attitude of those who know (*panditāḥ*), for they "lament not for those who have passed and those who have not passed", (*gatāsūn agatāsūṁś ca na anuśocanti*), 2.11b.

From this point on, Kṛṣṇa leads Arjuna to think (of Ultimate Reality) in accordance with the way gnosis itself behaves. The second chapter, described by the colophon as *sāṁkhya-yoga* in verses 12 through 30, provides an initial expression to the way one should think about Ultimate Reality insofar as the provoking factor of thought here is the existential problem of human mortality and the anxiety which accompanies it. Clearly, there are many ways in which this problem itself can be resolved, no doubt with corresponding implications to one's view of Ultimate Reality, and they can range all the way from nihilism to gnosis of the Vedāntic kind. There is no automatic reason for preferring the latter unless it institutes itself, to do so, however, being the first thing we note about the way it behaves. And thus gnosis takes the first step in raising thought towards itself. The initial expression of the way one should think on this matter begins with the statement: "Never have I not been, nor thou, nor these leaders of people; and none among us will hereafter not be", (*na tu evā'haṁ jātu nā'saṁ, na tvaṁ ne'me janādhipāḥ; na cai'va na bhaviṣyāmaḥ sarve vayaṁ ataḥ param*), 2.12. This is followed by a number of assertions of the indestructibility of the soul and of its unoriginatedness, with the refrain that one should not sorrow on account of that ontologically non-significant transition called death. Arjuna is summoned to view the destiny of embodied beings *sub specie aeternitatis* and thus to become free from anxiety.

Clearly, this view is only an alternative – one among many – that speculative thought may choose, although it is the most reassuring one. In order for it to be what Vedānta intends, this view has to be grounded in a deeper and self-certifying understanding of the Self, or *Ātman*. Speculation meets with it only by stumbling on it, causing the speculative thinker to be astonished. Therefore, the text says: "One meets with it as astonishing, another speaks of it as astonishing; even after hearing no one whatsoever knows it", (*āścaryavat paśyati kaścid enam, āścaryavat vadati tathai'va cānyaḥ, āścaryavat cai'nam anyaḥ śṛnoti; śrutvā'pi enaṁ veda cai'va kaścit.*), 2.29. This is, no doubt, encounter with gnosis itself but the astonishingness of that which is encountered continues to dominate the situation of thought and it lies in the fact that, although met with, spoken and heard, it is what is not *yet* known in the way other grounds of thought (either natural or ontological) are known.

Speculation stumbling on gnosis is a useful imagery. We can also liken speculative thought, that is, thought which is on the "look out", to an alert dog which scents an intruder and barks and wakes up the owner of the house. Gnosis comes like an unexpected stranger. We do not know the hour and manner of the stranger's coming but we will know when the dog barks and wakes us up. Speculation can be an activity that scents gnosis and with its own excitation can arouse the thinker.

Thought conducting itself in accordance with the way gnosis itself behaves is *Brahma-vidyā*, or the wisdom which has to do with *Brahman*. In many places in the *Gītā*, particularly in the second chapter which introduces *Brahma-vidyā* the word used for expressing it is *sāṁkhya*, but its use is invariably misunderstood by most writers on this text. The same wisdom or *vidyā* as it is carried over to the extended realms of *praxis* to the very terminus, i.e., action or *karma*, is designated by the companion word to *sāṁkhya*, i.e., *yoga*. Have these terms, *sāṁkhya* and *yoga*, used in the *Gītā* anything at all to do with the dualistic systems known by these names? Śankara for one says 'no'. The question and the answer apply also to some of the Upaniṣadic statements, one in particular in the *Śvetāśvatara Upaniṣad*, 6.13, which speaks of "the one among many" (*eko bahūnam*), "the eternity of eternities" (*nityo nityānām*), "the intelligence of intelligences" (*cetana cetanānām*), "that cause" (*tat kāraṇam*), "reached by means of *sāṁkhya* and *yoga*" (*sāṁkhya-yogādhigamyam*). In his *Commentary on the Brahma Sūtra* (2.1.3), Śankara adverts to this Upaniṣadic passage and observes: "In this statement, which is Vedic (i.e. Upaniṣadic) the words *sāṁkhya* and *yoga* denote gnosis and meditation respectively, as is to be inferred from their proximity (i.e., context). We will [of course] gladly allow those parts of the Sāṁkhya and Yoga systems which do not conflict (with the Upaniṣads)."[16]

However, on the surface the weight of evidence seems to be against what we have just said. How so? Let us consider the numerous occurrences of the words *puruṣa* and *prakṛti* which stand for the two central principles, or *tattvas*, of the Sāṁkhya system (accepted by the Yoga system also) and the detailed analysis of the three *guṇas* (strands) which constitute the second of these, viz., *Prakṛti*, or Matter. Add to that the obvious prevalence in the text of the typical ideas associated with Yoga. Now, the very word *sāṁkhya-yoga* as a hyphenated compound in relatively modern terminology appears in the colophon as the descriptive theme-name of the second chapter. This kind of evidence has persuaded many a scholar to consider the *Bhagavadgītā* to have some special connections with the Sāṁkhya and Yoga systems (which were hyphenated as a single twin system in later times). A well-known Indologist of the past, Richard Garbe, has gone as far as to argue that the *Gītā* was originally a Sānkhya-Yoga work, into which elements of the theistic Kṛṣṇa-Vāsudeva cult was poured and was later adapted to the requirements of Vedic religion.

Now, the principal error in this kind of assumption is this: a one-to-one correspondence between concepts and particular nomenclatures achieved much later in history is imposed upon an early text which was composed before such a correspondence came about. One of the most important facts to be borne in mind is that in the earliest Vedic and Vedāntic texts, and indeed in the commentaries too, terms were employed rather fluidly without that rigorous fixity of usage as we would expect to be the case in contemporary discourse. But what was really fixed is the inner world, or meaning as we would say. An inner world could be conveyed by a number of different synonymous terms, which again in other contexts could be synonyms of other terms with other meanings. This is the reason why total interpretation, or *mīmāṁsā*, is so very essential even to get at the meaning of terms, and it would be most undesirable to go about the business the other way around as literal-minded historians and philogists seem to do. Through interpretation we can introduce order into the realm of the terms according to meaning so that understanding of the text could be facilitated.

As we have shown, the initial statement of *Brahma-vidyā* in the second chapter covers the wisdom, both under the aspect of pure gnosis and as it is carried over to the realms of *praxis*, and these are respectively designated by terms *sāṁkhya* and *yoga. Praxis* is more clearly restated in verses 38 through 55. In the meantime there is an interregnum, to which we must turn.

Stanzas 31-38 constitute an appeal to Arjuna's self-esteem as a warrior to "take up arms and fight", although that self-esteem is on the verge of crumbling. [Such exhortations are scattered throughout the whole work.] Śankara states quite correctly that these stanzas reflect only "worldly considerations" (*laukiko nyāyaḥ*) and are "not" part of the teaching "as matters intended" (*na tu tātparyeṇa*). We must only assume that through the mouth of Kṛṣṇa Arjuna's own warrior self is made to speak and to assert itself, thus forestalling its premature disintegration and demise. And surely, the wise teacher himself as companion assists Arjuna in this regard. And we find this motif appearing again and again throughout the text, interspersed with *sāṁkhya* and *yoga*.

Stanza 39 marks the point of transition where *yoga*, i.e., the theme of carrying over *Brahma-vidyā* to the realms of *praxis* commences, in addition to *sāṁkhya*, or gnosis as such, with the words: "This is the theme of *sāṁkhya* that has been taught thee, now listen to the theme of *yoga*", (*eṣā te'bhihitā sāmkhye; budhir yoge tu imāṁ śruṇu*).

These two, i.e., *sāṁkhya* and *yoga*, are the fundamental themes of the *Gītā* and they dominate the entire text. They are mentioned together in 3.3 as two kinds of *niṣṭhā* (a word always wrongly translated "path" but might be better translated as "resolute observance"). Let us render that stanza as follows:

> In this world O Arjuna two kinds of resolute observance (*niṣṭha*) have been declared of old by me: resolute observance of gnosis as such (*jñana-yoga*) for the knowers (*sāṁkhyānām*); resolute observance of active effort [towards gnosis] (*karma-yoga*) for the effort-makers (*yoginām*). (*loke'smin dvividhā niṣṭhā purā proktā mayā'nagha; jñānayogena sāṁkhyānām karmayogena yoginām*).

Now, the word *yoga* has the concise meaning of effort, in the sense of a totally unicentred effort towards the highest and yet the most concrete of all spiritual goals. From hoary antiquity it has been gathering this meaning and the Yoga system but crystalizes it. However, it is based on a natural standpoint which requires the distinction between subject and object, sin and virtue and the sense of oneself being a doer and enjoyer. Śankara defines *yoga* as "that which consists in the performances of actions as a means to liberation, requiring a knoweldge of virtue and sin and the assumption that the self is distinct from the body as also the sense of being a doer (of action) and enjoyer (of fruits)."[17] According to this definition, what is elsewhere known as Śāṁkhya system also must, strangely enough, come under the caption *yoga* as against what is set forth by the term *sāṁkhya* (= gnosis as such) in the language of the *Gītā*. It is in the light of this that we must understand the statement by the teacher of the *Gītā* that he had declared the resolute observance of active effort to the *yogins*, or effort-makers, and that of gnosis as such to the *sāṁkhyaṇs*, or knowers. The generic meaning of *yoga* as effort, that is to say, unicentred effort towards the highest of human goals is modified in the *Gītā* in such a way as to reflect the fact that gnosis carried over into the area of active effort, be it that of thought or any other that is germaine to the definition of man as *puruṣa*, is decisively significant. Therefore, while *yoga*, or effort-making, in its generic definition would be radically distinct from *sāṁkhya*, or gnosis as such, in the new definition the former is perceived as that which has been charged with a destiny to "lead to", or more appropriately, clear the way for the latter. This truth is stated obliquely in 2.49: "Verily resolute observance of active effort is far inferior to the resolute observance of gnosis as such...; in gnosis as such take refuge...", (*dūreṇa hi avaraṁ karma buddhiyogāt ... buddhau śaraṇam anviccha...*). Śankara makes the meaning clear when he remarks on this: "The meaning is, 'therefore seek refuge in the wisdom of *yoga*, that is to say, the wisdom of *sāṁkhya*, which arises when *yoga* attains to maturity', in other words 'seek knowledge of Ultimate Reality'".[18] What Śankara means is that resolute observance of active effort is that which is charged with the destiny of clearing the way for the resolute observance of gnosis as such. The realization of such a destiny is what is meant by the term *siddhi* (attainment) associated with resolute observance of active effort, which in the *Gītā's* terminology is expressed by such various terms as *karma, karma-yoga* and *karma-niṣṭhā*, or often just by the term *yoga*. Hence Śankara explains *à propos Gītā*, 18.48: "It has been said that the *siddhi* reached by *karma* consists in attaining fitness for the resolute observance of gnosis as such."[19]

These two resolute observances, variously expressed (in various contexts) respectively as *jñāna, jñāna-yoga, niṣṭhā* and *sāṁkhya* for the one, and *karma, karma-yoga, karma-niṣṭhā* and *yoga* for the other, are alone distinctly recognized in the *Gītā* [*jñāna-yoga* for the knowers and *karma-yoga* for the effort-makers]. There is no third mentioned. So then, what about *bhakti*, in view of the so-called three-path scheme? We read about no resolute observance (*niṣṭhā*) pertaining to it. Accordingly, we have to conclude that the status of *bhakti* is different, not being a subject of resolute observance itself, though belonging to both gnosis as such, i.e., *sāṁkhya*, and to the effort, i.e., *yoga*, that goes with gnosis. Hence we have *bhakti-yoga* as one of the many dimensions that constitute the grand horizon of the *Gītā* as we shall soon see, and in a sense even the highest – and in a horizon which is intrinsically religious it cannot be otherwise.

Śankara, who wrote long before the three-path scheme was introduced follows the *Gītā* in strictly confining his interpretation to the two *niṣṭhās* (i.e., resolute observances, not understood as paths), and, no doubt, in doing so he conforms to genuine orthodoxy as laid down by the Mīmāṁsās. And orthodoxy does not envisage the possibility of holding *bhakti* (devotion) as an independent standpoint of exegesis or as an absolute basis of religion. Inasmuch as Rāmānuja approached both exegesis of texts and religion from *bhakti* he tried to break new ground, and for that reason his orthodoxy has always been a subject of debate. Śankara, on the other hand, worked within orthodoxy, even in his exaltation of gnosis at the expense of *karma*, or the totality of ritualistic and other auxiliary actions in accordance with Vedic injunctions. Accordingly, the choice was restricted to the two *niṣṭhās*. Śankara, while redefining both, advocated an unconditional and unqualified acceptance of gnosis as that which alone is in agreement with the nature of Ultimate Reality and final release (*mokṣa*). And he clearly called for the rejection of *karma* as what is not in harmony with Ultimate Reality and with final release. Nevertheless, he permitted a conditional, qualified and tentative use of *karma*, strictly under gnosis, but only as a dependent basis of religious and moral life and not as a standpoint of exegesis. Therefore, his approach to *karma-niṣṭhā*, unlike his approach to *jñāna-niṣṭhā*, is one of "no" to *karma* and "yes" to it in a qualified sense and of a transvaluation of *karma-niṣṭhā* eventually, (as distinguished from *karma* in the primary sense). Now, it is easy to see why he vehemently criticized some interpretations of the *Gītā* prevalent in his day, which gave equal standing to gnosis and to *karma* and considered them to be co-ordinate, expressing the position known as *jñāna-karma-samuccaya*, the word *samuccaya* implying exactly what we have just said, i.e., giving equal place to *jñāna* and *karma* and considering them as co-ordinate. This doctrine (*vāda*) Śankara vehemently criticizes on several occasions, particularly under *Gītā*, 2.10, a verse which simply marks the fact that Kṛṣṇa is there beginning his philosophical teaching (and again under 18.66). Śankara feels that the record must be set straight before ever entering into the teaching. However, it must be noted that even when Śankara says "no" to *karma*, he is actually only rejecting the authenticity of *karma*-philosophy, in view of the fact that such a thing existed then, and has always existed in the world of philosophy. Clearly, he is not saying "no" to *karma* as a fact of life and as a fact of nature. But he is denying to *karma* an intrinsic sphere of thought, which it claims, for thought belongs solely and singularly to gnosis.

THE TEACHING ABOUT THE TWO OBSERVANCES EXPANDED INTO A COMPREHENSIVE HORIZON

The teaching of the *Gītā* concerns the resolute observances of gnosis and active effort, the latter being understood as expression, concrete actualization and practical support of the former. They are not co-ordinate, because *karma-niṣṭhā* is entirely subordinate to *jñāna-niṣṭhā*. The contradiction comes only when they are held as co-ordinate, or even worse, when the subordinate becomes the superordinate, i.e., when it seeks to replace gnosis with some knowledge which results from human activity.

The teaching is expanded into a whole, comprehensive horizon, beginning with the third chapter of the *Gītā*. The horizon is coalescent with existence itself and *is* one of existence. It is formed of the dynamic substance of religion and morality and is put forth so as to be grasped and interiorized by thought. The horizon is formed by means of the deployment of a number of constitutive dimensions one after another. They are put forth by critically refining ideas and forces very much at work in the moral and religious life with which the text is in contact.

All along, while deploying these dimensions the *Gītā* frequently reiterates the essence of the teaching. As for the teaching, gnosis is regarded as the principal, and in fact the only, stream. The streams of *karma* are like rivulets and, no matter what their origin, must flow into gnosis: that is their authentic destiny. "All *karmas* without exception fulfill themselves in gnosis", (*sarve karmākhilam jñāna parisamāpyate*), as the *Gītā* itself says (4.33). The horizon as a completed whole not only covers and absorbs the entire world of moral and religious life but also makes it a cosmos by letting gnosis percolate into it. Here another aspect of *karma's* destiny is established, which is to be the path-clearer for gnosis. Thus, commenting on the words of the *Gītā* (4.42): "Take recourse to *yoga* (i.e., resolute observance of active effort, under gnosis) and stand up", (*yogam ātiṣṭho 'ttiṣṭa*), Śankara states: "It means that one must devote oneself to *karma* insofar as it is *the yoga* that clears the way for gnosis", (*yogaṁ saṁyag-darśanopāyaṁ karmānuṣṭhānaṁ kurvītyarthaḥ*).

This represents a radical transformation of *karma* (or *yoga*) and it lays the foundation for the teaching to expand itself into a comprehensive horizon. Now, there are many important dimensions, some of which are primarily dimensions of Reality and others are those of life-endeavour and thought-endeavour. The colophons often give clues to them. And yet they are all impartially subjects of both *theorea* and *praxis*. Thus to give emphasis, we not only can *see* the world-reality coming out of God and we *see* God as the Self of the world, but we also can *practise* them. We practise renunciation and we can also approach it as something to be grasped through seeing. To use a more convincing example, the Good that we see is also the good that we practise. The *Gītā* itself takes note of it in one instance when it explains the meaning of the word *sat*, comprehending both the meanings "Good" and "good", and more.

> For the Good/Reality/Being and for the good as practised this (i.e., the word) *sat* is used; also for praiseworthy action the word *sat* is employed, O Arjuna. (*sadbhāve sādhubhāve ca sad iti etat prayujyate; praśasthe karmaṇi tathā sacchabda pārtha ucyate.*), *Gītā*, 17.26.

Before the whole horizon is articulated the *Gītā* wants us once more to take a clearer look at gnosis. For that reason a restatement of it is given in Chapter 4.

Then let us turn to these various dimensions. These dimensions are treated as the principal themes of the chapters to follow (i.e., chapter 5 onwards), which are renunciation (*saṁnyāsa*), meditation (*dhyāna*), understanding (*vijñāna*), devotion (*bhakti*), discrimination (*vibhāga*, or *viveka*) and so on.

The dimension of renunciation (saṁnyāsa)

Accordingly then, first, (in Chapter 5) renunciation is unveiled. It is recognized that even the *praxis* of gnosis, insofar as it is active effort, involves a mode of action. But that mode of action exists which is entirely compatible with gnosis, and that is renunciation-action.

> He who acts, having relinquished (*tyaktvā*) attachment, resting his actions on *Brahman*, is not touched by sin (*lipyate na pāpena*), even as a lotus leaf (is untouched) by water. (*brahmani ādhāya karmāṇi sangam tyaktva karoti yaḥ lipyate na sa pāpena padmapatram ivā 'mbhasā.*), Gītā, 5.10.

The discourse on renunciation is carried over into the beginning of the 6th chapter, where (in the second stanza) renunciation is equated with active effort (*yoga*): "What they call renunciation (*saṁnyāsa*) that know to be yoga". Further on, in 18.2, a special definition is offered: "The sages regard renunciation as the giving up of actions prompted by desire", (*kāmyānām karmāṇām nyāsaṁ saṁnyāsaṁ kavayo viduḥ*). The very stanza also adds that this is the same as relinquishment (*tyāga*). There is a culprit and it is identified as imagination (*saṁkalpa*), which is a kind of false creative power. Renunciation is directed against it. Śankara points out that from imagination spring all desires (*samkalpa mūlā hi serve kāmāḥ*)[20] as well attested by Manu and the *Mahābhārata.*[21] This is the reason why *Gītā*, 6.2 adds to what was cited above: "No one ever becomes a *yogin* who has not renounced imagination," (*na hy asaṁnyasta saṁkalpo yogī bhavati kaśćana*).

Renunciation is, therefore, a particular *yoga*, an active effort representing the obverse of usual effort, and is to be understood as that which is left over when desire has been removed from all actions, while it is itself not an action, either positive or negative, for if it were it would contradict itself. It has being only in reference to all actions while it is itself not an action. The predication of renunciation on all other actions is what the *Gītā* means when it states (4.17), "the course of action runs deep", *gahanā karmaṇo gatiḥ*. [There is no other mystery in this statement, as some writers assume.] However, the active form of the word reflects the pervasive condition to which all human consciousness and language are subject. Hence it has the appearance of an activity. Śankara explains the predicament through a simile: "Activity is falsely attributed to the Self reflecting the egotistic feeling conveyed by the expression 'quiescent and *doing* nothing I sit happy' just as a person travelling in a boat sees the trees on the river banks moving in the opposite direction, although motion really does not pertain to the trees".[22] However, in the world of man's spiritual behaviour renunciation has a certain symbolic compatibility with gnosis, which no action has. Hence it is considered ideally akin to gnosis.

The dimension of meditation (dhyāna)

The dimension of meditation (*dhyāna*), briefly outlined in 5.27 and 28, is more fully unfolded in the 6th chapter. It begins with the insistence on "shutting out all external thoughts", "fixing the vision between the eye-brows" and "equalizing the in-breath and the out-breath", (*sparśān kṛtvā bahir bāhyāṁś cakṣus cai'vā'ntare bhruvoḥ*), 5.27. In the 6th chapter meditation is simply called *yoga* as if it is the paramount *yoga*. [This style is followed in describing each and every dimension in its context.] But its claim to be considered *the yoga* derives from a connection that possibly existed even in hoary antiquity and was well exemplified in later times by the Yoga system of Patañjali.

Following the already traditional view of *yoga* (continued later by Patañjali), the *Gītā* believes in the complete absorption not only of the mind but also of the body into the task of meditation, not so much in the sense of a means of realization so-called as, in fact, in the sense of a thorough-going self-testimony to total commitment that meditation itself symbolizes. And indeed it offers symbolic resistance to what lies at the root of mental tardiness and physical laxity.

Meditation is thought, the highest kind. It is highest thought we say but only in the sense of an activity that approaches receptivity, which is the essence of what really is thought inasmuch as thought is the extension of gnosis. The activity is only what we see of thought from the near side and it indeed dissembles what it is on the far side. As we have learnt already, if thought is the extension of gnosis, gnosis is the disposition of Ultimate Reality (i.e., of *Brahman/Ātman*). The steadiness, the concentration, the joy and the assurance of thought (here called meditation) rest on this fact. Hence the *Gītā* says:

> As a lamp in a windless place flickers not, to such a one is likened the meditator (*yogī*), who has mastered his thought, who in meditation (*yogam*) has become united with the *Ātman*;
>
> That in which thought has no other notion, restrained on account of the service of meditation (*yogasevayā*), where, beholding the *Ātman* through the *ātman*, In the *Ātman* he rejoices;
>
> That in which he finds this supreme delight, grasped by intelligence and beyond the senses, where, (thus) standing he no longer falls away from the Truth;
>
> That upon gaining which no other gain does he conceive to be greater, wherein standing not even by heavy sorrow is he moved;
>
> Let this disconnection from union with sorrow be known by the name of *yoga*; with certainty should be practised this *yoga* with heart undismayed.

(yathā dīpo nivātastho ne'ṅgate so'pamā smṛtā yogino yatacittasya yuñjato yogam ātmanaḥ;

yatro'paramate cittaṁ niruddhaṁ yogasevayā yatra cai'vā'atmanā'tmānam paśyann ātmani tuṣyati;

sukham ātyantikaṁ yat tad buddhigrāhyam atīndriyam vetti yatra na cai'vā'yaṁ sthitaś calati tattvataḥ;

yam labdhavā cā'paraṁ lābhaṁ manyante nā'dhikaṁ tataḥ yasmin sthito na duḥkhena guruṇā'pi vicālyate;

taṁ vidyād duḥkhasaṁyoga-viyogaṁ yogasaṁjñitam sa niścayena yoktavyo yogo'nirviṇṇacetasā.), Gītā, 6.19-23.

The dimension of understanding (vijñāna)

Chapter 7 ushers in the dimension of understanding. It is an anticipated outcome of meditation. Understanding, it is made clear, is possible through the First Principle, which is always one and the same, although the phenomena in which it is enfolded are diverse. The teacher of the *Gītā* speaks of it in the first person singular, as himself. Thus:

I am the taste in the waters, O Arjuna, light in the moon and the sun; I am the *praṇava* (*AUM*) in all Vedas, the sound in space, manhood in men.

The good odour in the earth and brightness in fire am I; I am the soul in all beings, and the power that burns in the ascetics.

Know, O Arjuna, that I am the eternal seed Of all beings; I am the intelligence of the intelligent ones, I am the splendour of the splendid.

I am the strength of the strong which is devoid of lust and passion, while I am the just desire in beings, which does not conflict with *dharma,* O Arjuna.

(raso'ham apsu kaunteya prahbā'smi śaśisūryayoḥ praṇavaḥ sarvavedeṣu śabdaḥ khe pauruṣaṁ nṛṣu.

puṇyo gandhaḥ pṛthivyāṁ ca tejaś cā'smi vibhāvasau jīvanaṁ sarvabhūteṣu tapaś cā'smi tapasviṣu.

bījam māṁ sarvabhūtānāṁ viddhi pārtha sanātanam budhir budhimatam asmi tejas tejasvinām aham.

balaṁ balavatāṁ cā'haṁ kāmarāgavivarjtam dharmāviruddho bhūteṣu kāmo'smi bharatarṣabha.), *Gītā*, 7.8-11.

Understanding has for its realm that which is controlled by the First Principle, the cause and the source of the universe, and hence what is called aptly by the name 'metaphysics'. However, it is maintained in the *Gītā* that though it is necessary for the mind to order all things around the First Principle, the First Principle itself is beyond understanding. "Me no one knows", (*māṁ tu veda na kaścana*), 7.26. That which is beyond understanding, nevertheless, communicates itself. Hence the significance of couching it in the first person singular pronoun (I, me, my) but in the way permitted only for the First Principle. Men make the quest for it with all their mind, with all their heart and with all their strength. Therefore, the quest is tantamount to worship and men set up what they arrive at as a deity (*devatā*). Men who are dead earnest pursue their quest with attentive reverence (*śraddhā*, a word not altogether adequately translated 'faith') as befits religious worship and no doubt their quests are justified rather than condemned by reason of their reference, however remote, to the hidden First Principle which can be only communicated by itself. "Whatever form any worshipper (seeker) with attentive reverence (*śraddhā*) wishes to worship I make that attentive reverence of his steady" (7.21). The truth is, while there is abundant basis for men to seek the First Principle (and earnest men actually do) there is no basis for them to really understand it, because that which moves them to the quest (not lightened to any one, *na prakāśaḥ sarvasya*) is a veil that confuses them in that it is the First Principle's own "creative" *māyā* (7.25).

The concept "First Principle" itself means that it is the Ultimately Real, as approached through phenomena. Understanding, therefore, is the grasp of the Ultimately Real through phenomena, and accordingly metaphysics is its realm, the meaning of the word to be literally taken as that which is beyond Nature (*meta ta physica*), signifying the fact that Nature (the world of phenomena) is its approach route.

The dimension of imperishable Brahman

Chapters 8-10 unravel the realm of metaphysics, because they describe Ultimate Reality (*Brahman*) in terms of its distributive presence in the universe of multiplicity. The description follows first of all the pattern made classic in the *Bṛhadāraṇyaka Upaniṣad* (3.6.1, etc.), that is, as the imperishable *Brahman* (*akṣara Brahman*), contrasted with the perishable character of things. Hence the imperishable *Brahman* constitutes the topic of the 8th chapter. [A discussion of imperishable *Brahman* as constituting the realm of metaphysics is to be found in our chapter on the Upaniṣads.] The teacher of the *Gītā* declares:

> What the knowers of the Veda call the imperishable, which ascetics free from passion enter, aspiring for which they walk environed in *Brahman*, that state I shall briefly declare to thee.
>
> (*yad akṣaraṁ vedavido vadanti viśanti yad yatayo vītarāgāḥ yad icchanto brahmacaryaṁ caranti tat te padaṁ saṁgraheṇa pravakṣye.*), *Gītā*, 8.11.

[The different use of the word *akṣara* meaning the syllable *AUM*, in 8, 13, must not be confused with this, but, as we observed in the context of the Upaniṣads, the two uses have an indirect relation too.]

The dimension of deepest mystery (guhyatamam)

In chapter 9 the metaphysics of imperishable *Brahman* and along with it understanding move into another dimension which is indicated by the term 'deepest mystery', *guhyataman* (stanza 1), and the term 'sovereign mystery', *rājaguhyam* (stanza 2). This is where understanding verily merges with gnosis, the way of which the teacher is going to declare, as stated in the very opening stanza:

> This, the most hidden (truth) I shall declare to thee, who are not inclined to cavil: gnosis [it is] together with understanding, by knowing which thou shalt be released from the inauspicious.
>
> (*idaṁ tu guhyatamaṁ pravakṣyāmi anasūyave jñānaṁ vijñāna sahitaṁ yaj jñātvā mokṣyase'śubhāt.*), *Gītā*, 9.1.

It is a mystery because it does not follow the law of understanding and is not something that logically issues from understanding even in the pursuit of the First Principle expressed as imperishable *Brahman*. And yet it is a mystery for the opposite reason also, that is to say, although not according to any expectation of speculation, i.e., that which is on the "lookout", understanding does indeed merge with gnosis. Hence it must be seen that understanding functioning in this way has the character of thought provoked by gnosis, of thought as the extension of gnosis. Mystery remains a mystery to thought in that gnosis continues to have to be recognized as a given, what could have come about only the way it has come about and in no other, in other words, only due to the revelation of the holy. And consequently the Reality revealed in this dimension remains concealed to that understanding which does not yet participate in gnosis. The particularity of a revelation, such as is the characteristic mode of the *Gītā's* teaching, calls for this peculiar companionship of gnosis and understanding, just as the revelation itself brings it about. This is a very special aspect of the thought which is the extension of gnosis. There is here a decidedly theistic character to the disposition of Ultimate Reality which is for us gnosis, and that character is expressed by the expression the *Gītā* uses here, i.e., "my divine *yoga*", (*me yogam aiśvaryam*), 9.5. And this too is a mystery, of which thought by itself cannot give an account. And because it is a matter of Ultimate Reality's own disposition expressed in a decidedly theistic, revelatory context, there is no way it can be expressed in language except by attributing to Ultimate Reality the character of first person (I, my, me, etc.). Śankara gives another reason for the use of these first person pronouns, that is "as a mere adoption of the world's mode of understanding" (*lokabuddhimanusaraṇ*).[23]

The dimension of [*self-*] *manifestation (vibhūti)*

The mystery is further pursued into the dimension of the [self-]-manifestation (*vibhūti*) of Ultimate Reality, in chapter 10. Also, the [self-] manifestation is the completion of the truth regarding the First Principle (as the imperishable *Brahman*) taken up in chapter 8 now that the dimension of the mystery of the particular and the unique has already interposed. Therefore, the instances of the presence of the imperishable *Brahman* in all parts of Nature and in all occurrences are re-counted here, now to be viewed in the light of Ultimate Reality's own [self-] manifestation. Thus:

> Of the world-epochs, I am the beginning and the end and also the middle, O Arjuna; of *vidyās* I am the spiritual *vidyā*; of those who speak dialectically I am the dialectic.
>
> Of the syllables I am the letter A; of compounds I am the dual; I am inexhaustible Time; I am the ordainer whose face is the cosmos itself.

(*sargāṇām ādir antaś ca madhyam cai'vā ham arjuna; adhyātmavidyā vidyānāṁ vādaḥ pravadatam̐ aham.*

akṣarāṇām ākāro'smi dvandvaḥ sāmāsikasya ca; aham evā'kṣayaḥ kālo dhātā'haṁ viśvatomukhaḥ.), *Gītā*, 10.32,33.

Towards the end of the chapter (10.40) Kṛṣṇa announces: "There is no end 'to my divine manifestations' (*divyānāṁ vibhūtīnāṁ*)", and adds "they are only described as 'illustrations' (*uddeśataḥ*)".

Now a brief comment on the word which we have translated as manifestation, or self-manifestation, namely *vibhūti*, may be made. The literature of the Yoga system has used it very differently. The third of the four chapters of Patañjali's *Yoga-Sūtra* is called *vibhūti*, a designation probably introduced by the ecommentary *Tattva-Vaiśāradī* of Vācaspati Miśra. The word is employed in the Patañjali tradition in the sense of super-normal powers that a practioner of Yoga is able to master. And that meaning clearly accords with the text of the *Yoga-Sūtra*. [Other related Yoga traditions also use the word in that sense.] However, *vibhūti* of the *Gītā* has nothing to do with such powers, as it actually stands for the unique [self-] revelation of Ultimate Reality as it relates to thought.

The dimension of devotion (bhakti)

Now comes the 11th chapter, which depicts one concrete, dramatic manifestation to Arjuna, for the sake of visually underscoring all that has been declared upto that point. And it also marks the transition to another dimension of apprehension beyond the metaphysics of understanding. It is that of devotion expressed by the word *bhakti*. This is the highest dimension and hence Śankara describes it as the essence of the whole teaching of the *Gītā* (*Gītā-śāstrasya sārabhūto'rtha*)[24] to which one is taken through the vision described in the 11th chapter, of Kṛṣṇa appearing before Arjuna in a splendid theophany of his cosmic form. This theophany introduces devotion (*bhakti*).

The dimension of devotion as has already been briefly introduced in the last stanza of this 11th chapter is then more fully stated in the following chapter which the colophon calls by the name *bhakti-yoga*. Śankara, commenting on 11:55 seeks to correct a wrong, popular notion about devotion in respect of the *Gītā*. The stanza speaks of "my devotee who serves me and looks upon me as his ultimate goal (*mat-karmakṛṇ matparamo madbhaktaḥ*)." Clarifying it, Śankara states, "A servant serves his master but does not look upon that master as his own ultimate goal. But "My devotee" works for "me" and looks upon "me" as his (own) ultimate goal."[25] The master, or the Lord (*Īśvara*) is none other than the Self. The ability to look upon the Self itself as the Lord, purged of the servility that normally pertains to the servant-master relation, is the true test of devotion, and it is to that dimension to which one is ushered.

> Greater are the troubles of those whose mind is set on the Unmanifest [than those who worship me], for, the way of the Unmanifest is hard to gain for the embodied beings.
>
> (*kleśo'dhikataras teṣām avyaktāsaktacetasām avyaktā hi gatir duḥkaṁ dehavadbhir avāpyate.*), *Gītā*, 12.5.
>
> [The Unmanifest stands for pure imperishable *Brahman.*]
>
> On me alone fix thy mind; let thy intelligence dwell in me; in me alone shalt thou abide henceforth. As to this there is no doubt.
>
> (*mayy eva mana ādhatsva mayi buddhiṁ niveśaya nivasiṣyasi mayy eva; ata ūrdhvaṁ na saṁśayaḥ.*), *Gītā*, 12.8.

Devotion simply strengthens the ground of man's metaphysical existence by taking it beyond the purview of the understanding that has yet not learnt to consort with gnosis. Metaphysical existence requires constant exercise in what results from understanding's consorting with gnosis, namely self-knowledge. Therefore, it is necessary that philosophical thought that is generated from gnosis returns periodically to all the realms of natural thought as well as of life for the sake of gathering their finest fruits and of placing them on its own trajectory. For this reason the *Gītā* now ushers us into certain dimensions, all of which are generally characterized by the attribute of discriminate wisdom or *viveka* as that has been, it is to be noted, the special vocation of the historical Sāṁkhya system to specialize in but also has been an intrinsic part of Vedānta. These dimensions are described in chapters 13-17. So, to these we shall now turn.

The dimension of fundamental discrimination

This dimension is described in the 13th chapter which enshrines the primary but all-too-easily-forgotten distinction (*vibhāga*) between the field (*kṣetra*) and the field-knower (*kṣetrajña*). The substance of this is stated thus:

> The field and the field-knower, those who with the eye of gnosis perceive their difference and the deliverance of beings from Nature, they attain to the Transcendent.
>
> (*kṣetrakṣetrajñayor evam antaraṁ jñānacakṣuṣā bhūtaprakṛtimokṣaṁ ca ye vidur yānti te param.*), *Gītā*, 13.34.
>
> [Note: 'the eye of gnosis' is an expression which does not yet mean gnosis.]

The knower is eternal and unchanging (namely, the Self as the Lord) and is in no way in bondage to the cosmos of becoming (*saṁsāra*). But the fact that, on the contrary, it appears to be so is due to agnosis (*avidyā*). Śankara explains correctly: "Thus it cannot be imagined that the knower of the field, the Lord, though [present] in all fields can have even the odour of becoming."[26] The exercise in self-knowledge as the essential character of metaphysical existence is meaningful only insofar as it signifies our overcoming a natural hindrance caused by the conditions of our phenomenal existence as it is given to us. In fact, the knowledge that such and such is the nature of existence as given is also the result of this exercise. In other words, that which is to be apprehended through discrimination is already prefigured in existence. We are obliged to give an account of the cosmos, that is to say, of becoming (all that arises), as it is the situation in which self-knowledge has to operate. As Śankara makes it clear, "all that becomes is due to the conjunction of the field and the field-knower".[27]

Discrimination between the field and the field-knower is an act of thought but of the thought that is grounded in gnosis. Nevertheless, it is an act and so much so cannot be a rejection of that source of all acts or becoming, namely the conjunction of the field and field-knower. Therefore, that particular act of thought is referential to this conjunction.

Philosophical thought in Vedānta, as we have already seen developing, is thought conducting itself in accordance with the way gnosis itself behaves. There is no doubt about this. But the regions in which thought so conducts itself are there by virtue of the afore-mentioned conjunction. So thought can establish its conduct only by keeping an eye on the way Nature (*Prakṛti*) itself behaves and by depositing the understanding it thus gains in the account of self-knowledge. The dynamic character of thought, that is to say, insofar as it is generated or provoked, even in respect of thought grounded in gnosis, has Nature alone to thank for, although in Vedānta's sense thought as grounded in gnosis is also a dialectical dissociation from Nature. Hence the *Gītā* leads us to the understanding of Nature's own fundamental behaviour.

The dimension of understanding of the discrete behaviour of the guṇas of Nature

The understanding of the way the *guṇas* (strands) of Nature behave is what essentially constitutes the understanding of Nature and is an indispensable ingredient for thought's achieving self-knowledge, to the end that it establishes itself in accordance with gnosis' own behaviour. This understanding is the next dimension to which we are led, and it occupies chapter 14. Its importance is announced in the very first verse, which characterizes it as the "highest knowledge" (*jñānānām jñānām uttamam*). But such characterization must not be taken literally, and certainly will not be so taken by those who know the Sanskrit style, which is often given to using hyperbolic adjectives in order to stress a point. The reason for doing that here, as Śankara aptly tells us, is not because this knowledge is actually the highest, but "merely in order to rouse interest in the mind of the hearer by praising it" (*parottamaśabdābhyām stauti śrotir-budhi-ruci-utpādanārtham*). To rouse interest in something by extolling it is a well-known convention in the Mīmāṁsā literature. The *guṇa* theory of Nature leads one from metaphysics to a metaphysical psychology, and it comes from hoary antiquity, from the mythical figure Kapila himself, but clearly like many another theory it was already in the air. As Śankara states in the context of a later passage (18.19): "Even Kapila's science of *guṇas* is indeed an authority as far as the *gunas* and their experience are concerned."[28]

The three *guṇas* are preliminarily described in stanzas 5-18 in the standard manner. Of the three, *sattva* is defined as light and hence skin to gnosis, *rajas* as passion (or energy) and *tamas* as darkness (opposite of *sattva*) or as inertia (opposite of *rajas*). Although they are alike in that "they bind the indestructible soul down in the body", (*nibadhnanti dehe dehinam avyayam*, stanza 5), *sattva* "gives rise to gnosis", (*sattvāt saṁjāyate jñānam*, stanza

17) and "those who stand thereon go upwards" (*ūrdhvaṁ gacchanti sattvasthā*, stanza 18). It only shows that *sattva*, while being part of bondage-creating *Prakṛti* is still a kind of vicegerent for the Spirit in our earthly life. Nevertheless, the higher value of *sattva* is only relative insofar as instrumentally it is superior, and it is restricted to the realm of becoming. It is the essence of discriminate wisdom for one to be able to see no other agency working in the realm of becoming than the *guṇas* (stanza 19), and so seeing one passes beyond the *guṇas* (*guṇān atīto bhavati*, Stanza 21).

The dimension of discrimination in the very realm of the Spirit

We are led to the next dimension, that of the Supreme Spirit (*puruṣottama*), in chapter 15. It is contrasted with the cosmos of becoming. It begins with the celebrated description of the upside-down tree called *aśvattha* and the exhortation to cut it down. The tree is a symbol of the cosmos. The very first verse tells us that its roots are above (*ūrdhvamūlam*) and branches below (*adhaḥśākham*), that its leaves are the Vedas (*chandāṁsi yasya parṇāni*). "He who knows it is a knower of the Veda" (*yas taṁ veda sa vedavit*). Cutting down of the tree is the act which completes the two progressive steps of discrimination between the field and the field-knower.[29]

However, the mandate of discrimination continues even further. For even in the realm of the Spirit there is need for clearly distinguishing between two ways of approaching it:

> Two-fold is the Spirit in this world, the perishable and the imperishable. The perishable is all these beings (i.e., in their totality), and it is said that that which is the unchanging is the imperishable.
>
> (*dvāv imau puruṣau loke kṣaras cā'kṣara eva ca; kṣaraḥ sarvāṇi bhūtāni kuṭastho'kṣara ucyate.*), *Gītā*, 15.16.

Discrimination goes even further. The highest level reached so far is that of the "unchanging, imperishable Spirit" (*kūṭastha akṣara puruṣa*) which is really none other than the highest point that can be reached by pursuing the metaphysics of the First Principle, as has already been outlined (before the framework of discrimination was put into operation, beginning with chapter 13, in terms of imperishable *Brahman*.)

The call now (stanza 17) is to go even beyond that highest point, in fact, to overcome and exceed metaphysics as such. So the

Gītā introduces "that which is called the *Ātman* that is [still] beyond" (*paramātme'ty udāhṛtaḥ*), "the Spirit that is the highest but other [to the former two]" (*uttama puruṣas tu anyaḥ*). The truth is even more clearly stated in stanza 18:

> Wherefore I exceed the perishable "Spirit" and am higher than even the imperishable "Spirit"; therefore in the world and in the Veda I am celebrated as the highest Spirit.
>
> (*yasmāt kṣaram atīto'ham akṣarād api co'ttamaḥ; ato'smi loke vede ca prathitaḥ puruṣottamaḥ.*)

The teaching pertaining to what has been spoken of here, i.e., the *Ātman*, is described in stanza 20 as "this the most hidden teaching", (*guhyatamam śāstram idam*). Commenting on this, Śankara observes, "the whole teaching of the *Gītā*, not only of the *Gītā* but of all the Vedas, is summed up in this chapter".[30] The reason for Śankara's making this emphatic and categorical statement is simply that finally *Ātman* has now been spoken, detached even from the metaphysics so inalienable from thought, because it is bound if not to the cosmos as such, at least to its ground in the imperishable *Brahman*. Even in this respect freedom has been achieved by thought as a genuine prospect, although only as a prospect.

The dimension of understanding in respect of a fundamental moral distinction

Discriminate knowledge continues to be applied as the essence of the phase of understanding that the text has been occupied with from the 14th chapter onwards. However, here in the 16th chapter a new dimension is being introduced: that of a fundamental, moral distinction in human nature, as between what is known as godly (*daivī*) and what is known as demoniac (*āsurī/rākṣasī*). This is an elemental distinction that goes far back to the past, much older than the Śāṁkhyan notion of the three *guṇas, sattva, rajas* and *tamas*, which are, no doubt, ethically as well as metaphysically conceived.

The unique aspect of what the *Gītā* is trying to do in this chapter is that, on the one hand, it draws from the primeval, elemental distinction (almost ethical dualism) in the Indian (perhaps universal) religious tradition and, on the other, tries to accommodate this very thing within a framework of the three-fold distinction of the Sāṁkhyan *guṇas*. The chapter not only discusses the two different moral natures of human beings in great detail but actually states that there are [only] these two, in the 6th stanza. "There are two created orders of beings in this world, the divine and the demoniac", (*dvau bhūtasargau loke'smin daiva āsura eva ca*). Śankara in his commentary makes it clear that what is meant by two is "two in number" (*dvau dvisaṁkhyākau*) and that the "two orders of created beings are the two orders of created *human* beings", (*bhūtānām manuṣyāṇām sargau sṛṣṭi*). This moral polarity is drawn specifically from ancient Brāhmaṇa literature, and the *Bṛhadāraṇyaka Upaniṣad* (1.3.1) clearly echoes it when it declares: "there are two classes of Prajāpati's creatures, the gods, and the demons", (*dvayā hi prājapatyā devāśca asurāśca*). [This distinction between the "godly" (*daivī*) and the "demoniac" (*rākṣasī/āsurī*) was made in an earlier place in the *Gītā* too, i.e., 9.12 and 13, but in the sense of religious rather than moral dispositions.] This dualism, although only potential, runs deep as Śankara bears witness, saying (*à propos* 16.6), "all must be divided into these two types", (*sarveṣām dvividhy-upapatteḥ*).

Of the two types, the godly (*daivī*) is one and the demoniac is the other, for which both terms *āsurī* and *rākṣasī* are synonymously employed. Because there are the three words (*daivī, āsurī*, and *rakṣasī*) Śankara at the beginning of his comment on chapter 16 speaks of (human) "natures" (*prakṛtaya*) in the plural (rather than dual). This may be interpreted merely as stylistic insofar as there are three words used in the *Gītā*, and nothing more may be made of it. The *Gītā's* own accommodation of this primeval, moral distinction of human natures in the framework of the *guṇa* theory has the eventual result of transposing the latter into the substance of the former. On the contrary, it would have been devastating to permit the cool, enumerative Sāṁkhyan metaphysics of Nature to absorb something so unassimilable, so obstinate, so elemental as the moral distinction in *human* nature expressed by the words 'godly' and 'demoniac' and all that it entails. [A non-Sāṁkhyan, non-technical connotation for "nature" (*prakṛti*) is maintained by both the *Gītā* and the commentator, along with the Sāṁkhyan, technical one. Such a freedom has never been sacrificed. But the three-*guṇa* analysis of Nature for the Sāṁkhya system is assimilated into the dualism of the godly and demoniac *human* natures clearly in a non-logistic way as evidenced better in the next chapter (chapter 17).] Accordingly, "godly" is equated with *sāttvic* as Śankara shows it to be the case (*daivī=sāttvikī*),[31] and that strictly for the sake of the resolute observance of gnosis (*jñāna-yoga*), which is the ultimate objective that all understanding is aimed to serve. And the demoniac is simply opposed to the *sāttvic* in reference to the project that is the main concern and includes both the *rājasic* and *tāmasic guṇas*. This is the way an accommodation is worked out, and accommodation here is assimilation.

The fundamental, two-fold moral distinction is the valid perspective for dealing with the three *guṇas* as just *sāttvic* versus *non-sāttvic*. The *sāttvic* is the godly. However, the list of qualities, both godly and demoniac are simply what are universally so regarded within the Indian and in much of the world's, tradition. There is no need for revelation or for a special use of gnosis to know what the godly, moral virtues are. Their practice itself is their revelation, and yet is an indispensable condition for the realization of gnosis. Ethics is the realm of pure practice based on its own *a priori*. For the *Gītā* it is as simple as that. Further, the *Gītā* perceives what is universally perceived, namely that they come as a whole group, in indivisible association with one another by means of an associative law of their own. The group thus consists of (Stanzas 1-3) fearlessness, purity of heart, steadfastness, giving, non-violence (which according to Śankara includes compassion for those who are suffering, *kṛpā bhūteṣu duḥkhiteṣu,*[32] truthfulness, uprightness, fortitude, humility, etc. The demoniac qualities (stanza 4), which are ostentation, arrogance, conceit, insolence, ignorance, etc., are the very opposite of the godly.

Furthermore, non-belief in a God who rules the world is identified with the demoniac attitude, while belief in God is the basis of morality, i.e., the godly attitude. The position is implied in the criticism of the demoniac world-view (stanza 8), according to which the world is devoid of truth (*asatyam*), without foundation (*apratiṣṭham*) and without a God (*anīśvaram*) and the product of sexual desire (*kāmahaitukam*).

The dimension of religious reverence

The discussion of moral distinction, which has occupied the foregoing dimension, ends with the need for belief in God as the ground of morality. That naturally takes us to the next dimension, which has to do with religious reverence, or *śraddhā*.

The word which we translate as "religious reverence" (also "attentive reverence") is *śraddhā*, the key word of the 17th chapter. It has a history coming down from the *Ṛg Veda* itself. In the

Ṛg Veda and other Vedas and in the Brāhmaṇas the word occurs many times. It is a compound of two words, *śrat*, or *śrad*, and *dhā*. The word *śrat*, or *śrad*, is related to Greek *καρδία*, *καρδίη*, the English 'heart' and probably the Latin *cred* (from which credo), carrying a meaning possibly akin to what we understand by 'heart' today. The word *dhā* has a variety of meanings in the Vedas, such as "to assume", "to have", "to give", and so on.

The *Gītā* in its description of *śraddhā* puts it in the company of *yajña* and *tapas*, all of which seem to stand together, yet signifying severally, man's whole-hearted attention, sacrifical dedication and unbounded exertion, for the sake of stretching and lifting his existence beyond the given limits. Hence in the 17th chapter *śraddhā, yajña* and *tapas* (i.e., whole-hearted attention, sacrificial dedication and unbounded exertion) are each shown to be of three types, according to the *guṇas*. However, only those who are of *sattva* are deemed truly religious and capable of reverence in the true sense.

> Men of *sattva* worship the gods; men of *rajas* worship supernatural apparitions and demons; and the others, the men of *tamas*, worship ghosts and bands of spirits.
>
> (*yajante sāttvikā devān yakṣarakṣasāṁsi rājasāḥ pretān bhūtagaṇaṁś cā'nye yajante tāmasā janāḥ*.), *Gītā*, 17.4.

Not only *śraddha, yajña* and *tapas* but even the foods eaten by people are classified according to the three *guṇas* to the point that the classification begins to look even artifical and trivial. But it has to be made for the sake of completing the structure of the threefold analysis with perfect symmetry. It would seem also that the pattern followed must be carried out to the end in keeping with the general religious tradition. However, the application of the three *guṇa* scheme seems merely to serve as foil for the essential and radical distinction between the godly (= *sāttvic*) and the demoniac, for the former alone qualifies as being fitted for true religious reverence, so indispensable a condition for the realization of gnosis.

THE CONCLUSION

Now that the horizon has been comprehensively delineated what remains is to bring the teaching to a conclusion. The teaching concerns gnosis and *karma* and the two *niṣṭhās* pertaining to them, and the horizon was developed through expanding the teaching.

The conclusion is stated in Chapter 18. It is a restatement of the teaching itself, including a summary review of the *guṇa*-theory and its applicability to the *karma* part of the teaching. While *karma-niṣṭhā*, as clearing the way for, and as auxiliary to *jñāna-niṣṭthā*, is discussed exhaustively and with approval, the grounds for any independent *karma*-philosophy are rejected.

The 18th chapter re-capitulates the entire teaching, according to which *jñāna-niṣṭhā* is the ideal of philosophical thought and existence, and in the spirit of that *karma-niṣṭhā* is being recovered as a genuine expression and auxiliary means, while the alternative view, of the latter being itself an independent "path"is rejected. Only *jñāna-niṣṭhā* is self-fulfilling because its object, gnosis, is eternally self-fulfilled, while *karma-niṣṭhā* fulfills itself in being redeemed and transformed by the former. What is *magna carta* for gnosis is for *karma* its commission and pathway to transform itself into the likeness of gnosis.

In order to see how this is so, it is necessary to pursue the general meaning as well as the particular use of the word *niṣṭhā* itself, which we have translated "resolute observance". In respect of general meaning, it may be said that it is a word that reflects the character of its object, that is to say, what is resolutely observed. Accordingly, *jñāna-niṣṭhā* reflects gnosis and its properties, and *karma-niṣṭhā* reflects *karma* and its properties. The general meaning of the word does not tell the whole story as far as the *Gītā* is concerned. Śankara shows that the word has a special usage in the text which makes it paradigmatically applicable to gnosis. In fact, he argues that the word is the same as *bhakti* (devotion) in respect of the special usage applicable to gnosis. [This in the context of 18:55, which says "by *bhakti* he knows me", *bhaktyā māmabhijānāti*), etc.]. He writes:

> In so far as the word *niṣṭhā* delivers the meaning of the self-arising and ripening of gnosis devoid of an opposition, and culminating in one's own definite experience of unity with the supreme *Ātman*, generated by the

> instruction of the scripture and the teacher, and by the auxiliary aid of the purity of intelligence, absence of egotism, etc., and accompanied by the renunciation of all works predicated on the notions of doer and deed, that is, [to repeat] in view of this culmination in definite self-experience, it (i.e., the word *niṣṭhā*) is spoken of as supreme *jñāna-niṣṭhā.*[33]

And Śankara adds that *jñāna-niṣṭhā* is the same as the highest of the five kinds of *bhaktis*, described in 7:16., that is, those of the virtuous men (*sukṛtina*), of the person in distress (*ārta*), of the seeker of knowledge (*jijñāsu*), of the seeker of riches (*arthārthī*) and of the one who is already in gnosis (*jñānī*) respectively.

Accordingly then, there is only one authentic *niṣṭhā*, which is *jñāna-niṣṭhā*, because resolute observance requires something not of man, something ontologically unchanging, unbecoming and undecaying as its object. This is the object which extends itself as its own resolute observance. And expressing the same in terms of thought, we may say that resolute observance of gnosis is thought as it authentically is insofar as thought is extension of gnosis.

However, to go back again to *karma-niṣṭhā*, it is not something to be viewed as in opposition to *jñāna-niṣṭhā*, because as Śankara says, the latter has no "opposition" (*pratipakṣa*). The authenticity of *karma-niṣṭhā* consists in its being assimilated into, and transformed by, *jñāna-niṣṭhā*, while it is inauthentic if in any sense it is viewed as an independent basis for philosophy, either co-ordinate with, or superior to, the latter. An independent *karma*-philosophy is the result of agnosis (*avidyā*), as Śankara argues in the context of his comment on the climactic utterance (*caramaśloka*) of the entire *Gītā* (i.e. 18.66):

> Abandoning all *dharmas*, take refuge in me alone; I will liberate thee from all sins; do not grieve.
>
> (*sarvadharmān parityajya mām ekaṁ śaranaṁ vraja; ahaṁ tvā sarvapāpebhyo mokṣayiṣyāmi mā śucaḥ.*)

Gnosis philosophy, understood in the above manner has vast consequences for our understanding of philosophical thought. We said just a few spaces above that the resolute observance of gnosis is thought as it authentically is insofar as it is the extension of gnosis. No doubt, if this be true a profound revolution in our comprehension of that activity, namely mental activity (*mānasa kriyā*), which has to do with thought, is called for. The highest "agent" of thought is the intellect (*buddhi*), and so much so thought is intellectual "activity". But under gnosis this activity as such is transformed into a receptivity in that the agent itself is transmuted into the similitude of that of which gnosis is the disposition. As Śankara puts it, "the intellect [as the agent in the activity of thought] in its purity puts on the sheer likeness of the *Ātman* (Ultimate Reality) in its disposition [to us] as gnosis (*caitanya*, or *jñāna*)".[34] [It must be added, that this putting on of the similitude of what is above each entity is carried on all the way down to the level of the body: the synthesizing mind then puts on the likeness of the intellect, the sense-organs that of the mind and the body that of the sense-organs.]

Having now discussed the essential gnosis-philosophy of the *Bhagavadgītā*, we have to return briefly to speak about the matter which we have characterized, based primarily on the authority of the great commentator, as part of the teaching, namely Kṛṣṇa's exhortation to Arjuna to fight the war as befits his warrior nobleman's *dharma*. In these urgings *Kṛṣṇa* is not acting as the teacher and personification of gnosis but as one through whom Arjuna's unexpressed quest finds expression. Kṛṣṇa, who in this respect is merely playing the role of companion is giving tongue to Arjuna's own inner, *dharma*-constituted phenomenal self, which is seeking itself. He has to gain it first in order to lose it by rising to gnosis. Find it and lose it he must in order to find *Ātman*. So the saying, "he that loses his soul shall find it", must be accompanied by another truth to be stated thus: "he who is in peril of losing his *dharma*-constituted self through *confusion of mind as to dharma* (*dharma-sammūḍha-cetaḥ*) must find it first so that he may lose it in gnosis and find the Self (*Ātman*)."

CHAPTER IV

GNOSIS AND PHILOSOPHICAL THOUGHT IN THE BRAHMA SŪTRA

The Brahma Sūtra (*Vedānta Sūtra*, or *Śārīraka Sūtra*), attributed to Bādarāyaṇa, is a different kind of text from the ones with which we have already tried to hold converse. It lays no claim, like the Upaniṣads or even like the *Bhagavadgītā*, to be a text through which *Vāk* speaks directly. In respect of gnosis it simply goes back to the Upaniṣads, which according to it is where *Vāk* speaks, and strings together (hence *sūtra*, meaning string, or thread),[1] in a systematic and logically ordered fashion, certain passages from them. It follows a central thread of connections so that we can call the result the bare outline of a system. A system must have a development, and in the case of the *Brahma Sūtra* the development obeys both the inner logical progression discernible as being inherent to the theme of *Brahman* itself and the outer logic of a philosophical discourse, which is the same as Reason in its public form.

However, the skeletal text of the *Sūtra* is a series of what reads like codes, which would make no sense at all to those who attempt to read it independently, that is to say without the benefit of the light thrown by "commentaries". It is quite clear that it came into existence for use within groups where Vedānta in its wider setting was studied and discussed.

Śankara's *Bhāṣya* ("Commentary") is not only the oldest of the existing ones but the authentic and original expansion of the *Sūtra* into a full-fledged system. There have been commentaries by later *ācaryas* like Rāmānuja, Madhva and others, who either modified Śankara's interpretation or offered a totally different one. Śankara's position, as is well-known, is characterized by the absoluteness of gnosis over against *karma*, with its various implications, serving as the so-called path to *mokṣa*, as well as by the transcendence of *Brahman* elevated above all qualities, or *guṇas*, not to speak of his rigorously non-dualist (*advaita*) view of Reality such that he denied being to anything other than *Brahman*. Śankara's standpoint thus outlined has also its corollaries in his doctrines of *Avidyā* and *Māyā*. Just as a whole mighty line of Śankara's successors developed enormous logico-metaphysical arguments to defend his philosophy in its entirety, others, both the Vedāntists of different persuasions and opponents of Vedānta alike, in the several centuries that followed produced countless works, some of them very great measured by the yardstick of logical skill and acumen, with the purpose of refuting it.

Within the Vedānta tradition itself, in view of the fact that all thought actually turned around the system that Śankara had built, some centuries after his death there arose a concern with the authenticity and veracity of his interpretation of the *Sūtra* (as also of the other foundation texts of the tradition). Thus other commentaries came into being, which refuted his interpretation. However, the question as to which *Sūtra* commentary is faithful to the text is meaningless because the text in itself is not independently interpretable. So the different commentaries must actually themselves be taken as just the core texts of different philosophico-theological systems, written in imitation of Śankara's own example. There can be not much debate about the fact that without Śankara's *Bhāṣya* there would have been no possibility of his challengers writing their own commentaries on the *Sūtra*. Śankara's Commentary belongs with the *Sūtra*, making the latter come to life. Paul Deussen quite correctly observes: "We must ... renounce the attempt to keep Bādarāyaṇa's teaching and Śankara's interpretation of it separate from each other."[2] Accordingly, he looks upon the two texts together as an indivisible whole for his "systematic exposition".[3] In fact one can even go further, and describe Śankara's *Bhāṣya* as the real philosophical work which used the *Sūtra* as a path-finder like a mariner's compass. [Henceforth we shall speak of them as one single text.]

THE ARRANGEMENT OF THE TEXT

We spoke earlier of the development of the system which heeds both to the progression of the inner logic of the theme of *Brahman* and to the outer logic of discourse. Between these two there is a deeply conspired co-ordination which can be unravelled in the arrangement of the text itself, quite clearly an evidence of its systematic character. There is, however, also something not within the purview of a system which is also witnessed in the text, and that we must describe as the accord worked out between the way gnosis (*Brahma-vidyā*) itself behaves and the way thought conducts itself. Thus we see that there is system here but also something deeper than system.

The text is composed of four *adhyāyas* or chapters, each of which is divided into four *pādas*. Each of these *pādas* is, again, divided into *adhikaraṇas* or topical sections, in which are grouped together a number of individual *sūtras*. The first *adhyāya*, i.e., *samanvaya*, text-arrangement, seeks to bring together passages from the Upaniṣads gleaned from different places which set forth the theme of *Brahman* (*Ātman*) from various perspectives. The second, called *avirodha*, meaning removal of objections based on presumed contradictions in the way the central theme has been set forth, seeks precisely to do what the word says. It is in the cooperation between *samanvaya* and *avirodha* that the fundamentals of the accord between the way gnosis itself behaves and the way thought conducts itself consists, and this accord is the basis of all *praxis*, a matter taken up next. The third chapter, *sādhana* or *praxis* is an exhaustive enterprise of refining the ritual, moral and meditative techniques aimed at realizing *Brahman*-gnosis. Indeed these techniques were already there and had been employed in the service of other goals. The fourth, *phala*, or fruit, is actually a continuation and conclusion of *praxis*. It schematizes the types of actualized goals, no doubt in religious terms continued to be called *mokṣa*, or *nirvāṇa*, but equally to be appropriated philosophically, through the thought which is the extension of gnosis. It is correct also to say that the possibility of philosophical thought is kept as a trust in the concrete religious life, and no doubt the obverse is also true, that is to say, the religious life must be held in the safe-keeping of philosophical thought.

Let us again remind ourselves that all that we say about the text is with respect to the whole text, i.e., as expanded into the *Bhāṣya* by Śankara. Both the system and, even more significantly, the accord between gnosis and thought are manifest only in the *Bhāṣya*, which also provides us with an initial access route to gnosis, as, decidedly, we cannot reach it from nowhere but only from where we are. And yet in constructing the access route it is not forgotten that thought moves towards (and reaches) gnosis only because that thought which has the capacity to do so is gnosis extended.

The extension of gnosis as thought is the greatest mystery of all in Vedānta as philosophy. The mystery is, by nature, never to be resolved, because its continuance is what makes the entire project of the quest of Vedānta as philosophy possible. As such, on the one hand it comes to our view as the hidden reason why gnosis extends itself as thought rather than remain unextended and, on the other, confronts us with the fact of the obscuration of gnosis. However, when we are really held by it, as by the question of Ultimate Reality itself, individual boundaries, and even those between so-called subject and so-called object become meaningless. That is why the two words in Vedānta which are used to express this mystery, i.e., *māyā* and *avidyā* defy such boundaries, and is why these words are as much epistemological as metaphysical (specifically cosmological). However, the difference between *māyā* and *avidyā* appears to be non-existent for the most part except in a very subtle respect: *māyā* rather expresses the mystery with reference to the transcendent, namely as power (*śakti*) of the Divine, while *avidyā* expresses the same in terms of the structure of consciousness, especially in its struggle to know Ultimate Reality. [And later, cosmologically they are also treated as synonyms.]

Therefore, in the initial access route to the philosophy of gnosis which Śankara constructs in the *Bhāṣya* (by way of a preface) he points to *avidyā* and opens it up for everyone's profound consideration insofar as that is what confronts everyone the moment interest in Ultimate Reality is awakened. The word *avidyā* is itself very significant as in its formation it is privative, thus having the import of absence of knowledge (any knowledge) and therefore equivalent to 'ignorance' and synonymous with other terms in Sanskrit such as *ajñāna* and *apramā*. And yet it is already loaded from the start as that which signifies the structure of consciousness in which knowledge (gnosis) of Ultimate Reality is absent, a condition, however, that spurs the quest for that which is absent. [Here we must translate *avidyā* as 'agnosis'.] In this manner it is shown to be already the venue of a primordial dialectic, a setting of the stage for the entry of gnosis.

The confrontation of every man with *avidyā* in his consciousness is shown to be primordial. The first step in philosophical thought, therefore, is to completely explore the nature of this confrontation directly, that is to say, intuitively. However, such exploration can turn out to be perilous unless it is, for the sake of its own fruitfulness, oriented prospectively towards the discovery of man's own essential being as *Ātman* (*Brahman*). Only in that prospect can the darkness of agnosis be overcome. And therein lies the only hope of recovering meaning in the form of liberation (*mokṣa*), nonetheless a liberation through that which is essential for man, namely thought.

THE CIRCLE OF GNOSIS PHILOSOPHY

The deeply conspired co-ordination between the inner logic of the *Brahman* theme and the outer logic of discourse, and the still deeper accord between gnosis and thought are worked out through the drawing as it were of a circle of gnosis philosophy. The point from which the circle is drawn is where gnosis is revealed through the speaking of *Vāk* and the point at which the drawing of the circle is completed is where that revelation is confirmed in realization. What compels the drawing of the circle is the imperative of the task which thought that has its ground in consciousness sets for itself, namely, the discovery of Ultimate Reality. However, in drawing the circle, as far as thought is concerned, it has at its disposal only the *modes* of gnosis which it appropriates. They are also what underlie the possibility of the circle, whereby the conduct of thought accords with the behaviour of gnosis.

Now, the modes of gnosis are two, the revelatory and the realizational, or put very simply, that which belongs with the showing and that which belongs with the seeing. The genius of Vedānta, particularly as worked out explicitly by Śankara in the *Sūtra Bhāṣya*, is that it establishes the fact that showing and seeing are ultimately one and the same but with the qualification that their convergence is achieved by thought via the project of the gnosis circle. The circle may be drawn as narrowly or as widely as is required in a given project – and it will be very wide if the project is co-terminus with the cosmos (the All) itself. Reason (basically called by such names as *tarka, yukti, nyāya*, etc.) actually is on the side of showing. The traditional limbs of the Indian Science of reasoning (*tarka-śāstra*), called the *pramāṇas*, must, accordingly, be placed on the side of showing. The *pramāṇas* (sources of knowledge or means of producing knowledge) in their customary phenomenological ordering begin with *pratyakṣa*, a word which is often wrongly translated 'perception'. But *pratyakṣa* (*prati* + *akṣa* literally, that which is before the eye) means 'appearance' (this word taken in its neutral connotation, that is, not set in the Appearance-Reality framework), signifying the coming before the eye of the thing itself. It is a showing which, no doubt, instantaneously becomes one with the event of perception, but is not perception *per se*. [The acid test which proves it is the fact that if *pratyakṣa* is used it is always for the thing which appears and not the perceiver.] Of the original three limbs of the *pramāṇa-śāstra*, after *pratyakṣa* comes *anumāna*, usually translated 'inference', and then comes *śabda* (what *Vāk* speaks), also called, more concretely, *śruti*, i.e., that of *Vāk's* speaking which has been "heard" and preserved as the Vedas. As for *anumāna*, it is the fundamental limb in the process of argumentation designed to show, not, however, some structural logical relation but always the actual things which are directly aimed at. [This is a unique feature of all Indian logic.] It is just as true of *pratyakṣa* as of *anumāna* that it is the thing that shows itself and it is not the thinker who shows anything. Likewise again, *śabda*, meaning sound and hence word, is that by which someone's appearance or presence is announced or otherwise made known. Therefore, basically, it is a form of *pratyakṣa*, which is the reason why in traditional Vedānta works beginning with those of Bādarāyaṇa and Śankara frequent references to *pratyakṣa* are made in the sense of *śabda*.[4] And of course through *śabda* it is *Brahman's* appearance, or presence, that is made known rather than just things as in *pratyakṣa* in general. In this sense *śabda* is the highest and, for that reason, the most philosophically problematic as well as productive kind of appearance, because that which appears this way, i.e., knowledge of the Ultimate Reality, is the focus of all questions in philosophy. [It is also significant that the last of the limbs added by some Mīmāṁsā and Vedānta works is *anupalabdhi*, meaning non-presence and hence the exact opposite of *pratyakṣa*, eventually equated, perhaps not correctly, with *abhāva*, i.e., the non-existent thing. And this *anupalabdhi* too was drafted as a source of knowledge, with perfect justification, no doubt.] All this being so, it would also have been clear by now that in Vedānta inasmuch as *śabda* itself is a limb of *pramāṇa-śāstra*, or *tarka-śāstra*, and inasmuch as all these limbs are also means for the thing (even *Brahman*) to appear there is no room for conflict between Revelation and Reason.

To reiterate, the modes of gnosis, i.e., revelational and realizational, which belong respectively with showing and seeing, are as much the essence of the way gnosis itself behaves as of the way thought conducts itself. But this can be said only in the light of the accord between the way of the one and the way of the other having a philosophical reality, that is, in other words, in the light of thought's finding itself as extension of gnosis. Thought is extension of gnosis as much in the latter's revelational mode as in its realizational mode. The drawing of the circle of gnosis is merely an expression of the fact that thought is already the extension of gnosis in both of the latter's modes, and is not by any means the act by which thought *becomes* the extension.

Now, this accord tells us, as in the case of gnosis so in the case of thought, that there is a showing (revelational) mode and a seeing (realizational) mode, although always it must be borne in mind that what essentially underlies both of them is one and the same and that they are different only as modes. Thus, just as through the use of the *pramāṇas* the showing is carried forward by thought, so there is something else by which the seeing is carried forward *in* thought, and the idea is expressed by a number of terms such as *dhyāna, nididhyāsana, upāsana*, etc., all of which have the generic meaning of 'meditation'. This meditation or meditative thought occupies the centre of what is called *sādhana*, or *praxis*, and it is thought conducting itself as though it were a means to realization. As we enter the text of the *Sūtra* and its *Bhāṣya* we shall see how these two modes of thought correspond to the modes of gnosis, and how both are integral to the gnosis circle. We will also notice that the circle is drawn in a perfectly coherent and systematic manner in this text, which for that reason alone has become "the standard work of the Vedanta school",[5] and we should add, its standard-bearer, that is, the one by which all other works are to be judged.

ACCESS ROUTE TO THE GNOSIS-CIRCLE: ŚANKARA'S CELEBRATED PREFACE

By his brief but extraordinarily powerful preface, Śankara lays an access route to the philosophy of Vedānta, aimed at every thinking person as an invitation to enter the gnosis circle which he is about to draw. It consists in a radical examination of the ground of consciousness from which naturally all thought that has to do with the question of Ultimate Reality is launched. It is in fact a critique of the ground of consciousness. The critique is made possible by the anticipation of gnosis, which like the early morning sun puts under its beam of light a fundamental element in consciousness which is operational in thought's quest for Ultimate Reality. That element is shown to be the innate and primordial power of consciousness to distinguish between the subject and the object. Therefore, it is the basic tool of all thinking. Hence, Śankara writes:

> The object of awareness (*viṣaya*) and the subject that is aware (*viṣayin*), denoted by the words *yuṣmat* [the basal form of the pronoun meaning 'you'] and *asmat* [the basal form of the pronoun meaning 'I'] respectively, which in nature are as different as light and darkness, cannot transform themselves into each other, and neither can their respective properties (*dharmas*) be mutually exchanged. Therefore, the superimposition (*adhyāsa*) of the objects which are within the range of the denotation of the word *yuṣmat* and its properties upon the subject which is within the range of the denotation of *asmat* and in essence is consciousness must be deemed a [dynamic] fiction (*mithyā*). Likewise also is the superimposition of the properties of the one upon the properties of the other. Nevertheless, it is a natural course in the world's transaction, resulting from "the fiction which is agnosis" (*mithyājñāna*) that there is [such] mutual superimposing of the subject and the object along with their respective properties, although they are absolutely different from each other. And there is also this imagining 'I am this', 'this is mine' on account of the fact that "truth and non-truth have intimately paired with each other" (*satyānṛte mithunīkrtya*).[6]

The preface points out the existence of a strange anomaly here, namely, the lack of a proper coordination between the way language functions through denotation of its most basic terms and the way consciousness actually operates in thought. This is demonstrated as a vicious condition which fundamentally inhibits our natural ability to arrive at even empirically reliable knowledge of things and of ourselves. And how great would this limitation be if the knowledge we seek is that of Ultimate Reality, whether taken as objective or in terms of the Self (*Ātman*)! And further, because of the pairing of truth and non-truth the shifting of our intuitions as between true and false [refer, in our Introduction, to the discussion of "thought as the penetration of the hidden depths of reality"] ceases to be a real possibility.

Śankara does not believe that this condition is correctible from *within* the immanent structure of consciousness by way of some further critique or therapy. Hence he does not endorse any programme in such a direction as though that were to constitute philosophy. He understands this condition to be but part of a universal condition that embraces everything, including those things which we naively assume as being primordial and hence a priori. This universal condition is described by Śankara as the mutual "superimposition" (*adhyāsa*) of self and not-self, and is designated by the term *avidyā*. "Learned men consider this superimposition to be of the nature of *avidyā*," (*tametamevam lakṣaṇam adhyāsam panditāḥ avidyeti manyate*). It is called *avidyā*, or *agnosis*, because it is that which by positing itself as the very antithesis of *vidyā* (*jñāna*), or gnosis, confronts it and is confronted by it. Indeed, it is by virtue of this confrontation that man discovers himself as the being whose phenomenal essence is the desire for gnosis. The discovery is made possible by the grace of *Vāk*, and thereby *agnosis* itself is grasped as what is marked for dissipation. Hence Śankara concludes the Preface with these words:

> It is for the sake of destroying the cause of this vicious condition (or *anartha*, to be paraphrased as 'viciously cyclic condition') and for attaining the knowledge of the unity of the Self that all Vedānta (Upaniṣadic) statements originate. In what manner is this the purport of all Vedānta statements we will endeavour to show in this Vedāntic system.[7]

This vicious condition is not to be construed as the usual predicament of logic, what is technically called *anavasthā* (going back forever without reaching a place for repose), but a deep existential one which causes the gravest self-disorientation in our search for a foot-hold. Hence it is described precisely in that sense as *anartha-hetu*. [There is a bonus to be obtained by following Śankara's analysis, which is this: Through *Vāk* a co-ordination between the way language functions and the way consciousness operates even in everyday life may be aimed at so that the meanings of words in their denotational field can be caught correctly by means of the intuitions of consciousness. This possibility will turn out to be no small boon in every kind of communication and its benefits will be obvious and will be a tremendous aid to philosophy even when it is approached as what has its ground in consciousness (forgetting the gnosis ground for the time being) as it will save thought from all that initial effort which occupies the bulk of the enterprise known by the name of philosophy.] Now this vicious condition can be put an end to by only the gnosis circle, into which thought is ushered.

A PRELIMINARY STATEMENT BASED ON THE FIRST FOUR SŪTRAS

The first four *sūtras* (the *catussūtri* as they are customarily called) are taken as one whole, based on which a complete initial statement of Vedānta as that philosophy in which the way of thought accords with gnosis is given. It is a brief preliminary account of how gnosis behaves vis-à-vis thought's quest for Ultimate Reality and how thought may conduct itself responsively.

The very first *sūtra*: "Then, therefore the desire for *Brahman*-gnosis", (*athā'to brahma-jijñāsā*), is examined from the point of the fundamental character of man's existence to be grasped philosophically, as what is unconditionally oriented towards the liberating knowledge of Ultimate Reality. This truth, no doubt, is to be always taken in conjunction with that with which it primordially corresponds (as the foundation of all *a prioris*), namely that the essential disposition of Ultimate Reality (towards us) is gnosis. Try as hard as we may we shall never succeed in escaping the equation of this correspondence, which, however, positively viewed is, the first firm step that thought can take for releasing itself from the strangle-hold of the existential vicious condition, the *terminus ad quem* reached by thought as it tries to grasp Ultimate Reality from the ground of consciousness alone.

Over against this equation of correspondence may be placed (for the sake of an instructive contrast) an ends-and-means approach for which the paradigm is provided by none other than the other line of Vedic exegesis, i.e., Pūrva-Mīmāṁsā, or Karma-Mīmāṁsā. This line of exegesis is known for its elevation of the potencies of *karma*, or the rite, that in effect sums up all of man's manly effort, taking it beyond its mundane frame to the region of the transcendent. The rite, on the one hand would appear to be an absurd, humanistic epic calculated to be the only way for man to grasp for himself the utterly elusive meaning of his own and the universe's existence – and indeed nothing less than the totally "absurd" epic of human rite can be adequate for this. But on the other, the absurdity of it is removed by the fact that the epic is the enactment of a transcendent knowlege which comes via *Vāk*. Śankara now faces head-on this epic heorism of the rite and says 'no' to it from the vantage point of *Brahman*-gnosis, for he sees ultimate truth as lying even beyond it, which is what he wants to show. He, however, does not object to the "absurdity" of the rite, for he too shares the view that the absurdity of the absurd is dissolved in a transcendent knowledge. The moot question for him is the nature of transcendent knowledge itself, as to whether it generates an epic of the rite or an authentic epic of gnosis, under which the rite, and with it the whole sphere of human action, would also find its proper place.

At this point we must recall how the *Bhagavadgītā* (according to Śankara at least) rejects the resolute observance of action and affirms the resolute observance of gnosis. It is the opportune moment now to link action (*karma*) discussed in that text with the principal philosophy of Karma-Mīmāṁsā. Need it be said that in either context *karma* is not spoken of primarily in the everyday sense of action, but in the sense of the epic of the rite, the way to grasp the transcendent, elusive meaning of all existence and hence as the action which embraces, supercedes and also sanctifies all human action.

[At this point we cannot but recall how the *Bhagavadgītā* rejects the resolute observance of action and affirms the resolute observance of gnosis. The action that is rejected is the same as the *karma* laid down by the Pūrva-Mīmāṁsā.]

According to Pūrva-Mīmāṁsā, the knowledge that it gives has placed ultimate, efficient, salutary action (the rite) within man's power. The rite is, no doubt, an acknowledgement of the transcendent and it is also the means by which man can project himself unerringly to his final destiny. Śankara in rejecting *karma* rejects all the assumptions that underlie it.

It is the common understanding of all the systems of Indian philosophy that our review of Ultimate Reality reflects – and is reflected by – the means (called means of liberation, or *mokṣa-sādhanam*) that are envisaged to reach it, that the two agree with each other. And it is also a truism that there is no view of Ultimate Reality as pure intellectual vision, divorced from a means that assuredly takes us to it. The question, however, is not only what the means are but *how* we take even that which is known to be the true means. According to Vedānta, that alone is true "means" which is no longer measured by the criteria of means. This is the crux of its debate with Pūrva-Mīmāṁsā and is the essential reason for its rejection of the means-ends structure as such. Vedānta, therefore, takes the position, that in its case the view of Ultimate Reality is such that the "means", i.e., gnosis, already belongs with Ultimate Reality (as its own disposition towards us), which accordingly ceases to be any kind of means in our sense. Hence Śankara writes: "Only by means of gnosis is Ultimate Reality to be reached. And the reaching of Ultimate Reality is man's highest end (*puruṣ-ārtha*), attainable through the destruction of that vicious condition (*anartha*), namely *avidyā*, which (writ large) is the seed of the entire chain of phenomenal becoming (*saṁsāra*)." Hence gnosis is described as *pramāṇa* namely, that which gives itself as the "means of knowledge". It should be noted that it is called not *a pramāṇa* but just *pramāṇa* and hence is not to be understood in terms of the scholastically organized *pramāṇa-śāstra* where it is a stock word and used in the weak sense of the science pertaining to the "means of knowledge". On the contrary, in the present context it occurs in the uniquely strong sense that is attached to the original *pramā*, or the true knowledge of the entity that goes with gnosis (*jñāna*) itself. *Pramāṇa* in its original sense must be taken as meaning gnosis projecting itself into the realm of "means".

The epic of gnosis versus the epic of the rite

Let us briefly advert to the central issue which has been looming over the debate between the two Mīmāṁsās, i.e., Vedānta and Pūrva-Mīmāṁsā, to be put in the form of the question: which is true, the epic of gnosis, i.e., that which expresses the epic aspect of gnosis, or the epic of the rite? The two systems ostensibly have a common foundation, namely the Vedas, although they do differ as to the portions through which *Vāk* itself is held to speak (i.e., the Upaniṣads for the one, the Karma-kāṇḍa, or Brāhmaṇas, for the other). The scope of this debate, a mortal combat in fact, cannot be confined to the two systems, nor to the history of Indian philosophy. Everyone has a stake in its outcome, for thinkers everywhere are tacit participants in it and not just spectators. For which is true, the epic of gnosis or the epic of the rite? As for the latter, need it be said that it expresses the final meaning of all philosophies which put action in the forefront of thought, whether in the form of grasping action or liberating action? It is only that Pūrva-Mīmāṁsā expresses these philosophies in the perfect universal language, that is, of the rite, working out from the very start the absolute integrity between word and meaning as stated at the very beginning of the fundamental systematic text of the system, Jaimini's *Mīmāṁsā-Sūtra*, in these words: *likavedayoḥ śabdārthaikyam* ("In the world and in the Vedas there exists unity of word and meaning"). No other similar philosophy which invests so much in action has created such a perfect language of rite as has Pūrva-Mīmāṁsā.

Śankara's 'no' to Pūrva-Mīmāṁsā must be extended to a whole lot of philosophies throughout history, particularly today. Pūrva-Mīmāṁsā presents not only an epic of the rite but a humanistic one, which, however, is so thoroughly humanistic that, far from rejecting the gods, it assigns them a place in its grand and universal scheme of action, reality and meaning – and man, not a creature subject to fear, holds the key to it in his hands because he is master of the rite.[9]

Śankara carefully works out the alternative epic, that which expresses the epic aspect of the gnosis circle. In this task he has the entire Upaniṣads, the *jñāna-kāṇda*, from which to draw inspiration. The Upaniṣads themselves were a gathering of the gnosis elements trapped in the sacrificial (*yajña*) material of the Vedic Mantras as well as the Brāhmaṇas. The most luminous example is found at the very beginning of the *Bṛhadāraṇyaka Upaniṣad*, where the most heroic[10] horse sacrifice symbolism is transposed into gnosis, commencing with the words: "AUM, verily the dawn is the head of the sacrificial horse", (*aum, uṣā vā aśvasya medhyasya śiraḥ*).

The epic of gnosis will also eventually restore the rite itself, within gnosis, to its rightful place, not as an epic (and certainly as a humanistic one), and with it the entire sphere of action, including most of all the active form of thought, so that we may "do" thinking too, as we surely must. It is in this spirit that Śankara shows the way to re-claim that pinnacle of the Indian epic literature, i.e., *Bhagavadgītā* episode of the *Mahābhārata*. His work in this respect is a clear pointer as to how the popular epics as a whole may be viewed as enactments of gnosis; wherein lies the fulfilment of *dharma.*[11]

Knowing the known as the essential movement of the gnosis circle

The epic which implements and enacts the gnosis circle is construed as a movement in the direction of knowing that which is known. This is the theme to which Śankara turns at the end of his comment on the first *sūtra*. A fundamental predicament with regard to the quest for Ultimate Reality is expressed: "It is either absolutely known or not known at all. If absolutely known then it need not be desired to be known; if not known at all it would be impossible to desire to know it", (*tatpuna brahma prasiddham aprasiddham vā syāt*; *yadi prasiddham na jijñāsitavyam*; *aprasiddham naiva śakyam jijñāsitum iti*).

This is a predicament of the most serious kind, which puts the whole enterprise of philosophy under question. For, how indeed can one investigate Ultimate Reality if it is not already self-evident, and if self-evident why investigate? Is it possible that this question is aimed at other ways of conducting thought in the quest for Ultimate Reality than in accordance with gnosis, in view of a whole chain of implications and entailments that can emanate from it? Śankara seems to let the question answer itself within the terms of gnosis. In doing so, however, he directs attention to Ultimate Reality itself, which is described as "eternally pure, eternally knowing and eternally free" (*nitya-śuddha-buddha-mukta-svabhāvam*), as well as "omniscient and wrapped in almightiness" (*sarvajñam sarvaśakti-samanvitam*). "The word *brahman* itself", Śaṇkara contends, "has the meaning of eternal purity, etc.", (*brahma-śabdasya hi vyutpadyamānasya nityaśuddhatvādayo'rtaḥ pratīyante*). Because of this it must be deduced that it is a word that is the fullness of meaning which informs our thought about Ultimate Reality.

And *Brahman* indeed exists. Its existence is made available to thought by reason of manifesting the meaning of what that word itself brings in our deepest self. Accordingly, Śankara observes, "Brahman's existence is made available (i.e., to thought) on account of its (i.e., the word's) meaning having come from the root *bṛhate* it expands into greatness) and on account of the self-hood of everyone", (*brhaṭer-dhātorarthānugamāt, sarvasya ātmatvāñca brahmāstitva prasiddhih*). This is the great correspondence or attunement to be looked for as that which, according to Vedānta, makes philosophy what it is. This is the correspondence between expansion into infinite greatness (of Being) that the word *brahman* itself connotes and the indispensable reference of all meaning, in other words the self of everyone who thinks. And the word *brahman* stands conclusively for *Vāk* as it is on its way to meet our thinking self, and thinking is nothing but welcoming and receiving *Vāk* and bringing it home to the destination to which it has set its face of its own accord. [And as for *Vāk*, because of its association with the Vedas, it is likely to project the notion that only those who have the privileged position in relation to the Vedas will have access to it. But in the case of the self, no such privileged standpoint is recognized because "everyone knows selfhood and no one thinks 'I do not exist'", (*sarvo hi ātmāstitvam pratyeti na nāham asmīti*). "Everyone" (*sarva*) is absolutely everyone, "the whole world" (*sarva loka*).]

The Upaniṣadic equation of the self and *Brahman* (*ātma ca brahma*) is restated by Śankara in this place, and it indeed acquires a new dimension of significance for philosophy, by reason of the location of the meaning of what *Vāk* itself says within the self of the thinker, which, inasmuch as it is the inescapable reference of that meaning, grasps infinite Being unto itself, as itself and not as another. However, this is not as in the natural paths of thought (as we have discussed in our Introduction) a mere boundary-making for the unbounded that is *Brahman*. On the contrary, it is removal of boundary from the self, and consequently from thought too.

No doubt, in this new dimension to which thought has been raised through bringing to the forefront the revolutionary significance of the equation of *Brahman* with the self, an unprecedented possibility has been indicated. Consequently, it speaks to all thought that raises the question of Ultimate Reality and helps it to give a coherent account of its conduct beyond its natural competence. Thus in opening the way for all thought to such a self-revelation gnosis ceases to have to remain in some splendid isolation. Therefore, the truth that the gnosis circle exemplifies paradigmatically, namely, that only the known can be desired to be known (*jñātam eva jijñāsitavyam*) can be transported, and be made integral, to all philosophy that asks the question of Ultimate Reality. In fact, the dictum that only the known can be desired to be known, that it is the real objective of all philosophical quest, serves as the essential truth pervading the entire movement of the gnosis circle. The philosophy of the gnosis circle will serve to awaken all philosophy to this awareness.

It is, therefore, not the case that the gnosis circle runs its course without contact with other ways of engaging in philosophy. The truth, on the contrary, is that it merges with all other streams of thought and yet is working in them from within. Further, it is not the case that the gnosis circle, because it operates with a clear vision of the goal of thought, will cause open-ended questions, the essence of philosophy, to be dried up. Here again the truth is just the opposite, for the desire to know what is at its base already known is the ground of infinite questioning. And indeed there is no other ground which is able to sustain such questioning. That is the reason why the term 'infinite' is used so as to mark that ground, which is itself what is infinite in the true sense, and, consequently, the endless act of asking questions produces an invincible sense of our approaching the highest truth, or rather of its closing in upon us. [Hence also the compact of questioning with adoration.] That means that the word 'infinite' does not stand for a mere quantitative march of tiresome and endless distances. We must recall that the very arrival of that which laid the theoretical base for the gnosis circle, i.e., the truth that *Brahman* is *ātman*, in the Upaniṣads was preceded by such asking of questions – and now it is deeply revived by Śankara. It is this quality which makes philosophy the inexhaustible self-expression of the gnosis circle, for, as such it is not a movement from one definite point to another definite point but the swallowing up of every beginning and of every end that are part and parcel of other ways of thought which naturally launch us into philosophy. The gnosis circle takes over what had been launched from other grounds. Finally then, to let thought be the extension of gnosis, to let it conduct itself in accordance with the way gnosis itself behaves, to be qualitative and inexhaustible in the questionings which constitute philosophy and yet be *knowing* all the time, to take over all thought that has been launched from other grounds, that is the nature of the epic of gnosis.

The gnosis circle and the exegis of what Vāk itself has spoken in the Upaniṣads

We say that *Vāk has spoken*. Clearly, there is a retrospect which characterizes thought's involvement in the gnosis circle, because

Vāk's speaking comes to us via the Upaniṣadic sentences which are already there, and because of the historic character of our existence and of our knowledge – the past being the medium – we put its arrival in the past. The Vedāntic tradition, is, however, careful not to constrict the past as such to the chronological past, which is the reason why it is open to us in the present and is indeed present. The exegesis of the Upaniṣadic sentences, which are already there and, by defying the concrete determination of time, comes to us in the present, is itself the way our thought can conduct itself in accordance with the way gnosis itself behaves, that is to say, in the manner of *Vāk's* speaking.

The exegesis of Upaniṣadic sentences

The gnosis circle is undergirded by the exegesis of what *Vāk* has spoken in the Upaniṣads. The task envisaged thereby is that of bringing our natural thought, through criticism, into the orbit of gnosis, having taken into account the variety of ways in which men without the benefit of gnosis approach the question of Ultimate Reality and with it the question of the self. These men range all the way from the naive persons and the *lokāyatas* (materialists) who contend "that the mere body endowed with sensibility is the self" (*dehamātram caitanyaviśiṣṭam ātmeti*) to those who think "that there is a God who is omniscient and omnipotent but is different from the self" (*asti tadvyatirikta īśvara-sarvajña-sarvaśaktiriti*). Only a bare sampling is provided as possible ways in which man can think on the subject which is "indefinitely large" (*bahavo vipratipanna*). [Besides, man's final blessedness is in jeopardy here, because attainment of that goal is the deep-seated reason why man investigates Ultimate Reality at all.] In view of all this, Śankara writes at the end of his comments on the first *sūtra*, announcing the nature of the task of exegesis as follows: "Hence now begins via an essay on the desire for *Brahman*-gnosis the project of going reflectively over the sentences of the Upaniṣads, using the tool of Reason that accords with them so as to be of service in the cause of ultimate blessedness", (*tasmāt brahma-jijñāso'panyāsa-mukhena vedāntavākya-mīmāṁsā tadavirodhatarkopakaraṇa niḥśreyasa-prayojana prastūyate*). [The word *mīmāṁsā* has the meaning of going reflectively, or thoughtfully, over something said by *Vāk*.]

Because *Vāk's* speaking is at once revelation and concealment there arises the need for going reflectively over what has been said in the Upaniṣads. To this end is Reason drafted into service as a tool (*upakaraṇa*). A tool is only as good as the use to which it is put and that depends on, on the one hand, the user and, on the other, the purpose or goal. A tool is a tool because, unlike an instrument (*yantra*), it never takes over the direction of its own use. In Vedānta, Reason is, on the one hand, a cement that secures the connections among points in the passage of thought through the gnosis circle and, on the other, the clearing house of the points themselves as they are developed in that circle. It is that which carries thought towards its destiny, which is accord with gnosis. It is not fitted to see anything other than the environs of connections which include the connection of thought with gnosis in their ultimate accord, as that too is a point to be cleared in the clearing house. And it is not fitted to see gnosis as such, much less to clear it. Nevertheless, it is called upon to critically examine the point at which thought links itself up with gnosis the latter prerogative, while never to be surrendered, is always liable to be mistaken as though it were a power able to pass verdict upon gnosis. However, it has been universally the case that Reason oversteps its boundaries and under the guise of speculation often claims to be the instrument, and sometimes the sole instrument, of discovery of Reality.

While it is true that there is in the Indian tradition no word which has either the depth or the force that Reason has in the Western tradition, there nevertheless are a number of different terms which serve as partial equivalents. [Quite the obverse is the case with *jñāna*, for which 'gnosis', though cognate philologically, is only a weak translation. Especially is it the case in Vedānta where *jñāna* has a depth and force not found in any Western term including 'gnosis'.] However, such words as there are in Sanskrit reveal both their legitimate role in which Vedānta sees Reason and its tendency, recognized even in antiquity, to overstep it. The words which Sanskrit supplies in this respect are *tarka, yukti, anumāna* and *nyāya* itself (and sometimes even *pramāṇa*, depending on the context).

To take the word *tarka* first, it comes from the root *tark*, meaning to conjecture, to guess, to suspect, to infer, to try to discover, to ascertain, to argue out (either in public debate or in one's own mind), to speculate, to recollect, to have in one's mind, to intend, etc. Some of the earliest instances of its use are in the *Kaṭha* and *Maitrī Upaniṣads*. In *Kaṭha* 1.2.9. its power is assessed negatively: "Not by *tarka* is this (i.e., knowledge of *Brahman*) attainable (*naiṣā tarkeṇa matirāpaneya*).[12] But in *Maitri* 6.18 and 20 it is listed as a member of the six-membered Yoga (*ṣaḍangayoga*) which carries thought towards its destiny, meaning accord with gnosis.

This reference in the *Maitrī Upaniṣad* leads us to the word *yukti*, for it has the same root *yuj*, to unite, to fit, from which *yoga* also comes. The *Māṇḍūkya Kārikā* of Gauḍapāda (an elaboration of the *Māṇḍūkya Upaniṣad*), at 4.25 clearly elevates *yukti* as a *darśana*, or seeing, and at 3.23 employs the commonly used compound, *yukti-yuktam* (united in *yukti*) in an uncommon sense.

Again, *anumāna*, usually rendered 'inference' comes from *anu* + *mā* (*mīyate*), meaning to measure after. In *Maitrī Upaniṣad* 6.1, we have the word used in verbal form: "The course of the inner self is measured after by the course of the outer self", (*bahir ātmakyā gatyāntarātmano anumīyate gatiḥ*); and "the course of the outer self is measured after by the course of the inner self", (*antarātmakyā gatyā bahir ātmano anumīyate gatiḥ*). The very form of the word shows that *anumāna* is not self-initiating or self-impelling Reason, for it merely measures after something that has presented itself. Although in Vedānta what it is a measuring after is gnosis which gives itself or appears by itself, it is always predicated, even in other philosophies, upon the things or events which on their own come into view, that is to say, became *pratyakṣa.*[13]

Finally, the word *nyāya*, from *ni* to lead, guide, + *aya*, has the sense of returning a thing into itself in the manner of a cyclic movement, and hence acquires the meaning of the *rational* process by which the *ārchē* of what presents itself in its appearing or *pratyakṣa* is manifested by securing the connections among points in the passage of thought through the circle. In this sense it originally meant exactly the same as *mīmāṁsā*. The *Āpastamba Dharma Sūtra*[14] has two passages where the words *nyāya* and *nyāyavit* are used simply to refer to Pūrva Mīmāmsā and not to the Nyāya system of Gotama. In Pāṇini's *Sūtra* we find the same usage.[15]

Śankara uses all these words in both their positive and negative meanings. [In fact the proper ordering of his usages of these and related words would itself be a significant task. That indeed is true of other words he uses too, not excluding *pratyakṣa, pramāṇa* and even *jñāna*.] Reason when positively understood is taken as functioning within the gnosis circle, as fitting or cementing the connections among points within it and as manifesting thought's link with the ground of gnosis itself. That is how Śankara is able to say that certain views are *nyāyyam* (what is properly *nyāya*) while certain other views are not *nyāyyam.*

CAUSE THE PRIMORDIAL QUESTION

The question of cause, which is primordial in the order of human inquiries spurred by the shock of wonder, is taken up in the second *sūtra* and the comments upon it. The *sūtra* says: "Whence the origin etc., of this," (*janmādyasya yataḥ*). Put in the form of a readable sentence it is rendered thus: "(It is that) whence (comes) the origin etc., of this (world)." Only origin is explicitly mentioned but with "et cetera" (*ādi*) it is understood to be stylistic abbreviation for origin, subsistence and destruction, (*sṛṣṭi/janma, sthiti* and *bhangam/saṁhāram*). The locus classicus of these is in the description of *Brahman* in *Taittirīya Upaniṣad* 3.1.1: "That from which these creatures are born, by which after birth they live, and which on departing they enter, that desire to know, that is *Brahman*", (*yato vāco imāni bhūtani jāyante, yena jātāni jīvante, yat prāyanti abhisaṁviśanti, tad vijijñāsasva, tad brahmeti*).

This *sūtra* speaks about the cause of the world (*jagat-kāraṇam*), in its formally expressible three-fold aspect of "whence?" "whereby?" and "wither?", with another aspect not formally expressible implicit, i.e., the question "wherefore?", or "why?" Man is a being fated to ask the question of cause, because he sees himself as an effect. What it is he and his world are effects of he knows not; nevertheless, it is impossible for him to find rest without knowing it. This is the anguish he carries with him from cradle to grave. The question of the cause of the world is primordial among those questions which result from the impingement of wonder, and is instantaneously formulated in our space-time oriented mind with which we do intellectual thinking as "whence?" "whereby?" and "whither?" The question of the cause of the world is primordial in that it is indissociable from our space-time oriented mind's earliest moments of its grasp of the world and thereby of consciousness, upon which it is grounded. It gave birth to metaphysics centering on the question "what?" [But behind all these there has always been lying, being laid by *Vāk* (*Logos*), the question "why?"]

Metaphysics is not the only expression of the causality mode of our thinking, for every branch of science is likewise an expression of it, depending upon the particularity of the phenomenon investigated. Every science, however, had been reared in a metaphysical cradle in that the particular phenomenon, whether the physical world or the *psychē*, was examined under an intractable whole, which is the province of metaphysics.

It is possible that, as Kant says, space and time are forms which the mind imposes upon the world. However, we do not know the history of this imposition, nor the point at which it originally occurred. We must assume that the origin of this imposition is conterminous with the genesis of phenomenal human consciousness itself, although it certainly is not a determinate moment. Therefore space and time are indissociable from the human mind which is the ground upon which we even inquire into the origin of space and time, and consequently whenever we raise the cause question *à la* the origin etc. of the world the space-time orientation of the question becomes inescapable. The *Brahma Sūtra* and the *Bhāṣya* recognize this predicament, and accordingly they use the space-time orientation of the cause question and with it the same orientation of the intellect itself as a ladder by which to climb beyond it, and to force the issue thereby of the real Cause (which is Ultimate Reality itself).

Vedānta sees something still anterior lying behind even the forms of space and time as self-constitutive, but elusive to all investigations. This it calls *avidyā*, which being beginningless is what makes even the moment of the first advent of the forms of time and space indeterminate and indeterminable. Nevertheless, gnosis is its termination (*nivṛtti*). In that sense *avidyā* is also writ large as cause of the world and of our phenomenal self-hood. [Buddhism too views *avidyā* as the cause of *duḥkha* (suffering), as the first link in the causal chain of twelve links. But it has no way of speaking of another Cause in the way Vedānta is privileged to do.]

The metaphysical inquiry into the cause of the world may be undertaken as a speculative activity, which would be natural for the human mind or as led by what *Vāk* itself says about Ultimate Reality, i.e., in accordance with gnosis. In the Indian world speculations of various kinds had their own vogue, of which the most prominent products were the Sāṁkhya theory of *Prakṛti* and Vaiśeṣika theory of atoms. On the contrary, Vedānta which starts from the ground of gnosis, endeavours to tame speculation with the help of what *Vāk* itself says.

Śankara approaches the question of the cause of the world from a point beyond anything that speculation can reach, i.e., from the standpoint of what *Vāk* itself says. As such he treats this question as a phenomenally conditioned way of asking about *Brahman*. To speak of *Brahman* as the Cause is, however, not so much an answer to a previously directed question as the revelation, *via Vāk's* speaking, of the questioning mode of *Brahman*-gnosis itself. And yet our previously directed question, which naturally and irrepressibly springs from the ground of human consciousness, far from having to be midsdirected, is led so as to enter the questioning mode of *Brahman*-gnosis. This is the essence of Vedāntic thinking on the subject of Cause. That is why Śankara remarks: "*Brahman*-gnosis brings about thinking on the meaning of what *Vāk* itself says", (*vākyārtha vicāraṇādhyavasāna-nirvṛttā hi brahmāvagatiḥ*).

In order to lead our thinking on the subject of Cause away from the speculative orientation and into the questioning mode of *Brahman*-gnosis Reason is to be regrasped and the power of connections among points in thoughts' passage to gnosis, including most of all the last point linking it with gnosis. There should be no hesitation in doing this, "because", to reproduce Śankara's own words, "the Upaniṣads themselves take the help of Reason" to this end, (*śrutyaiva ca sa sahāyatvena tarkasya abhyupaipatvāt*). This is why Śankara states further: "It is seen that a person's intelligence is helpful to him", (*puruṣa-buddhi sahāyyam ātmano darśayati*).

The affirmation of the questioning mode of Brahman-gnosis

The questioning mode of *Brahman*-gnosis has profound implications for the very speculative approach to cause. How strange that all speculation results in some metaphysics, with a conjectured First Cause passed on as the foundational reality from which the entire chain of being is the deduced! And yet this fact must not be used as an argument against the free exercise of the human intellect in search of the cause. How then is the irrespressible freedom of thought appropriated except by approaching it as gnosis' own self-extension? At the same time, the course of those who see thought, grounded as it is for them in mere knowledge of transcendental commands, as nothing more than an appendage to the rite, must also be resisted.

The possibility of a conflict between what *Vāk* itself speaks (i.e., Revelation) and Reason is abolished in Vedānta by removing the falsely speculative vocation from the latter. But this must not be so interpreted as to mean that Revelation is some kind of authority for man's moral and religious conduct, i.e., in the performance of the rite, which is the way that the other orthodox, *Vāk*-based system, i.e., Purva-Mīmāṁsā, understands it. On the contrary, for Vedānta, which puts itself forward as the true Mīmāṁsā, Revelation is nothing but the manifestation through *Vāk* of something that is already there on its own, namely gnosis, whose destiny is realization, i.e., playing out the reality of the Real (*satyasya satyam*). Hence Śankara writes:

> It is not the case that what *Vāk* speaks may be grasped in isolation as in the case of how we should conduct ourselves in the rite, but it is the case that what *Vāk* speaks (i.e., *Brahman*-gnosis) is to be taken in conjunction with the possibility of its realization. That (i.e., the latter) is the path of approach because *Brahman*-gnosis is what must culminate in actual experience and because as an object of inquiry it is an already existing entity. When we view Revelation merely as source of the knowledge of the rite there is no reference to experience (i.e., realization) and what *Vāk* speaks is presumed to be mere (external) authority, the essence of it all coming down to action by man which, however, for its motivation must depend solely upon man (i.e., his will).[16]

At this point the *Bhāṣya* only seems to turn tangentially, by way of a digression as it were, to Pūrva Mīmāṁsā, in order to criticize it in reference to the deep implication of the inquiry into cause, for thought. And yet far from being actually a tangential detour, this criticism of Pūrva-Mīmāṁsā also points simultaneously to the impotence of a speculative system like Sāṁkhya to adequately answer the former's thesis that the real goal of philosophy ought to be the appropriation of the Force/Power by way of the understanding of the Vedic injunctions and the performance of action in accordance with it. Pūrva-Mīmāṁsā is a system which wants to break with the causal mode of our thinking. It bases itself on a radical stance that the world may better be assumed as what has always been there, or, in its own words as "what has never been not thus" (*na kadācit anīdṛśam jagat*). This no doubt reflects a heroism which is part of its approach to philosophy as the epic of the rite. A mere speculative system like Sāṁkhya which does not know the secret of interiorizing thought as experience will indeed have no answer to such a mighty challenge. Therefore, the statement, "because *Brahman*-gnosis is what culminates in actual experience and as an object of inquiry is an already existing entity", is addressed to both these opposing systems.

For Vedānta inquiry into cause is *not intrinsically part of Brahman*-gnosis even in its questioning mode. Nevertheless, it belongs with *Brahman*-gnosis insofar as it is a legitimate inquiry which is launched from the ground of human consciousness and as such falls within the proper scope of *Vedānta-vākya-mīmāṁsā*. That is the reason why Śankara states that this *sūtra* concerning origin is not to be looked upon as though it were put forward "for the sake of producing a speculative essay (on cause)" (*janmādi-sūtram na anumānopanyāsārtham*) but "for the sake of showing forth what has been revealed by Vedāntic sentences" (*vedānta-vākya-pradarśanārtham*).

The place of the concrete myth in the inquiry into Cause

There is no room for a speculative essay on cause in Vedānta. Nevertheless, here is just emerging a gigantic essay, based on the exegesis of revelation, which is going to take up a large part of the *Bhāṣya*, as it comes to grips with, and transforms, all that is inescapable for the natural paths of thought. Following the lead of revelation through *Vāk*, it has already become clear that gnosis is the only ground from which we can authentically approach the question of Cause. But it is also the case that when the question is pursued concretely the Cause which is seen from the perspective of gnosis is seen as the all-knowing Cause. Gnosis becomes fused with the Cause, creating a mythic ground for further conduct of thought in this respect. The concrete "myth" of the omniscient Cause is alone adequate to carry forward the thought on the subject of Cause . That is the reason why Śankara concludes his comment on *sūtra* 2 with the observation that many passages of the Upaniṣads can be adduced, which refer to "the Cause that in its own essential (concrete) form is all-knowing" (*sarvajña-svarūpa-kāraṇa*).

The "myth" of the omniscient Cause makes thought concrete and thus enables it to move forward, and, therefore, the next *sūtra* 3 is introduced, which says: "On account of the origin of/in the Vedic texts", (*śāstra-yonitvāt*). This *sūtra* declares that the omniscience of *Brahman* is to be maintained on account of the fact that *Brahman* itself is the source of the Veda and that, obversely, the Veda is the source of our knowledge of that.

In the preceding *sūtra* speculative Reason as a means of arriving at the Cause even if that were to correspond to *Brahman* conceptually has been rejected because this conceptual modality, like all others, is deemed non-significant in that it merely reflects some people's preference and nothing more. Further, if we had freely arrived at the notion of *Brahman* as a conceptual product, then our concept-forming mechanism's self-reference would be held as the fundamental source of the knowledge and it will supplant *Vāk's* showing. In order to offset such a course *Vāk* has been summoned to reveal its own source in that it is none other than the disposition of *Brahman*, i.e., gnosis. This disposition eventuates in *Brahman's* self-communication through *Vāk*, and it is concrete insofar as it comprehends not only the secrets of our destiny, but also the secrets of our (and the world's) origin. Creation of the world is itself deemed an antecedent revelation and it is recalled concretely through what *Vāk* says. This procedure binds our destiny and our origin together under one single Force/Power (*śakti*), which makes out the Omniscient One (*sarvajña*) to be also the Omnipotent One (*sarva-śaktimān*), both concepts being constantly coupled together by Śankara. [We can easily notice that there lies here a message to Pūrva Mīmāṁsā also, which, by-passing the cause question, had concentrated on the Force/Power that takes us to our destiny, having rated that as the essence of *Vāk's* communication.]

The concreteness of the myth of the Omniscient One is essential for our being able to give a proper account of gnosis as the disposition of Ultimate Reality and consequently of our being able to think of Ultimate Reality in accordance with the way gnosis itself behaves, in that it offers itself as the non-shifting ground upon which we can anchor our thinking. Divine omniscience is such that in knowing all it communicates itself with all, wherein is to be located the very mystery of creation. Consequently, Cause and revelation become inseparable. Therefore, that which is the Cause is also the source of revelation, and accordingly it also becomes evident, obversely, that our knowledge of *Brahman* as the Cause in respect of both the creation of the world and of revelation is based on the *concrete* revelation itself (*Veda*) which presents to us the concrete myth of the Omniscient One.

Hence Śankara explains:

> *Brahman* is the source, i.e., the Cause of the Vedic texts, beginning with the *Ṛg Veda*, comprising many *vidyās*, which like a torch illuminate all things and are themselves the effulgence of the Omniscient. Now such texts as these, that is, of the nature of the *Ṛg Veda*, etc., with their many branches, wrapped in the quality of omniscience, do not occur apart from the Omniscient. It is well known in the world that the human authors from whom any science proceeds, for instance, Paṇini and others from

> whom Grammar arose, possess far more knowledge than the texts they have written. What, then, can be said about the Great Being, who is the source from whom, as if without effort, i.e. in the manner of sport and like a person's breathing out, are born the *Ṛg Veda*, etc. [cf. *Bṛhadāraṇyaka Upaniṣad*, 2.4.10.], which are the basis of all classes and modes of a phenomena that we diversely encounter in the gods, human beings and animals? And unsurpassed omniscience and omnipotence belong to that Great Being. Alternately (interpreted), it (the *sūtra*) would also mean that the Vedic texts beginning with the *Ṛg Veda*, as described above, are the source of our knowledge of *Brahman*. The contention is that the source of our knowledge of the source (Cause) of the world (i.e., *Brahman*) is the Veda.[17]

Maintaining the omniscience of *Brahman* on account of its being the source of what *Vāk* says through the Veda entails the understanding of the latter as itself the source of our encounter with that omniscience. This entailment is articulated as though it is an alternative interpretation of the *sūtra*. It is for this reason that Śankara focusses attention on it and makes the remark (cited at the end of our last quotation): "Alternately (interpreted), it (the *sūtra*) would also mean that the Vedic texts beginning with the *Ṛg Veda*, as described above, are the source of our knowledge of *Brahman*. The contention is that the source of our knowledge of the Source, of Cause (*Brahman*) is the Veda." The knowledge that *Brahman* is the Cause is the first item of *Vāk's* expression of gnosis as a directive revelation through its own speaking. It is, however, so not by virtue of what gnosis itself is but rather by virtue of the predication of all our natural thinking on the subject of cause (i.e., by way of the question "what?", "whence?", "whereby?" and "wither?" or "unto what?", with the implicit question "wherefore?", or "why"), that *Vāk* authenticates this knowledge and at the same time *Brahman*-gnosis authenticates *Vāk*. This fact is expressed by the double meaning of the *sūtra*.

Śankara vigorously argues in favour of *Brahman*-gnosis as the essence of what *Vāk* speaks through the Veda as against the means-ends structure of *karma*, or the rite. The proponents of *karma* naturally appeal to Jaimini, the founder of their tradition of Vedic interpretation, who had laid down: "As the Veda has *karma* as its purpose those parts of it which do not conduce to that purpose are meaningless" (*āmnāyasya krīyārthatvāt ānarthakyamatadarthānām*), *Mīmāṁsā Sūtra*, 1.2.1. Based on this dictum, the followers of Pūrva Mīmāṁsā must, as Śankara observes, conclude that "the Vedānta passages (which speak in the language of *Brahman*-gnosis) are devoid of meaning", (*ato vedāntānam ānarthakyam*). At best they would deem such passages as "merely supplementary to *karma* injunctions and prescribe the meditative act as just another kind of rite", (*krīyā-vidhiśesatvam-upāsanādi-krīyāntara-vidhānārthatvam*).

Śankara continues to speak of *Brahman* as the Cause but in such a way that the Cause question is itself taken into gnosis. But it is necessary to recall that Śankara has been, from the commencement of the *Bhāsya*, actually addressing two conflicting positions – represented by Sāṁkhya and Pūrva-Mīmāṁsā. As for the latter of these two, Vedānta is united with it in a position based on the common ground of *Vāk's* speaking. As for the former, the opposition of Vedānta to it is of a different character, the common ground being that which characterizes all authentic rise of thought from the ground of consciousness, namely, the pressing interest in the problem of Cause. [It is easy to see, as we proceed through the text of the *Bhāṣya*, that other systems like Vaiśeṣika atomism and some schools of Buddhism are also brought in for examination as great variants of the position paradigmatically represented by Sāṁkhya.]

Now, moving to *sūtras* 3 and 4 Śankara is rather addressing Pūrva-Mīmāṁsā. We notice a movement from the common ground of all authentic natural thought, i.e., that wherefrom the burning interest in the problem of Cause is pursued, to the standpoint of revelation, i.e., the speaking of *Vāk*, which is shared by Vedānta and Pūrva-Mīmāṁsā alike. Nevertheless, Pūrva-Mīmāṁsā and Vedānta also stand separated as it were by a wide chasm. Hence it is that Śankara inveighs against the followers of Pūrva Mīmāṁsā and proposes the need for a truer grasp of what *Vāk* speaks as it has to do with the Cause (*Brahman*). The crucial issue in understanding the text is the "sequential connections", which is taken up next.

Sequential connections (samanvaya)

The *Sūtra* 4 says: "But such it is (i.e., as stated about the Cause) on account of the sequential connections (of revealing statements of the Veda)", (*tat tu samanvayāt*). It serves to show once again that *Brahman* is the Source of the world and of the Veda, and also that for this knowledge has, phenomenally speaking, the Veda alone as its source. Hence Śankara elaborates it (restating the whole thesis around the notion of Force/Power for the benefit of Pūrva Mīmāṁsā, for which it is primary though in a different sense, as we have shown before):

> That the Omnipotent Cause of the origin, subsistence and dissolution of the world is *Brahman* is known from what *Vāk* speaks through the Upaniṣads. How is it so? Because that is the way of sequential connections. That follows from the purport of all Upaniṣadic statements insofar as their meaning is discerned. Accordingly, (it is said): "In the beginning, dear one, this was Being itself, one only without a second"; "The *Ātman* was this in the beginning, one only"; "That alone is this *Brahman*, without an earlier, without a later, without an inside, without an outside"; "This *Ātman* is *Brahman*, who perceives all"; "This is the immortal *Brahman* itself, in front"; and so on. It is not fitting to suppose any other meaning for passages like these inasmuch as it is determined that their sequential connections concern the essential nature of *Brahman.*[18]

Sequential connections and thought

As the *Bhāṣya* progresses through the stations set up by the first four *sūtras* we notice a clearer manifestation of the way thought is enabled to conduct itself in accordance with the way gnosis itself behaves. This is the essence of the *samanvaya*, or sequential connections, which are being steadily and systematically deployed. The question of Cause, which is the one that natural thought primordially grapples with, has now entered a new phase, thanks to the Upaniṣadic texts that speak of it. At this point we must recall our earlier observation: "In order to lead our thinking on the subject of Cause away from speculative orientation and into the questioning mode of *Brahman*-gnosis Reason is to be re-grasped as the power of connections among points in thought's passage to gnosis, including most of all the last one linking it with gnosis." Now we are able to see that this prospect is open to thought only because of *Vāk*, so that thought can ride on its back, so to say, and realize the connections in exactly the way in which *Vāk* manifests the connections in the things it speaks through the Vedic texts. As a result, thought's upward motion and gnosis's "downward" extension are seen to coalesce. [And further, thanks to this fact, thought is not thwarted by the barriers of unanswerable questions it is fated to ask or by the abyss of not-knowing it must encounter. And it is never pushed aside into some realm of Practical Reason so as to make do with what is less than the Absolute. By the grace of *Vāk*, thought is enabled to break through the barriers such as the antinomies of Reason it constantly erects for itself in its quest for Ultimate Reality.]

Because *Vāk* provides the connections, thought can find its passageway to its own natural base, namely, consciousness, carrying gnosis with it. That is how the identity of consciousness and gnosis, so fundamental to Vedānta, is also realized. That is how the supreme utterance of *Vāk*, namely, "That thou art", serves as the perfect expression of the gnosis circle which thought is enabled to follow. In this manner the last link of thought, i.e., that which connects it to gnosis, is manifested also as its first link, i.e., that which connects it to consciousness. Without this, the very origin of thought in consciousness, even when approached in terms of the shock of wonder, must remain ever hidden and impervious to the most penetrating analysis, whether psychological, linguistic or ontological. But in terms of the gnosis circle as guided by the connections which *Vāk* provides we are enabled to get behind everything and begin our journey of thought from the absolute ground.

It is the belief of Vedānta that the question of Cause followed up to the end, on the basis of the speaking of *Vāk*, holds out the hope for thought's entry into the gnosis circle, of which the highest expression is the great statement of the Upaniṣad, "That thou art". But it is noticed that *Vāk* has been used by Pūrva Mīmāṁsā in a way that deflects thought from entering into that circle, and Pūrva Mīmāṁsā hence proposes the epic of the rite in its place as the authentic subject-matter of philosophy. In the philosophy of the rite the only "cause" worth caring about is the Force/Power dependent on the rite, as it will, it is believed, enable man to reach his destiny. Hence in refutation of this Śankara writes:

> What *Vāk* speaks is not to the end of dealing with the essential character of (man's) being a rite performer. The Upaniṣadic statements such as "then by what should one see and by whom" reject the causality of *karma* and its fruits. Nor can *Brahman*, despite the fact that in essential nature it is absolutely real, be an object encountered by the eye because the identity of *Brahman* with one's own self cannot be known except by virtue of *Vāk's* saying "That thou art". (The opponent, however, argues that) an instruction which does not command us either to give up something or to take on something (as a positive act) is pointless. (But) the fact that (such is not the case) is not a fault, because the highest human end to be obtained (or destiny to be realized) is only the knowledge of the oneness of

> *Brahman* with our own self, and it has nothing to do with either discarding or accepting something, and yet it expells all sorrow. Even though there is discussion of deities (i.e., dynamic principles) and of meditation pertaining to them in the course of what *Vāk* itself speaks, there is no contradiction (of our position). Even in the face of such discussion *Brahman* does not become a supplementary subject-matter (or epiphenomenon) of *karma*-injunctions. For in view of the fact that there is nothing either to discard or to accept in what is just unity, all notions of duality such as *karma*, the causal agent etc., are done away with.[19]

Śankara's extended essay on Cause devotes itself largely to showing (*vis-à-vis* Sāṁkhya) that *Brahman* is the Cause, on the one hand, and, on the other, to refuting the rite – oriented approach to philosophy (*vis-à-vis* Pūrva Mīmāṁsā). What is said about all other systems can be placed as appendices to this twin enterprise.

In showing that *Brahman* is the Cause, our ordinary, human investigations concerning the mystery of ours and the world's existence, (hovering around the question "why?", or "wherefore?") are led not so much to where an answer could be had in accordance with the way we ask it as to a point from which a perfect existence in thought is made possible without needing any other concrete answer than that *Brahman* is the Cause. That point is gnosis. Apart from it, thinking would be merely like being stretched on the anvil of the unknown to receive the relentless hammer-blows of the question "why?". Under gnosis thought has no greater vocation, no greater end to serve than to lead everything that comes along, every question that arises, to that point, hence following the circle of gnosis. [And no doubt, that which responds to the notion of Cause is merely the entrance door to *Brahman*, which in reality transcends all relations of cause and effect.]

However, goal-seeking man, paradigmatically represented by the utilitarian religious man, best typified and perhaps summed up by Pūrva Mīmāṁsā, is under perennial temptation to turn away from what is beyond our ken to know, and hence to follow some humanistic, positive path which orients thought to the problem of *how* we can reach our destiny or fulfill ourselves. However, for Pūrva Mīmāṁsā the humanism to be adopted is not ordinary or secular but transcendental inasmuch as both the vision of human destiny and the knowledge-how come from *Vāk*. [The belief in the absoluteness of *Vāk* continues to be the reason for Pūrva-Mīmāṁsā's polarity-in-kinship type of relation with Vedānta.] But

Śankara points out that such a project, transcendental though it be, is in fact based on a mere humanistic techné, while the Vedāntic project of *Brahma-vidyā* is not based on any humanistic techné, (*na puruṣa-vyāpāra tantrā brahma-vidyā*). On the contrary, he adds, "*Brahma-vidyā* is a science of the thing itself inasmuch as (the certainty of) its knowledge is not unlike what results in the encounter with any object by virtue of its own presence", (*pratyakṣādi-viṣaya-vastu-jñānatvāt vastu-tantraiva*). [Now, one may detect an apparent contradiction between this last statement and the one included in the previous quotation to the effect: "Nor can *Brahman*, despite the fact that in essential nature it is absolutely real, be an object encountered by the eye, because the identity of *Brahman* with our self cannot be known except by virtue of *Vāk's* saying 'That thou art'." However, there is no contradiction because the non-objectivity of *Brahman* still holds and what is now affirmed is the certainty with which we can know the thing itself, which is not unlike, or less than, that of our knowledge of the things that present themselves to the eye. And let it not be forgotten that what is said by *Vāk* (i.e., *śruti*) is always rated a higher kind of *pratyakṣa*, or presence before the eye.] Hence it is concluded: "It is not possible to suppose by any reasoning whatsoever that Being, *Brahman*, that is to say, the knowledge of *Brahman*, follows as a consequence of something (some rite) that is *to be* accomplished, (*evam bhūtasya brahmaṇastajjñānasya vā na kayācid yuktyā kāryānupraveśa kalpāyitum*). In conclusion, the reality of *Brahman* is not to be treated as an epiphenomenon or something that is generalised as a notion, mounted as it were on the transcendental, humanistic project which constitutes the epic of the rite. [A subtle and hardly noticeable opposition of *Brahman*-gnosis (*tat-jñāna*) with *Brahman* as Being (*evam bhūta*) occurs here. In some places *Brahman* and *Brahman*-gnosis are used as synonyms, and this has peculiar relevance in light of the Pūrva-Mīmāṁsā explanation of them as epiphenomenon of the rite.]

Summary of the comments on the first four sūtras

Śankara's comments on the first four *sūtras* are the seminal expressions of the Vedānta system, which he will work out in detail in the subsequent pages of the *Bhāṣya*. They served as the foundation on which his own immediate commentators and their commentators developed their own accounts of the system.[20] This is a witness to the self-sufficiency of this seminal statement.

These comments constitute the essential thesis of that which is elaborated as a monumental essay on Cause. And the examination of Cause, let us repeat, is simply an entrance door to the problem of Ultimate Reality and it itself, in the form in which it formally appears, is not the real subject-matter to be thought. It is only a surrogate that *stands in* for Ultimate Reality. It represents our way of approaching *Brahman* on account of the history of our thinking, grounded as it is in our phenomenal consciousness and attended by everything that that fact entails.

The exposition of *Brahman* as the Cause, given principally in terms of criticism of Sāṁkhyan speculation and Pūrva-Mīmāṁsā exegesis of *śruti* simply lays down what it is that we should understand as Ultimate Reality. This two-pronged criticism tells us: (a) that we must observe circumspection in approaching Ultimate Reality, which requires us to use texts that understand themselves as uniquely privileged channels of approach, and (b) that the exegesis of these texts must have as their proper goal not the understanding of texts themselves but the understanding of Ultimate Reality. [Now, this latter is a unique feature of Vedāntic hermeneutics, which is the reason why hermeneutics becomes a genuine tool of philosophy, and Śankara carries it out in a thorough-going and consistent manner.] These two serve as the fundamental paths for the investigation of Cause, and for the development of the gnosis circle.

THE UNFOLDING OF THE SYSTEM IN THE MAIN BODY OF THE *BHĀṢYA*

Our dialogue with the *Bhāṣya* is being conducted with the aim of discovering the unique way in which philosophical thought is grounded in gnosis. We shall continue to adhere to that aim as we approach the main body of the *Bhāṣya*, beginning at the 5th *sūtra* of Chapter I, from which point on the system unfolds itself in truly epic proportions. All important schools of India, both Vedic and non-Vedic, and their central doctrines are comprehended in the vast and highly complex debate that ensues from this. All the traditional sciences pertaining to language, etymology, interpretation and speculation, not to speak of the boundless resources of

Vedas, Epics and Purāṇas, are brought into play in this monumental task. However, as we are not undertaking a comprehensive study of this great text as a whole, and as our approach is determined only by the underlying purpose of our dialogue, which is the discovery of the relation between gnosis and philosophical thought, it would be imprudent for us to so broaden our scope as to cover the entire range of the debate. The individual items of this debate are covered by many a scholastic treatise in the post-Śankara literature. Our task rather is to raise afresh something that has not received adequate attention in the past and to do so in such a way as to bring it into a philosophical purview as we have set out to do from the beginning.

The great hermeneutical essay on Cause continues through the unfolding system of the *Bhāṣya*. [And Cause, as we have said "stands in" for Ultimate Reality.] Gnosis is what has directly to do with Ultimate Reality, and thought is what has its ground in gnosis and returns to it by a circular path. The nature of the gnosis circle has already been shown by way of the comments on the first four *sūtras*, and it is now begun to be drawn on a much larger scale using debate with the views of other schools as a means of expression. Now, the views of these other schools, no doubt, offer themselves concretely inasmuch as they belong to actual schools. However, they are also speculative possibilities *per se*. Thus Śankara remarks as he steps forward to draw the gnosis circle on the larger scale of a fully unfloded sytem, seṃinally expressed already *via* the principle of sequential connections:

> We have already stated how the Upaniṣadic passages, which are useful for the knowledge of *Brahman*, and of which the sequential connections have to do with knowing *Brahman* in one's own self, with no relation whatsoever to the rite, would actually lead to that gnosis. We have also stated how *Brahman* is omniscient and omnipotent and is the Cause of the origin, preservation and dissolution of the world. The followers of Sāṃkhya as well as others, for whom the cause is some other posited being and insofar forth are to be known by other means, interpret the passages of the Upaniṣads (too) as confirmation of their supposed causes.[21]

Accordingly, in drawing the circle of gnosis on a larger scale, the ways in which we would naturally think when we investigate Ultimate Reality are recounted from the beginning onward and are integrated with thought that has its ground in gnosis. [Vedānta expresses itself as much by exegeting what *Vāk* itself says as by criticizing other schools in respect of their quest for Ultimate Reality, for which, as we have seen, the notion of Cause always stands in. In the history of Indian philosophy Sāṁkhya reigned as the paramount classical school devoted to the investigation of Cause which may very well be considered to have been its unique vocation. It is this fact that Śankara acknowledges when he describes it as the principal stalwart (*pradhāna malla*), by immobilizing whom, by virtue of the Nyāya maxim of *atideśa* (extension of scope), lesser stalwarts like the Vaiśeṣika atomism are also automatically disarmed.[22] Vedānta as philosophy has to be understood in two ways: firstly, as the exegetical presentation of what *Vāk* itself says, and secondly, as a series of systematically developed *vādas*, or logically laid positions. The latter are always presented in relation to some other position or cluster of positions. That is how such nomenclatures as *brahma-vāda* (*vāda* pertaining to *Brahman*), *advaita-vāda* (*vāda* of non-dualism), *māyā-vāda, avidyā-vāda*, etc., are employed. All of them are rebuttals of some existing *vādas*, which constitute the bulk of both Indian metaphysics and dialectics. Take away these interlocuting *vādas* and there will be no more reason to express Vedānta in any other terms than the exegesis of the texts which directly speak of *Brahman*. In other words only *Vāk* would remain. But then, it is also to be remembered that discourse is the body in which philosophy dwells among human beings and, as such, thought is fated to engage in *vādas*, even down to the level of disputations, which happens to be the lowest end of the meaning scale of that word. The philosophy of Vedānta uses Sāṁkhya and other systems as opponents, through debating with whom it spells itself out systematically.]

Being and Thinking

In drawing the gnosis circle on a large scale the first item considered is the relation between being and thinking, which is taken up in the group of *sūtras* (1.5.11), called *īkṣaty adhikaraṇam*, or, section on thinking. These *sūtras* furnish the key to refuting the Sāṁkhyan view that the ultimate material principle called *Pradhāna*, regarded as co-eternal with, and independent of, the other ultimate principle *Puruṣa* (Spirit), is the Cause of the world. Thus *sūtra* no. 5 says "On account of the word 'thinking', (*pradhāna*) is not (the Cause); it is not mentioned in the Vedic texts", (*īkṣater na aśabdam*). Commenting on this, Śankara observes:

In Vedānta it is not possible to find the Cause of the world in *Pradhāna*, as Sāṁkhya contends. Indeed it (i.e., *Pradhāna*) has no basis in the Veda. How so? Because of the word 'thinking'; because of our hearing (in the Veda) of 'bethinking'. That is how we hear the Upaniṣad when it tells us: "Being alone, dear one, was this in the beginning, one only without a second", (*Chāndogya* 6.2.1). And it further says: "That one bethought to itself 'I shall make myself into many' and it created resplendent heat, etc.", (*Chāndogya* 6.2.3).[23]

The key word is *īkṣati*, which comes from the root *īkṣ*, to see, to behold, to bethink to oneself, to muse, to contemplate, etc. In *Chāndogya* 6.2.3 and *Aitareya* 1.1.1, Being is said to have 'bethought to itself' (*aikṣata*). [In *Praśna* 6.3, the expression is *īkṣām cakre*, with the same meaning.] The Upaniṣads tell us, and the *sūtra* repeats, that *īkṣa* is the causal relation within which Being holds everything to itself. And the fact that everything is so held becomes also, simultaneously, the holding on the part of all that is held. That which separates the holding and being held is constantly under assault, and that marks the character of gnosis, which is such that thought comes to its own when it recovers its ground in gnosis.

Here we learn something about thought in its essential character of being the access to Ultimate Reality which it is in its philosophical vocation. In this vocation, thought's quest for Ultimate Reality is also a quest for its own ground, to which it is simultaneously beckoned. Only by knowing its own ground can thought know itself, and thereby it also knows that it is more than what it appears to itself, that it sees itself only superficially.

However, the prospect of this critical self-knowledge resides not in what it can construct for itself unaidedly but in what comes outside itself, that is to say, through the speaking of *Vāk* about its origin. And *Vāk* says that Ultimate Reality through its essential disposition, i.e., gnosis, (primordially) put forth thought, wherein the reverse movement which we know as thought is reposed. This *sūtra* and the others in the *īkṣati* section while expressed in the form of an account of the genesis of the world is also an account of the origin and destiny of thought, for every statement about *Brahman* knowing itself the real purport thereof is to generate knowledge on the part of human beings. And that is done in the most authentic way of *Vāk's* speaking, i.e., via the myth of the Omniscient Creator. That is the reason why Śankara argues that the word *īkṣate* is used "in a way paralleling the (Pūrva Mīmāṁsā) use of the word *yajate* (he, she, or it sacrifices), and that, accordingly, its meaning, far from being derived from its root, is to be sought in (its capacity to *produce*) the object", (*īkṣater api ca dhātvartha nirdeśo'bhipretaḥ yajateritivat, na dhātunirdeśaḥ*). Thought, therefore, is a productive agent and is similar to sacrifice in its utterly heroic, ontological function. But there are two important differences. Firstly, for *īkṣate*, in view of the fact that the account of the genesis of the world is simultaneously an account of the origin and destiny of thought, its epistemological meaning is yielded only in its reverse application such as this statement expresses. In other words, what it really intends to say something about is man's thought insofar as it seeks Ultimate Reality. Secondly, inasmuch as what it "produces" is not something that has not been there but what is already there pre-eminently (i.e., as gnosis) its productivity is infinitely greater and therefore, infinitely more heroic.

Thought at its root is gnosis itself. Only in a secondary way of talking can we even speak of gnosis having an object which it illuminates or of itself as an object that is sought. That is why Śankara compares our speaking of thought in reference to Ultimate Reality (or in our own language as the extension of its disposition, i.e., gnosis) to our speaking of the Sun's shining even though there is no object for that activity.[24]

Sāṁkhya, which is the classical philosophy of Cause outside the Upaniṣads, is an account of the origin of the world. And it is forced to begin the account with a doctrine of the Being whose thought is the Cause (origin) of the world. In this enterprise it found it necessary to appropriate the Upaniṣadic myth of the Omniscient Cause, the originating thinker, which is Being itself. Although not taken in essential Upaniṣadic sense, Sāṁkhya borrows this myth from the Upaniṣads because it serves Sāṁkhya's purpose. And, no doubt, the myth could only come by virtue of what *Vāk* itself has spoken. It could not be invented. And once it is accepted in any form and with whatever definition, it would help one to penetrate the haze that surrounds the problem of origin – which, no doubt, is surrounded by haze. However, seeking its own definition, Sāṁkhya substituted *Pradhāna* in the place of *Brahman* as the Being that is to be understood as the originating thinker.

Śankara recounts the Sāṁkhyan appropriation of the myth of the Omniscient One in a very telling manner. Sāṁkhya, whose dualism has separated conscious Spirit (*puruṣa*) and non-conscious Matter (*Prakṛti*, or *Pradhāna*), so radically that the former plays no part at all in the genesis of the world and of thought (being completely devoid of any such ability) has to seek to ground the myth of the Omniscient Creator in *sattva* (meaning goodness, buoyancy, transparency to light and finally, capacity to reflexively appropriate consciousness), which is one of the three *guṇas* (qualitative strands) that constitute the latter. Accordingly, Sāṁkhya, Śankara tells us, considers *Pradhāna* itself to be that which functions as the Omniscient Being. This Śankara argues is not possible. And so he writes: "As it is devoid of a witnessing consciousness, the function of *sattva* cannot be expressed by the verb 'to know'. And non-conscious *Pradhāna* is not (by definition) a witness. Hence *Pradhāna* cannot be considered omniscient", (*asākṣika sattva vṛttiḥ jānāti na abhīdhiyate. na ca acetanasya pradhānasya sākṣitvam asti. tasmāt anupapannam pradhānasya sarvajñatvam*). In conclusion, "only *Brahman* is properly the supreme omniscient Cause of the world", (*sarvajñam mukhyam brahma jagataḥ kāraṇam iti yuktam*).

Since, however, the crux of the matter is how we understand the word 'to think' (and with it the word 'to know') ascribed to Being, Sāṁkhya has a logically consistent clue to offer. It says that the word *īkṣati*, to think, must be taken as figurative (*gauṇa*), or as just imprecise common usage (*aupacārika*), along with other such usages which we cannot do without. Hence as Śankara points out, for Sāṁkhya, the statement "Being thought" is of a piece with other well-known figurative expressions like "the sea is angry". Sāṁkhya's appropriation of the myth of the Omniscient Creator, strange as it may seem, is logically accountable on the basis of the figurative interpretation of the word 'to think'. The myth itself, however, serviceable as a place to put the anchor in developing an explanation of the origin of the world, is in fact for Sāṁkhya something to be approached as no more than a useful metaphor. And how frequently both metaphysical and scientific theories are anchored, in the last analysis, on assumptions of a metaphorical character. For instance, how naively we speak so often of "Nature's own design", "History's own purpose" and so on! No doubt, neither our daily life nor our thinking, not to speak of theoretical speculation, will be possible without the unique privilege that metaphor confers, the highest of which is the sustention of myths which serve as places to put the anchors necessary for theoretical explanations. This indeed is to be granted. However, Sāṁkhya's appropriation of the myth of the Omniscient Creator goes beyond that. It is taken over from the Upaniṣads. But although in the Upaniṣads the myth of the Omniscient Creator is intentionally concrete, Sāṁkhya has made it metaphorical through its interpretation. Now, the essential distinction between the Vedāntic and Sāmkhyan interpretations of the statement, "Being thought", (and their approaches to the myth of the Omniscient Creator) is one between the concrete and the metaphorical. [And we say 'concrete', rather than 'literal' which is a category that has no place at all in the understanding of Vedic texts, and consequently in its philosophy.]

The myth of the All-knowing one is held as indispensable for thought about origin. It has its basis in Ultimate Reality itself as made known in the speaking of *Vāk*. Could it also be constructed either from our speculation which relies on our habitual metaphorical language as well as from a metaphorical exegesis of what *Vāk* itself has spoken? Sāṁkhya, however, produces a new justification for the metaphorical exegesis of the Upaniṣadic statement, "Being thought", for it occurs in a context where we also read that the products of that thinking, viz., resplendent heat (*tejas*), water (*āpaḥ*) and food (*anna*), also thought. The latter could admittedly only have a figurative meaning, for resplendant heat, etc., as is well-known, cannot think. The answer is in the next *sūtra* (no. 6): "(*Vāk's* saying that Being thought) is not metaphorical because of the word *ātman*", (*gauṇaścet na ātmaśabdāt*).

In the comment on this *sūtra*, Śankara makes a distinction between primary sense (*mukhyārtha*) and figurative sense (*gauṇārtha*), which corresponds exactly to "concrete intention" and "metaphorical intention" respectively. He shows that the statement of the Upaniṣads, "It (Being) thought", is a concrete expression of the concrete myth of the Omniscient Creator (which is *Brahman* itself) because the same passage says that it (Being) as the *jīva-ātman* primordially entered its first creations, viz., resplendent heat, water and food. The identity between Being and self (*ātman*) is expressed subsequently more clearly in the famous passage, "That is Being, That is the *ātman*, That thou art, O Śvetaketu", (*Chāndogya* 6.9.1-6.16.3, stated in a refrain).

The key is furnished by the word *ātman*, the self, which may more properly, in this context, be taken as self-hood, or subjectivity, as that is the essential factor which makes it possible to attribute thought to Being. [The double reference of the word *ātman*, which we have become acquainted with in the Upaniṣads, i.e., as pertaining the human beings and to *Brahman*, needs to be recalled here. In this sense, subjectivity comprehends both the human self and *Brahman*, the Ultimate *Ātman*.] If we should continue to speak of thinking as an "activity" of Being and should do so without heeding to subjectivity, our speaking should remain metaphorical. But *Vāk* speaks concretely and not figuratively when it says, "Being thought".

Sāṁkhya is the paramount instance of a philosophy which fails to grasp subjectivity. But philosophy can be saved from sinking deeper into the quick-sand of metaphorical speaking and thinking, that is insofar as they have to do with Ultimate Reality, only by grasping the subjectivity of the Being that thinks, which, however, only *Vāk* can bring home to us. [Nevertheless, there is a legitimate order of metaphorical speaking and thinking and that belongs to everyday life, on the one hand, and to the realm of the rite, on the other. But this should not be mistaken for the domain of the quest for Ultimate Reality.]

The more we think and the more we speak, the more is unfolded, *provided* the ground of our thought is gnosis and the ground of our speaking is *Vāk*. The word *vikṣepa*, used in the sense of unfoldment, or opening up, stands as much for the world's becoming as for philosophy's expansion into a structure. In that way the expanded essay on Cause is a running commentary on the unfoldment of the world of variety from the Being that bethought to itself. In any other way philosophy will only be a series of speculative structures governed in the last resort by metaphors which do not know that they are metaphors and what they are metaphors of. In order to be a real, running commentary such as indicated and not a series of disparate, speculative structures, it has to hold fast to its ground. That is what Śankara shows with unrelenting rigour.

Now, to run with the unfolding world in its course, to be a true commentary, is what philosophy does as its vocation of dwelling among human beings, that is, through discourse. It has another and deeper vocation, expressed by the word *mokṣa* or freedom. In this word *mokṣa*, a new way of revealing the ontological depth of subjectivity is introduced. We observed above that self-hood is subjectivity and that it is the essential factor which makes it possible to attribute thought to Being. Now, subjectivity which has already been pre-figured by the notion of witness (*sākṣī*), and reinforced further by showing that it is the self-hood of Being as Thinker, to which an entity like *Pradhāna*, devoid of subjectivity, cannot lay claim, is now invited to show its ultimate sign, leaving no room for any more quibbling about it. That sign is decisive. Accordingly, subjectivity is now to be understood as that which is essentially oriented towards *mokṣa*. Hence the next *sūtra* (no. 7) says: "On account of there being an instruction unto *mokṣa* (in what *Vāk* has spoken) for one who resolutely observes it", (*tanniṣṭasya mokṣopadeśāt*).

What is resolutely observed is gnosis, which is the essential disposition of Being (i.e., *Brahman*) itself, expressed by *Vāk* in the words, "it bethought to itself". Our resolute observance (*niṣṭhā*) is thought, which is our responsiveness in like form to the disposition of *Brahman*. And *Vāk* performs two functions, i.e., that of unconcealing gnosis and of directing our thought to respond in like form, or, in other words, in accordance with it. By virtue of *Vāk's* showing the path, thought carries in itself *the ultimate sign of subjectivity*, i.e., *mokṣa*, as the "goal" to which it is directed. This signifies no ordinary existential orientation of thought, for the impulsion to *mokṣa* (*mumukṣatva*) is identical with the desire to know Brahman (*Brahmanjijñāsā*). This is fundamental to Vedānta's ontology of human existence and it is a realistic ontology, where the subject of freedom, i.e., the self, is real and concrete because *mokṣa* is real and concrete. On the contrary, Sāṁkhya, which also understands itself as a serious philosophy of freedom, is actually too afflicted by an inability to provide an authentic view of freedom because it has no authentic theory of the subject of freedom. Consequently, it is forced to push its figurative interpretation further and further, right up to the concept of freedom itself, resulting in a metaphorical view of freedom, and the consequence, from the Vedāntic point of view, can only be incalculable spiritual detriment. Hence Śankara writes:

> If the sacred text, which is the source of perfect spiritual knowledge, were to instruct a person, who, though still ignorant, nonetheless, desires freedom (i.e., *mokṣa*) to the effect that the non-conscious (i.e., *Pradhāna*), known to be not-self, is in fact self (i.e., the subject of freedom), that person would, in a way, reminiscent of the (proverbial) blind man catching hold of the bull's tail, (instead of taking the bull by the horn, that is), be thwarted in his effort to realize the goal of human existence and be thrown into meaninglessness.[25]

The expression we have translated as "the goal of human existence" in a conventional manner is *puruṣārtha*, which may be quite correctly rendered "the meaning of human existence". The opposite of it is "meaningless" (*anartha*) as mentioned in the same statement. It is quite clear that the *puruṣārtha* that is intended here is *mokṣa* and *mokṣa* alone, the ultimate goal, or meaning, of human exixtence. Now, if, as we have said above, subjectivity is that which is oriented towards *mokṣa*, it has to be defined by the same orientation. That means the definition has to be derived from the concrete actuality of *mokṣa*, which is the goal towards which the subject, *puruṣa*, is oriented and the criterion by which its meaning is defined. In this present context it is appropriate to understand *puruṣa* as "subject". The unique nature of the *puruṣa* derived solely from the concrete actuality of *mokṣa*, concerning which *Vāk* gives instruction, is what should be referred to by the word "subjectivity" (for which, however, the text itself gives no equivalent, which is not surprising). From the Vedāntic standpoint, Sāṁkhya, or any such philosophy, which approaches freedom in any other way and without the benefit of the directing instruction of *Vāk* will forever miss subjectivty and be thrown into meaninglessness. [It is necessary at this point to clarify that the Sāṁkhyan use of the word *Puruṣa*, according to its dualistic ontology, is not at all the same as *puruṣa* in the sense of subject or, more precisely, subject-of-freedom, in the way it is used here. This distinction we mark by writing the former with a capital 'P' and the latter with a small 'p'.]

Now, we have already been ushered into the realm of subjectivity. We have just been shown that *the subject is the being that is oriented towards its own freedom* insofar as subjectivity cannot be attributed to a being like *pradhāna*, which is described as working for another being's freedom. Therefore, subjectivity construed in this way is the rock against which the entire understanding of the project of liberation as metaphorical must be dashed to pieces. Existentially, subjectivity is the unconditional disposition towards *mokṣa* on the part of the subject, which means that, in other words, we must describe subjectivty as *being-unto-freedom*. Furthermore, *such a disposition on the part of the subject of freedom is itself possible only in the amplitude of Ultimate Reality's own disposition which we call gnosis*. And it is revealed as a direction-giving instruction by *Vāk*, i.e. *moksopadeśa*.

In the foregoing three *sūtras* of the *īkṣati* section, we have been led from Being and its thinking, through the self, to freedom, all the way learning to eschew the metaphorical in favour of the concrete. At length we have gained a new understanding of subjectivity, that is, as being-unto-freedom. Let that truth be stated directly and then obversely in the following way: the subject is the being that is oriented to its own freedom; only that which is oriented towards its own freedom can be considered being.

In the light of this we can understand why Śankara refutes the strange theory of freedom that Sāṁkhya propounds, which involves a complete dissociation between the subject of freedom and the agent of freedom. For Sāṁkhya the subject of freedom is *Puruṣa*, the spirit which remains in splendid isolation from all activities of *Prakṛti*, or *Pradhāna*, including the very creation of the conditions which call for the project of liberation. The *Puruṣa* of Sāṁkhya remains a mere spectator, although in some strange way it is the subject of freedom as well as the beneficiary in *Pradhāna's* struggle for freedom.[26]

If the subject and the agent were utterly distinct and eternally different the whole project of liberation would become artificial, conducted as it is on the basis of an artifice. An agent of freedom which is not the subject and is not even remotely a beneficiary of freedom can only be an artifice. Clearly, what is true of the project of liberation must apply to thought as well, which too becomes artificial. When an artifice is set up in order to account for the project of liberation and for thought, the authenticity of both is at stake.

For Vedānta the subject of the project and the agent are one and the same, i.e., the self, more aptly expressed by the adoption of the word *puruṣa*. If it is otherwise, as held by Sāṁkhya, the agent would be an artifice and as such it is to be eventually discarded. That is the reason for the next *sūtra* (no. 8): "*Vāk* does not say (anything) about (the agent) having to be discarded", (*heyatva avacanāt ca*)".

Śankara in his comment on this employs the metaphor of the invisible *Arundhatī* star, raising the question whether an artifice can be the focus of freedom-striving through gnosis:

> As a person points to the *Arundhatī* star by pointing to another first making him believe that some other celestial body in its proximity is *Arundhatī*, although it is not, and while pointing so also instructs him that he should later reject it in favour of the real *Arundhatī*, so it would seem (if Sāṁkhya were right) that *Vāk* would tell (one who strives for *mokṣa* that (ultimately) what had been pointed to as the focus of freedom-striving is not the self (i.e., the subject to which *mokṣa* pertains). But *Vāk* does not tell us so.[27]

The word *heya*, "to be discarded", which comes from the sacrificial lexicon suggests not only the idea of throwing away something into a disposal bag as it were, but also that of which the usefulness is exhausted and hence that which is no longer fit to be associated with what is sacred. For Vedānta the agent is not *heya* as it is identical with the subject of freedom.

The discussion up to this point has been occasioned by the original question as to what is the Being that thinks, finally leading up to the notion of subjectivity as being-unto-freedom, where the agent is none other than the subject. It is not there as something eventually to be thrown away, for the contrary is the case. So now, the same truth is stated in a positive way in the next *sūtra* (no. 9) thus: "Because of *Vāk's* speaking about absorption of the agent into the Self", (*svāpyāyāt*).

Based on this *sūtra*, Śankara elucidates the meaning of the being, at once the subject of freedom and agent, of which *Chāndogya Upaniṣad*, 6.8.1, says: "When this *puruṣa* sleeps, dear one, it verily becomes one with its own Self, becomes absorbed into its own Self. Therefore he is said to be sleeping. It is absorbed into itself", (*yatra etat puruṣaḥ svapīti nama satā somya tadā sampanno bhavati, svapīto bhavati. tasmādena svapītyācakṣate, svam hi apīto bhavati*). With the aid of the etymology which the Upaniṣadic passage itself has provided, Śankara analyses the word *svapīti* (to sleep) thus: "*sva* and *ī* preceded by the prefix *api* means to be absorbed", (*apipūrva-svaiter layārthatvam prasiddham*).

In *Vāk's* speaking about the absorption of the agent of the project of liberation (which it does because the agent is itself the subject of the project) we have been led to clarification of subjectivity, i.e., as being-unto-freedom. And subjectivity is marked by the sign it carries, viz., *mokṣa*. It has also been made clear to us that we have no other authentic way of knowing ourselves as being. Now, the dual meaning of *sat* as Being and as being, is something that we have noted as we have moved forward from the initial *sūtra* of the *īkṣati adhikaraṇa*.

The understanding of human subjectivity as being-unto-freedom has been brought to us through a series of steps marking the systematic unfoldment of the meaning of Ultimate Reality, i.e. *Brahman*, as the Being that thinks. It is, however, easy to be misled into believing that the understanding of human subjectivity is the goal to which the unfoldment has been taking place and that, therefore, we may now kick off the ladder by which we have climbed to that understanding. But such a belief would be thoroughly un-Vedāntic as it is not the case that human subjectivity is henceforth going to constitute the supreme subject-matter of philosophy. For nothing but nothing can ever take the place of absolute *Brahman*, which is what makes everything else authentic. Subjectivity is marked out from other entities like *Pradhāna* because the subject and agent of freedom, the *ātman*, (small 'a') is enfolded in the undifferentiated self-identity of *Brahman*, and as such absorbed into it, *svāpyāyāt*). Paradoxical as it may sound, it is precisely this capability to be absorbed entirely into the Absolute that makes subjectivity authentic. The authentic subject is not some single one (*Der Einzige*) that stands apart from *Brahman* because it becomes itself only in the denial of itself within the sovereign perspective of *Brahman*. The essence of its individuality too rests in that denial, which is the highest sacrifice that a being is capable of making, viz., giving up its beingness, its *sattā*. This is the existential way of thought conducting itself in accordance with the way gnosis itself behaves. [When beingness goes Being remains.]

Now, the obverse side of subjectivity in its relation to the Absolute is also worthy of attention, namely, that only in subjectivity, or in other words, only by the silencing of all objectivities does Ultimate Reality show itself. *Pradhāna* is not only alien to this way of Ultimate Reality's showing itself, but stands in its way. These two sides of the same truth continue to be presented formally by the endless reiteration that *Pradhāna* is not the Cause of the world, the concept 'cause' standing in for that which constitutes the highest subject-matter of philosophic inquiry. *Brahman* alone remains that subject-matter and that fact is affirmed from all possible standpoints, exhaustively catalogued in subsequent portions of the text. There we find a complete mapping out of the world of concepts, no doubt with a considerable predominance of those of cosmology as might legitimately be expected. In anticipation of that are stated the last two *sūtras* (no. 10 and 11) of the present *adhikaraṇa*: "On account of the uniform direction in which the texts move", (*gatisāmānyāt*); and, "because we hear (*Vāk* say so)," (*śrutatvāñca*).

Śankara cites a few passages from the Upaniṣads, merely for initial instantiation, to show that "by means of the (inner) essay pertaining to the uniform movement of the Upaniṣadic texts they are interpreted as arguing, or laying, that conscious Being (i.e.,

Brahman is the Cause", (*gatisāmānyopāsanena ca sarvo vedāntāḥ cetana kāraṇa vādina iti vyākhyātam*). [The significance of *cetana* ("conscious Being") presumably is that it generates authentic subjectivity, in which alone can Ultimate Reality show itself.] It is also necessary to note that a new hermeneutical principle, i.e., the uniform direction in which the texts move (*gatisāmānya*, or *gatisāmānyatā*) has been enunciated, and it is carried through from now on. This principle, no doubt, functions within the framework of sequential connections (*samanvaya*), but rather as a way of demonstrating by discourse (*vāda*) the absolute truth of *Brahman*, and as such it is "accompanied by demonstrative reason" (*nyāya pūrvakam*), as Śankara writes.

At this point we notice that a wider stage is being set for Vedānta as philosophy to express itself, that is to say, conduct itself in accordance with the way gnosis itself behaves. The stage is wide, but at its centre is placed the quintessential concepts and symbols of the Veda which may serve as vehicles for philosophy's fuller self-expression through discourse, especially discourse with those whose thinking is already nurtured by these concepts and symbols, however imperfectly. As vehicles for philosophy's self-expression henceforth they are going to constitute the body of what continues to be regarded as the essay on Cause, which as we know is a discussion of *Brahman*.

Now, for a modern man too, who is not nurtured in any way by the quintessential concepts and symbols of the Veda, and who draws the substance of his discourse (and hence of his thought) from the lived and experienced world alone, and from anything beyond it only to the extent that it is already dissolved into that world, this new stage set has some relevance on account of its potential repercussions that go beyond its boundaries, and they are not difficult to tune into.

For the wider discourse has been introduced what may be broadly expressed as a "second level" for the conduct of philosophical thought, besides the essential or original "level" in which thought is envisaged as direct response in like form to gnosis, and where what *Vāk* is speaking as it itself wants to speak is alone norm, rendering man's own speaking in response to it a kind of denial of all that is drawn from the concepts and symbols of the Vedas, no less than those drawn from the world (and hence *neti, neti*). But then comes a second level which both permits and warrants a different kind of speaking and thinking.

This new stance may be called a "two-level" approach to thought. Is this a mere ontological accommodation or a bending to the needs of discourse in that it is the form in which philosophy dwells among human beings? That is not the case because it is not a tactic for facing a contingency, and in that sense the stance itself is not new. Rather, in its essence it is the articulation of what is already there in the integral composition of the Vedic texts. Hence Śankara writes: "*Brahman* is comprehended in two "modalities", as qualified by the limiting adjuncts of name, form, change and modification, and in the opposite manner, that is as devoid of all adjuncts", (*dvirūpam hi brahma avagamyate nāma-rūpa-bheda-vikāropādhi-viśiṣṭam, tadviparītam ca sarvopādhi vivarjitam*).

This takes into account a beginningless condition in which thought happens, one which even brings it into being, that is, as the extension of gnosis, through a refracting medium, as it were. That condition is *avidyā (agnosis)*, which envelopes thought all around as well as permeates it from within. It is this *avidyā* that gives thought a sense of autonomy and by the same token (on the reverse side) gives the thinker, i.e., the subject, an unconquerable sense of loneliness, as if gnosis is not there. However, Vedānta does not approach *avidyā* nor the autonomous-cum-lonely situation of thought from the inside but rather, as it becomes it, from the ground of gnosis. [Here we may also recall our discussion at the beginning of this chapter how consciousness is put in a beam of light from gnosis, whereby *avidyā* is manifested *ab initio*.] For the objective is to grasp the condition in which thought is held and hence to redeem it.

The point from which the process of redemption begins is the understanding of *avidyā* as already put under gnosis (and decidedly not before) as a *splitter* in the very operation of thought, whereby the thinker and the thought (i.e., *Brahman*) stand, as it were, apart and facing each other as subject and object, which is precisely what Śankara says in the following words (obviously speaking from the ground of gnosis): "There are thousands of sentences which show *Brahman's* two modalities, predicated on the difference between gnosis and *avidyā*; in the condition of *avidyā Brahman* bears the differentiating sign of thinker and the thought", (*iti ca evam sahasraso vidyāvidya-viṣaya-bhedena brahmaṇo dvirūpatam darśayanti vākyāni. tatra avidyā avasthāyām brahmaṇa upāsya-upāsakādi-lakṣaṇaḥ sarvo vyavahāraḥ*).

This point is driven home by him by appealing to the paradigm statement on duality in the *Bṛhadāraṇyaka Upaniṣad* (4.5. 25): "Where there is duality as it were, there one sees another... but where the *Ātman* is all this, then whom can one see and by whom is seen?", (*yatra hi dvaitamiva bhavati tad itara itaraṁ paśyati...yatra tu asya sarvam ātmaivābhūt tat kena kaṁ paśyet*). The validity of duality is accepted as an essential and realistic part of the process of grasping the condition in which thought is held and of redeeming it. [By the same token dualism is rejected as detrimental to this process.]

The rest of the text of the *Bhāṣya* can be understood from this point on with the two levels of thought as the key. In a formal way these two levels are called "higher" (*para*) and "lower" (*apara*), *Brahman* too being described accordingly as *para Brahman* and *apara Brahman* or *nirguṇa Brahman* and *saguṇa Brahman*, respectively. However, this formal distinction ought not to be literally applied in philosophy. For if that which is indicated by the word *para* carries the implication of *neti, neti*, then as far as any description of *Brahman* or the expansion of discourse is concerned, that is the end of the road. No deductive, tautological structure is possible such as is essential for a theological ontology. We cannot even attribute perfection to *Brahman* because that would be nothing more than an exercise in tautology based on certain innate concepts. [All perfections are conceivable for the human mind, whereby a Supreme Being can be tautologically envisioned so as to hold all those perfections, rejecting all imperfections.] However, this is where the *Sūtra* and the *Bhaṣya* show their sources. They do not follow the logical path of *neti, neti* alone in disregard of "thousands" of Vedic statements where *Brahman's* perfections such as Supreme Cause, Creator, the Omniscient, the All-powerful, etc., are mentioned. Thus *neti, neti* itself is re-linked to them and is interpreted not as just Void (which would be the case if the path followed were independent of the Veda) but as the highest expression of fullness (*sampūrṇam*) in comparison with which the very Vedic descriptions of *Brahman* in positive terms appear as depleted (*nyūnam*). In this way this linkage between the two levels is something not to be missed. This is what makes the bodying forth of Vedāntic philosophy possible. And yet *neti, neti* is implanted within the heart of the structure of perfections even though drawn from the Vedas. But that structure is essential for discourse. However, because of *neti, neti*, while discourse is being made, it is also being unmade. But the unmaking is within the making, and the more is made the more is unmade. This is essential for the gnosis circle, and that is the course the essay on Cause is to follow.

The Being that is to be known: the Question approached through Cosmology

The *sūtras* 6-11, which we have just discussed, have been the basis for considering the question as to the Being that thinks. Now, beginning with the *sūtra* no. 12, preparation is being made to raise the complementary question, what is the Being that is *to be known*, and hence commands thought absolutely? The clearly anticipated answer to both is: it is *Brahman* which thinks, therefore knows, and is to be known, therefore to be thought. The two questions are the two complementary sides of what is but one, formally expressed as the question of Cause. According to Vedānta, these two are inseparable and they must, therefore, not only appear but appear together in every investigation of Being. And further, insofar as they are the two sides of what is but one, i.e., the question of Cause, they both point to the same Being, i.e., *Brahman*, than which there is no other.

The fact that we are led to the same Being in answer to different questions reveal an underlying connection between the questions themselves as having also originated from the same Being, a fact which makes it inevitable for them to be grasped as complementary. Here we also learn the inner meaning of gnosis, defined by us as the disposition of Ultimate Reality, which may now be expressed as *the amplitude between the two poles of Being*, i.e., *as the one that thinks, therefore knows, and as the one to be known, therefore to be thought*. And as for thought, also defined by us as the extension of gnosis, it may be expressed as *the tuning into, or as attunement with, this amplitude*. Here, then, in this amplitude of gnosis we find the inner space for what Heidegger has described as the attunement (*Gestimmtheit*) or tuned correspondence (*gestimmte Entsprechen*) between being and Being. (And here we also begin to perceive the deeper possibilities of what we have described as thought approached from gnosis as the ground. This also gives us a clue to Śankara's definition of Vedānta as philosophy, which too we cited in our Introduction: "It is the vision of Ultimate Reality in which there is no distinction between gnosis, what is to be known and the knower" (*jñāna-jñeya-jñātṛ-bheda-rāhitaṁ paramārtha-tattva darśanam*). [We cannot, however, pretend that these deeper possibilities are to be directly addressed to Heidegger's formulation of Being and the correspondence between being and Being, for it moves in a different path from what we envisage in the framework of Vedānta. And no philosophical formulation can be corrected from the standpoint of another philosophy. In any case, what is aimed at here is *Vedānta's* own self-articulation in such a way as to be seized as philosophy.]

Now that our attention has been drawn to Being in the form of the question as to what it is that is to be known – shifting from the original pole of Being as that which thinks, therefore knows, – the path of thought to that end is going to be discussed. That path, as already shown in a preliminary way, is cosmology – and cosmology, because, as a form of investigation, it conforms to man's inherent and natural way of thinking.

However, the cosmology that is going to be used is not a speculative cosmology reared on some *a priori* considerations. In that sense what is undertaken is the critical use of an already existing sacred cosmology, Vedic cosmology that is, rather than the production of a cosmological theory *ab initio*. The latter kind of undertaking would be entirely alien to Vedānta, which turns away from speculation that is not already grounded in what *Vāk* has spoken, that is to say, not actually found in the Vedic texts – such is the framework within which it operates. However, this turning away is not an indication of aversion but of a positive will to penetrate to what is beyond the specific speculations that lies unattendedly behind them. We may describe that which lies behind as the matrix of speculative possibilities. Out of this matrix come all particular speculations. And *Vāk* calls it to itself. This is the call (*āmantraṇa*) of *Vāk* and as such it marks its entry into this hidden matrix.

The call, however, is not made through some generic categories or even through some *a prioris* but through the concrete, quintessential concepts and symbols of the *Vedas*. That there are generic categories and *a prioris* is by no means denied. On the contrary, it is understood that they find their usefulness in the call of *Vāk* to the matrix of speculations.

As for these Vedic concepts and symbols, it is not necessary to attribute any *a priori* virtues to them because, on the one hand, they themselves are the means by which *Vāk* calls all cosmological speculative possibilities to their matrix, and, on the other, the *a prioris* themselves find their usefulness in that call. However, their choice is not arbitrary because as a group of terms they have always done duty in the Vedas as the basis of that holistic structure of experience and perceptions which the Vedic community had accepted as the sacred cosmos – and the Sāṁkhyans too share in that community.

The fundamental question is, what is the cosmology that is organized upon this nucleus of terms for? It is, no doubt, agreed by the participants in the on-going debate that it is certainly not for the sake of knowing the cosmos, at least not for the sake of knowing the cosmos alone. For Vedānta and for Sāṁkhya alike cosmology is the path that thought takes in its quest for something else, i.e., Ultimate Reality, which is the one to be known. For Vedānta this something else, this Ultimate Reality, is *Brahman*, for Sāṁkhya it is *Pradhāna*, both predictably enough.

The absolute difference in the ontologies of what is to be known, to which cosmology provides a passage-way, is already prefigured in the respective understandings of cosmology itself. In Sāṁkhya there is no call of *vāk* to the hidden matrix of cosmological speculations (and, therefore, Sāṁkhya is described as *aśabdam*, i.e., devoid of *Vāk's* speaking.) As such, Sāṁkhya is wedded to one speculative system, regarding it as literally true. And so it is bound to interpret the cosmology expressed by the nucleus of Vedic concepts and symbols accordingly and to look upon the concepts and symbols as categories, in fact as *a priori* categories. For Vedānta *Brahman* alone remains the only Being to be known, the one absolute goal of philosophical thought, the quintessential concepts and symbols of the Vedas, the nucleus of terms, upon which the sacred cosmology rests, having to be understood merely as surrogates for *Brahman*. [It is on account of this rigorous grounding in *Brahman* as the Being to be known that Vedānta eventually reinterprets cosmology itself in terms of (1) *Vāk*, otherwise known as the Veda (the eternal IDEA), and (2) *Avidyā* – in a mutually complementary way.]

The nucleus of terms first considered in the *Brahma Sūtra* is chosen not arbitrarily but on account of the evident fact that it forms the core of the holistic, structured Reality maintained by the Vedas, which also conforms to the deepest spiritual aspiration of man. The terms, accordingly are:

That which is of the nature of bliss (*ānanda-maya*), 1.1.12-19; The Being within the source of light symbolied by the Sun as well as within the organ of perception of light symbolized by the eye (*antasthaḥ*), 1.1.20-21; Space/Ether (*ākāśa*), 1.1.22; Life-force (*prāṇa*), 1.1.23, 28-31; Light (*jyotiḥ*) 1.1.24-27.

While Sāṁkhya interprets them as standing for *Pradhāna*, Śankara equates them with *Brahman*. Each of these terms, according to Śankara, is a surrogate, i.e., within the sacred cosmology, for *Brahman*. At the end he gives a gist of his argument, hermeneutically grounded in the Vedas and the Vedic sciences (actually as he enters the next *pāda*), in these words:

In the first *pāda* of the first chapter it has been stated that in the light of the *sūtra*, "whence the origin etc. of this", (1.1.2) that *Brahman* is the Cause of the world comprehending space/ether, etc. The properties of *Brahman* insofar as it is the Cause of the world, such properties as all-pervasiveness, omniscience, omnipresence and omni-self-hood have been all but explicitly declared. After showing, based on consideration of Cause, that certain words known (ordinarily) to possess other meanings are in fact surrogates for *Brahman*, certain expressions and statements in like manner susceptible to doubt have also been determined as bearing testimony to *Brahman*.[28]

These expressions and statements, according to Śankara's own declaration at the end of the above remark, are examined in the *pādas* 2 and 3, i.e., the 32 *sūtras* of the former and 43 of the latter. The original group of five is now supplemented by a much larger set of concepts and symbols, among which, to select but a few instances, are: "the inner controller" (*antaryāmin*), 1.2.18-20; the invisible (*adṛśya*), 1.2.21-23; "that which is encountered in the form of the universe" (*vaiśvānara*), 1.2.24-32, etc. All these without exception indicate *Brahman* and not *Pradhāna*, nor, for that matter, the individual self (*jīva*), which has been newly offerred hypothetically, as an alternative object of philosophical quest, along with *Pradhāna*.

In the possibility that *jiva* could be thought of as the being to be known, i.e., the object of philosophical quest, the existence of a new loophole has been discovered and it has to be plugged. This line of thought, it is shown, is based primarily on misinterpretation of one of the great passages of the Upaniṣads, i.e., *Chāndogya* 3.14.1 and 2: "All this, verily, is *Brahman*. Let a man meditate calmly on it as *tajjalān* (i.e., that from which everything arises, by which it is sustained, and to which it returns). Verily man is the essence of his resolution. Just as a man resolves in the world so he becomes. Therefore let him resolve", (*sarvaṁ khalu idaṁ Brahma tajjalān iti śānta upāsīta. atha khalu kratumayaḥ puruṣo. yathā kratur asmin loke bhavati tathātaḥ pretya bhavati. sa kratuṁ kurvīta*). The first several *sūtras* of the second *pāda* are actually devoted to combating the tendency (which probably existed in fact and not only as possibility) to elevate self-knowledge approached in this subjectivist way to the place that rightly belongs to Self-knowledge in the sense of *Brahma-vidyā*.

And it is inordinately strange that such a view should go hand in hand with the view that the knowledge of *Pradhāna* is the true objective of philosophy. Śankara suggests that there are also lesser entities like *Vāyu* (Air), on behalf of which such claims have been put forward, as pointed out in comments on 13.1.

All these misunderstandings had arisen on account of the word *sva* ('own self' in a generic, logico-metaphysical sense). That problem is pointed out in the very first *sūtra* of the third *pāda*: "Because the term 'own self' is used in reference to that which is the abode of heaven, earth, etc., (*dyubhvādi āyatanaṁ svaśabdāt*).

In the course of an acute discussion of the term 'own self', the question is raised whether in the Vedas it is employed in a generic sense, as though it were a purely grammatical formation, a reflexive pronoun used substantively. The answer is given: "no, that is not the case". Śankara writes definitively:

> According to the statement in question, the Supreme *Brahman* is alone fit to be the abode of the world comprising of heaven, earth, *antarīkṣa, manas*, and all the life-forces, i.e., the sense-organs woven into its fabric. How is it so? Because of the term 'own self' and because it means what the word *ātman* itself means. The word *ātman* occurs in these passages: "Know the one only Being – the *Ātman*, (*Muṇḍaka Upaniṣad*, 2.2.5). The word *ātman* can be correctly understood only if we take it to mean the supreme *Ātman* (i.e., *Brahman*) and not something else. In some places in the Vedas *Brahman's* being its (i.e., the world's) abode is expressed by the term 'own self': "All these created things have their roots in Being, have their abode in Being, and have Being as their corner-stone,[29] (*Chāndogya Upaniṣad*, 6.8.4).

The contention clearly is that whatever prior or extraneous meaning we may have in our mind for the term 'own self' it will not serve any purpose in understanding the Vedic use of it unless we learn to derive its meaning from the supreme *Ātman, Brahman,*

Being. Even a most primary word like this, which is formed in the immediacy of our self-consciousness, is restructured by *Vāk*. That is because *Vāk* cuts through the very illusion which makes what is really mediate appear to us as immediacy, that is in our condition of agnosis. This of course calls for our thought, even in respect of our primary words, to be tuned into the amplitude of gnosis.

After considering a series of other words which express the sacred cosmology, at a further point, i.e., at the opening of the last *pāda* of Chapter I, Śankara observes:

> In the wake of the declaration as to the desire for knowledge of *Brahman*, *Brahman's* identifying sign was stated, i.e., "whence the origin etc., of this". As to the possibility raised (by some) that the identifying sign is equally applicable to *Pradhāna*, that has been set aside on the basis of the *sūtra* which says that the attribution of thinking to *Pradhāna* is not according to *Vāk's* speaking. By the discussion we have just completed it has been shown, in view of the *gatisāmānya* of the Vedic texts, *Brahman* and not *Pradhāna* is the Cause of the world. (But) this is far from established (they say), because in some traditions of Vedic hermeneutics certain other words prevail which seem to suggest that *Pradhāna* is the Being to be known.[30]

These "certain other words" are analysed in the 28 *sutras* of the 4th *pāda* of Chapter 1. The most crucial one is *avyakta* (meaning, the unmanifested). Now, this lead word was appropriated by Sāṁkhya as an explanatory synonym for *Pradhāna*. Śankara shows through a very lengthy analysis (etymological, linguistic and ontological) that this equation had been carried out on the basis of a false assumption and that in fact the word *avyakta* simply means what it says: "the unmanifest". This identification, he argues, has become part of, as well as support for, a faulty metaphysics. He declares at length, "It is not *Pradhāna* that is spoken of as the Being to be known, nor is it what the word *avyakta* indicates."[31]

Now, if *Brahman* continues to be the Being to be known, what is the meaning to be assigned to *avyakta*? The answer comes in Śaṅkara's categorical statement: "*avyakta* is *Avidyā*."[32]

Reconception of Cosmology on the twin basis of Avidyā and the Veda, with the view to the question, "what is to be known?"

Now that in this 4th *pāda* of the First Chapter *Avidyā* has been introduced in the context of the cosmological inquiry centred on the question as to the Being to be known, we must discuss it in that context, but in doing so we must also bring into view that complementary part of the new basis of cosmology, i.e., the *Veda*, which although introduced in the previous *pāda* had been held in abeyance by us with the intent of taking up the two together, as we are going to do now. [The origin of the world from the *Veda* was first propounded in 1.3.28; and the origin from *Avidyā* is enunciated by Śankara himself (rather than by the *Brahma Sūtra*), first in his comments on 1.4.3. and repeated in other places, particularly under 2.1.14.]

Brahman has already been established as the only Being to be known. And a cosmology has to be developed which will sustain this with unerring clarity. It was sought to be achieved by first providing an "acceptable definition of *avyakta*, i.e., as what denotes the antecedent potential stage of the cosmos at which it is not yet manifested by names and forms", (*jagadidam anabhivyakta-nāma-rūpaṁ prāgavastham avyakta-śabdārham*, 1.4.3.).

At this juncture we may turn to our own statement on the concept of *avidyā* (as agnosis) which we made in the individual, phenomenological sense, earlier on in our present chapter, defining it as being of the nature of mutual superimposition (*adhyāsa*) of self and not-self. Let us reproduce part of our remark: "It is called *avidyā*, or agnosis, because it is that which by positing itself as the very antithesis of *vidyā* (*jñāna*), or gnosis, confronts it and is confronted by it. Indeed, it is by virtue of this confrontation that man discovers himself as the being whose phenomenal essence is the desire for gnosis. The discovery is made possible by the grace of *Vāk*, and thereby agnosis itself is grasped as what is marked for dissipation." From that phenomenological framework of understanding we have, in light of the inquiry into Cause, moved to the cosmological framework. And we have in the meantime been enriched by the governing myth of the Omniscient Creator. Hence now, Śankara discusses *Avidyā* in the cosmological framework (and accordingly we write the word with a capital 'A') and it is in that framework that he argues that the antecedent condition of the world is not some kind of mindless, blind mechanism but something that can only be imputed to a conscious Creator who thinks the world into existence. [It is that same fact which guarantees that *mokṣa, mukti*, is eternal and that the released souls are not thrown back into the *saṁsāric* cycle, a matter about which

Sāṁkhya can say nothing cogent. Therefore, according to Śankara the dependence of this antecedent condition upon the conscious Creator "must be held to be necessarily so", (*sā ca avaśyam abhyupagantavyā*). Also, the potentiating power of the seed (of the cosmos) is of the nature of *Avidyā* and it is indicated by the word *avyakta*, and it has its basis in the highest Lord (the Omniscient Creator) and is of the nature of *Māyā* and is the great slumber in which the *saṁsāric jīvas*, unaware of their own essence, continue to sleep.[33] The famous *Śvetāraśvatara* passage (4.10) is also cited: "Know that the cosmos is *Māyā* and the maker of *Māyā* is the mighty Lord", (*māyām tu prakṛtiṁ vidyāt māyinaṁ tu maheśvaram*). [There has always been much confused thinking in most traditional and contemporary interpretations as to whether *Māyā* and *Avidyā/avidyā* are absolutely synonymous with each other our not. Now with the key we have appropriated it is easy to see that as approached phenomenologically, i.e., as an element in our consciousness, which has been put under the beam of the light coming from gnosis (as we have stated earlier), *avidyā* is not the same as *Māyā*, while as approached cosmologically, *Avidyā* and *Māyā* are the same. The intervening myth of the Omniscient Creator has helped to bring forward the altered connotation. That is the reason why we must move with *Vāk* as it speaks, if we should achieve true hermeneutics.]

Now, the *Avidyā*-basis of the cosmos must be taken in conjunction with its *Veda*-basis. The *sūtra* 1.3.28 says about the cosmos that "it was generated from that" (*ataḥ prabhavaḥ*). Śankara comments: " 'From that' means from the logos of the Veda", (*ata eva hi vaidikāt śabdāt*). [We recall our identification of *Veda* with the IDEA, rather than with the Vedas.] This logos, *Vāk*, it is stated, "is without beginning and end but is eternal" (*anādi-nidhanā nityā*). Then there are names and forms and it is stated that "it is through them that beings and the rites were put into existence", (*nāma-rūpe ca bhūtānām karmāṇām ca pravartanam*). The myth of "the Omniscient Creator, who through the logos of the Veda created (all this) in the beginning", (*vedaśabdebhya eva ādau nirmame sa maheśvaraḥ*), is also brought in.

This myth connects the account of the genesis of the cosmos from the *Veda* with the parallel account of the genesis from *Avidyā*, both through the potential seeds of becoming, known as name and form. In order to perceive this let us move forward to 2.1.14, in the course of the comment upon which Śankara observes: "The names and forms which are imagined through *Avidyā* and which are, as it were, of the essence of the Omniscient Lord of all, and which are not definable as either identical with or different from Being (i.e. *Brahman*) and are the seeds of the entire cosmos of *saṁsāric* existence are the *Māyā*-power of the Lord".[34]

We see now that cosmology reconceived on the basis of *Avidyā* (or *Māyā*) and the *Veda* (IDEA) has a very clear relation to gnosis in respect of that which is to be known, therefore to be thought, in exactly the way in which cosmology based (as at the start) on the truth that *Brahman* is the Cause has also the same relation to gnosis, i.e., in respect of that which thinks, therefore knows, and that which is to be known, therefore to be thought. We have also learnt that that which thinks, therefore knows, and that which is to be known, therefore to be thought, mark the amplitude, the tuning into which is what must be called thought, i.e., insofar as it has to do with Ultimate Reality.

Earlier on in our present chapter when we introduced "the circle of gnosis philosophy" we spoke of two modes of gnosis, which underlie the possibility of the circle, whereby the conduct of thought accords with the behaviour of gnosis. We spoke of these as the revelatory mode and the realizational mode, the one belonging with showing and the other belonging with seeing. In terms of that distinction it may seem that the amplitude of gnosis is exclusively concerned with the revelatory, or showing, mode. But we will correct that impression by reproducing a statement we made in that earlier context: "The genius of Vedānta, particularly as worked out by Śankara in the *Sūtra Bhaṣya*, is that it establishes the fact that showing and seeing are ultimately one and the same but with the qualification that their convergence is achieved by thought via the project of the gnosis circle." The realizational or seeing mode of gnosis has the same amplitude as we have described above, and thought in relation to that mode too is nothing but tuning into it.

However, the sighting of the convergence of the showing mode and seeing mode of gnosis, into whose amplitude thought is the tuning into, is carried forward, through successive steps of further showing and further seeing, as essential to the unfolding of the system in a formal sense, and to the drawing of the circle of gnosis philosophy in a deeper, spiritual sense. The first entails *avirodha*, which, as we stated at the beginning of this chapter, means removal of the objections based on presumed contradictions in the way the central theme (i.e., *Brahman*) has been set forth. The second entails *praxis*, or *sādhana*, which also as we stated, is an exhaustive enterprize of refining the ritual, moral and meditative techniques aimed at realizing *Brahman*-gnosis that naturally leads to the fruit, or *phala*, actually a continuation and conclusion of *praxis.*

The Showing mode of Gnosis continued through Reason, and Criticism of other schools' use of Reason

Vedānta appropriates Reason for carrying forward the showing mode of gnosis, in other words, for extending Revelation. In this way, gnosis whose intrinsic means of showing is Revelation (as what is spoken by *Vāk* of its own accord, hence with that literal meaning called *āgama*) becomes also discoursible in the accepted, natural way in which human discourse about Ultimate Reality is conducted, i.e., through reasoning.

But has not Reason an authentic realm of its own, taking into consideration the fact that *Vāk*, logos, is the common ground of Reason and Revelation? Then why should Reason's function be merely carrying forward what Revelation has shown? And do we not also know that *Vāk* is the ground of the structured reality comprehending the cosmos, and therefore it is not possible that it could be approached and re-shaped by the corresponding logos structure of the mind, leading us to ontological. Reason (such as has prevailed in the Western tradition from Parmenides down)? In this manner can we not think of a correlation between Reason and Revelation starting from their very depth in the way some Western theologians like Paul Tillich have attempted to do in the Western tradition?

At the first look the answer to all these questions would seem to be affirmative. But when the matter is looked into more deeply, it will be clear that the first appearance is false. For Vedānta speaks of *Vāk* in two ways, i.e., as the ground of all structured reality, including the cosmos, and again as that which communicates gnosis, namely *Vāk* as it speaks. No doubt, as the ground of all structured reality, *Vāk* harbours the potentiality of what could have been philosophically sought out by the mind as ontological Reason, grasping within its embrace the seeking out also, thus generating a *history* of Reason (as in the West). But Vedānta did not turn to this path. Why did it not? But before we ask this question, we may ask the prior question "why it or any tradition should necessarily have?" In asking why a particular tradition did not, we assume that the experience of another tradition that actually did so turn, i.e., the Western, is norm. But we soon learn that there is no such thing as norm for great philosophical traditions, that there are only uniquenesses. That from logos as ontological Reason the West initiated and developed a great *history* of Reason, which exploded in a number of directions such as theology, science, ideology and politics, to name but the principal ones, and also continued to occupy the centre stage of the history of philosophy, is undoubtedly part of its uniqueness. No doubt, Reason in this tradition often bursts forth beyond itself, especially breaking into thought's relation to Being and yet without abandoning itself but by only rethinking its ground, often agonizingly.

Vedānta's uniqueness is that it has concentrated on *Vāk* as it communicates gnosis. And hence it turns to Reason as a means for further carrying forward what *Vāk* by itself shows. Accordingly, only in this specific sense is its criticism of other schools' use of Reason to be understood, and no doubt, these schools too had not concerned themselves with ontological Reason nor had they anything that, unlike Vedānta, has even such a potentiality. In brief, in Vedānta's criticism of other schools' use of Reason what is criticized must be understood as *reasoning*, which is a universal factor in all natural thought, seen to be moving in the forefront of all thought that has its ground in human consciousness (as we demonstrated in our Introduction). Understood in this manner, Vedānta through its criticism seeks to lead Reason and its power into the trajectory that moves in the direction of gnosis. All this becomes clear from Śankara's celebrated statement (in 2.1.11) in criticism of other schools' use of Reason, the major part of which, as being relevant to the present discussion, is cited below:

> Reasonings which are not grounded on what has come on its own (*āgama*), i.e., what *Vāk* has spoken (and speaks), and are undertakings based on mere assumptions of persons (who use Reason) are unfounded. As they are mere assumptions they are far from definitive. We see in the world that conjectures labouriously made by adepts (at this way of using Reason) are proven false by greater adepts, and those made by the latter are also in turn disproved by yet others, and therefore it is not possible to believe that these reasonings have a solid foundation and that they are definitive. This is so on account of the variations in human thinking.... (Some people may protest that Reason is self-validating and argue): Its unfoundedness

(on anything but itself) is its beauty, and it is precisely on account of this that flawed (or bad) reasoning is to be rejected and flawless (or good) reasoning to be achieved. (And they add:) There is no philosophical principle (i.e., *pramāṇa*) that encourages a person to remain in an unenlightened state that may have prevailed before. Hence the lack of a ground for Reason (i.e., other than itself) is far from being a defect. (To this we reply:) Let us, for argument's sake, assume that this is correct. Even then there is a certain predicament (arising from the nature of the practicular object to be known), and there is no way out of that. For, although for some objects Reason's self-groundedness may be deemed sufficient, as far as the object to be known, with which we are presently occupied (i.e., Ultimate Reality itself), our contention that this way of using Reason leads us to a predicament from which there is no escape still holds good. It is not possible to make assumptions, unfounded on what has come on its own (i.e., *āgama*) the basis for thinking on the supremely grave question of Being-as-it-is, which, put in other words, is itself the project of freedom (i.e., *mukti-nibandhana*). Being-as-it-is cannot be grasped through its (possible) appearance because it is formless (and hence does not appear), nor can it be deduced from signs (i.e., *lakṣaṇā*) because it has none. And all those who take freedom in its unconditional character understand that gnosis culminates in freedom. That transcendent gnosis is undifferentiated, because it is the disposition of Being itself. (By way of analogy it may be said that) in the empirical world (too) the truth of a cognition depends on all people cognizing an object in an identical way. In that sense it too is transcendent as in the uniformly cognized form of fire (e.g., its hotness). (However, concerning empirical entities which do not appear but can be deduced only from signs,) mutual differences among men are a scandal. It is all too well known in the world that a position taken by one disputant is controverted by another and the latter's position in turn by a third. How then can such unsettled knowledge take the place of gnosis?[35]

In this criticism Śankara is taking Reason, that is, strictly in the way in which it is understood in the present frame of discourse, to the limits of its possibility in order to argue out what it can do and what it cannot do. Its authority in establishing clear-cut knowledge of empirical appearances, by following their own signs, is acknowledged. However, this is so only in principle, for in actual fact the disagreement among thinkers even with respect to uniformly available empirical cognitions is a scandal. But it is also pointed out that that authority cannot be extended to knowledge of Ultimate Reality as there is no appearance of it which is to be known, and there are no lead signs. The only thing that appears, or presents itself, is that which has come of its own accord (i.e. *āgama*), in other words what *Vāk* has spoken. That, then, is the *pratyakṣa* in this respect. No doubt, that has its lead signs too. It would be a misuse of Reason to by-pass this thing which appears and to speculate on the nature of Ultimate Reality by inauthentically extending Reason's authority, although for the most part only theoretical and seldom realized, into the realm of the Ultimate. By the same token, it has its proper use, which is to carry forward the showing mode of gnosis, and that consists in *Vāk's* own speaking. This way we are led to the conclusion of Śankara's statement:

> Hence it is established that knowledge of Ultimate Reality is brought by the Upaniṣads. Inasmuch as there is no such knowledge outside this there is a predicament that faces the Reason that seeks ultimate freedom without it. Therefore, on the ground of what has come of its own accord and carried forward by Reason as it follows its own deductive path, it is now confirmed that the conscious *Brahman* is the Cause of the world and of Nature itself.[36]

We have just completed outlining the showing mode of gnosis, terminating in the way Reason is used for it. It is important while noticing the depth of Śankara's discussion of Reason, that we should perceive that it is not aimed at leading Reason to its source in *Vāk* (logos), the structure of all reality and of speaking itself but at *Vāk's* specific speaking by which gnosis shows itself. The desire for freedom (*mumukṣatva*) which is the same as the desire for knowledge of Ultimate Reality (*brahma-jijñāsā*) is, however, its sign present in human consciousness. This sign is what makes that which comes of its own accord (i.e., *āgama*, or the Vedas) an appearance, a presence, or *pratyakṣa*, which in turn addresses that which carries the sign, i.e., human consciousness, the sign itself revealing consciousness's inherent structural orientation. It is because of this that gnosis serves as the ground of thought.

[Śankara's criticism continues, and passing to other schools from that paradigmatic non-Vedāntic school, i.e., Sāṁkhya, in relation to which the essentials of gnosis and philosophical thought in Vedānta, predicated primarily on the Cause question, have been set forth. The criticism, however, is carried on through the rest of the second chapter, beginning at 2.1.12, covering all other important schools such as Vaiśeṣika atomism, Buddist aggregationism, "nihilism" and mentalism, Jaina pluralistic pan-psychism, and Bhāgavata creationism. However, as the criticisms of these schools, albeit important in other respects, have no immediate bearing on the question of gnosis and philosophical thought in the way we have set up for investigation we shall not touch upon them in this work.]

The Seeing, or Realizational, mode of Gnosis, the New use of Cosmology, and the Return of the Rite

We stated early in this present chapter of ours that the two modes of gnosis, i.e., the revelational (showing) and the realizational (seeing) are as much the essence of the way gnosis itself behaves as of the way thought conducts itself, and we added that this can be said only in the light of the accord between the way of the one and the way of the other having a philosophical reality, that is, in other words, in the light of thought finding itself as extension of gnosis. We also spoke about how both these modes of gnosis and their extensions as thought are integral to the gnosis circle. Having discussed the one, let us now turn to the other, i.e., the realizational, which is the subject-matter of the last two chapters of the *Brahma Sūtra* and its *Bhāṣya*, entitled *Sādhana* (*praxis*) and its *Phala* (fruit).

The third Chapter, *Sādhana*, as Śankara states at the beginning of his comment on it, deals primarily with certain *vidyās*, the word *vidyā* (also from *vid*, to know), having the meaning of practical "knowing-how", hence very similar to the original meaning of the Greek *epistēmē*. A *vidvān*, therefore, in the oldest sense of the word is an *epistamenos*, "one who knows how", again, as in the Greek tradition.[37]

It is made clear repeatedly that *vidyā* in the sense of *praxis* has nothing but what it itself is in the theoretical sense to draw from. And there is no interval at all between the *theōrea* and the *praxis*. Hence, *vidyā* is its own *praxis*, which entails the "know-how". However, one noteworthy feature of it is the re-introduction of cosmology, no doubt *Avidyā*-based cosmology, for the particular conduct of thought that is entailed in *praxis*, i.e., what is called *upāsana*, or concrete meditation. In this respect thought involves the use of tools (*upakaraṇa*) such as *prāṇa* (life-breath) and other cosmological entities formed as means. This matter Śankara discusses at the very opening of the third chapter. "It follows", he states, that, as has already been said, "certain tools (of thought) for the human being, which are different from his self, also spring from *Brahman*", 3.1.1.[38] The use of these tools for *upāsana* (meditation) constitutes the main feature of the "know-how" of *Brahma-vidyā*. In fact the bulk of the third and fourth chapters is an elaborate discussion of this theme. That the apparent differences in the tools do not imply any differences among the *vidyās* (insofar as they are all expressions of the same *Brahma-vidyā*) is dealt with in *pāda* 3 of the third chapter, beginning with the first *sūtra*: "In view of the declaration in the entire body of the Upaniṣads (i.e., pertaining to *Brahma-vidyā*) all *vidyās* are identical", (*sarva-vedānta-pratyayam codanādi aviśeṣāt*).

Cosmology provides the tools for meditation, but because the cosmology is *Avidyā*-based the thinker can use the tools without fear, provided he knows it to be so, and this is the essence of the Vedāntic "know-how". For indeed, with the rising of gnosis, *Avidyā* will be dissipated. Hence, Śankara states in 3.2.21:

> Inasmuch as it is said that the cosmos superimposed on the one only Being, i.e., *Brahman*, through *Avidyā* is to be dissipated by means of gnosis, it would be sufficient for one (i.e., the thinker) to be made to know: "*Brahman* is one only without a second" (*Chāndogya* 6.2.1); "That is the Truth, That is the *Ātman*, That thou art" (*Chāndogya* 6.8.7-16). Then gnosis (i.e., in the seeing mode) will spring up of itself and counterpose itself against *Avidyā*.[39]

In thought conducting itself in accordance with gnosis in its realizational or seeing mode, what has been held in abeyance at the beginning of the epic of gnosis, i.e., the rite, returns, not, however, as an epic of its own and certainly not as a humanistic epic as in Purva-Mīmāṁsā. This is the same as saying that thought, or thinking, itself enters the sphere of the rite, which entails the doing of something but no longer as a means to an end.

But why the doing, why the rite? If thought is to be a doing, is to be an entry into the sphere of the rite, is not its accord with gnosis likely to be broken, because gnosis has been consistently defined as "not a humanistic project", (*na hi tat puruṣa-tantram*), but a "project of the thing (Being) itself", (*vastu tantram-eva hi tat*).[40] The answer lies in regrasping the whole sphere of the rite anew, under gnosis, one in which meditational "action" dominates. However, meditational action takes us to the last step in the epic of gnosis.

All the traditional rites such as "the rites proper to a person's station beginning with the lighting of the sacred life", (*agnīndhā-nādi-āśrama-karmāṇi*), 3.4.25, are now appropriated as *vidyās.*

These rites, it is maintained, based on 3.4.33, are "cooperators" (*sahakārī*) in the attainment of the fruit. Now fruit, or *phala*, is a theme of the utmost importance for Vedānta, and the fruit is freedom (*mokṣa, mukti, nirvāṇa*) itself. For the gnosis circle must be consistent with the definition of the subject, i.e., man, as being-unto-freedom, and such consistency of thought's conduct stands as a witness to the absoluteness of gnosis. Under gnosis the rites are oriented to the one fruit, i.e., freedom.

Thought, inasmuch as it is the attunement with the amplitude of gnosis and inasmuch as gnosis is not an epiphenomenon of the rite, has in itself an orientation to the concrete fruit. Only in such orientation is the attunement with the amplitude of gnosis possible, for here all that is vague, merely metaphorical and abstract is eschewed.

Once again, why the rite? In fact, Vedānta does not actually give a reason. It simply grasps what is already there, in the particular manner in which it exists in a particular tradition and outlines a new use for it. On the other hand, while declining to give a reason for the existence of the rite, it gives a number of explanations of its use. Among them is the fact that they, the daily, natural religious performances, or *nityakarmas*, are helpful for the soul's self-purification and that they are cooperators in the project of *mokṣa*. Many are the statements where "the rites are described as being able to consume impurities of the soul because gnosis is the highest goal."[41] Often, it is also argued that recommendations to perform rites are spill-overs of the praise (*stuti*) of gnosis – and in this way a new "place" for them is found.[42]

On the whole, we see that gnosis says "no" to the rite in terms argued for by Pūrva Mīmāṁsā, and yet says "yes" in terms of itself, but always subordinate to the acquisition of certain interior wealths of the meditator such as calmness, and most of all the desire for freedom (*mumukṣatva*),[43] the last of which is considered the highest wealth. The performance of the rite is treated as a spontaneous aspect of the way one who resolutely observes gnosis and is resolutely on the way to freedom comports himself. It is not something to be observed for any merit of its own. The text naturally ends with a declaration of the certainty of eternal freedom for one who resolutely observes gnosis, a freedom that is the accepted goal of all spiritual investigation and striving, whose finality and ultimacy are also unequivocally stressed. That is how the text ends.

A Concluding Supplementary Remark

The subject-matter of our investigation has been gnosis and the question of thought. In this just completed chapter of ours we have investigated it with the help of the *Brahma-Sūtra* and its *Bhāṣya*. The text itself has said much about gnosis by its own flow, or *gati*. And in this very flow we have had to find gnosis as the ground of thought as well. We have been summoned not only to understand what the text apparently says but to question it so that it speaks again in the very amplitude of gnosis, which we have learned cannot be tuned into in any other form than as thought. It is true, however, that we have certainly not been left in any doubt that as the text comes to a close its clearly directed appeal is to ultimate spiritual freedom. Could it be otherwise? Certainly not, in view of the absolute integrity and finality of the system. Ultimate Reality, gnosis, freedom – these three have a certain relation to one another, which cannot be anything short of identity. The system itself unfolds merely so that this identity may be revealed – as gnosis, of course – and also so that all of our thinking as well as striving, i.e., all that has had its origin, broadly speaking, in consciousness, may be brought into its orbit, thereby facilitating our realizing this identity of the Real, gnosis and freedom.

Such, no doubt, is the ordinance of gnosis. However, the fact that philosophy, while placing itself within this ordinance, also heeds the call of thought, which when followed down to its ground is perceived as nothing else but gnosis, is the reason why it unavoidably hears another clearly directed appeal of gnosis, which relates to thought itself directly. It is no doubt the case that the ability to heed this call of thought (albeit, according to Vedānta, having its ground in gnosis), and set out in the direction from which the call keeps coming, is what makes philosophy philosophy. All philosophies are together in this. It is also unavoidable that in investigating the source of the call philosophy reaches a ground beyond the realms where thought is recognized as thought, which is a new, self-manifesting ground. [We described in our Introduction three different grounds, i.e., consciousness, the correspondence of being to Being and gnosis.]

But, that thought proceeds from gnosis is also a new fact. As such, it investigates gnosis and questions it. The questioning of its own ground is the questioning of all things, and it must go on without ceasing and yet without anticipating a realized knowledge weighing heavily upon the questioning. When we concentrate on freedom as that to which gnosis moves, it might seem that questioning is far from the way of Vedānta, other than in the technical sense as steps towards ultimate certainty of saving knowledge. That is why we must return again and again to the questioning mode of *Brahman*-gnosis that we have spoken about. In other words, we are here talking about gnosis itself as the ground of questioning in that it is the ground of thought. And questioning is not in the technical sense of working one's way towards anticipated certainty of saving knowledge. On the contrary, we are here considering the full implication of gnosis as the ground of thought, which already comprehends the certainty that technical reasoning merely searches for. It is this ground which must hold that inexchangeable essense of philosophy that we call questioning. In other words it becomes the house of all questions (and of all *scepsis*). Philosophy, therefore, is more fully understood in this way as the habitation of the attunement with the amplitude of gnosis. It furnishes the scope for our being questioningly involved in the realization of knowledge and at the same to be involved in the questioning, no longer with the certainty of knowledge as a deadweight, but with gnosis itself as a freeing agent. This is how the known is to be known, this is how the Real is realized. This is how the question "why" along with the "why" of the "why" will continue, and the circle of gnosis philosophy, instead of remaining a closed circle, will become open again in order to be carried further forward, and yet in a new way that will hold, contain and ground the anguish as well as the darkness of questioning.

Our remark that the circle of gnosis philosophy, instead of remaining a closed circle, will become open again in order to be carried further forward can be illustrated by the very transitional character of the great essay on Cause with its principal interest in a sacred cosmology essentially designed to give man a firm place from which to conduct thought in response to gnosis. Even in that essay the circle keeps on opening itself to emerging, deeper possibilities of thought in response to more arresting appearances of gnosis which brought forward the definition of gnosis as the amplitude between the two poles of Being (the one that thinks, therefore knows, and the one that is known, therefore thought), and of thought as the attunement with that amplitude.

The essay on Cause, which served as the framework for debates with Sāṁkhya and other traditional Indian systems come to a point of bounding over itself. By tracing the development of the essay to that point where that framework itself was transcended, the challenge was how to seize what could ensue therefrom as the opening again of the gnosis circle for continued conduct of thought, albeit in deepest accord with the way gnosis itself behaves.

Here it has become insistently clear that coming into the ambience of that Western tradition which is characterized by the gravity and single-mindedness with which it has asked the question of thought, under Being, is not only unavoidable but is immensely needful and useful. By attending to that tradition, gnosis philosophy is enabled to question itself about thought even in the very act of approaching it from the ground of gnosis, and to develop an unprecedented perspective on the possibility of thought coming to pass in the appearing of gnosis. In that way it also no longer needs to remain a mute outsider to the tradition that pursues the question of thought as the central question of philosophy.

Finally, it must have become amply clear why our present work has had to go about its business by means of a dialogue with the very foundations of the Indian gnosis philosophy. No study of any later work would lead to the same possibilities. By the same token, once the tradition has been seized at the source subsequent developments will also find their place in the stream, within critical limits.

NOTES AND ADDITIONAL REFERENCES

1 – TO INTRODUCTION

1. *Note*: For instance, speaking of Western-European philosophy, Heidegger states parenthetically "and there is no other, neither a Chinese nor an Indian philosophy", *What is Called Thinking?*, Translation (of *Was Heisst Denken?*) by J. Glenn Gray, New York, Harper & Row, 1968, p. 224.
2. Martin Heidegger, *What is Philosophy?* translation (of *Was ist das – die philosophie?*) by W. Kluback and J.T. Wilde, New York, Twayne Publishers, 1958, pp. 29-(30)-31.
3. *Ibid.*, p. 21.
4. *Ibid.*, p. 67.
5. *Loc. cit.*
6. Cf. the excellent analysis of "The Concept of Phenomenon" in Martin Heidegger, *Being and Time*, translated by J. Macquarrie and E. Robinson, New York, Harper & Row, 1962, p. 51, (*Sein and Zeit* No. 29).
7. *mala gar philosophou touto to pathos, to thaumazein. ou gar allē archē philosophias ē autē. Theatetus*, 155d-.
8. *dia gar to thaumazein hoi anthrōpoi kai nun kai to prōton ērxanto. Metzphysics*, A2, 982 b. 12.
9. *What is Philosophy?*, pp. 82-83.
10. *Ideas*, translated by W.R. Boyce Gibson, New York, Collier Books, 1962, (23A) p. 82.
11. *yato vāco nivartante aprāpya manasā saha, Taittirīya Upaniṣad*, 2.4.1.
12. Italics ours.
13. *What is Philosophy?*, p. 27.
14. *Ibid.*, p. 33.
15. *Ibid.*, p. 69.
16. *Loc. cit.*
17. *Ibid.*, p. 71.
18. *Ibid.*, p. 73.
19. *Ibid.*, pp. 73 [74] -75.
20. *Ibid.*, p. 77.
21. *Ibid.*, p. 79.
22. *Ibid.*, p. 79.
23. *Loc. cit.* Schon die griechischen Denker, Platon und Aristoteles, haben darauf aufmerksam gemacht, dass die philosophie und das Philosophieren in die Dimension des Menschen gehören, die wird die Stimmung (in Sinne der Ge-stimmtheit und die Be-stimmtheit) nennen, p. 78.
24. *Ibid.*, p. 85. Das Erstaunen ist die Stimmung, innerhalb derer den griechischen Philosophen das Entsprechen zum Sein des Seienden gewährt war, p. 84.
25. *Ibid.*, p. 49.

26. *Loc. cit.*
27. *Loc. cit.*
28. Cf. *Ibid.*, p. 57.
29. *Ibid.*, p. 61.
30. Heidegger, *Was ist Metaphysik?* (8th Edition) Nachwort, p. 43.
31. *Essays in Metaphysics*: Identity and Difference, translation (of *Identität und Differenz*) by Kurt F. Leidecker, New York, Philosophical Library, 1960, p. 58. Cf., *Identität und Differenz*, p. 64.
32. "Plato and Heidegger", *The Question of Being*: East and West Perspectives, edited by Mervyn Sprung, University Park and London, Pennsylvania State University Press, 1978, p. 53.
33. *Commentary on Māṇḍūkya-kārikā*, 4.1.

2 – TO CHAPTER I: THE *ṚG VEDA*

1. *What is called Thinking?*, p. 178.
2. *Dhātukośa*, M.R. Kale, *A Higher Sanskrit Grammar* (1894), reprint, Delhi, etc., Motilal Banarsidass, 1967, p. 124.
3. *Ibid.*, p. 205.
4. *ata eva ca nityatvākṛter-devāter-jagato vedaśabda-prabhāvatvāt vedaśabda-nityatvam api pratyetavyam, Brahma-Sūtra-Bhāṣya*, 1.3.29.
5. *yajñena vācaḥ pradavīyam āyan.*
6. Cf. translation by H.H. Wilson, reprinted, Calcutta, Punthi Pusthak, 1961, pp. 221-2, (*Viṣṇu Purāṇa*, 3.4.1).
7. See *The System of the Vedanta*, p. 51.
8. A.Y.P.S., 1.33. Cf. Jaimini, *Mīmāmsā-Sūtra, taccodakeṣu mantrākhyā śeṣe brāhmaṇaśabda.*
9. *Note*: The number 10473 for *ṛks* is based on the authority of Erkara Raman Nambūdri, the greatest living scholar of the Vedas. See his *Āmnāyamadhanam*, Tanavūr, Malappuram Jilla, Kerala, India, Anadi Books, 1976, p. 36.
10. See Sāyaṇa's introduction to his *Ṛagbhāṣya.*
11. *What is Called Thinking?*, pp. 232-233. *Note*: The idea of long preparation that Heidegger speaks about is very well known to Yoga. Thus the *Yoga Sūtra* (1.14) speaks of preparatory exercise (*abhyāsa*) for a long time (*dīrgha-kāla*) and regularly undertaken (*nairantarya*) as a pre-condition for intuition.
12. The introduction to the *Ṛgbhāṣya*: *tatko vā ṛṣi iti vicāraṇayā ṛṣati mantrān paśyati tapasā iti ṛṣi iti. vyutpatyā mantradraṣṭureva taccabdena grahaṇam. ata eva ṛṣayo mantra draṣṭāraḥ sāmpradayikī prasiddhiḥ.*
13. See Yāska, *Nirukta*, beginning of Ch. 7.
14. 1.41.6
15. 7.32.13.
16. 1.40.5.
17. 7.7.6.

18. 10.134.7
19. *What is Called Thinking?*, pp. 138-9.
20. *Ibid.*, p. 140.
21. *Ibid.*, p. 141.
22. *Ibid.*, p. 143.
23. 10.88.14.
24. *What is Called Thinking?*, p. 117.
25. *Śakti and Śakti*, Madras, Ganesh, 6th ed., 1965, p. 484.
26. See Arthur Avalon (Sir John Woodroffe), *Principles of Tantra*, Madras, Ganesh and Co., 3rd ed., 1960, pp. 494-5.
27. *What is Called Thinking?*, p. 10.
28. *Amarakośa, pradhamakāṇḍa, śabdādivarga.*
29. *What is Called Thinking?*, p. 10.
30. 10.67.3.
31. 9.26.2.
32. 10.67.4.
33. See *Āmnāyamadhanam*, p. 128.
34. This same idea is exactly expressed by Bhavabhūti in *Uttararāma-caritam* thus:
    āvirbhūta-jyotiṣām brāhmaṇānām ye vyavahārasteṣu mā samśayābhūt bhadrā hi eṣāṁ vāci lakṣmir niṣannā naite vācaṁ viplutārthaṁ vadanti.

3 – TO CHAPTER II: THE UPANIṢADS

1. The *Commentary on the Kena Upaniṣad*, 4.7. *upaniṣad, tādātmya-lakṣaṇena sāmīpyena nitarāṁ brahma gamayitvā ahaṁ māṁ iti granthīn śithilī kṛtya avidyāṁ saṁskāraṁ sādayati vināśyati iti upaniṣad brahma-vidyā.*
2. *upaniṣaditi vidyocyate. tacchīlānāṁ garbhajanmajarādi niśādanāt tada-vasādanāt vā brahmaṇo vā upanigamayitṛtvād upaniṣaṇṇaṁ vā asyāṁ paraṁ śreya iti*, Sureśvara in the introduction (*Saṁbandhavārtika*) to his famous sub-commentary on Śankara's *Commentary on the Bṛhadāranyaka Upaniṣad*. Sureśvara follows up this definition elaborately, beginning with the statement: "Here the word *upaniṣad* has the meaning of the transcendent *Brahman*-knowledge", (*atra copaniṣad śabdo brahma-vidyaikagocaraḥ*), stanzas 3-8.
3. *Loc. cit.*
4. For example, see Introduction to the *Commentary on the Kaṭha Upaniṣad*.
5. See *Chāndogya*, 3.11.5; *Bṛhadāranyaka*, 6.3.12; *Śvetāśvatara*, 6.22; *Muṇḍaka*, 3.2.11; *Maitrī*, 6.29. *Note*: The problem of the qualification or eligibility (*adhikāra*) to learn the Upaniṣads develops out of this. Essentially, it is the character of the knowledge that automatically excludes those who are not qualified. See *Sureśvara*, Supra, Stanza 12.
6. *Kena*, 4.6.7.

7. The expression is composed of four parts, *tad, ja, ti, an,* meaning *that* from which all things *originate*, to which they *return* and in which they *subsist*.
8. *Bṛhadāraṇyaka*, 2.4.5.
9. *Chāndogya*, 7.1.2, 3.
10. *brahma stomaṁ ghṛtamadass akran, Ṛg Veda*, 2.39.81.
11. *brahma stomaṁ maghavā somaṁ ukthā bibrateti, Ibid.*, 4.22.1.
12. *Ibid.*, 6.45.7.
13. *Ibid.*, 10. 141.3.
14. *Six Systems of Indian Philosophy*, pp. 68 ff.
15. *Geschichte der Philosophie*, I, pp. 240 ff.
16. *Religion and Philosophy of the Vedas and the Upaniṣads.*
17. *Philosophies of India*, pp. 77-8.
18. *yajñakarma-codanāt brāhmaṇam.*
19. *Religion and Philosophy of the Vedas and the Upaniṣads.*
20. *Ibid.*, p. 454. *Note*: One cannot agree with Keith, however, that in the Brāhmaṇas sacrifice is magic pure and simple (*loc.cit.*), while he himself writes: "... taken as a whole it is impossible to deny the name philosophy to an ordered view of the universe [that is in the Brāmaṇas] fully thoughtout, and within its fundamental limitations, logical and complete", (*Ibid.*, p. 455). How could magic be credited with such things?
21. *Śatapatha Brāhmaṇa*, 8.4.1.3, here taken from translation of Julius Eggeling.
22. *Ibid.*, 11.2.3.6. Cf., *Aitareya Brāhmaṇa*, 2.1.1.
23. *Ibid.*, 10.3.5.11, 12.
24. Cf. *Tāṇdya Brāhmaṇa*, 8.8.8-10. *Aitareya Brāhmaṇa*, 1.19.1, *Śatapatha Brāhmaṇa*, 11.2.3, etc.
25. 10.6.3.1.
26. *Geschichte der Philosophie*, I.2.84 ff.
27. Cf. 7.8.2; 1.37.7; 10.92.13; 10.168.4.
28. 10.168.4.
29. *sūrya ātmā jagataḥ tasthuṣaśca*, 1.115.1.
30. *ātmā yajñasya*, 9.6.8.
31. *ātmā yañjasya pūrvyaḥ*, 9.2.10.
32. 10.163.5, 6.
33. 4.2.3.1; 9.2.1.2.
34. 4.2.3.1.
35. 11.2.1.2.
36. 3.8.3.8.
37. 10.3.5.13.
38. 10.6.3.2. (J. Eggeling's translation, adapted to make the distinction between *Ātman* and *ātman*.)
39. *Commentary on Chāndogya Upaniṣad*, 6.8.7: *ātma śabdasya nirupapadasya pratyagātmani gavādi śabdavat nirūḍhatvāt.*
40. *The Philosophy of the Upaniṣads*, p. 39.
41. *Commentary on Brahma Sūtra*, 2.1.14. *sa ātmā tat tvam asi, śvetaketo, iti ca śārīrasya brahmabhāvopadeśāt, svayaṁ prasiddhaṁ hi etat śārīrasya brahmātmatvam upadiśyate, na yatnāntaraprasādhyam. ataśca idaṁ*

brahmātmatvam abhyupagamyamānaṁ svābhāvikaṁ śārīrātmatvasya bādhakaṁ sampadyate, rajjvādibuddhaya iva sarpādibuddhīnām.

42. *Kaṭha Upaniṣad*, 1.2.23; *Muṇḍaka Upaniṣad*, 3.2.3.
43. *ataśca na bhinnākāra-yogo brahmaṇa śāstrīya iti śakyate vaktum. bhedasya upāsana arthatvāt abhede tātparyāt, Commentary on Brahma Sūtra*, 3.2.12.
44. *athāta ādeśaḥ neti neti, na hi etasmād iti, neti anyat param iti. atha nāmadheyaṁ satyasya satyam iti.*
45. *nanu kathamābhyāṁ neti neti nirdeśābhyāṁ satyasya satyaṁ nirdikṣitamiti ucyate-sarvopādhi-viseṣāpohena yasmin na kaścit viśeṣo'sti nāma vā rūpaṁ vā karma vā bhedo vā jātirvā guṇo vā taddvāreṇa hi śabdapravṛtti bhavati. na caiṣām kaścidviśeṣo brahmaṇyasti. ato na nirdeṣṭum śakyata idaṁ tad iti. gaurasau spandate śuklo viṣaṇi iti yathā loke nirdiśyate tathā. adhyāropa nāma-rūpa karma-dvāreṇa brahma nirdeśyate vijñānamanāndaṁ brahma vijñānaghana eva brahma ātmā iti evamādiśabdaiḥ. yadā punaḥ svarūpameva nirdidekṣitaṁ bhavati nirastasarvopādhiviśeṣam tadā na kenacidapi prakāreṇa nirdeṣṭum. tada'yam eva asti upāya yaduta prāptinirdeśa pratiṣedhadvāreṇa neti neti nirdeśaḥ, Commentary on Bṛhadāraṇyaka Upaniṣad*, 2.3.6.
46. *etena sadākhyenā'tmanā'tmatvāt sarvam idam jagat*, Comment on 6.8.7.
47. *sad eva idam agra āsīt evam evadvitīyam, tadd haika āhuḥ, asad evedam agra āsīd ekam evādvitīyam tasmāt asataḥ sad jāyata kutas-tu khalu, saumya evaṁ syāt, iti hovāca, katham asataḥ sajjāyeti, sat tu eva, idam agra āsīt ekam evādvitīyam.*
48. *Commentary on Kaṭha Upaniṣad*, 1.1: *brahma-vidyāyām upaniṣadcchabda-prayoga-darśanāt upaniṣad-cchabdena brahma-vidyocyate.*
49. *svaṁ praśnaṁ nyāya-prakāram atītya āgamena praṣṭavyāṁ devatāṁ anumanena mā prākṣīḥ, Commentary on Bṛhādaraṇyāka Upaniṣad*, 3.6.1.
50. *Bṛhadāraṇyaka Upaniṣad*, 2.4.14; *yatra hi dvaitam iva bhavati, tad itara itaraṁ jighrati, tad itara itaraṁ paśyati, tad itara itaraṁ śṛṇoti, tad itara itaram abhivadati, tad itara itaraṁ manute, tad itara itaraṁ vijānāti. yatra tu asya sarvam ātmaivabhūt, tat kena kaṁ jighret, tat kena kaṁ paśyāt, tat kena kaṁ śṛṇuyāt, tat kena kam abhivadet, tat kena kaṁ manvīta, tat kena kaṁ vijānīyāt? yenedam sarvaṁ vijānāti, taṁ kena vijānīyāt, vijñātāram are kena vijānīyat?*
51. This simile is very reminiscent of Plato. See *Phaedo*, 24-28; *Phaedrus*, 246f; *Republic*, IV, 433. Further, inspite of differences, *nous* in Plato seems to be identical in what it does, with *vijñāna* of the *Upaniṣads.*
52. *Taittirīya Upaniṣad*, 2.5.1.
53. *Māṇuḍūkya Upaniṣad*, 13: *nānta prajñam, na bahiṣprajñam, nobhayataḥ prajñam, na prajñāna-ghanam, na prajñam, nāprajñam, adṛṣtam, avyavahāryam, agrāhyam, alaksaṇam, acintyam, avyapradeśyam, ekātmapratyaya-sāram, prapañcopaśamam, śāntaṁ, śivam, advaitam, caturtham manyate, sa ātmā sa vijñeyaḥ.*

4 – TO CHAPTER III: THE *BHAGAVADGĪTĀ*

1. *tadidam gītāśāstraṁ samastha-vedārtha sārasaṃgraha-bhūtam.*
2. *tadartha-āviṣkaraṇāya-anekair-vivṛta-pada-padārtha-vākyārtha-nyāyam-api-atyanta-viruddhān-ekārthatvena laukikair-labhyamāṇam-upalabhya-aham vivekato'rtha-nirdhāraṇārthaṁ saṁkṣepato vivaraṇaṁ kariṣyāmi.*
3. *dve akṣare brahma-pare tu anante vidyāvidye nihite yatra gūḍhe; kṣaraṁ tu avidyā hy amṛtaṁ tu vidyā vidyāvidye īṣate yas tu so'nyaḥ.*
4. See *Gītārahasya* (E.T.), pp. 30-36.
5. *Essays on the Gītā*, p. 73.
6. S. Radhakrishnan, *The Bhagavadgītā*, pp. 13-14.
7. *Op. cit.*, p. 12.
8. R.C. Zaehner, *The Bhagavadgītā*, p. 1.
9. *Op. cit.*, p. 2.
10. *Op. cit.*
11. *Op. cit.*
12. *sarvopaniṣado gāvo dogdhā gopālanandanaḥ pārtho vatsaḥ sudhir bhoktā dugdhaṁ gītāmṛtaṁ mahat.*
13. *Gītā*, 1.45.
14. *Ibid.*, 2.7.
15. F. Nietzsche, On the *Geneology of Morals*, trans., W. Kaufman, pp. 36-7. *Note*: Nietzsche and the *Bhagavadgītā* seem to say the same thing, from opposite standpoints, leading to opposite conclusions. Yet the fact that there is a common ground is noteworthy.
16. *"tatkāraṇaṁ sāṁkhyayogādhigamyam" iti vaidikam eva. tatra jñānaṁ dhyānaṁ ca sāṁkhyayogaśabdābhyām abhilapyate. pratyāsatter iti avagantavyam. yena tu amśena na virudhyate tena iṣṭameva sāṁkhyayoga-smṛtyoḥ sāvakāśatvam.*
17. *ātmano dehādi-vyatiriktasya kartṛtva bhoktṛtvādi-apekṣo dharmādharma viveko-pūrvika mokṣa-sādhana-anuṣṭhāna-lakṣaṇo yogaḥ, Commentary on Gītā*, 2.10.
18. *yata evam yoga-viṣayām buddhau tat paripāka-jāyāṁ vā sāṁkhya buddhau śaraṇam-āśraya-prāpti-kāraṇam-anviccha prārthayasva paramārtha-jñāna-śaraṇe bhavet-ityarthaḥ.*
19. *yā ca karmajā siddhiruktā jñāna-niṣṭhā-yogyatā lakṣanā.*
20. Comment on *Gītā*, 6.4.
21. "The source of desire is imagination, and sacrifices are of the form of desire", *saṁkalpa mūlaḥ kāmo vai yajñāḥ saṁkalpabhāvāḥ, Manusmṛti*, 2.2. "O desire I know thy root, thou art born of imagination", *kāmā jānāmi te mūlam saṁkalpāt-kila jāyase, Mahābhārata, Śāntiparva*, 177.25.
22. *ata ātma-samavetatayā sarva-loka-prasiddhe karmaṇi nadīkūlastheṣviva vṛkṣeṣu gati-prātilomyena akarma karma-bhāvaṁ yathābhūtaṁ gatyabhāvamiva vṛkṣeṣu yaḥ paśyet, akarmaṇi ca kārya-kāraṇa-vyapāro parame karmavadāt-manyadhyāropite tūṣṇīm-akurvan-sukhamāse-ityahaṁkārābhisaṁdhi-hetutvāt tasminakarmaṇi ca karma ya paśyet,* Śankara, *Commentary on Gītā*, 4.18.
23. Comment on 9.5.

24. Comment on 11.54.
25. *matparama karoti bhṛtyaḥ svāmi-karma na tu ātmanaḥ paramā pretya gatiriti svāminaṁ pratipadyate, ayaṁ tu matkarmakṛtmām eva paramāṁ gatim pratipadyate iti matparamaḥ.*
26. *evaṁ ca sati sarva-kṣetreṣvapi sato bhagavataḥ kṣetrajñasya īśvarasya saṁsāritva-gandhamātram api nāśakyam*, Comment on 13.2.
27. *sarvam utpādamānaṁ kṣetra-kṣetrajña-saṁyogādutpadyate ityuktam*, Introductory comment on chapter 14.
28. *guṇasamkhyāne kāpile śāstre tadāpi guṇasaṁkhyānaṁ śāstraṁ guṇabhoktṛviṣaye pramāṇameva.*
29. See J.G. Arapura, "The Upside-down Tree of the *Bhagavadgītā*", *Numen*, vol. XXII, Fasc. 2.
30. *sarvo hi gītāśāstrartho'sminnadhyāye samāsenoktaḥ, na kevalam gītāśāstra eva, kiṁ tu sarvaśca vedārtha iha parisamāptaḥ.*
31. In the Comment on 16.1.
32. In the Comment on 16.2
33. *jñānasya svātmotppatti-parapāka-hetu-yuktasya pratipakṣa-vihīnasya yadātmānubhava-niścayāvasānatvaṁ tasya niṣṭhāśabdābhilāpāt śāstrācāryopadeśena jñānotpatti-paripākahetuṁ sahakāri-kāraṇam buddhi-viśudhyādi-amānitvādi cāpekṣya janitasya kṣetrajña-paramātmaika-jñānasya kartṛtvādi-kāraka-bheda-buddhi nibandhana-sarva-karma-saṁnyāsya-sahitasya svātmānubhava-niścaya-rūpeṇa yadavasthānaṁ sā parā jñāna-niṣṭheti-ucyate.*
34. *buddher-ātma-sama-nairmalyādyupapatter-ātma-caitanya ākārābhāsatvopapttiḥ*, in Comment on 18.50.

5 – TO CHAPTER IV: THE *BRAHMA SŪTRA*

1. "Because of the stringing together of the passages of the Upaniṣads like flowers, therefore it is called *sūtra*" (*vedānta-vākya kusuma granthānarthatvāt sūtrāṇām*), Śankara's *Bhāṣya on the Brahma Sūtra*, 1.1.2. [Hereafter this text will be referred to as just the *Sūtra Bhāṣya* or *Bhāṣya.*]
2. *The System of the Vedānta*, (English translation), p. 27.
3. *Op. cit.*, p. 4.
4. For instance *Bhāṣya*, 1.3.28 says "*pratyakṣa* is *śruti.*"
5. Deussen, *op. cit.*, p. 4.
6. *Bhāṣya*, opening sentences: *yuṣmadasmat-pratyayagocarayor-viṣaya-viṣayinos-tamaḥ-prakāśavad-viruddha-svabhāvayor-itaretara-bhāvanupapattau siddhāyām-taddharmāṇām-api sutarāmitaretara-bhāvānupapattiḥ. ityato'smatpratyayagocare viṣayiṇi cidātmake yuṣmatpratyayagocarasya viṣayasya taddharmāṇāṁ cādhyāsaḥ, tadviparyayeṇa viṣayiṇastaddharmāṇām ca viṣaye'dhyāso mithyeti bhavituṁ yuktam. tathāpi anyonyasminn-anyonyātmakām anyonya-dharmāṁśca-adhyasyetaretarāvivekena. atyantaviviktayor-dharma-dharmiṇor-mithyājñāna-nimittaḥ satyānṛte*

mithunīkṛtya, ahamidam, māmedamiti naisargiko'yam lokavyavahāraḥ.

7. *asya anartha heto prahaṇāya ātmaikatva-vidyā-pratipattaye sarve vedāntā ārabhyante. yathā ca ayamarthaḥ sarveṣāṁ vedāntānāṁ tathā vayam asyāṁ śarīraka-mīmāṁsayāṁ pradarśayiṣyāmaḥ.*
8. *jñānena hi pramāṇena avagatum iṣṭam brahma. brahmāvagati tarhi puruṣārthaḥ, niḥśeṣa-saṁsāra-bīja-avidyā-anartha nirbahaṇāt, Bhāṣya,* 1.1.1.
9. *Note*: All Vedic knowledge is regarded as a refuge from fear. In the *Chāndogya Upaniṣad* (1.4.2) we read: "Verily the gods when they were afraid of death entered the three-fold knowledge (i.e., the three Vedas) for refuge. They covered themselves with the Hymns (*chandobhir achādayan*); because they covered themselves with these, therefore these are called *chandas* (*chandasāṁ chandas*)." Ancient etymology refers to the origin of this word as *chad*, to cover. See Śankara's *Gītā Bhāṣya* 15.1. This is carried forward as mastery of the whole circumstance of fear by Pūrva-Mīmāṁsā, and as total fearlessness (*abhayam*) consequent on gnosis by Vedānta. Other traditions like Buddhism have advanced other kinds of knowledge for the same fearlessness.
10. *Note*: Gnosis too has its own kind of heroism in its epic. Śankara puts it in terms of the rite (also called *pravṛtti*) but calls it by the name *nivṛtti* (non-rite) which constrasts with the former in meaning. It has its own corresponding life-style, i.e., *saṁnyāsa*, or the estate of the renunciant, which is a *ritual* – of existence – without the rite.
11. Tilak's *Gītārahasya* may be viewed as a latter-day attempt to put the *Gītā* back into the framework of the epic of the rite, with modernistic, political overtones.
12. *Note*: the word *tarka* is used here in its fundamental sense and not to be taken in the sense of *tarka*, the 8th of the 16 principles, or *padārthas*, of the *Nyāya Sūtra.*
13. The *Nyāya Sūtra* of Gotama, the basic text of the Nyāya system, outside Vedānta though it is, declares at 1.1.5, that *anumāna* which is three-fold springs from *pratyakṣa.*
14. *Āpastamba Dharma Sūtra*, II. 4.8.13; II. 6.14.13. (Cf. G. Buhler's translation in *Sacred Laws* in *Sacred Books of the East Series. Note*: Many Mīmāṁsā works retain *nyāya* in their title. Jaimini's *Nyāya-māla-vistāra*, a celebrated work, designates all the theses it propounds as *nyāyas*. The appropriation of the word by the Nyāya system of Gotama clearly has created a confusion.
15. III. 2.122.
16. *na dharma jijñāsāyām-iva śrutyādaya eva pramāṇaṁ bramajijñāsāyām. kiṁtu śrutyādayo'nubhavādayaśca yathā sambhavam iha pramāṇam. anubhava-avasānatvāt bhūta-vastu viṣayatvāt ca brahmajñānasya. kartavyehi-viṣaye na anubhava-apekṣā asti iti śrutyādīnām eva prāmāṇyaṁ syāt*

sarvārthavadyotinaḥ-sarvajña-kalpasya yoni kāraṇaṁ brahma. na hi īdṛśasya śāstrasya ṛgvedādi-lakṣanasya sarvaguṇānvitasya sarvajñātanyataḥ sambhavo'sti. yad-yad-vistārārthaṁ śāstraṁ yasmāt puruṣa-

viśeṣāt sambhavati, yathā vyākaraṇādi pāṇinyādir-jñeyaikadeśārtham api, sa tato'pyadhikara-vijñāna iti prasiddhaṁ loke. kimu vaktavyamaneka-śākhā-bheda-bhinnasya tasya devatiryaṁ-manuṣya-varṇāśramādi-pravibhāga-hetor ṛgvedādyākhyasya sarva jñānākārasya aprayatnenaiva līlānyāyena puruṣaniḥśvasāvad-yasmān-mahato bhūtādyoneḥ sambhavaḥ, "asya mahato bhūtasya niḥśvasitam etad yad ṛgvedaḥ" (*Bṛhadāraṇyaka Upaniṣad*, 2.4.10) *ityādiśruteh. tasya mahato bhūtasya niratiśayaṁ sarvajñatvam sarvaśaktimatvaṁ ca iti. atha vā yathoktaṁ ṛgvedādi-śāstram yoni kāraṇaṁ, prāmaṇam asya brahmaṇo yathāvat-svarūpādhigame. śāstrādeva pramāṇāt-jagato janmādi-kāraṇaṁ brahmādhigamyata ityabhiprāyaḥ, Bhāṣya*, 1.1.3.

18. *tad brahma sarvajñaṁ sarvasakti jagadutpatti-sthiti-laya kāranaṁ vedānta-sāstrād eva avagamyate, katham? "samanvayāt". sarveṣu hi vedānteṣu vākyāni tātparyeṇaiva tasya arthasya pratipādakatvena samugatāni. "sadeva saumya idam agra āsīd, ekam evādvitīyam"* (*Chāndogya Upaniṣad*, 6.2.1); *"ātmā vā idam ekam eva agra āsīd"* (*Aitareya Upaniṣad*, 1.1.1); *"tad etat brahma apūrvam anaparam anantraam abāhyam. ayam ātmā brahma sarvānubhūh"* (*Bṛhadāraṇyaka Upaniṣad*, 2.5.19); *"brahma eva idam amṛtam purastāt"* (*Mund. Upaniṣad*, 2.2.12); *ityādīni. na ca tadgatānāṁ padānāṁ brahma svarūpa viṣaye niścite samanvaye'vagamyamāne'rthāntara-kalpanā yukta, Bhāsya*, 1.1.4.

19. *na ca teṣāṁ-kartṛ-svarūpa-pradipādana-paratā-vasīyate. "tat-kena kaṁ paśyet"* (*Bṛh.*, 2.4.14). *ityādi-kriyā-kāraka-phala-nirākaraṇa-śrute. na ca pariniṣṭa-vastu svarūpatve'pi pratyakṣādi-viṣayatvam brahmaṇaḥ "tat-tvam asi"* (*Chānd.*, 6.8.16) *iti brahmātma bhāvasya śāstram-antareṇa-anavagamyamānatvāt. yattu heyopādeya-rahitatvād-upadeśānarthakyamiti naiṣa doṣa. heyopādeya-śūnya-brahmātmāvagatamādeva sarvakleśa prahaṇāt puruṣārtha-siddheḥ devatādi-pratipādanasya tu svavākya-gatopāsanārthatve'pi na kaścid-virodhaḥ. na tu tathā brahmaṇa upāsana-vidhiśeṣatvam sambhavati. ekatve heyopādeya-śūnyatayā kriyā-kārakādi dvaita vijñānopamardo-papatteḥ, op. cit.*

20. Padmapada, one of the four disciples of Śankara wrote a commentary called *Pañcapādika*, on the first four *sūtras*, reputedly at the master's own behest, and it is the start of a whole commentarial line known by the name *Vivaraṇa*, taking its name from the commentary on it, namely, the *pañcapādika-vivaraṇa*, by *Prakāśātman*. This last work again, gave rise to a chain of works by a whole succession of commentators, the *Pañcapādika-vivaraṇa-prakāśikā*, by Nṛsimhāśrama; the *Vivaraṇa-prameya-saṁgraha* by Vidyāranya; and so on.

21. *evam tāvad vedānta vākyānāṁ brahmātmāvagatiprayojanānāṁ brahmātmani tātparyeṇa samanvitānām antareṇāpi kāryānupraveśaṁ brahmaṇi paryāvasānam uktam. brahma ca sarvajñaṁ sarvaśakti jagadutpatti-sthiti-nāśakāraṇam iti uktam. sāṁkhyādayastu pariniṣṭhaṁ vastu pramāṇāntara-gamyam eva iti manyamānāḥ pradhānādīni kāraṇānāntarāṇi anumimānāḥ tatparatayaiva vedānta-vakyāni yojayanti, Bhāṣya*, 1.1.4.

22. Cf. *Bhāṣya.*, 1.4.28.

23. *na sāṁkhya-parikalpitam acetanaṁ pradhānaṁ jagadaḥ kāraṇaṁ śakyaṁ vedānteṣu āśrayitum. aśabdaṁ hi tat. katham aśabdatvam? īkṣateḥ-*

īkṣitṛtva-śravaṇāt kāraṇasya. katham? evam hi śrūyate: "sadeva saumya idam agra āsīt ekam eva advitīyam" ityupakramya; tad aikṣata bahusyāṁ prajāyeti. tat tejo asṛjata, Bhāṣya, 1.1.5.

24. *asatyapi karmaṇi savitā prakāśa iti kartṛtva vyapadeśadarśanāt. evam asatya api jñāna karmaṇi brahmaṇaḥ 'tadaikṣata' iti kartṛtva-vyapadeśopapatter na vaiṣamyam, Bhāṣya,* 1.1.5.
25. *yadi ca ajñasya sato mumukṣoḥ acetanam-anātmānam ātmeti upadiśet pramāṇabhūtaṁ śāstraṁ sa śraddadhānatayān-ghago-langūla-nyāyena tadātmadṛṣṭiṁ na parityajet, tadhā puruṣārthāt vihanyeta, anarthaṁ carcet, Bhāṣya,* 1.1.7.
26. *Sāṁkhya-Kārikā* (62) runs as follows: [Hence] there is no being bound, none freed and none in the transmigratory cycle; only *Pradhāna* in manifold conditions is bound, freed and in transmigration, *tasmān na badhyate'ddhā na mucyate nāpi saṁsarati kaścit saṁsarati badhyati mucyati ca nānāśrayā prakṛtiḥ*).
27. *yathā arundhatīṁ didarśayiṣuḥ tat samīpasthāṁ sthūlaṁ tārām amukhyāṁ pradhamam arundhatī iti grāhayitvā tāṁ pratyākhyāya paścāt arundhatīm eva grāhayati, tadvat na ayam ātmā iti brūyāt. na caivam avocat, Bhāṣya,* 1.1.8.
28. *Prathame pāde "janmādyasya yataḥ" ityākāśāde samastasya jagato janmādi-kāraṇaṁ brahmeti uktam. tasya samaṣtha jagat-kāraṇasya brahmaṇo vyāpitvam, nityatvam, sarvajñatvam, sarvaśaktitvaṁ sarvātmakatvam ityevaṁ jātīyakā dharmā uktā eva bhavanti. arthāntara-prasiddhānāṁ ca keṣāṁcit śabdānām brahma-viṣayatva hetu-pradipādanena kānicid-vākyāni spaṣṭa-lingāni saṁdihyamānāni brahma-paratayā nirṇitāni, Bhāṣya,* 1.2.1.
29. *yade tat-asmīn-vakye dyauḥ pṛthivī antarīkṣaṁ manaḥ prāṇā ityevam-ātmakaṁ jagadotatvena nirdiṣṭam, tasyāyatanaṁ paraṁ brahma bhavitum arhati. kutaḥ? svaśabdāt ātmaśabdād iti arthaḥ. ātmaśabdo hi iha bhavati: "tamevaikaṁ jānatha ātmānam" iti. ātmaśabdaśca paramātma parigrahe samyagavakalpate nārthāntara parigrahe. kvacinca svaśabdena-iva brahmaṇa āyatanatvaṁ śrūyate: sanmūlāḥ saumya imāḥ sarvāḥ prajāḥ sadāyatanāḥ sadpratiṣṭhāḥ. Bhāṣya,* 1.3.1.
30. *brahma-jijñāsām pratijñāya brahmaṇo lakṣaṇam-uktam "janmādyasya yataḥ" iti. tallakṣaṇaṁ pradhānasya api samānam-ityāśaṁka tadaśabdatvena nirākṛtam: "īkṣater na aśabdam" iti. gatisāmanyaṁ ca vedānta-vākyānāṁ brahma-kāraṇa-vādaṁ pratividyate na pradhāna-kārana-vādaṁ pratīti prapañcitaṁ gatena grandhena. idaṁtu idāmīm avaśiṣtam āśaṁkyate. yaduktaṁ pradhānasya aśabdatvam. tadasiddham. kāsucit śākhāsu pradhāna-samarpaṇābhāsānāṁ śabdānāṁ śrūyamāṇatvāt, Bhāṣya,* 1.4.1.
31. *tasmāt na pradhānasya atra jñeyatvam avyakta-śabda nirdiṣṭatvam vā, Bhāṣya,* 1.4.5.
32. *Bhāṣya,* 1.4.3.
33. *avidyātmikāhi bījaśaktir-avyaktaśakti-nirdeśyā parameśvarāśrayā māyāmayī mahāsuṣuptiḥ. yasyāṁ svarūpa-pratibodha-rahitāḥ śerate saṁsariṇo jīvāḥ. Op.cit., Bhāṣya,* 2.1.14.
34. *sarvajñsya īśvarasya ātmabhūta iva avidyā-kalpite nama-rūpe tattvānyatvābhyām anirvacanīye saṁsāra-prapañca-bijabhūte sarvajñasya īśvarasya*

māyā-śakti-prakṛtir-iti, Bhāṣya, 2.1.14.

35. *yasmāt nirāgamāḥ puruṣotprekṣa-mātrā-nibandhānas-tarkā apratiṣṭhitā bhavanti. utpreksāyā niraṁkuśavtvāt. yathāhi kaiścit-abhiyuktair-yatnenotprekṣitās-tarkā abhiyuktatarair-anyair-ābhāsamāna dṛsyante, tairapi utprekṣitāh santaḥ tatoranyair-ābhāsyanta iti na pratiṣṭhitatvaṁ tārkāṇāṁ śakyaṁ samāśrayitum. puruṣamati vairūpyāt...ayam-eva ca tarkasya alamkāro yadapratiṣṭhitatvaṁ nāma. evaṁ hi sāvadya tarka parityāgena niravadyas tarka pratipattavyo bhavati. na hi pūrvajo mūḍha āsīdityātmanāpi mūḍhena bhavitavyam iti kimcid-asti pramāṇam. tasmāt na tarka-pratiṣṭhānaṁ doṣa iti cet evaṁ api avimokṣa-prasangaḥ. yadyapi kvacid-viṣaye tarkasya pratiṣṭhitatvam upalakṣyate, tathā'pi prakṛte tāvad-viṣaye prasajyata eva apratiṣṭhitatva-doṣāt-anirmokṣas-tarkasya. na hi idam atigambhīraṁ bhāvayāthātmyaṁ muktinibandhanaṁ āgamam-antareṇa utprekṣitum api śakyaṁ. rūpādya bhāvāddhi na ayam arthaḥ pratyakṣasya gocaraḥ, lingādyabhāvāñca na anumānādīnām iti ca uvācāma. api ca samyag-jñānān moksa iti sarveṣām mokṣa-vādinām abhyupagamaḥ. tañca saṁyag-jñānam eka-rūpam. vastu-tantratvāt. eka-rūpena hi avasthito yo'rthaḥ sa paramārtho loke. tadviṣayaṁ jñānaṁ saṁyag-jñānam iti ucyate. yathā agni rupeṇa iti. tatraivaṁ sati saṁyag jñāne puruṣāṇāṁ vipratipattir-anupapannā. tarkajñānānāṁ tu anyonya-virodhātma prasiddhā vipratipattiḥ. yaddhi kenacid-tārkikeṇedam eva saṁyag-jñānam iti pratipāditam, tadapareṇa vyutthāpyate tenāpi pratiṣṭhāpitaṁ tato'pareṇa vyutthāpyata iti prasiddhaṁ loke. katham ekarūpānavisthita-viṣayaṁ tarka-prabhavaṁ saṁyag-jñānaṁ bhavet, Bhāṣya*, 2.1.11.

36. *ataḥ siddham-asya-eva upaniṣadasya jñānasya saṁyag-jñānatvam, ato'nyatra saṁyag-jñānatvānupapattes-saṁsārāvimokṣa eva prasajyeta. ata āgama-vaśena-āgamānusāri-tarka-vaśena ca cetanaṁ brahma jagataḥ kāraṇaṁ prakṛtiśceti sthitam, loc.cit.*

37. On *epistēmē* and *epistamenos* see Heidegger, *What is Philosophy?* p. 57.

38. *tatra ca jīva vyatiriktāni tattvāni jivopakaraṇāni brahmaṇo jāyanta ityuktam.*

39. *atha avidyādhyasto brahmaṇi-ekasminn-ayaṁ prapañco'vidyayā pravilāpyata iti brūyāt, brahma-eva-avidyādhyasta-prapañca-pratyākhyānenāveditavyam "ekam evādvitīyam brahma", "tatsatyaṁ sa ātmā tattvamasi" iti. evam āvedite tasmin vidyā svayam evotpadyate. tathā ca avidyā bādhyate, Bhāṣya*, 3.2.21.

40. Repeated again under 3.2.21 from 1.1.4.

41. For instance, 3.4.26.

42. For instance, 3.4.14; 3.4.27, etc.

43. See 3.4.27.